CRIPPLED EAGLE

CRIPPLED EAGLE

A Historical Perspective of U.S. Special Operations 1976-1996

by
Rod Lenahan

Including:
JTF 1-79 The Iran Rescue Operation
Its Precedents and Aftermath

Narwhal Press
Charleston/Miami

Library of Congress Catalog Card Number: 98-065032

ISBN: 1-886391-23-8 (Paperback)
ISBN: 1-886391-22-x (Hardcover)

FIRST EDITION

Cover illustration incorporates the author's original photograph of the U.S. Embassy Compound wall in Teheran and images of the front and back of the Humanitarian Service Medal awarded to members of the JTF 1-79 who participated in the rescue attempt of 24 April 1980.

This book is available through: Narwhal Press, 1629 Meeting Street, Charleston, SC 29405; and though the American Military Museum of Charleston, 40 Pinckney Street, Charleston, SC 29401.

Printed in the United States of America

DEDICATION

This work is dedicated to the American soldiers, sailors, marines and airmen who will face the next challenge. Hopefully, our nation will permit them to be fully prepared.

Crippled Eagle

ACKNOWLEDGMENTS

This work could not have been completed without the help of a host of comrades, some of whom are mentioned in the work. Others, for security and privacy reasons, are not.

I owe a special debt to Colonel Charlie Beckwith, U.S. Army, and Colonel Jim Kyle, USAF, for plowing the road and providing their personal perspectives in Delta Force *and* Guts To Try. *The same tribute goes to Colonel Jerry Boykin for the fruits of his academic research, which are reflected in the chapter on the Congressional Crusade.*

Special thanks go to former Marine, professional comrade and friend, Jim Magee for reading, commenting and rereading of the numerous editions and evolutions of the manuscript.

Thanks also are on tap for Keith Nightingale for his "vignettes from the field," and for Jesse Johnson for his "Delta Reports."

Lastly, my thanks to RS, GP and LL, true friends who volunteered to be "Reader" Guinea pigs, and to the editors, artists, and staff at Narwhal Press who brought this together in book form.

I thank them all, and gratefully recognize all their contributions, apologize for any omissions, and take full responsibility for any errors.

-- *Rod Lenahan*

A Historical Perspective of U.S. Special Operations 1976-96

CONTENTS

Part I

Lays out the plateaus and stumbling blocks from 1976 through early February 1980 and the extensive efforts of men, imbued with a "can-do" attitude, forced to generally "make do."

Part II

Documents the final months of preparation for the Iranian hostage recovery mission and the events of March and April 1980 when the force is committed.

Part III

Describes the tremendous scope of the follow-on efforts that took place from May 1980 through January 1981, a period of dedicated effort to make up for previous years of neglect and to be ready to go again. Part Three closes out with a review of the conditions under which the hostages were held, and where they were on the night of the rescue attempt.

Part IV

Traces the ebb and flow of progress and obstacles that transpired subsequent to 1981, then closes with a summary portrait of the units that constitute today's United States Special Operations Forces.

Part V

Reviews some of the myriad operations and deployments that SOF have been involved in during the first ten years of the existence of the United States Special Operations Command and its joint approach to the use of SOF. Provides profiles of some members of JTF 1-79 and concludes with a Personnel rooster as of 24 April 1980.

Crippled Eagle

ILLUSTRATIONS

Following Page 132

PREFACE

An increase in both the frequency and the violence of international terrorism was heralded in the international media and on TV sets around the world in September 1970. The event was the highjacking of five commercial airliners by the Palestinian Liberation Organization (PLO) and the explosive destruction of four of the aircraft, nearly simultaneously, at Dawson field in Jordan.

Two years later, during the '72 Olympics, just outside Munich Germany, another PLO team raided the quarters of the Israeli Olympic team, killing one athlete and taking another ten team members hostage. All of the hostages were killed by the terrorists during a quickly organized and poorly executed hostage rescue attempt by German police at an airport outside of Munich.

In the wake of each new incident, another government began to create a counter-terrorist force. Many times, the cadre and the recruits for the force came from the country's airborne or other special-purpose military forces.

The West German government recognized the need for such a force in the wake of the '72 Olympic incident. At the time, Germany was also facing major internal domestic terrorist threats, in the form of the Red Army Faction and the Baader Mienhof gang. The German leadership elected to create a dedicated national police, para-military counter-terrorist unit, vice a military reaction force. The unit included personnel with specialized assault, communications and intelligence skills, and had its own specially equipped vehicles and emergency airlift, both fixed and rotary wing, available on an on-call basis. The unit known as Grenzschutzgruppe - 9 (GSG 9) was trained to operate within German national territory as a special surveillance, VIP-protection, and national counter-terrorist reaction team. The German national government, sensitive to the ghost of the Nazi Storm Trooper, did not plan to unilaterally employ the force -- Group Nine (as it came to be called) -- on another nation's soil. However, they did envision a situation where the force would be employed with the permission and assistance of the host nation. Both France and Italy, also faced with internal domestic threats, followed the police model and fielded a specialized National Police unit.

The Israelis, on the other hand, facing both internal and external threats, were prepared to employ their forces wherever needed. This was a direct reflection of the Israeli experience in fighting this type of undeclared war. The mission was given to the Ministry of Defense (MOD) and the Israel Defense Force (IDF). The MOD/IDF elected to create several forces with different levels of training. The lowest level of training was given to virtually all Israeli combat units in order to provide an immediate reaction capability at the local level throughout the entire country. Higher levels of training were given to selected elements of the Airborne units and the Golani Brigade, with a smaller cadre of military personnel receiving extensive target take-down and close-quarters combat training focusing almost exclusively on counter-terrorist operations and hostage recovery. The hard core of the Israeli external capabilities came from within the military parachute and raider units of the Israeli Defense Forces (IDF), and a C-130 squadron of the Israeli Air Force (IAF). These forces made their quasi-public debut in the summer of 1976 following an aircraft highjacking incident that began on 27 June 1976. On that date, a PLO team hijacked an Air France airliner with more than 100 passengers on-board; fifty of the passengers were Israeli. After refueling in Muammar Qadaffi's Libya, the aircraft flew south into central Africa and landed at Entebbe Airport in Uganda. The choice of Uganda was not an accident or a whim, but was in accordance with a pre-coordinated agreement between the terrorists and Ugandan President Idi Amin.

During the first 36 hours, the terrorists released the non-Israelis, while continuing to hold actual or suspected Israelis and the French flight crew hostage. A composite Israeli strike force (IDF/IAF) was hastily assembled, a plan developed and rehearsed. Seven days after the initial highjacking, on the night of 3/4 July 1976, the Israelis conducted a bold airlanding-raid at Entebbe. The Israeli force secured the release of the hostages with the loss of one member of the assault forces and two hostages. In the process, they killed most of the terrorists and some 20 Ugandan soldiers. Refueling of the Israeli aircraft that carried the force into Entebbe had been recognized as the weak link in the Israeli plan. Even though tactical refueling expediencies were prepared, unforeseen circumstances on the ground at Entebbe precluded their employment. Fortunately, after some late-hour negotiations, the government of neighboring Kenya allowed the Israeli force to land in Kenya and refuel the IAF aircraft for the long trip back to Israel. Although this action was a great relief, a premature public announcement by the Israeli political leadership put the mission in jeopardy. An announcement of the successful rescue effort was made while the rescue aircraft were still over Africa and several hours from the safety of Israeli airspace or fighter protection. Advised of the premature announcement, the rescue force took extra measures to minimize the possibility of being detected by foreign radars.

The events of Entebbe quickly came to be a benchmark for the development of an American military Counter-terrorist capability. Given the global vulnerability of U.S. interests and citizens, the United States needed a force or forces that could react to a situation virtually anywhere in the world. Only days after the Israeli raid, General Jack Hennessey, the

Commander In Chief of the United States Readiness Command (REDCOM) received a phone call from a senior officer in the Pentagon. The tall, distinguished ramrod Army General took the call on his feet in his 2nd floor office of Building 501, REDCOM Headquarters, on MacDill Air Force Base, near Tampa, Florida. After the usually pleasantries, the Pentagon caller queried, "can we" ("we" being the United States) "do that?" General Hennessey's reply ran along the lines of -- "I have the forces, but they do not have the training."

American military counter-terrorism planning and preparation, as we know it, began shortly thereafter; however, its effectiveness was often stymied and short-changed throughout the following three years (1976-1979) by a combination of factors, inluding a nonchalant ("it can't happen here") attitude to the terrorist threat by the State Department, and an antipathy against anything "joint" within some higher elements of the service hierarchies. The situation was compounded a mix of "not invented here", and a "what's in it for me?" competitiveness at the mid-level of some service force structures. Lastly, in some quarters there was a misplaced perception that the U.S. Armed Forces could throw together a task-organized unit when needed.

In February 1979, during the early days of the post-Shah Iranian Islamic Republic, an unruly mob, led by members of the Iranian Peoples Militia, swept onto the American Embassy grounds in downtown Teheran and took many of the Americans working on the grounds captive. After more than four hours of dialogue between the American Ambassador and the fragile interim Iranian civil government, the captors were persuaded to free the Americans and the need to employ American force was avoided. Subsequently, the embassy staff was downsized and all family members were evacuated to the United States. Tensions and political turmoil continued to increase in Iran between the competing factions. On 4 November 1979, less than nine months after the initial takeover, Iranian Islamic militants, using a "protest" crowd composed largely of women as a deception screen, again overran the American Embassy in downtown Teheran. This time, there was no quick settlement and more than 100 people were taken hostage, including 67 Americans.

After five months of diplomatic and economic efforts failed to secure the release of the remaining 53 American hostages, President Carter directed an American military Joint Task Force (JTF 1-79), composed of Army, Navy, Marine and Air Force personnel to launch a rescue mission. The American mission was aborted midway through its first phase (i.e., the force insertion phase) during the early hours of 25 April 1980. The decision to abort was made based on logistic deficiencies. Specifically, the number of operational helicopters needed to effectively conduct the operational phases of rescue had dropped below the minimum number required. The disappointment of the withdrawal was compounded and magnified by the accidental collision of one of the helicopters and a C-130 aircraft during the withdrawal operation. The crash resulted in a conflagration of burning fuel, electric wiring and exploding ammunition. The fire took the lives of eight members of the rescue force in its first two minutes. Learning of the American attempt the next morning, the Iranian hostage-takers began making plans to disperse the Embassy hostages in small groups to multiple locations throughout the country.

The service attitudes of the previous months and years changed substantially after the fiery calamity in the Desert. Planning and preparations for a "second effort" picked up steam almost immediately, in accordance with a verbal directive from President Carter on 28 April to "get ready to go again."

This second, much bigger effort began the revitalization of our national special operations capability to an almost unparalleled level. However, after the initial nine months of "catch-up" in 1980, progress quickly slowed in 1981 following the release of the hostages, and the road became bumpy with bureaucratic impediments through 1987. Substantial progress was made in the following ten years, as witnessed by the growing contributions of American Special Operations Forces in a wide variety of peacetime, contingency and wartime missions. Regrettably, some deficiencies still persist.

What follows is the story of the evolution of U.S. Special Operations Forces (SOF) capabilities from near extinction in the mid-seventies through the low point of Desert One to the high ground of the '90s.

For readers not familiar with military and government acronyms, a special glossary has been appended to the text (page 265).

INTRODUCTION

PROJECT RICEBOWL
THE HIGH AND LOW OF SPECIAL OPERATIONS

As night descends on the ship and the artificial lights begin to take effect, they start gathering. First in individual movements, later in small groups, they begin appearing. They move to places on the hangar deck and stand against the bulkheads, watching, hoping they won't be spotted as being too obvious and being asked to leave. Some find places on the stairwells and catwalks overlooking the hangar deck where they can see but not be seen. Their focus is the eight helicopters that are being slowly wheeled from their anchor points to the elevators.

The eyes follow each movement of the aircraft and observe each movement of the pilots and crew as they walk around their craft and climb aboard. The observers say nothing, but watch intently, as if they were for the first time ushered into a church service in mid-ceremony. They have come from all over the ship to watch. From the galleys in mid-meal so they would not miss this. From their bunks deep within the ship. From the reactor spaces far below the waterline and from their relatively comfortable accommodations in officer country they came. Until a very short while ago they had no conception of what these helicopters, these space-users would do. As if by some unseen messenger, the carrier crew has individually received notice as to what is happening and each man wants to be a part of this moment. Sailors stand with hands over their mouths and with anxious eyes. Little human sound is heard, only the ceaseless vibrations of the ship itself and the whir and clank of the machinery that is making things happen. Much is thought, but little is said. Individually, they sense something important is about to happen

As the eight helicopters are aligned on the flight deck, the audience moves slowly to gain a vantage point. Topside, however, controls are much more stringent. Most still remain standing on the hangar deck and search for a vantage point up the elevator frame or deck opening. Only the ingenious or those with a job can directly see the task at hand. Two sailors squat behind a fire extinguisher between two large horizontal antennas, hoping the bulk will obscure them from critical view.

One by one, the helicopters launch into the darkening sky, turn perpendicular to the flow of the ship, and glide off into invisibility. The audience stands transfixed as the last black dot disappears, then the watchers begin to slowly return to their original places. Still, no one is talking, only thinking, and some are praying.

Crippled Eagle

Less than twelve hours later, in the early morning hours of 25 April 1980, the day turned to one of sadness and shock, trauma and determination. On that day, the best and boldest of America's Special Operation Forces came face to face with the results of 15 years of neglect and the unpredictable forces of nature.

On a barren stretch of flat, wind-blown desert 400 miles inside a hostile country, eight American servicemen gave their lives that day in an attempt to achieve the freedom of other American citizens. The servicemen were there because the Government of Iran had been defying international law and illegally holding 53 American citizens hostage for nearly five months.

Many have said it was also the beginning of a revitalization of U.S. Special Operations Forces (SOF). In fact, it was the mid-point in a slow uphill struggle, which in many ways is still continuing today.

PART I

CHAPTER ONE
The Years Before

The November 1979 takeover of the United States Embassy in Teheran came as a surprise and shock to most of the world, although there were plenty of strategic warning signs. The U.S. government had recognized the growing threat of international terrorism much earlier in the decade. In the summer of 1975 the Secretary of Defense, through the Office of the Joint Chiefs of Staff, had directed the development of a generalized Concept Plan (CONPLAN) to react to a range of terrorist actions; however, no forces were assigned to the plan or specifically trained for the mission. Shortly after the Israeli raid at Entebbe in 1976, the Joint Chiefs of Staff (JCS) directed General John "Jack" Hennessey, Commander-In-Chief (CINC) of the U.S. Readiness Command (CINCRED) to review, revise and expand the initial CONPLAN and develop a force capability.

This directive came about as part of a telephone call between a senior officer at the JCS and General Hennessey within days of Entebbe. The JCS call had begun with the question, "Do we have a plan to do that?" CINCRED's response was a reminder that a plan had been prepared and had been submitted to JCS for review the previous fall. This response was followed by a second question, which asked, "Can we, do we have the forces to do, what the Israelis just did?" General Hennessey responded that he had the forces, but that they did not have the specific training. After this brief dialogue, the JCS speaker asked General Hennessey to send someone to the Pentagon to recover the plan, rework it on a priority and very limited need-to-know, "close-hold" basis, and resubmit it "fleshed out" within 45 days.

General Hennessey immediately gave the requirement a high priority and simultaneously directed two actions. The first task went to his Director of Intelligence (J-2). The J-2 mission was to assemble all available information on the Israeli hostage incident and recreate the events of those seven days leading up to the raid at Entebbe. General Hennessey stressed that he wanted particular attention paid to the behind-the-scenes military and political planning, preparation and problems experienced by the Israelis. Less than ten days later, a time-line composite of the Israeli preparations and actions had been constructed by a team of five Readiness Command (REDCOM) J-2 intelligence analysts and was briefed to General Hennessey and his senior staff.

The second task went to the Director of Plans (J-5) to revise the original 1975 CONPLAN submission. The J-5 convened a planning team consisting of representatives from each of the principle REDCOM staff directorates: operations, logistics, communications, intelligence and personnel, and two operational capabilities that General Hennessey had under his command, Army Rangers and the Air Force Special Operations Wing. During the early planning discussions, consideration was given to having each of the overseas unified theater commands (European, Pacific, Atlantic and Southern Commands) build and train a highly specialized counter-terrorist force. Due to a lack of uniform force capabilities in the different theater commands and the cost associated with this option, the final guidance directed REDCOM to create a single joint capability that could respond to a challenge anywhere in the world. Each overseas command was encouraged to create its own immediate reaction, "*in extremis*" force. The theater commands typically assigned this mission to one of their existing service forces as one of many, extra, on-call missions.

REDCOM was a downsized version of its predecessor, U.S. Strike Command (STRICOM). Strike Command had been created in the early 60's in the wake of the 1958 Beirut Intervention and the earlier Suez Canal Crisis of 1956. Its mission was to enhance joint force training among the American military services and provide a cadre for two standing contingency focused Joint Task Forces (JTF-7 and JTF-11). One was focused on the Middle East and Africa and the other on the Pacific theater. The STRICOM JTFs were deployed numerous times during its tenure, usually for joint and combined training with the forces of allied or friendly nations. Its most striking real-world effort was the international intervention and rescue evacuation of the Congo and Brazzaville in the midst of a major civil conflict in 1963/64. During the force drawdown of the mid-seventies following the Vietnam pullout and the general change toward a less forceful military posture, STRICOM was deactivated and replaced by the smaller Readiness Command. The REDCOM mission was essentially the same as its predecessor -- Joint Force Training. However, this was to be conducted within the limits of four major, JCS-sponsored exercises a year. And instead of two full-up, standing JTF staffs as STRICOM had possessed, REDCOM was authorized one scaled down JTF cadre staff which was to be the nucleus for a world wide contingency response staff.

Most of the REDCOM counter-terrorist planning team were already part of the command's deployable Joint Task Force cadre and routinely worked together. The collective REDCOM planning team totaled about 15 personnel. In addition, a planning cell from the two field units (the Army Rangers and the USAF 1st Special Operations Wing) that would be employed under the plan were included. Representatives from their parent service headquarters (Army Forces Command for the Rangers and the Tactical Air Command for the 1st SOW) also participated. The collective team also included operationally-oriented representatives from both the Defense Intelligence Agency (DIA) and the National Security Agency (NSA). Their role was to ensure that the mechanisms of these agencies were prepared to provide national level intelligence support on a worldwide basis. The Command's CIA liaison officer also participated, pledging an undefined degree of support.

The planning team worked for several weeks fleshing out the CONPLAN until it reached a point where the plan was more akin to an executable Operations Plan (OPLAN) than the normal paper thin CONPLAN, although the document cover and official designation still labeled it as a CONPLAN.

During the process of structuring the force and laying out the "troop list," General Hennessey requested the participation of Navy Special Warfare Elements, (Sea Air Land -- SEALs, and Army Special Forces -- Green Berets). These forces were to be integrated into the planning and training program as on-call forces and attached to the JTF during mission preparation and execution as specialized strike elements. General Hennessey was denied the services of both of these capabilities. The Navy, which had no operational forces assigned to REDCOM, stated that the SEALS were Fleet assets and were not available to support joint operations. The Army's Special Forces community said that the Green Berets were stretched too thin conducting training missions with allied nations; none could be spared for inclusion in the REDCOM plan.

Rebuffed but not discouraged, General Hennessey and his planners accepted these limitations and pressed on to create a quick reaction Counter-Terrorist Joint Task Force (CT-JTF) from the assets available to the command. For this mission, these forces were the only two battalions of Army Rangers that existed and the USAF-only Special Operations Wing (SOW). Elements of the Joint Communications Support Element (JCSE); a JCS communications element also based at Mac Dill that had a worldwide contingency response capability was tasked to provide the major communications support.

Many of the REDCOM planning representatives became the core staff of the CT Joint Task Force. Designated JTF-7X (X-ray), the staff was quietly created to manage the planning and execution of any subsequent counter-terrorist mission. The JTF-7X cadre was imbedded within the deployable staff of the "White World" Joint Task Force Seven, the Command's joint training and quick reaction conventional JTF.

In an effort to enhance the training and capabilities of the forces, REDCOM requested additional munitions funds from the Army to support the Ranger's' need for more live fire practice and to procure some accuratized, close range pistols and long range sniper weapons. The standard Ranger weapon was the M-16 rifle. Although a superior infantry weapon, it was not the weapon of choice for this type of close-in mission. At the same time, a request went to the Air Force seeking additional flying hours to support the long haul transport and air assault training requirements associated with delivering and recovering the force.

Both requests were turned down by the respective service staffs with the comment that funds were not available and that Command would have to "make do" by taking it out-of-hide. With these handicaps imposed, the forces began joint training as part of the Readiness Command Joint Readiness Exercise (JRX) training program.

The first, and smallest, joint exercise of many that were to occur during the next three years took place in the fall of 1976 in Yakima, Washington, as a subset of a much larger REDCOM JRX. It involved terrorist role-players actually breaking into the exercise director's kick-off reception, kidnapping several senior REDCOM staff officers, and holding them hostage in a remote site. The reaction force involved the JTF-7X cadre staff, a planning cell, and a Ranger company from the 2nd/75th Ranger Battalion. The JTF staff employed tactical reconnaissance assets (RF4C aircraft) to locate the detention site. Once the actual location was confirmed, the Rangers developed and tested several alternate assault and extraction tactics. Under cover of darkness and with the support of an Army helicopter detachment, the Rangers assaulted directly inside the enemy compound totally to the surprise of the terrorists. This resulted in the quick freeing and extraction of the hostages back over the triple rolls of concertina barbed wire that surrounded the hostage site.

Shortly after this initial exercise, a combined REDCOM, JCS and DIA team traveled to Israel and spent more than a week with members of the Entebbe planning and execution staff, learning of some of the planning and security challenges and operational near-mishaps the Israelis had faced. The REDCOM members of the team included the JTF-7X cadre for Operations, Intelligence and Planning. The DIA representative, Lt. Colonel Jack McDonnell, USAF, had been the DIA representative to the REDCOM Planning group, and the JCS representative, Colonel Bud Skoins, was the Chief of the JCS Special Operations Division (SOD). Upon completing the visit, the REDCOM participants briefed the results to General Hennessey and his senior staff in a closed-door session. During the visit, the team obtained glimpses of some Israeli training techniques and learned of several near mishaps (tactical, logistic and political) that had occurred during the Israeli operation. The American team also confirmed that the event reconstitution prepared by the REDCOM intelligence team was not only accurate, but contained some facts which the Israelis chose not to disclose during the visit. At the conclusion of the briefing and the ensuing discussion, General Hennessey directed that a similar detailed analysis be conducted on all future terrorist incidents that drew a counterforce reaction and the results examined for pitfalls and positive lessons.

The formal REDCOM Joint Readiness Exercise (JRX) Program was part of the JCS Five-Year Exercise Plan and was budgeted in accordance with the planning and scope of four large-scale, multi-force exercises conducted each year. This limited number of JRXs (one per quarter) was insufficient to allow the CT-JTF to attain or maintain proficiency in the range and variety of missions they could be called upon to perform. Through a collaborative arrangement with the senior Army component command, Forces Command, which was responsible for the "service" aspects of Army training, an existing Army service training (and testing) program nicknamed EDREs (Emergency Deployment Readiness Exercises) was used to fill the JTF-7X training gap. Both Ranger battalions were part of the EDRE program, with one of the battalions always on alert. This unit, known as the Ranger Ready Force (RRF), was prepared to respond to real-world contingency operations within 18 hours of alert. Each EDRE also had an Air Force air support element that provided the strategic and tactical airlift needed to marshal, move and execute the Ranger mission.

A small cell of EDRE planners was brought into the "need-to-know" circle that was the CT community at the time. These cells, one at Fort Stewart, Georgia, and one at Fort Lewis, Washington, were responsible for supporting the two Ranger Battalions (the 1st-75 Rgr Bn at Fort Stewart and the 2nd Rgr Bn at Fort Lewis). This support included obtaining use of the exercise site, developing the exercise scenario, ensuring all the essential exercise support was arranged, and providing bad-guy and hostage role-players as well as safety referees. Working with the REDCOM exercise planners, Air Force staffs of the Tactical Air Command (TAC) and the Military Airlift Command (MAC), this "exercise team" set the stage and arranged the "props" in accordance with the mission scenario. All of this pre-planning and field-coordination was done, without the knowledge of the "players" (i.e., the JTF 7X cadre, the Rangers, the 1st SOW, the JCSE Quick Reaction Team, and the REDCOM Deployment Cell (D-Cell) which provided security and field support).

Each exercise scenario was developed and conducted against the backdrop of real-world events and a set of political and military constraints. By the conclusion of the third exercise, the JTF 7X cadre had refined the standard JTF deployment and operating procedures and developed an integrated approach to the planning and preparation for a real-world CT mission. These procedures were used, evaluated, amended and refined after each exercise. By the conclusion of the fifth exercise, validation of procedures and situational refinements were the key hallmarks. In each subsequent exercise, the scenario became more complex, the situation more demanding, and the development and application of solutions more realistic. This included the expanding involvement of several national agencies, such as the Defense Mapping Agency (DMA), the Defense Intelligence Agency (DIA), and the National Security Agency (NSA).

The DMA provided quick reaction photo and map graphics of the exercise site for tactical planning use. The DIA provided similar materials and topographic analysis of the real-world backdrop location. Simply stated, DIA provided a real-world description of the backdrop country, region and environment, while DMA provided the details on the actual CONUS-based field training (i.e., exercise site). NSA resources were used to enhance the planning and execution security procedures of the JTF and the operational forces. NSA teams monitored various communications links and, acting as a hostile power, attempted to identify the JTF command and control structure, and monitor the mission planning and the actual deployment. These intercept efforts resulted in a NSA attempt to identify the participants and reconstruct the events. Subsequent to the exercise, this NSA reconstruction was compared to the actual sequence of events; the results were used to change or develop procedures to further reduce the operational and communications signature of the JTF and the operational forces.

Operational air support quickly expanded beyond the 1st SOW and the Tactical Air Command. It included both the Military Airlift Command (MAC), which provided strategic airlift (C-141s and C-5 transports), and the Strategic Air Command (SAC), which provided both air refueling (KC-135s) and strategy reconnaissance (i.e., SR-71 and U-2) support. The JTF-7X team leader and Chief of Staff was Air Force Colonel Turnipseed. His day-to-day job was head of the JTF branch and the Chief of Staff of the "White World" JTF staff, a perfect dovetail to his role in the 7X team. The first JTF 7X J-3 (Operations Boss) was Lieutenant Colonel Bobby Davis, a tall, lanky paratrooper who had earned his first set of spurs during the Korean War. The first Communicator was Major Scotty "Ranger" White, the second being Major Peter Dieck, who subsequently assumed command of JSCE as a Lieutenant Colonel. Pete Dieck was replaced as the JTF 7X J-6 by one U.S. Navy Captain Norton, a multi-faceted jewel. Captain Norton brought not only superior technical, planning and leadership skills, but also his superior intellect, a great personality and joviality. He was equally at ease playing a naturally bearded and rotund Santa Claus all year long, or conducting prolonged negotiations dialogue with "terror role-players," who themselves were adept at this form of psychological gamesmanship, since they were typically Army psychological warfare specialists.

On 23 May 1977, the tranquillity of the Dutch countryside was shattered when two teams of Moluccan nationalists took over an elementary school and commuter train in northeast Holland. They demanded autonomy for their homeland, a south Pacific Island grouping which was a Dutch protectorate. Working within the borders of Holland, an amalgamation of Dutch Army, Navy, Marines and Federal police were employed to isolate, surveil and ultimately assault the two sites. The school was stormed on the fourth day of the crisis in an operation that used armored personnel carriers to gain access to the interior of the school by crashing through the interconnecting glass corridors. Some aspects of the final rehearsal for the assault on the train were published in the media; however, their significance apparently did not reach the Moluccans on-board the train. The commuter train was assaulted at dawn on Day 20, the 11th of June, by a unit of Dutch Marines after Navy underwater specialists had planted listening devices on-board the train and explosive charges in the surrounding area. The Marines received fire support from Army and Police marksman, as well as a diversionary (simulated) aerial bombardment by Air Force fighter aircraft. The Marines succeeded in clearing the train at the cost of two hostages and six Moluccan nationalists. This event was also analyzed in detail and briefed to the JTF 7X staff per General Hennessey's earlier guidance. The principle lesson learned was that "more" is not necessarily better in all circumstances.

The West German test came five months later, nearly six years after GSG-9 had been created and 2,700 miles from German soil. In October 1977, a Lufthansa airliner carrying more than 70 German citizens was highjacked over the Mediterranean shortly after it took off from the island of Majorca. After chasing the hijacked aircraft for four days through six countries, suffering through two media compromises and two "training aborts," a GSG-9 team stormed the aircraft as it sat on the ground at Mogadishu. The assault was conducted under the cover of darkness and with the permission and cooperation of the Somali government. The German force rescued the hostages with only one injury to themselves, none to the hostages, and the capture of the four terrorists, who were turned over to the Somali government. This event was also examined in detail; the full scope of the "chase," the negotiations, and the "take-down" were reconstructed and lessons extracted. The most significant lesson concerned the use of "rubber" bullets; as used by GSG-9, the "rubber" bullets proved to be ineffective in a situation where it is imperative to quickly and totally neutralize an armed terrorist. One of the terrorists, a woman, sustained more than a dozen hits and was still strong enough as she was being carried away on a stretcher to raise her arm in a clenched-fist gesture of protest.

In the wake of the German success at Mogadishu in 1977, the same question that followed Entebbe was asked again -- "Can we do that?" This time, the REDCOM answer was a flat "No!" It was explained that the type of surgical takedown (undetected assault and rapid penetration of a commercial airliner) required specialized knowledge and equipment, constant training, and dedicated personnel. Again, a request from REDCOM was issued to the service headquarters for Special Forces and SEAL participation in the CT training program. Again, the answer was "No!" However, both services began to develop their own counter-terrorist capabilities, the Navy using the SEALS of Naval Special Warfare Group Two in the Norfolk area, and the Army using the Special Forces community at Fort Bragg. The Navy began close-quarters shooting training using waxed red dye bullets in their training encounters with "terrorists" at a remote training site where they had converted a double-wide mobile home to a combination "hostage detention and rescue site." The Army had a bolder initiative brewing.

At the same time that REDCOM was creating JTF 7X, Colonel Charles A. "Charlie" Beckwith, a burly Special Forces officer, had been tasked by Major General Bob Kingston to resurrect a concept paper on a counter-terrorist force that Beckwith had prepared in late 1975. Beckwith was occasionally known for shooting from the hip, but was a bulldog when given a mission. In this case, the mission became a crusade.

Beckwith, the Commander of the Special Forces School at the time, had been advocating the creation of an anti-terrorist capability, similar to the British Special Air Service (SAS), since the mid '60s. He had served an exchange tour with the British Special Air Service (SAS) in 1962 and was enamored of the British style of training and the product it produced. General Kingston, the Commander of the JFK Special Warfare Center at Fort Bragg, had also served with the SAS and was of the same mind as Charlie and also believed that the United States needed to create a dedicated counter-terrorist force.

Charlie's concept of CT was a low-visibility counter-terrorist night action by a relatively small, specially trained force equipped with unique weapons and equipment, which covertly infiltrated the target area, then conducted the terrorist neutralization action. Charlie, with the guidance of General Kingston and the encouragement of General William De Puy, the Commander of the Army Training and Doctrine Command (TRADOC), immediately began the long process of refining the proposal and developing a Concept Briefing. The initial effort was briefed to General De Puy in mid-November 1976, then reworked and rebriefed toward the end of January 1977. After some additional modifications, directed by General De Puy, the concept was presented to General Kroesen, the Commanding General of Forces Command (FORSCOM) in early May 1977. Although there was some staff resistance to the proposal at FORSCOM, General Kroesen, who knew of General Hennessey's efforts with the REDCOM CTJTF, said he would support the proposal when it was briefed to the Army Chief of Staff, General Bernard Rogers.

The proposal was briefed to General Rogers in the Pentagon on 2 June 1977. General De Puy, General Kroesen and Lieutenant General Edward C. "Shy" Meyer, the Army Deputy Chief of Staff for Operations and Plans (DCSOPS) and Major General Kingston were the principals in attendance. General Rogers recognized the need expressed in the briefing and directed General Meyer to lay out a plan and a cost estimate to create the force. General Meyer, with General Kingston's concurrence, turned this task over to Colonel Beckwith. Beckwith was asked to prepare and submit a cost estimate and a proposed Table of Organization and Equipment (TO&E) to General Meyer within ten days. Charlie complied, but it was not until mid-September 1977 that he received a telephone call from General Meyer's office advising him that the package had been approved. Charlie now began the long arduous task of building all the paperwork necessary to create a new unit. The process was slow, until GSG-9 went into action in mid-October.

The events at Mogadishu put a high flame under the need to create a fully trained American surgical takedown force. Charlie's game plan was to develop an American version of the German capability, although the organization and initiation had a British organizational flair (squadrons and troops, vice companies, platoons and squads). This was due to Colonel Beckwith's experience with the British Special Air Service (SAS), which employed these smaller-sized force modules. The sixteen-man troop was the key block. Several troops made a squadron, while a troop could be broken down into four four-man squads, or eight two-man teams, or some combination thereof, depending on the mission. According to his vision, the force would be a surgical capability designed to operate as a national military SWAT team. His concept called for concurrence of the host country, and, with CIA assistance, his force could be quietly positioned immediately adjacent to the target. The force would execute the tactical assault essentially within an isolated and protected cocoon. Charlie said he needed 24 months to screen and properly train a force, and lots of money. He got his 18-24 months and two bags of money and, eventually, carte blanche to recruit throughout the Army for an organization officially to be known as 1st Special Forces Operational Detachment Delta (1st SFOD-D). Almost from its infancy, it became known simply as "Delta." This was now the fall of 1977.

With the official green light in sight, and a renewed sense of urgency, General Jack Mackmull, the new JFK Center Commander (General Kingston having been transferred to Korea the previous June) and Charlie set about arranging a trip to Europe to touch base with the SAS and GSG-9. However, in late October, before leaving on the European trip, the Army team was briefed by two members of the REDCOM JTF-7X cadre on the GSG-9 operation at Mogadishu, including the events of the previous several days of the chase. At the time of the briefing, the REDCOM staff was deployed on a large-scale, joint-readiness exercise in the Florida panhandle. It was raining hard that afternoon when the REDCOM JTF-7X Operations and Intelligence staff officers were called out of the field to the hangar that housed the Exercise Director Staff. The REDCOM officers were told to bring their deployment kits and to be prepared to brief "the plan." The REDCOM team went through the events of Mogadishu and then started to brief the status of JTF-7X. The visitors, all senior Army officers, were wearing camouflage fatigues sans name tags. The visitors, who had not been introduced and did not make any move to introduce themselves, did not exhibit any interest in hearing any thing about JTF-7X, its capabilities or procedures, and terminated the briefing after being presented only the review of the "chase and the takedown."

The official message which provided the authority to activate Delta was dated 19 November 1977; however, neither Charlie nor General Mackmull saw the message until after they returned from their European trip in December. General Hennessey, as CINCRED, also received the activation message. He promptly requested that General Mackmull come to Tampa and brief him. After the briefing, and somewhat agitated by the actions (and non-actions) of the Special Forces community during the past year or so, and the long lead time required to develop Delta (24 months), General Hennessey (who still had the responsibility for the DOD CT response) gave General Mackmull a mission. He told General Mackmull that he was holding Mackmull responsible for providing a surgical response capability if the need arose before Delta was operational. General Hennessey wanted a group trained for such surgical missions as urban hostage barricade and aircraft recovery situations now, not eighteen months down the road. General Mackmull got the message and assigned the responsibility for developing this interim capability to the Commander of the 5th SF Group, Colonel Robert Mountel. Colonel Mountel, a compact, dynamic and dedicated officer, did his job well. Within a two-month period, he and his Operations officer, Lt. Colonel Joe Cincotti, had created a capability from within the existing SF elements at Fort Bragg and were training hard. Again, it was "out of hide," and operated on a homemade but very demanding shooting range. This highly diverse and skilled team was nicknamed Blue Light.

In addition to its own individual shooting, surveillance, and hand-to-hand combat skills training, Blue Light participated in several of the

REDCOM JTF-7x CT-EDREs. In one of these, the target was a guarded and well illuminated airliner (with aircrew, hostages and terrorists on-board) parked on a hardstand within a hostile, guarded military airbase. Blue Light elected to be inserted under cover of darkness by a high-altitude, five-mile offset parachute drop to the east of the objective. The Ranger force targeted against the hostile guard force, its barracks, armament and the base control tower had been inserted five miles to the west several hours earlier. Blue Light, using steerable square chutes, landed quietly in the darkness 300 meters beyond the airfield and circled around to the north for its approach to its final assault locations. In the meantime, the Rangers had closed to several points along the western perimeter and taken up their positions without being detected by the terrorist guard force. Upon a given signal, both forces conducted their complimentary missions successfully, and evacuated the area along with the hostages before hostile reinforcements could arrive.

***

The REDCOM Joint Task Force 7X team was now well experienced in planning these operations and employing the available forces. The CONPLAN now had some meat to it; command, communications and intelligence procedures had been worked out and documented in manuals and Standard Operating Procedures (SOPs). In addition, a detailed review was conducted of each exercise and refinements made. On the international scene, and in keeping with General Hennessey's original guidance, an in-depth analysis had been conducted of all major terrorist actions going back to the mass aircraft highjacking (and demolition) by the PLO in September 1970. This collection of case studies continued to be prepared and added to in the wake of every major terrorist incident, particularly those where the target government responded with military or paramilitary force.

One of these events began on 18 February 1978, when two PLO gunmen shot and killed an Egyptian VIP in Nicosia, Cyprus, and took 30 people hostage. The terrorist pair bartered the hostages to obtain a plane and crew, releasing the majority of the hostages at planeside. After flying around the Middle East for 30 hours and refueling in Algeria, the aircraft returned to Larnica Airport in Cyprus where negotiations began for the release of the remaining two hostages in exchange for the safe passage (disappearance) of the gunmen out of Cyprus. An Egyptian parachute unit had been dispatched by Cairo and arrived at Larnica in mid-afternoon. The Egyptian C-130 was allowed to land and was parked nearly 300 hundred yards from the aircraft holding the terrorists and their hostages. After waiting several hours and shortly after learning of the possibility that the terrorists were about to be granted safe passage out of Cyprus, the

Egyptians attempted to storm the hostage plane. Most of the Egyptian force was cut down in a hail of bullets from the Cypriot National Guard, killing fifteen of the Egyptians as they moved over the open tarmac between the two planes. Subsequently, the hostages were released, the terrorists disappeared, and the surviving Egyptians were hospitalized, then flown back to Egypt. The REDCOM analysis concluded two major findings. First, Egyptian emotions overcame logic and good planning, with the assault being executed in desperation and without full knowledge of the operational environment. Second, the Cypriot authorities, some of whom, including the lead negotiator, were sympathetic to the PLO cause, had not cordoned off the Egyptian aircraft, an action that would have reduced the possibility of a confrontation. Instead, they had covertly moved elements of the Cypriot National Guard into concealed positions from which they could intervene if the Egyptian forces attempted an assault. The Cypriots also had stopped the Egyptian attaché from advising the Egyptian Commander of the Cypriot positioning action.

This collection of counterforce analyses eventually included seven events concluding with the French/Belgium rescue operation into Shaba province in Zaire in the spring of 1978. The analytical focus in all cases was on the planning and preparation, and the force closure and extraction movement as well as the engagement. These real-world analyses and the JTF's exercise experience showed that no two incidents were the same. Each incident was unique in some aspect, each was more difficult than its predecessors, and a single cookie-cutter approach could not be applied. Moreover, the analysis showed that smooth working support procedures, superior intelligence, a short command line, and strict security were of as much importance as a superbly trained assault force.

The 7X cadre would normally gather on a biweekly basis to review world events and discuss the possibilities. "What ifs" of specific terrorist groups targeting U.S. interests with Embassy takeovers were always high on the list. Basic planning products for more than two dozen U.S. embassies were prepared by DIA and DMA, at the request of the 7X staff from 1977 through 1979. Other scenarios examined and exercised included aircraft and special weapons recovery missions.

The training scenarios were, for the most part, the Entebbe type, that is, a non-permissive (hostile) environment. This involved planning how to penetrate hostile airspace, insert the force, close with the objective locations undetected, execute the mission with surprise, skill and precision, and extract quickly and safely. This meant that the air planners of the 1st SOW, TAC and MAC had to get the force to the insertion point (and back) safely. The Rangers had to close on the objective, accomplish the area seizure, and establish a security cordon. Then Blue Light did the hostage rescue within the security donut provided by the Rangers, sometimes with an assist from an orbiting AC-130 gunship from the 1st SOW.

Several general officers alternately served as the JTF Commander during the 1976-1979 time frame. One of these was Major General Jim Vaught, the Commander of the 24th Infantry Division headquartered at Fort Stewart, Georgia. Most of the exercises were of the no-notice variety and ranged from a 72-hour reaction time down to 24. The distances were always long, sometimes extending from Florida to Washington State, then to New Mexico, sometimes from Florida to small islands off Hawaii. The weather was always the extreme, Death Valley in August, Wisconsin in December. The challenge was always how to get there and close on the target undetected, accomplish the mission and extract within the time allowed.

During the initial planning stage, a detailed options development and review was conducted by the planning cadre. Both the options development and review process included inputs from the air and ground forces that always attached a liaison officer. An evaluation was done on each option against a set of mission criteria, and the results and recommendations presented to the Commander for his selection and planning guidance.

Airlift was always a problem because of the cost and the limited number of special operations aircraft in the inventory. The greatest deficiency was with helicopters. The standard UH-lH (Huey) could not carry many troops very far. In addition, neither the Huey nor the Army OH-58, or the Air Force H-3 could fit into a C-130 or C-141 without being dismantled. The Army Blackhawk was still years away from delivery as was the Air Force long-range, night, low-level MH-53J (Pave Low). Both production schedules kept slipping because of low budgetary priority. The CH-46 could carry a good load, but did not have the range, and, except for one Marine Amphibious Unit, the flight crews did not have the requisite low-level night experience. In addition, neither the Army nor Marine CH-43s could fit in a C-130 or C-141 and even required disassembly to be transported in the huge cavity of the wide bodied C-5.

The J-3 Special Operations Division (referred to as SOD) was the JCS office that had staff cognizance for the plan and its execution (should it be activated). This team of special operations personnel was equally involved at their own level. In addition to moving the plan through the formal peacetime review process known as "deliberate planning," the JCS SOD cell, as well as the DIA, often had representatives participate in the field exercises. It was during one of these exercises that the first American lives were lost in CT training. A USAF C-135 Command & Control aircraft, on loan from TAC for an EDRE exercise and participating for the first time, failed to clear a mountain ridge after takeoff from Albuquerque. It pancaked into the side of the hill, killing the entire crew and a JTF staff cadre that was in a training status. A total of 16 soldiers and airmen died in the mishap.

This was not the only mishap to befall the training program. Some were inflicted deliberately as learning tools. One such example occurred during a major CT-EDRE in December 1977. The objective (training) site was located in northern Wisconsin and involved a dual target mission. One target, an aircraft with "terrorists and the hostage air crew" on-board, was to be "taken down" by Blue Light while a Ranger element was to simultaneously assault a warehouse several miles away that was being used by the "terrorists" to hold the "aircraft passengers hostage." The weather was extremely harsh and the ground was covered with ice. The insertion mode was to be an offset nighttime parachute drop into a drop-zone several miles from the two objective sites. Closure with the targets was to be by foot within a three-hour window.

During the pre-mission briefing by the senior ground force commander, it became apparent to some of the JTF-7X staff that the ground tactical plan, particularly the closure segment, had not been thoroughly developed. The briefing of the movement and closure plan was very general, with no specifics beyond a meaty hand on a map and the words "we will land here and move to here." This was not the degree of detail normally witnessed in the final pre-mission brief. Concern was further heightened by the rough terrain to be covered, the harsh winter weather, and the fact that the "terrorists" were being supported and screened by a host country military force. In the play of the exercise, this force was not a paper simulation. It consisted of a full battalion of Army Combat Engineers who were stationed on the training site and who, as it turned out, had been told of the JTF plan and the timing of the assaults by the senior exercise controller, an Army major general.

During the night parachute insertion, several jump injuries were sustained. These included a sprained ankle by the mission leader, Blue Light's operations officer, Lt. Colonel Joseph Cincotti. However, he and the Blue Light force moved overland with the Ranger blocking force to the airfield and conducted the aircraft takedown, although not as smoothly as anticipated. In the meantime, a Ranger squad which had the mission to reconnoiter the warehouse site captured an Opposition Force (OPFOR) soldier who told them of the advance briefing given to the OPFOR by the senior exercise controller. As the Ranger squad was observing the warehouse, the squad learned that the main Ranger force with the warehouse takedown mission could not reach the location in time and they would have to execute the rescue assault. Having been charged with this new responsibility, the squad leader created a diversionary action that revealed the composition of the terrorist force and confirmed the location of the hostages within the warehouse. Armed with this crucial information, the squad successfully conducted the warehouse mission, "accidentally" exploding a noise simulation training grenade at the feet of the senior controller who had briefed the OPFOR as they made their assault. However, in the exercise, "HOTWASH," it was lack of detailed planning and attention to the ground closure plan that was the major learning point.

In a subsequent field exercise, an equally forceful lesson was impressed on all concerned by another mission "failure." This occurred after a successful closure and takedown, but as a result of a poor extraction. The reason was the lack of attention to and failure of the operational forces to rehearse the extraction plan and consider the potential "what ifs." Some of the JTF staff recognized the value of these "failures" as legitimate ego-deflators and valuable lessons, even if some of the "failures" were partially set up by the control group.

In late May of 1978, JCS SOD coordinated the attendance of a host of senior government officials, including Ambassador Anthony Quainton of the State Department's Office of Counter-terrorism and the new Director of the FBI, Judge Webster, at the execution phase of a CT exercise. The exercise involved a blackout C-130 landing and an assault on an Air Force DC-9 configured as an airliner with military Psychological Operations (PYSOPS) personnel playing the role of terrorists and military support personnel assuming the role of hostages.

The terrorist role-players had been holding the crew and passengers for 36 hours, during which time JTF-7X set up surveillance and began a live, unrehearsed negotiations dialogue. The interactions among the role-players, the surveillance and the negotiation teams and the JTF Command section were not scripted, but had become a set of normal procedures for the JTF-7X staff. The aircraft assault was conducted by Blue Light and successfully completed in 90 seconds. Judge Webster was so impressed with the capability that, in spite of security concerns normally surrounding the existence of the DOD capability, within three days the *Washington Post* had a story describing the exercise and noting Judge Webster's attendance. Blue Light remained the operative Counter-terrorist force for the next two months, until 1st Special Forces Operating Detachment-D (Delta) was initially "certified".

The initial certification of Delta and the stand down of Blue Light came in July 1978 at the conclusion of a Delta field exercise. The senior exercise evaluator was Lieutenant General Volney Warner, Commander of the XVIII Airborne Corps. The linchpin of the certification was the unit skills portion of a large-scale field exercise which required Delta to simultaneously take down two targets -- a hijacked airplane and a terrorist-held building. The exercise was designed to test all of Delta's intelligence, operations and command and control procedures as well its tactical proficiency. During the planning phase, Delta flooded the exercise controllers with reams of questions -- Essential Elements of Information/Requests for Information (EEI/RFIs). The controllers did not have the answers, at least not in the detail Delta wanted. Eventually, Charlie badgered the control group into allowing him and a few of his staff to conduct a "Leaders Reconnaissance" of both targets. It turned out that he and some of his troops knew the target building well, a major plus for Delta. Although the target aircraft, an old propeller transport, had not been in the Delta training repertoire, the reconnaissance was sufficient to identify its blind spots and the location and type of doors and emergency windows. About 4 A.M., after closing with both targets undetected, Delta successfully executed both "take downs" in seconds, passing the certification. Following the normal "Hot Wash," Charlie suggested to General Meyer (who had come down from Washington to witness the field exercise) that there was no longer a need for Blue Light. General Meyer agreed and Blue Light was deactivated shortly thereafter. Regrettably, the rivalry and animosity between Colonel Beckwith and Colonel Mountel extended beyond the two individuals. None of the Blue Light Team applied for, nor were they asked to test for, Delta.

Colonel Beckwith, ever sure of his independence and Delta's unique position as a pure Army entity and asset, and not overly fond of things "joint," did, however, observe two JTF 7X quick-reaction exercises, and eventually Delta participated with the 7X in one field exercise. During this period of Delta's developing maturity (e.g. between its initial certification in July 1978 and its final certification in November 1979, just before the American Embassy in Iran was overrun), individual relationships did develop between some of the Delta staff and a few members of REDCOM JTF cadre. This was particularly true within the communications and intelligence staffs. At one point in the fall of 1978, Colonel Beckwith hosted a visit by General Hennessey to Delta's Compound." During the visit, Delta conducted a "room clearing" demonstration in the specially constructed $90,000 shooting house, and General Hennessey witnessed some close-in hand-to-hand training drills. The visit also included a tour of the Delta armory. This was not the standard military arms room where weapons and ammo were stored. This was a well-equipped and well-staffed facility created specifically to maintain and modify the close-in assault and standoff sniper weapons used by Delta. The armorers were justifiably proud of their skills, and it showed. General Hennessey was duly impressed, commenting on the armorers' superior skills to the two members of 7X cadre that accompanied him on the visit.

During the 1978-1979 time frame, operational procedures and techniques as well as planning, logistic, communications, and intelligence mechanisms were developed by both 7X and Delta. The JTF focused on denied-area penetrations and non-permissive environments; Delta on the close-in permissive environment, SWAT team type of action. The respective procedures were documented, practiced, critiqued and revised during numerous quick reaction exercises and several real-world false alarms. Several of the latter came close to requiring U.S. military action, and there was some "leaning forward," but these situations were either resolved peacefully, or another nation with greater interest exercised its counter-force option.

One of these "leaning forward" events occurred in the winter of 1978. Iran was in a high state of turmoil and a highly questionable transition period, from the formerly stable military-political secular government of the Shah to an unknown revolutionary anti-western regime with a strong Islamic fundamentalist bent. The DOD was concerned about the growing instability and unrest and the potential for much of the advanced U.S. weaponry that had been sold to the Shah finding its way into hostile (USSR) or unstable (Libya) hands. In December 1978, JCS dispatched a team of Special Operations planners, led by Colonel Jerry King, USA, the Chief of the JCS Special Operations Division's Unconventional Warfare Branch, to Europe. The team included several members of the REDCOM JTF 7X cadre, including the J-2. The purpose was to assist the European Command planners (members of the U.S. Special Operations Task Force Europe - SOTFE) with the development of contingency options to recover, disable or destroy the most sensitive military equipment, if that became necessary. The equipment ranged from elements of the American NIKE Air Defense System to fighter aircraft air-to-air missile guidance systems and Navy Command and Control systems. During this week-long effort, extensive research was conducted on the installations and systems of concern and target folders were prepared. Fortunately, none of the installations were in urban build-up areas, simplifying the development of force insertion and extraction options.

However, given the large number of Americans and other westerners in Iran at the time, and not wishing to create any animosity with the fragile interim Iranian civilian government or the growing religious right, the State Department recommended no action be taken and military planning was suspended.

Less than three weeks later, on 16 January 1979, the Shah abrogated power and left Iran. Two weeks after that (on 31 January), Ayatollah Khomeini, who was vehemently opposed to the Shah and had been living in France since his exile more than 15 years earlier, returned to Teheran to the tumultuous welcome of hundred of thousands of chanting Iranians. The turmoil increased steadily in the ensuing weeks, as the civil government became weaker and the religious fundamentalists stronger.

On the 14th of February, the American Embassy compound was overrun by a mob composed mostly of Islamic Revolution Militia, known as the Pasdaran. Most of the Americans barricaded themselves in the compound buildings and several groups prepared to defend themselves with weapons. However, after some four hours of dialogue between the U.S. Department of State, the American Ambassador on scene and officials of the interim civil government, the militia was persuaded to withdraw from the compound. An armed confrontation was avoided, as was the need to employ American military forces.

Subsequently, the Embassy staff was reduced and all families were evacuated during the next few months. Many of those who remained thought (hoped) that the worst was over. The Embassy community consisted of several divergent groups, each with their own set of values and viewpoints on the situation and the world. There were the diplomats, the economic consulars, the CIA officers, the military attachés and the somewhat separate, Military Assistance Group which coordinated directly with the Iranian Military High Command. The Iranian military structure at the time was considered by some to be the only stable force in the country.

The U.S. State Department advised President Carter that it was better to continue a diplomatic presence, maintain as many avenues of communication as possible, and seek to develop others with the emerging regime. State reasoned that to pull up stakes would allow the Soviets unimpeded access to the region. Some American advisors believed that, just as the Shah had been a buffer against Soviet influence in the area, it would be folly to surrender any potential the United States might have to achieve a similar relationship with the new Iranian government, whomever that might be.

Both the JTF-7X and Delta staffs considered Iran a potential trouble spot. Both had identified the American Embassy as a likely target. It had been on REDCOM's potential list for more than nine months and had been used as the backdrop for a major REDCOM JRX. Delta, via Army channels, suggested to the State Department that the Embassy warranted a detailed security survey. The Teheran embassy was already high on the DIA/REDCOM list of eleven such locations. The survey would have allowed a detailed set of blue prints, diagrams, and photographic documentation to be collected and available should the need arise. The State Department turned down the Army (Delta) offer just as they had turned down similar entreaties by DIA and REDCOM.

During the early months of 1979, Colonel Beckwith and Delta began working with both DOD and non-DOD agencies, including the FBI, the

CIA and the Defense Nuclear Agency. Several "Delta-only" training exercises were conducted with each of these organizations. Some of these were conducted in metropolitan settings, including San Francisco and New York. In keeping with Charlie's view of counter-terror operations, virtually all of the training scenarios reflected a "permissive non-hostile environment," where the surrounding area was controlled by friendly elements, be they local, state or federal authorities, or a cooperative foreign government.

In the spring of 1979, a first occurred. The JTF 7X cadre and 1st SFOD-Delta conducted a collaborative exercise. It was conducted on government property, on an island in extreme southern Florida, essentially in the middle of a military family housing area. The scenario painted a picture of a well advanced, highly volatile terrorist group that claimed it possessed a nuclear weapon and threatened to detonate it on a given timetable, injuring hundreds of civilians and threatening an adjacent metropolitan area unless their demands were met. The background information indicated that there were elements of truth in their claim. Several pounds of plutonium had been stolen a few months before from a research laboratory and the theft had not been publicly acknowledged. A real situation of this nature would have involved nuclear weapons specialists from the Defense Nuclear Agency, called NEST (Nuclear Emergency Search Team). In keeping with the real-world training philosophy of both REDCOM and Delta, a NEST team participated in the exercise. The NEST role was twofold: confirm the probability of the terrorists possessing nuclear material, and then to dismantle any such device once Delta had effected the takedown. A wide range of surveillance and sensor techniques were applied during the planning phase to pinpoint the precise location and guard posture of the terrorists and the most probable location of the nuclear device, a NEST training model which emitted the essential characteristics of a true device. Two of the observers positioned in the JTF/Delta command and observation post during the takedown were General Hennessey and Ambassador Anthony Quainton. The exercise was concluded satisfactorily with the rapid neutralization of the terrorists and no loses to Delta.

In the three years following the withdrawal of U.S. forces from Vietnam (1973-1976), Special Forces (SF) strength had dropped from seven plus, very robust active-duty, SF Groups to three under-strength groups. It was to remain at this level for the next seven years. The nominal size of a full-up group approximated 1,400 soldiers. During the low period of the late 70s, the actual numbers dropped to half the TO&E strength. Similar situations existed in the Air Force, and to a lesser extent in the Navy. The Air Force Special Operations AC-130 gunships were not funded in the active force budget beyond 1979, and were scheduled for deactivation or transition to reserve status that in other situations (such as reconnaissance platforms) was a death knell. Also, the MC-130 Combat Talons (long range force insertion platforms) were old machines and were not scheduled for any significant new modifications or Service Life Extension Programs (SLEP). Air Force deep-penetration helicopters were virtually non-existent, except in the "White Hatted" Air Rescue Service which was operated in small detachments. There was a general feeling among pilots and crews in the Air Force that SOF was not a career-enhancing assignment. At the same time, the Navy was about to decommission the last of its special warfare/operations-capable submarines.

One can conclude that the creation of Delta Force was an anomaly. The trend was clearly toward downsizing, as evidenced by the fact that not only had the size of SOF been reduced but also that SOF funding had been cut by 95 per cent in the 1970s. Still, the activation of Delta Force was a beginning, although it was not necessarily a change in institutional service attitudes, given that its birth was the product of a few individuals, not an institution.

***

In the spring and summer of 1979, the military personnel machine began to churn out the normal set of rotational reassignments as it did every year. At the top of the Army pyramid, General Rogers, the Army Chief of Staff, was posted to Europe to assume duties as the U.S. Commander-in-Chief, Europe, and dual-hatted as the Supreme Allied Commander of Europe, the senior military officer in NATO. Lieutenant General Meyer, the Army Deputy for Operations and Plans, was promoted to full General and appointed to replace General Rogers as the new Army Chief of Staff. Colonel Beckwith also received orders. Charlie was alerted for an assignment to Europe. His projected move was to occur later in the year, in early winter. He was to assume command of the EUCOM Joint Special Operations Staff. Called Special Operations Task Force Europe (SOTFE), this cadre of special operations personnel was the senior special operations planning element for the United States European Command. Two other Army officers, both former Ranger Battalion Commanders, Lt. Colonels Wayne Downing and Joseph Stringham, who were very familiar with the Rangers, the 1st SOW and JTF 7X, were selected to attend senior service schools.

Many of the original REDCOM JTF-7X cadre were also reassigned, due to the normal three-year rotation cycle. This included the primary communications, operations and intelligence planners. Several were transferred to the Washington area, as was General Vaught and a number of his EDRE planning staff from Fort Stewart who had been instrumental in developing the exercises and the logistics support. The JTF-7X Operations Officer, LTC Bobby Davis, was assigned to the alternate National Military Command Post at Fort Richey, Maryland. The former chief communicator, LTC Peter Dieck, was assigned to the Army staff, while the JTF-7X J-2 was assigned to JCS's Special Operations Division, not as an intelligence officer but as an International-Political Affairs Officer in the Special Plans Branch. In addition, the former Blue Light Intelligence Officer, a seasoned Special Forces officer, received orders assigning him to DIA.

Most of these individuals thought that they had left the world of counter-terrorism operations behind them, at least for a while. Little did they know that the skills and experience they had acquired working on JTF-7X and with the Rangers, Blue Light (and Delta), and the Air Force Special Operations forces, would soon be put to a major test.

CHAPTER TWO
The Take Over
(and Initial Reactions)

It was mid-morning on Sunday, the 4th of November, a work day in Iran. The Chargé D'Affairs, the senior American Diplomat, left the Embassy compound at about 09:30, exiting through a throng of demonstrators, which had become somewhat of a routine occurrence in the past few months. He had an appointment at the Ministry of Foreign Affairs (MFA) some twenty blocks away at 10:00. The mob was composed mostly of Iranian women each wrapped in the traditional Islamic body-concealing robe called a Chador, chanting religious and anti-American slogans. They did not appear to pose any particular danger.

At approximately 10:25, several male demonstrators climbed over the main gate of the American Embassy compound. Once inside, they quickly opened the gate while two Iran National Police officers assigned to protect the Embassy stood by and watched, doing nothing to stop the intruders. Once the gate was opened, several hundred Chador-clad figures carrying placards and banners surged into the compound. The invasion of this sea of humanity was immediately reported to both the State Department Operations Center in Washington and to the Chargé at the Ministry of Foreign Affairs (MFA) via telephone. Both lines remained open and a dialogue continued between Foggy Bottom and the besieged Embassy staff and the Chargé for the next several hours.

Part of the invading crowd assembled in front of the multi-storied brick Chancery building and continued to chant anti-American slogans while other groups swept around the Chancery and headed directly toward the senior staff residences and the Consulate building located behind and to the left of the Chancery. A smaller group led by a young male splintered off and proceeded directly to the rear of the Chancery building and began to force an entry through a basement window. The group that reached the Consulate building focused its efforts on an attempt to gain entry through an unbarred, second story bathroom window.

Word of the presence of demonstrators on the compound quickly spread among Embassy personnel, but there was no panic. The Chancery and consulate buildings were immediately locked and secured by the on-duty Marine guards. The off-duty Marines, living in the Bijon Apartments immediately behind the compound, were notified and told to remain where they were and offer no resistance. Within a short period of time, the Marines were taken prisoner by several male militants.

The State Department Regional (Embassy) Security Officer (RSO) instructed the on-duty Marines to initiate the established emergency defense plan. Upon learning that some of the crowd had penetrated the basement of the Chancery, the RSO went down to the penetration point and began a discussion with the student leader, finally convincing him to withdraw the group. Meanwhile, all Embassy personnel within the Chancery had moved to the second floor, and sequestered themselves behind locked doors.

The RSO left the Chancery with the student leaders through the same window the penetrators had used to gain entry, then headed to the Consulate building past the row of small staff cottages to investigate the situation at the Consulate. He found the building secure and the occupants safe. The attempted penetration by the militants through the second floor window had been thwarted by an alert Marine guard. The RSO then returned to the front of the Chancery with the student leader.

Due to the small number of demonstrators and its location on the perimeter of the compound, most of the consulate occupants were able to leave the building (and the compound) undetected. However, the last group, consisting of five Americans, was captured a few blocks from the compound by a combination of students and Pasdaran. Two Iranian National police stood by and did not interfere with their capture. The group was escorted back to the compound and led to the Ambassador's residence where they were handcuffed and placed under the surveillance of armed guards.

After reentering the Chancery, the RSO received permission from the Chargé to go back outside and attempt to diffuse the crowd in front of the building. He left his flak jacket and weapon with the Marine guard and again departed the Chancery building. The RSO renewed his dialogue with the students with the intent of allowing them to conduct a symbolic protest, in the form of a "sit-in" on the Embassy grounds. During these discussions, two older males emerged from the crowd. The crowd now contained a growing number of older males, some of whom were carrying clubs painted with "Down With America."

The two older individuals brusquely ushered the young student leader aside, took the RSO's radio, put a gun to his head and told him to order the door to the Chancery opened. The RSO told his captors that such a decision would have to come from the Chargé. The RSO then shouted to the Marine inside the building, who had been covering him, to call the Chargé and tell himChargé that the situation was "just like February 14th." The RSO was led away to a building in the adjacent Embassy Motor Pool area. Once there, he was tied and placed under armed guard.

Approximately ten minutes later, the RSO was taken back into the basement of the Chancery through the original student penetration point. Meanwhile, the students had started a fire on the first floor of the Chancery in an effort to dispel the effects of a tear gas grenade that had been accidentally discharged by one of the Marines as the Americans retreated to the higher floors.

The RSO, now tied and blindfolded, was led up to the second floor. He was then forced to relay the militants' demands via phone to the last group of "free" Americans who had locked themselves in the secure vault area and were busy destroying classified material. After some delay, during which the overall situation was discussed via telephone, between those in the secure area and the Chargé, the Chargé directed the vault holdouts to open the door and surrender. Reluctantly, the order was obeyed. The door was opened and the last Americans were taken captive.

As the Americans were taken prisoner, they were blindfolded and their hands tied with precut, pre-knotted nylon rope. During the initial capture of each group, particularly those who held out in the secure and vaulted areas, a degree of rough handling was experienced.

As various portions of the Chancery came under the control of the militants, the rooms were ransacked and symbols of America were defaced. Next came attempts, often at gun- or knife-point, to coerce Americans into opening safes, cabinets and locked desks. The takeover was completed by 3:00 that afternoon.

Initially, all the Americans were confined to either the Ambassador's residence at the rear of the compound or one of the four staff cottages. During the first three days, the captors conducted an identification and screening process of the Americans and other hostages. This sometimes involved a hostage being brought back to his/her work area to open safes and identify material.

Unknown to the Iranians, a handful of Americans who had escaped from the Consulate building early in the takeover-process had been picked up and were hidden by the Canadian Ambassador.

The White House, CIA, DIA and JCS had been informed of the mob action, the subsequent series of dialogues and surrender actions on a nearly continuous basis by the State Department via the National Intelligence Warning Network (NIWON). Shortly after news of the initial action reached the Pentagon and the European Command, Crisis Action Teams (CATs) and small planning cells were convened. One of these planning cells was convened within the Special Operations Division (SOD) of the Operations Directorate of the JCS J-3, another within the U.S. European Command headquarters in Germany, which had operational responsibility for U.S. military affairs in Iran. The eastern Iranian border with Pakistan marked the boundary between the U.S. European and U.S. Pacific Command's areas of responsibility.

Word of the Embassy takeover reached Colonel Beckwith (the Commander of Delta) at about 7:00 A.M. Sunday morning, East Coast time, the 4th of November. Delta had just concluded its second and final mission certification, a dual-target takedown set within a permissive environment with Delta doing its own reconnaissance and planning, as it routinely did. The targets were taken down successfully and nearly simultaneously. Delta had formally graduated, and operationally was less than twelve hours old.

Most of Delta had returned to Fort Bragg by 3:00 P.M. that afternoon and were involved in unpacking and cleaning their gear as Colonel Beckwith reviewed the AP and Reuters News Service dispatches that the Delta Intelligence Section had assembled. There was no official DOD message traffic on the incident, yet. Sunday night passed uneventfully. However, early Monday morning, Charlie received a call on the secure line from the staff duty officer in the Army's Special Operations Division requesting that Delta send a liaison officer to Washington to work with a JCS planning team.

On Day One, Sunday, the JCS planning team consisted of three officers from the JCS-Directorate of Operations, Special Operations Division (JCS-SOD). The team was headed by Jerry King an Army Special Forces Colonel, and included Air Force Special Operations pilot Lt. Colonel Bob Horton and Navy SEAL Commander Maynard Weyers. On Monday, the team was expanded by the assignment of an intelligence officer (IO), Lt. Colonel Lenahan, USAF, from another office in the Division. He had recently been assigned to SOD after completing three years with the REDCOM CT-JTF (JTF-7X) as its Chief of Intelligence. This initial cadre was augmented by noon with the arrival of two liaison officers from Delta. The senior of the two was Major Jesse Johnson, who in his vested, three-button, blue pin-striped suit looked more like a Madison Avenue advertising executive than a gun-toting counter-terrorist operator. The other officer was Captain Lewis "Bucky" Burrus. The pair did not go together, but their skills and personalities complemented each other; undoubtedly, they were selected by Colonel Beckwith as a mutual counterbalance. Bucky, a tall, raw-boned figure, had the persona of the good-old country boy from the backwoods. This hid his quick mind, his exceptionally fast reflexes, and his tactical planning skills as a CT operator.

The JCS-SOD planning cadre also drew support from three inter-linked functional groups of action officers. These included the rest of the JCS Special Operations Division, the Service Special Operations Staffs, as well as the DOD intelligence (DIA/NSA/DMA) contingency response structure. By midday Monday, all of these networks were focused on assisting the planning cell.

The principal task of the SOD cell was to monitor developments and assemble a picture of the situation in Iran, and conduct a feasibility evaluation of a range of insertion and extraction possibilities. The development of the ground tactical plan was under the purview of Delta, who would also have a major say in the selection of the final insertion and extraction options.

The SOD cell began receiving DIA analytical and imagery support immediately. This was soon followed by SIGINT (Signals Intelligence) feeds from NSA. This limited hard data was accompanied by a flood of speculation, rumor and opinions from the U.S. and international news media and a variety of international and national HUMINT (Human Intelligence) sources and agencies.

The immediate intelligence actions included: broad area photo research as well as pinpoint imagery collection; the production of special maps and gridded photo products; and focusing of NSA collection apparatus on the communications structure of the Iranian military and paramilitary forces to include the police communications network.

Blueprints of the Embassy buildings were obtained from the Department of State through the DIA liaison officers. The production of a three dimensional model of the compound was begun by a special support team of imagery interpreters and model builders at the National Photographic Interpretation Center (NPIC). This team of artists and technicians combined almost unsurpassed mathematical and craftsmen skills. The team was led for many years by a government civilian, Mr. Joe Montiminy and his able assistance Kenny Lane, who were past masters at their art but had never undertaken a project of the scope and detail required by the rescue planners. The Embassy model eventually grew to be more than 16 by 20 feet in size, with many of the buildings being floor-by-floor "take apart" cutouts. Other models to their credit included "Mary," the model of the Son Tay prison compound in North Vietnam, Khe Sanh Airfield, used to brief President Johnson on the siege, and more than two hundred others from Soviet Submarines to the Russian Space and Missile launch Complex at Turya Tam.

During the night, a secure teletype link was established between the planning team and Delta to carry the intelligence flow. This network was expanded as each operational entity was brought into the planning process.

A weather officer was assigned at the request of the planning cell intelligence officer. The IO had already reviewed the historical climatological data for the region and was aware, given the distances involved and the lack of weather stations in the most likely ingress corridor, that it would take weeks to build and validate an accurate weather forecast. This was to be the primary mission of the weather officer. Regrettably, the most experienced special operations weather officer (Air Force Lieutenant Colonel Keith Grimes) had been killed in the C-135 crash at Albuquerque during a REDCOM CT field exercise the previous year. The USAF weather institution had no one else of his caliber. A young Captain, Don Buchanan, was assigned as the JTF Staff Weather Officer (SWO). The daily compilation of weather data was begun. This data served as the basis for running one-, two-, and five-day forecasts. The forecasts were subsequently compared with the actual conditions that had occurred. Over a period of time, the difference between the predicted forecast and the actual weather decreased. Reconnaissance imagery was also used to compliment and validate weather data. This was particular true regarding forecasts of rain or snow. The reconnaissance imagery covered areas where there were no weather reporting sites.*

Other activities included a deliberate focus on the collection and evaluation of all open source reporting, regardless of media. This material included American television and foreign newsmagazines which often had data not presented in U.S. print or TV media. Another immediate priority was the production of all available hand-held photography of the city of Teheran and its environs. The DIA/CIA files included more than 1,500 hand-held photos. When the JTF print request hit the DIA production coordinator, a call was received asking for a reduction of the order. Please pinpoint specific locations. Would black and white versions of color pictures be acceptable? Could the number of copies be reduced? None of these curtailments were possible. Too much operational data would be lost. The photo laboratory processed the original request in less than 24 hours. These photographs, although many were unindexed as to precise location, proved to be of immense value throughout the next fourteen months. They provided the planners, the Delta operators and the reconnaissance teams with a ground perspective they could not have obtained through any other means.

All the available technical collection and research capabilities were quickly brought to bear in an attempt to fill critical planning voids and minimize the potential acceptance of unsupported human reporting as factual data. On-the-ground reliable HUMINT coverage was slim to nonexistent and the chances of immediate improvement were not promising. The collapse of the Shah's regime, the changing status of the Iranian leadership, and the hostile attitude of the population would make it difficult, but not impossible, to obtain reliable human source reporting.

---

* In most countries, weather is a human and economic concern, and therefore most civil weather stations are located near population centers or facilities that need weather observations to maintain, conduct or plan their operations (airfields, ports, farms, etc.). Rarely are weather stations located in uninhabited remote locations, thus much weather forecasting is based on an interpretation of general upper altitude weather movements (and patterns) derived from orbiting weather satellites. The ability of a weather forecaster not familiar with the history of the ground-level weather in a given area to accurately predict lower altitude and ground-level weather conditions from satellite observations is extremely limited.

Possible insertion and extraction locations, as identified from reconnaissance imagery, needed to be checked out on the ground. Of equal priority was definitive data on the specific hostage detention sites within the Embassy compound. Initially, the JTF looked to the CIA to fill these voids.

***

On the 6th of November, the Iranian militants claimed that five percent of the hostages were being held outside the compound in private homes as insurance against an American rescue attempt. The SOD planning cell intelligence officer took this to be a strong possibility, not just an unfounded claim, but the CIA liaison officers believed the latter. The first formal DOD options review was conducted on the 6th of November. This was the same day that Ayatollah Khomeini publicly stated his endorsement of the militants' action.

It was apparent to the small JCS/Delta coordination team that the situation was serious, and not likely to be resolved quickly. It was going to be a long hard pull. In the standard "can-do" tradition, the SOD planning team, aided by the service special operations and special plans staffs, began to come to grips with the hard-line realities of the "what if situations." Some of these were suggested by history, others by the rhetoric coming from Iran, which included threats to put the Americans on trial as spies and execute them.

Other JCS planning teams had also been convened, under the title of Operational Planning Group (OPG). These planning and option development groups were charged with looking at major force capabilities and retaliation options. This latter effort was spurred by the Iranian threat to kill the hostages. The SOD and OPG planning groups operated separately, but key senior officials flowed between the two to ensure compatibility and deconfliction. Deconfliction included operational planning, resource tasking, high level coordination interface, and adjudication of intelligence collection and production priorities. For this reason, the same DIA coordination team supported both planning efforts.

Significant planning and HUMINT collection problems were encountered as a result of the shifting range of perceptions held by various Washington constituencies. During the first few days, there was quite a bit of wishful thinking (outside of the rescue-planning cell) that the Iranian government would "step in" and free the Embassy staff as had happened nine months earlier. One set of perceptions presumed that the hostages would be released soon and there was little reason for concern.

This school of thought, and others, continued to shift the anticipated release date forward from hours to days, and then to weeks, as new milestones came and went. Milestones included: the first 72 hours; ten days;

Thanksgiving; a Red Cross visit; then Christmas, etcetera. Part of this school of thought was concerned that making any type of military preparations or taking any on-the-ground reconnaissance initiatives would jeopardize the possibility of negotiations and an early hostage release.

Part of the hopeful attitude held by the State Department and some officers of the CIA was aided by the selective release of three hostages on Day Fourteen (17 November), followed the next day by the release of another ten hostages. The first releasees included two women and a black Marine. The second group of releasees consisted of ten young black males, mostly Marines. The Iranian rationale for the releases had its roots in both propaganda and political gambits. The release automatically gave some life to the possibility of a negotiated settlement, while at the same time it showed the more serious side of the threat by retaining the more senior hostages, which was reinforced by the Iranian claim that the need for a trial persisted.

Early on, there was a plethora of senior officials, military and civilian, that visited the JCS planning area and, because of their rank, believed that they had a need to be kept abreast of events and the planning. By the fourth day, as the situation came to be recognized as a major challenge (not an opportunity for instant glory), the number of these erstwhile advisors decreased sharply as they distanced themselves from the potential "tar baby."

On the 7th of November, the Chairman of the Joint Chiefs, General Jones, hosted a senior level meeting to review the situation. Attendees included Harold Brown, the Secretary of Defense, the Army Chief of Staff, General Meyer, and Lt. General Philip Shutler, USMC, the JCS J-3, and others. After the senior SOD planner, Colonel Jerry King, a square-jawed, highly meticulous Special Forces officer with tremendous intellectual capacity presented the situation update and a summary of the planning options and potential mission challenges, it was agreed that the situation was too complicated for Delta to handle on its own. The complexities of planning a rescue, the scale of which had never before been undertaken, were huge. Tactically conducting a rescue in a twenty-seven acre compound consisting of more than sixteen buildings holding upwards of 67 possible hostages at five different locations guarded by a force numbering more than 150, which in turn was supported by bands of armed zealot irregulars, was daunting. Coupled with the above was a hostile (or at least questionable) government status and an unpredictable civilian population that was in the throes of a social revolution. Compounding the problem was the fact that the rescue objective was located in a congested urban center more than 1,600 miles from the nearest American military base. The American Embassy was located almost dead center in the Capitol City, which held the potential to be a very nasty hornet's nest, once disturbed. The city of

Teheran stretched more than sixteen miles from north to south and ten miles east to west in a dense network of narrow streets and highly populated areas. Within these confines, there were no less than seven major military bases, more than 100 police stations, and an unknown number of armed neighborhood militia groups. In a nutshell, the situation was more challenging than any exercise, or series of "what ifs" problem-solving intellectual excursions ever conducted by REDCOM, Blue Light or Delta, or faced by the Israeli Defense Forces or the German CT-unit GSFG-9.

It would take a melding of a wide range of talent and expertise to pull this one off. A formal organization one echelon above Delta, a joint task force, would be needed to coordinate all the aspects of the rescue effort. It would have to operate from the Pentagon. No one knew how long the situation would drag on. Both strategic and tactical surprise (i.e., mission success) were highly dependent of the utmost security and concealment of all preparations. What the planners did know was that this "exercise" was not a 72-96 hour, "grab your rucksack and rifle and go for it" training EDRE. This was for real, for the long haul, and very serious. And, just as the continuing REDCOM analysis had stated, each situation was different from its predecessors and always more difficult. The opposition had learned from previous events and applied the lessons to make the next more difficult. This challenge made the events of Son Tay, Entebbe and Mogadishu and the earlier planning for the recovery of the sensitive American equipment from the Iranian military bases seem simple by comparison.

While various insertion and extraction concepts were being explored, Delta was wrestling with some of the key factors confounding their tactical planning. The most critical factor was the exact location of the hostages. Were they all in the compound? If so, were they in two buildings or scattered throughout several? Were hostages being held in the Chancery or the basement warehouse called the Mushroom Inn? Regardless of which set of answers was correct, the possible tactical solutions were limited by the size of Delta force. Essentially, Colonel Beckwith had only one fully trained "Troop," about 40 shooters. More were in training, but even those farthest along were four to six weeks from completion of training that could not be cut short. They had to learn and hone the skills they would need the most. No shortcuts were allowed.

Complicating all the physical and logistical challenges faced in developing a viable option was the political issue of final staging locations. The force could not be launched directly from the United States, or even Europe, and be landed in the middle of downtown Teheran ready to conduct the mission. Some closer location or locations would have to be found. One possibility was to launch from an aircraft carrier, but the Navy refused to consider putting a carrier inside the Arabian Gulf. Navy planners contended that maneuvering room was limited and such a placement would subject the carrier and its escort vessels to a possible air attack from Iran. Thus, the closest launch point for a carrier-based force would be outside the gulf and up to a hundred miles off the southeast coast of Iran, making a rescue effort a round trip of more than 1,500 miles. This was too much for any helicopter in the American fleet to accomplish without refueling.

Additionally, given a nominal ground speed of 120 miles per hour, just the inbound transit could take more than six hours. The long flight duration would also take a toll on both the helicopter aircrews and the rescue force. Even assuming quick mission success on the ground, the outbound recovery transit could take another four to six hours. This would be plenty of time for the Iranian Air Force to launch fighters to intercept the slow-moving choppers. These straight-line travel calculations did not even consider another critical factor -- the need for darkness to mask the insertion and extraction flights. Even in November, darkness could fully cover only one leg of the mission. By May, there would be barely enough darkness to cover the inbound transits, dictating a two-night operation. All of these factors raised the probability of an early discovery or a two-day mission profile. Insert on Night One, hide during the following day, and then conduct the ground rescue and air extraction on Night Two.

Beginning on the 10th of November, the Defense Mapping Agency (DMA) delivered the first of the many special map and photo-gridded products they were to prepare during the next fourteen months. The typical graphic included a map insert delineating the area of concern, an overview photograph and one or more enlargements of key sub-areas. Products were made for both hostage detention sites and all areas of future operational activity. The first products focused on the Embassy, the city, and a potential extraction airfield south of Teheran, which had been identified by the EUCOM Special Operations-Hostage Recovery planning team led by Major James Magee, USMC.

On the same day, an Air Force officer, Major Harry Johnson, who was assigned to the Embassy but who had been on leave in the United States when the compound was overrun, was assigned to the JTF. In going over the blueprints of the various compound buildings (which had been obtained from the State Department earlier), he noted that many of the drawings were inaccurate due to interior modifications made in the past few years. This prompted a joint review of the blueprints and the building models with two State Department personnel who had also recently served in Iran. This three-man team updated the blueprints and the models were corrected. (Two weeks later, Major Johnson was assisted in a second review by another Air Force officer. Captain Neil Robinson brought a new set of insights to the review. Robinson, an Air Force academy graduate and Intelligence officer with the body of a Golden Gloves champion, was one of the black hostages released as part of a propaganda ploy by the militants ten days later.)

In parallel with the JCS planning effort, the EUCOM hostage recovery cell had been busy developing, evaluating, and refining various rescue options. On 10 Nov 79, the EUCOM J-3 Deputy Director, submitted the EUCOM options by secure phone to Brigadier James H. Johnson, USA, his planning counterpart in the JCS-J-3 for evaluation. Within thirty-six hours, JCS asked EUCOM (and the U.S. Pacific Command) to send a planning representative to Washington to assist in option development. The two commands responded quickly; their respective planning representatives Liaison Officers (LNOs), Major Magee for EUCOM and Colonel Jim Keating, USAF from the Pacific Command were en route to Washington within twenty-four hours.

The next day (11 Nov), it was learned from the media, and confirmed by the State Department, that four foreign diplomats had been allowed to visit the compound and had seen most but not all of the hostages. The diplomats visited hostages in six different buildings within the compound, none of which was the multi-story masonry-and-brick Chancery, the building where more than half of the hostages had been seized. The diplomats were told that five percent of the hostages were being detained in a private house off the compound as insurance against a U.S. rescue attempt. If true, as suspected by the SOD planners, this meant that the hostages were being held in at least three separate locations outside of the compound. One was the unidentified site the diplomats had been told of. The second was the Iranian Ministry of Foreign Affairs (MFA), where three Americans including the Chargé had been detained under guard since the Embassy takeover. The third was the location of the "Invisible Canadian Six," whom the State Department and CIA refused to acknowledge even existed. Thus, a total of nine distinct locations (6 in and 3 off the compound), of which at least two were unknown, contained American personnel.

The planning cell intelligence staff had been carrying the missing six Americans as unlocated but safely outside the hands of the Iranians. When this topic was discussed with the CIA Liaison Officers, the planning cell J-2 was told not to be concerned and to quietly drop the six from the hostage tracking board. This was done at the overt level, but tracking was quietly maintained off stage. At the same time, the planning cell J-2 was concerned about the Chargé and his two companions in the Ministry of Foreign Affairs (MFA), being overlooked given the intense focus on the Embassy compound.

The topic of the Chargé and his two companions was not welcome when brought to the attention of Colonel Beckwith, who contended that he had his hands full handling the compound with its potential for numerous sub-holding sites. He did not want his planning made any more complex or his force capability watered down by having to take on another location. At the same time he did not want another ground force brought into play. He resisted this need for a long time, but eventually had to accept the reality of the two rescue locations (Embassy and MFA). He had also initially resisted the potential involvement of Rangers as a security force, but acquiesced to the need to develop and exercise several insertion and extraction scenarios. Eventually, he and the Ranger battalion commander, Lt. Colonel Sherman Williford, struck up a positive relationship. Williford designated a planning cadre (representatives from Operations, Intelligence and Communications) and a specific Ranger company for the mission. Knowledge of the mission was limited to the planning team. Several members of the Ranger team, including Colonel Williford, Captain David Grange (Operations), and Captain Johnie McClellon (Intelligence), were familiar with the planning and security procedures from their REDCOM Counter-terrorist JTF-7X training exercises.

Meanwhile, the selection of a qualified General Officer to Command the JTF had begun in a dialogue between General David Jones, CJCS and General Meyer, the Army Chief of Staff. General Meyer had been an early proponent and supporter of Delta long before Charlie received the full green light in November 1977, but Meyer realized that the Embassy situation was beyond the capabilities of Delta alone. Meyer recommended General Jim Vaught, recently reassigned to the Army Operations Staff in the Pentagon, as his candidate to command the JTF. In addition to General Vaught's experience as an Army Division and JTF Commander, he had an appreciation for raid planning.

At the time of his selection, General Vaught was airborne, en route to Europe on a long-planned business trip. As soon as General Jones concurred with the nomination, General Meyer flashed a message to General Vaught's European reception party to have Vaught contact him as soon as he arrived. The message that General Meyer passed to General Vaught in their initial transatlantic telephone call was brief and to the point: Vaught had been selected to head the rescue effort, he would have a JTF staff of his choice, and Delta would be available. Meyer instructed Vaught to get back to Washington ASAP, preferably by the next available direct flight. The next flight was an Air France Concorde, which Vaught charged to his personal credit card. Eventually he was reimbursed, but only after a long paper battle with the bureaucrats who administer the DOD policy of "cheaper is better" when it comes to air travel.

Upon reaching Washington on Monday the 12th, General Vaught went directly to the Pentagon and the office of General Meyer and from there directly to the office of the Chairman of the Joint Chiefs of Staff, General David Jones. In the meantime, the number of staff personnel involved in supporting the initial planning assessments had been expanded to approximately 25 officers, which included support cells from three service staffs. The Chief of the SOD Unconventional Warfare (UW) Branch, Colonel Jerry King (who was also the senior rescue planner) worked with one of the Army staffers. They prepared a roster of all these individuals along with a notation as to their current role and background, and a recommendation as to their future role in the JTF.

The roster was provided to General Vaught when he returned from his meeting with General Jones. Within a day, he had reviewed the list and made his selections, adding a few officers with particular skills or knowledge. There was little change in the cadre staff positions; however, some key positions remained unfilled.

Two of these unfilled positions were the Chief of Staff and Director of Operations (J-3). The chief of the SOD UW branch, Colonel Jerry King, had been working both these positions in his role as lead planner and action officer. He remained in this dual capacity, although early on there were suggestions to bring in any one of three Army officers to be the J-3. All three candidates were familiar with the JCS CONPLAN and the REDCOM JTF 7X operations. Two were former Ranger Battalion Commanders . Both were then attending senior service schools. The Army staff thought their abrupt removal would cause unwarranted questioning and speculation. The third candidate, the former REDCOM JTF 7X J-3, was assigned to the alternate National Military Command Center at Fort Richey as a Command Post Team Chief. His transfer was not looked on favorably, either. Of all the people, available Jerry King had the background, drive, stamina, brains and personality to pull it off. He was Special Forces and Ranger qualified, tough and level-headed with a tremendous operational grasp, and had staff, command and troop experience. Like the majority of the JTF, he had seen combat service in Vietnam. He also had been the JCS team leader on the earlier Iranian weapons neutralization contingency planning of the previous December, as well as the JCS observer on several REDCOM 7X exercises.

A shrewd judge of character and highly knowledgeable of the organizational and talent needs of a JTF staff, King began to match capabilities with responsibilities. Within 72 hours, a total headquarters of 32 people had emerged. The team was large enough to get things done efficiently, yet small enough to preclude the generation of unnecessary paperwork or wasted effort. Given its size and compactness, King was able to closely monitor both the staff elements and the operations planners. Like a Roman galley Captain, he verbally beat the drum or flogged the laggard who seemed to be drifting from the mainstream of requirements

The support personnel, part of the 32, came with the local furniture. Most important was the administrative clerk, Navy Yeoman Bill Collins. Extraordinarily efficient, capable of dealing with and manipulating divergent Officer personalities, and a very hard worker, Bill Collins also had a major additional benefit -- a wife who cooked fantastic meals for 32 people on short notice. The Yeoman's catering service became a much appreciated and essential part of the work and the morale system. This type of unsolicited dedication and commitment to the mission and team was not mentioned in any Service manual.

One key position that initially was unfilled was that of senior air planner and coordinator. The Air Staff recommended Colonel Jim Kyle, who had orders transferring him to Kirkland Air Force Base, New Mexico, but who was still at his old duty station in Hawaii. Kyle was contacted at his quarters on 11 November, kissed his wife goodbye, and boarded a plane for Washington that night. After meeting with his Air Staff point of contact the next morning, and then passing muster with "Hammer" (General Vaught's cover nickname), Colonel Kyle began to assess the strengths and weakness of the air equation. He quickly pinpointed that, in addition to the need for more blackout landing practice, the greatest weakness was the lack of a reliable refueling plan.

The strategic distances involved -- the United States to the Middle East, and from whatever Middle East launch sites were chosen, into Iran and back out -- were horrendous. The Middle East tactical legs were of the most concern. The most beneficial estimate of the air distances involved in the tactical leg exceeded 2,500 miles. This was not a great challenge for C-130s, the most probable part of the fixed-wing equation; but, if helicopters were to be involved, as the planning probabilities indicated, then some innovative refueling measures had to be worked out.

On 12 November 1979, the rescue force was officially constituted as a Joint Task Force by General Jones, under the innocuous designation JTF 1-79.

The staff lineup reflected the following roll call:

Commander .... Major General Jim Vaught, USA
Special Advisor .... Lt. General Phillip Gast, USAF*
Air Deputy Senior Air Planner....... Colonel Jim Kyle, USAF
Chief of Staff .... Colonel Jerry King, USA
Operations Planner (Training)........ Commander Meynard Weyers, USN

---

* Former Commander of the US Military Advisory Group, Iran and de facto JTF 1-79 Deputy Commander (in-waiting)

Operations Planner (Air-Flow)....... Lt. Colonel Bob Horton, USAF
Communications Officer.............. LTC Peter Dieck, USA
Logistics Officer......................... LTC John Barnett, USA
Personnel Officer .... Chief Petty Officer Bill Collins, USN
Field Training Coordinator........... Major Keith Nightingale, USA
Intelligence Officer .... Lt. Col. Rod Lenahan, USAF
Intelligence Officer .... Major Dick Friedel, USA
Intelligence Officer .... Captain Tim Casey, USA
Delta Liaison Officer.................. Major Jesse Johnson, USA
Delta Liaison Officer.................. Major Bucky Burruss, USA
EUROPEAN Command LNO....... Major Jim Magee, USMC
PACIFIC Command LNO .... Colonel Jim Keating, USAF
NSA Liaison Officer .... Commander Bud Fossett, USN
NSA Liaison Officer .... Mr. Robert Spencer
DMA Liaison Officer .... Colonel John O'Meara, USA
CIA Liaison Officer .... Aron Able (Pseudonym)*
CIA Liaison Officer .... Bob Baker (Pseudonym)*

The National Security Agency (NSA) had appointed a full-time liaison officer, Commander Bud Fossett, and DMA had done the same, Colonel John O'Meara. Both CIA and NSA had also installed secure Teletype links from their respective headquarters to the JTF spaces. Information from this flow, as well as imagery analysis from several photo interpretation teams (DIA, CIA, Army and Air Force), together with a summary of media reporting and a three-day weather forecast, was analyzed and combined every morning. The result of this effort was the daily intelligence message that was sent to all of the field components. This same network was extended to the field training sites and, eventually, to the rescue staging and launch sites.

The original SOD intelligence planning team member was selected to be the JTF J-2, just as he had been the previous three years with the Readiness Command's CTJTF. The other two intelligence officers were Army. One was the former S-2 of Blue Light (Captain Tim Casey) and the other (Major Dick Friedel) had been the Intelligence control officer for the Ranger CT Emergency Deployment Readiness Exercises (EDREs). The three had worked together in the past year during various exercises, and had also worked with the Ranger S-2, the Delta S-2, and one of the DIA liaison officers. A similar relationship existed between the JTF J-6 Communications officer (LTC Peter Dieck) and the Delta communications officer (Major Jorge Torres-Cartenga). Both of these officers were highly knowledgeable and cooperative team players with imagination, experience

* The JTF was supported by two Liaison officers from the CIA, who coordinated JTF interface with both the CIA and, in turn, the State Department.

in both tactical and long haul strategic communications, and mission dedication. One of their earliest collaborative adventures involved climbing on the roof of the Pentagon on a cold, windy November night. There they unobtrusively installed a long-haul radio antenna, and secured 300 feet of black connector cable to the roof, eventually dropping it down the courtyard wall into the SOD spaces and running it through another 80 feet of ceiling to the JTF communications center which they had just set-up.

Most intelligence requirements were formulated by the JTF in anticipation of the individual force element needs based on a projection of their unique mission information requirements. In addition, information requirements (EEI- Essential Elements of Information) came in from the field components by message or courier. JTF requirements for National Agency (DIA-DMA-NSA-CIA) support were usually handled on a face-to-face basis with the respective liaison representatives, occasionally by secure phone followed by a classified message. Responses were normally by message or other hard copy form, and, on occasion, by secure phone. Intelligence data came directly into the JTF from the originating agency, and, in the case of CIA, HUMINT reporting also went directly to 1st SFOD-Delta through arrangements previously made between Delta and the CIA. Delta also received some imagery directly from CIA under the same set of previous arrangements. The CIA imagery and the accompanying analysis were focused on activity within the compound, while the JTF focus extended to the entire country. The expanded JTF Imagery requirements were supported throughout the effort by two teams -- one was geography focused and one was installation and activity focused. The former, headed by Anne G. Love, a geographer extraordinaire, and Charlie A. Nomina, an inexhaustible searcher, examined and re-examined the broad expanses of the Iranian countryside for drop zones, landing areas, pickup points and hide locations. The other team, known as "F Troop," was located in the basement of the Pentagon and headed by a wiry-haired dynamo named Arthur Gomes, Jr. This team provided analysis and readout support on a daily and special task basis.

The day the JTF was formally created and sited in the JCS (SOD) office complex, the rescue planning effort was given the name "Operation Ricebowl." This was both a security and deception move.

The term RICEBOWL was chosen by General Vaught to avoid a hint of linkage with Iran, hostages or rescue. "Ricebowl" was specifically selected to infer an Asiatic operation. A major emergency relief operation was ongoing in Cambodia and General Vaught hoped that any speculation (about aircraft movements -- the most overt of the early actions) would link our activities to that effort. This was particularly germane as some of the initial air movements involved SOF C-130s of the 1st Special Operations

Squadron operating out of Okinawa and Guam. This concern about the project name was legitimate, as most of the staff had seen examples of "clever" project names which, when examined, had a direct relationship to the uniqueness of the project or to the nature of the unit involved. These selections reflected the age-old normal human characteristic of seeking a sense of importance, recognition and association. This operation would not fall into that ego trap.

The term "Ricebowl" and about a dozen more key words constituted a "no speak" list. Words such as mission, rescue, hostages, embassy, compound, operation, Delta, Rangers, 1st SOW, Iran (anything which might peak the interest of a casual listener) were forbidden outside the physical spaces of the JTF and Delta planning areas. This restriction definitely included car pools, commuter buses, airplanes, airport and hotel lobbies, restaurants, bars, taxicabs, and the Pentagon hallways. Most of the out-of-town members of the JTF wore civilian clothes or uniforms without unit patches, as did many of the military and civilian employees who worked in the Pentagon, thus helping to maintain a low profile.

JTF 1-79 had a single purpose and mission -- prepare a plan and train a force to rescue the American citizens illegally held in Iran, and be prepared to execute it "ON ORDER." Its mission, unlike the several other planning efforts also underway, was to save lives. Most of the other efforts conducted by JCS OPGs (Operational Planning Groups) were designed to support the execution of retaliatory and preemptive operations should the situation dictate, such as hostages being killed, etcetera. These were all "big" force options involving the commitment of conventional air, naval and ground forces. General Jones and a few other officers, including the JCS J-3 Lt. General Philip Shutler, Brigadier General Johnson (J-33), and General Vaught, were aware of all the options. However, the planners within each of the OPGs and the Rescue JTF were not privy to the detailed plans of any other group. DIA provided intelligence support to all the groups and had, on Day One, identified two officers to serve as the interface with the OPGs and the rescue staff.

In addition to "the" rescue-planning cadre, several other sub-teams were created to investigate ideas and options on how the rescue force, identified at this time as a Delta force of 40 plus "operators" (also called "shooters"), could be inserted into Iran and close on the Embassy in Teheran undetected. Strategic closure was the immediate problem. Tactical closure with the Embassy compound would be worked out later. These concept and feasibility teams were closeted separately in several adjacent offices within the SOD spaces, but outside of the separately secured Unconventional Warfare (UW) Branch area, which by now had become the inner sanctum. This formerly innocuous L-shaped office suite had evolved into a combination JTF operations center, planning room, and the hub of most information and activities.

Each of the "Options Teams," as they were called, was given a general parameter for their particular effort. Some of these efforts were geographically focused, others transportation mode focused. Several possibilities emerged, one being insertion overland by truck, another by air insertion using CH-47 helicopters. Another cell focused on the options for fixed wing air insertion. A wide range of possibilities surfaced: commercial infiltration (what about weapons?); parachuting the force in (what about broken legs and getting to the compound?); and airlanding and seizing an airfield in or near Teheran (how do you maintain surprise until you close with the Embassy?).

The Options teams worked imaginatively and aggressively from 13 through 18 November. The options examined also included overland (bus, truck, train, etcetera) from each of the neighboring countries. Helicopter launches from each, maritime infiltration via the Persian Gulf and the Caspian Sea, and both airland and parachute entry were considered. Each team worked separately and each was provided all the intelligence that was available or that could be collected or produced. Maps, topographic studies, and reconnaissance photography were the mainstay. The teams included a person familiar with the logistic nuances of the possible options and launch environments, plus officers familiar with the mobility and operational needs of the strike force.

The feasibility of each concept was evaluated against several factors. These factors included such questions as -- Could it be done undetected? Did we have the assets and means to make it work? What was the transit time, hours or days? What was the impact of the winter weather? What would be the condition of the rescue force when they arrived? What were the options for recall if necessary? What mobility was required once the force was on the ground? These were but a few of the factors considered. The ground insertion option was one that received immediate attention.

The task was to investigate and develop a Ground Transport Option. What busses, trains and planes transit Iran? What are their schedules? Where do they start and where do they end? Who gets on-board? How do they get on-board? Who checks the passengers? How are they checked? How do people eat, drink, and dress? And, of course, how can we take advantage of this information to transit a bunch of American-looking Americans into Iran and out again with the hostages? Various people who had been there before were interviewed and quizzed on the environment. Trucks look pretty good, in some regards. We could buy some local-looking trucks, put our people in them and drive to town. Where do we start? We can choose Turkey, Iraq, Pakistan or Afghanistan as a jump-off point. Further investigation yields some small problems. Apparently, no country is willing to overtly support us. No one was quite sure how long the trucks would have to stay on the road or how the customs checks worked. Processing at border check points sometimes took days. Winter weather creates special problems and the occupants would require food, water, heat, air, and relief facilities.

A former aide of General Vaught's, now a civilian international businessman, was brought in. The man knew Turkey and General Vaught. He studied the road map, the topographic charts, the imagery of the border, and other data, compared notes and came up a judgment that trucks were not viable for inserting the force but had a strong potential, with far fewer problems, for the transit of some scouts. The results, pros and cons were briefed to General Vaught. He concurred and would discuss the possibilities with the Chairman at their afternoon meeting.

During these early days of option investigation, a steady stream of strangers occupied the outer lobby, waiting to talk to a staff principal regarding a single piece of archaic knowledge that only such a visitor would know. The pieces of the puzzle were coming together slowly with the aid of many people, most of whom had no precise idea of what they were supporting and were smart and polite enough not to ask. Train schedule for Bangladesh? Lamb carcass traffic in Turkey? What were the customs procedures at the Dogubazet checkpoint? When are the Sunni holy days? Commercial flight routes? No information was rejected and virtually every idea was considered. That was one of General Vaught's best traits -- he was open to anything and had the sense to take some time to examine it before judging its worth. His interest was the mission, not the trappings or protocol. People -- military, government and civilian -- who wouldn't normally ever meet a General were providing ideas. Every feasible option and some unfeasible options were explored looking for a part of the entry solution.

Another equally crucial issue concerned how to get between 150 and 200 people, some of whom may be incapacitated or injured, out of the middle of a major metropolitan area once the alarm was sounded. The only feasible means was vertical extraction by helicopters. The choppers would then fly the rescue force, and their precious human charges, to an American-controlled transfer-point where they all could be quickly and safely transferred to a faster long haul mode of travel for the final leg of the rescue effort.

Each option and idea was reviewed and discussed with COMJTF and the forces that would be called upon to execute the option. Gradually, the options narrowed themselves to a long-range air insertion, a covert ground closure, and a rapid vertical extraction from the city followed by a transfer of the hostages and the rescue force to several strategic airlift platforms for the final leg of the extraction.

***

In mid-November, the newly created JTF issued a Preliminary Intelligence Assessment that led off with the following statement regarding the Embassy situation:

> *1. The current (hostage) situation (in Iran) is the result of several weeks of detailed planning and is sanctioned by the Ayatollah Khomeini. The situation has been and will continue to be orchestrated by the Shiite religious leadership using the students and the Revolutionary Guards as propaganda and security apparatus.*
>
> *2. The situation at the compound has now settled into a routine with demonstrations periodically staged outside the Chancellery Gate on Takhi-E-Jamshid Blvd. Crowd size varies from 50 curiosity seekers to several thousand at lunch and prayer time when announcements go out via the radio and the local public address system."*

***

During this formative period, the JTF staff employed the organizational and planning framework of the existing JCS CONPLAN created by the REDCOM planners. This included the structure of the JTF and concepts for operational planning, force deployment, communications, logistics, intelligence and supporting cover actions. Given the complexity of the mission challenge, many of these procedures -- particularly the logistics, communications, intelligence and deception measures -- were stretched, modified, and expanded periodically as the situation redefined itself over time. The other DOD agencies that were in the support role, such as DIA, NSA and DMA, also employed the framework and procedures outlined in their previously developed supporting plans to the basic JCS/REDCOM CONPLAN.

Due to strict Operational Security (OPSEC) considerations, all JTF planning was conducted in the UW branch office located within J-3 SOD. Initially, fewer than twenty people were read-in to JTF activities. With the exception of those individuals on distribution for the *Situation Book* (Generals Schutler and Johnson - JCS J-3, the Chairman General Jones, Dr. Harold Brown the SECDEF, and the President), no one outside of the JCS J-3 SOD spaces was made aware of the details of the ongoing planning, much less the creation of JTF-1-79.

***

One of the first JTF Point Papers to be added to the SECDEF/CJCS *Situation Book* addressed some of the most time-consuming chores facing the JTF and was titled accordingly.

TIME CONSUMING ACTIONS TO ENHANCE BASE CASE SUCCESS

A. Obtain additional intelligence on compound and city activities.
B. DELTA continues to train, review mockup, study intelligence and review planning.
C. Define and develop communication and other requirements to support insertion/extraction.
D. Determine feasibility of inserting 15 man advance element by covert/clandestine means.
E. Determine if better way to insert through covert means.
F. Establish close definite contact with 3rd country with help in Iran, for insertion, aid in objective area and extraction or movement to safe haven.
G. Improve communications capability for positive control at each decision point.
H. Develop detailed deception plans, to include method of creating diversions, neutralizing radio/TV stations and developing capability to shut off commercial power.
I. Assure vehicle availability both for insertion/extraction use.
J. Identify multiple extraction assault landing areas.
K. Arrange for safe havens for all if assault extraction delayed or unsuccessful.

***

The EUCOM LNO (Major Magee) reported to the JCS J-3 SOD, on 14 Nov 79, and proceeded to brief the JCS J-3, Lt. General Shutler, USMC; Brigadier General Johnson, USA, General Vaught, Col. Kyle, and Col. Jerry King on the EUCOM developed options. The briefing included force closure estimates, capability comparisons, and success estimates. To no one's surprise, the EUCOM conclusion was that "none of the courses of action assures a high probability of freeing the hostages or avoiding substantial casualties to the assault force." Following the briefing, Major Jim Magee and the PACOM LNO, Colonel Jim Keating, who had also arrived, were sworn to secrecy and briefed by Colonel King on the JTF option developments. Magee was then assigned to work with the J-3 team and assist in refining the "Helo Option" along with representatives of Delta, 1st SOW, and other planners from JCS J-3 SOD, and the Department of the Army Staff Special Operations Staff. Colonel Keating worked with Jim Kyle on the strategic deployment plan. The two command Liaison officers were a pair of different but complementary bookends. Both were solid soldiers, highly versatile quick thinkers with extensive joint service experience in special operations and the capabilities and limitations of their theaters. In addition, both had the utmost confidence of their respective four-star theater commanders.

Initial planning concentrated on an "Emergency Option" to be implemented if the Iranian militants killed one of the American hostages. This option quickly took on all the trappings of a prescription for war. It included airborne assaults to seize one or more of Teheran's three airfields, an overt fast-moving armored movement and forced entry into the American Embassy compound, and neutralization of any Iranian resistance, followed by a devastating fighting withdrawal to an extraction airhead under active American fighter/attack air cover. This was an option of last resort in the minds of the planners. Once the initial "Emergency Option" planning was completed, JTF focus shifted to the detailed examination and development of other options which held the promise of bringing all (or most) of the hostages out alive.

By mid-November, a preliminary "Bare Bones" Concept Paper was added to the "Book." The paper was only one page and short on verbiage. It contained only eight dot points and was simply titled CONCEPT.

CONCEPT

a. 75 Delta military personnel required to assault compound (high risk but entry is "doable" providing intelligence is accurate and surprise is achieved).
b. Insertion of one or more Delta persons into country day or two in advance of insertion.
c. Delta team trains at special stateside location. Transportation to Europe by C-141, to Iran by special MC-130.
d. Air refuelable Combat Talon (low-level covert infiltration aircraft) MC-130s from Pacific and CONUS.
e. Delta team inserted by MC-130s. Delta team rest for 24 hours in Tehran.
f. Assault compound in middle of night. Free hostages and proceed to pick up point.
g. MC-130s make blackout, night assault landing, pick up personnel and fly to 3rd country.
h. Extraction most difficult part of operation is very high risk.

A few days later, Colonel Beckwith sent thc following ***"OPS IMMEDIATE"*** message to General Vaught. Datelined 19 November, it shows the focus of Beckwith's concept of operations at this stage of the planning. The "assets" he refers to are two former Iranian security officers who, when the Shah abdicated, left Iran for their own safety and were placed under contact by the CIA.

O 191715R NOV 79
FM CDR DELTA//BECKWITH
TO COM JTF//MG VAUGHT
SUBJECT: PLANNING CONSIDERATIONS

1. WITH REGARD TO INFILTRATION, I SPENT THREE HOURS THIS MORNING WITH ASSET XXX, AND MOST OF THE AFTERNOON WITH ASSET ZZZ. BASED ON DETAILED MAP STUDY AND ASSETS PERSONAL EXPERIENCE ON THE GROUND I NOW BELIEVE THAT THE BEST OPTION OPEN TO US AT THIS TIME, BASED UPON THE CURRENT SITUATION, IS TO ENTER IRAN BY COMBAT TALON. AIRLAND 35-40 KM EAST OF TEHRAN AND QUICKLY TRANSFER PERSONNEL AND GEAR TO THREE TRUCKS WHICH CAN BE PROVIDED BY XXXX. MOVE BY TRUCK TO THE EMBASSY COMPOUND, CROSS THE WALL AT TWO SEPARATE POINTS, RESCUE THE HOSTAGES AND EXFILTRATE THE COMPOUND BY HELOS. IN THE EVENT THE MISSION GOES SOUR AND EXTRACTION FROM THE COMPOUND BECOMES IMPRACTICAL, DELTA WOULD MAKE EVERY EFFORT TO MOVE TO THE STADIUM.

2. BOTH ASSETS BELIEVE THAT TRUCK INFILTRATION FROM TURKEY OR PAKISTAN TO TEHRAN IS TOO RISKY. ZZZZ DEPARTED TEHRAN 10 NOV 79. THIS ASSET FURTHER RECOMMENDED THAT THREE DELTA PERSONNEL DRIVE TRUCKS FROM LZ TO TARGET. I WILL SUBMIT A PROPOSAL TO YOU LATER WHICH ENVISIONS FIVE DELTA PERSONNEL TO PRECEDE FORCE AND GET INTO POSITION IN-COUNTRY. ONE DELTA MAN IN OP AND ONE ON LZ. THIS MAN TO SELECT LZ AND LINK UP TRUCKS WITH DELTA FORCE.

3. I HAVE REQUESTED AN 18 WHEEL VEHICLE AT THIS SITE TO TRAIN SELECTED PERSONNEL TO HANDLE TRUCKS. ZZZZ RECOMMENDED WE USE LARGE 16 WHEEL TRUCKS, PREFERABLY MACK OR MERCEDES.

BT

These planning efforts concentrated on a rescue effort based on an undetected closure with the Embassy compound and the Ministry of Foreign Affairs (MFA) utilizing RH-53D helicopters, MC-130's transports, Delta Force, and Rangers. The RH-53D was judged to be the only helicopter with the range and payload for a mission that could be as much as 1,000 nautical miles one-way. The MC-130s were selected due to their unique penetration capabilities. Delta was selected as the surgical ground force due to their specialized Counter-terrorist, hostage-recovery training. The Rangers were selected because of their training and special skills for various security missions, and for seizure of an extraction airfield. By late November 1979, all courses of action had been scrubbed down and two versions of a "preferred option" were selected for full-scale development.

The preferred (or deliberate) option envisioned seven RH-53D helicopters being disassembled and flown, via C-5 transport aircraft, to an

American staging base on the island of Diego Garcia south of India in the Indian Ocean. Then, the RH-53Ds were to be reassembled and prepared to be flown under their own power out to the aircraft carrier *USS Kitty Hawk* that was on patrol duty in the Indian Ocean.

The initial plan called for the Delta strike teams and Navy/Marine RH-53 helicopter flight crews to be deployed to Diego Garcia by C-141 transports. Delta would then be flown out to the *Kitty Hawk* on-board small Navy fixed wing transports capable of landing on the carrier flight deck. The flight crews would fly the helos on-board. As the *Kitty Hawk* steamed toward its launch location, the JTF staff, the Rangers, a JCSE communications detachment, the 1st SOW MC-130s and AC-130s gunships, and MAC C-141 Medical Evacuation aircraft, along with SAC flying gas stations (KC-135s) would move to staging bases throughout the region.

The plan envisioned a two-day operation: Delta would launch from the *Kitty Hawk* in the RH-53s at dusk; land in the Iranian desert at a pre-selected location; set up beacons for a fuel drop from the MC-130s; refuel the helicopters; relaunch and fly (still under cover of darkness) to a remote site southeast of Teheran. Delta would be dropped off at this site (and met by an advance party that had been infiltrated several days earlier). The advance party would then lead Delta to a safe haven where they would remain until the following night. After the Delta drop off, the RH-53s would reposition to another site, even more remote than the drop-off point, where the helicopters would be camouflaged and remain hidden until the next night.

After dark on Day Two, Delta would move via trucks to assault positions adjacent to the Embassy compound. On receiving the execute order from Colonel Beckwith, the strike teams would begin the assault using stealth and silenced weapons. As the assault order was given, the helicopter force would launch from their hide-site and make a beeline for the compound and the stadium adjacent to it.

As Delta assaulted the Embassy, a Ranger force (flown in on C-130s) would seize and secure the extraction airfield. Once the hostages were freed, they and Delta would be picked up by the RH-53s and flown to the extraction airfield. Throughout the operation AC-130 gunships, orbiting overhead, would provide surveillance and fire support to the ground force. Once all personnel were accounted for and on-board the MC-130s, the helicopters would be destroyed and the force would depart Iran on the MC-130s.

***

By the 19th of November, General Vaught had concluded his initial feasibility assessment and advised General Jones that he recommended a helicopter extraction option as having the greatest potential for success. The helicopter extraction option was the only viable means to remove more than 150 people (hostages and rescuers) from the middle of a dense and potentially very hostile metropolitan area.

By this time, the secure JTF teletype network had been fully established for some time, and had been extended between the JTF Headquarters and all the operational components which now included Delta, the 1-75th Ranger Battalion, and the 1st SOW. It was further extended to the Navy Helicopter detachment when it was constituted a few days later. The network was used for all staff functions -- command, operations, logistics, communications and intelligence. When the force deployed for the mission, this electronic umbilical cord went with it and was complemented by independently extending the NSA and CIA lines that had been feeding the JTF Headquarters. This three-way philosophy ensured the availability of a reliable communications alternative should one of the paths go down. Reliability was further enhanced by the ability to cross from one highway to another at several locations including the Pentagon, the CIA, and NSA Headquarters.

Since none of Delta force spoke Farsi, the native language of Iran, it would be necessary to find American military personnel who spoke the language, preferably individuals who had served in Teheran, were available for mission training, and would volunteer. A combination of screening the service personnel databanks for Farsi linguists, and assignment records for personnel who had served in Iran was initiated. Dialogue with the most recent attachés and former members of the Military Advisory Group yielded other candidates. Collectively, about twenty candidates were found. Their ranks and backgrounds cut across service lines from a senior Navy Captain, a mid-grade Army Captain to a junior Air Force enlisted man. Assessment of the potential driver/monitors began in mid-November. For most of the candidates, their initial contact with the JTF involved a phone call to arrange an informal meeting. Each candidate was handled individually by one of three JTF officers and there was no discussion of the JTF or a possible rescue effort. This first meeting largely focused on determining the level of the candidate's Farsi language skills, both speaking and oral comprehension. Based on the results the interviews, twelve candidates passed the language screening and were taken to various East Coast cities, for an evaluation of their temperament and truck-handling ability. In some cases, this involved rudimentary truck driver training. In other cases, it was learning how to handle a "stick shift" vehicle. Although no disclosure of the mission and no "recruitment pitch" was made during this phase of the screening process, the overall national focus on the situation in Teheran was clear, and Ted Koppel was making a name for himself every night on *Nightline*, lest one forget the hostage situation.

After this first field trip, the candidates, still being handled individually, were sent back to their home stations. This would be the pattern throughout the balance of the assessment, selection and training process -- a few days TDY to some location, then return to home station to await further instructions. Compartmented security was tight, and none of the candidates were advised of the mission, their precise role, or any of the still-developing operational details. In early to mid December, final assessment and selection occurred following several long days and nights of driving large trucks, including tractor-trailer rigs, through urban environments. This session also included the first of many sessions on vehicle maintenance and minor repair, from changing oil, water, spark plugs, filters and flat tires. At the end of this session, the candidates who had successfully completed the screening were put into small groups for additional training and further assessment. Part of the assessment and training process involved general military skills and weapons handling. During this phase of training/selection, the candidates were evaluated by members of "Delta" who were serving as weapons and tactics instructors.

Just prior to the first major field rehearsal, the remaining driver candidates were asked by their JTF contact to volunteer for the mission. All who were asked accepted. The others returned to their parent units with strict instructions not to discuss anything about the events of the previous several weeks. Those who remained were then briefed en masse on the broad outlines of the operation and their role in the mission. From then on, the driving role was played out during virtually all subsequent training exercises and mission rehearsals. Follow-on training included periodic trips to Fort Bragg, where the curriculum included weapons proficiency, extensive vehicle handling, and realistic role-playing at roadblocks and checkpoints manned by former members of the Iranian Secret Police. By this time, the drivers and their Delta "shotgun" counterparts were teamed up and fully integrated into the operational concept and training flow. In close coordination with the Delta assault elements, they spent much of January, February and March training at a variety of locations on specific aspects and excursions of the "going to town" closure phase of the mission.

***

Once the main ingredients and the general concept of the operation were known, cover actions and the development of deception plans were begun in earnest. The strict OPSEC and COMSEC measures that existed from the onset continued in force and were reinforced with each new person or action added to the JTF cast or repertoire. The same day the helicopter option was deemed feasible (19 Nov), the Iranian militants released three American hostages, two women and a young black Marine. During the course of the previous week, without any fanfare, they had released virtually all the non-Americans caught in the initial taken over.

The next day, the 20th, the militants released another ten Americans. This time the group consisted only of young black males, most of whom were Marine guards. These moves were an attempt to gain sympathy for the militant's cause among the "oppressed" peoples of the United States. The debriefings of the releasees allowed a reconstruction of the events of the takeover and confirmed some of the suppositions that the JTF intelligence team had about the initial hostage detention sites. Meanwhile, although a refueling site was yet to be found within the refueling ellipse of the 53s, JCS issued directions to the Navy and the Air Force on the 20th to prepare to deploy six RH-53 Sea Stallion helicopters to the Navy Indian Ocean Task Force.

Most efforts up this point had been directed toward providing the President with the capability to execute the deliberate (i.e., helicopter extraction) option during the period of the 2nd and 3rd of December 1979. It became obvious to General Vaught and all the planners that a launch must be conducted from Europe, or from waters immediately adjacent to Iran, for the helicopter option to be successful. Therefore, various support arrangements were envisioned as being required of EUCOM and its forces within the European and African Middle East littoral area, the most obvious being the establishment of a forward staging base. Egyptian President Anwar Sadat had graciously extended an offer of support and the use of Egyptian facilities to President Carter shortly after the militants took control of the Embassy compound. The Egyptian offer was now accepted and a barren, barely operational, fighter airfield, built by the Soviet Union in southern Egypt near the village of Wadi Kena, became the first JTF toehold in the area.

On Friday, the 23rd of November, a national level senior review was held in the small JTF Planning/Briefing room. A host of officials attended, including the Chairman of the JCS, General David Jones (now a regular visitor to SOD), Lt. General Shutler JCS J-3, and General Meyer, plus a host of others. There was standing room only for the late arrivals. The purpose was to update all the parties concerned as to the current status of the situation, the planning options examined, and the decisions made to date.

The primary outcome of this meeting was to request SECDEF approval to position a detachment of RH-53s on-board the "duty" Indian Ocean aircraft carrier, the *USS Kitty Hawk.* Preparations for the movement of the partially disassembled helicopters from the United States to Diego Garcia by

USAF C-5 heavy-lift transports had already begun, based on the Warning Order of the 20th.

Dr. Brown, SECDEF, approved the deployment and the C-5s soon departed the East Coast. The RH-53 airframes were unloaded at Diego Garcia, reassembled and flown out to the carrier under cover of darkness on the 25th. Their Indian Ocean "mission" was "mine sweeping" (which was in reality their normal Navy mission), and thus their appearance on the carrier would not be considered particularly unusual.

However, security guidelines dictated that no more than three of the helicopters could be on deck simultaneously. A small team of JTF aviation officers accompanied the aircraft to the carrier and remained on-board for several weeks. Responsibility for the maintenance and readiness of the helicopters was subsequently assumed by the duty carrier's aviation department. Eventually, the helicopters were transferred to two other carriers as these ships rotated into the Indian Ocean.

During the latter weeks of November and into December, while the rescue options were being developed and examined, the JTF intelligence team noted that the Iranians were using rumor and disinformation to deter a rescue attempt. Information was being circulated on the streets of Teheran that the walls and grounds of the Embassy compound had been mined and other defensive measures had been installed in and around the compound. Although the Iranians went to great efforts, with these and other deception measures, to deter a rescue, comparative analysis of data obtained from a variety of technical intelligence sources proved these Iranian claims to be false.

***

The question of funding arose early and persisted through much of the initial five months of preparation. One of the first official JTF memos to the Joint Staff dealing with the subject is presented below and provides a view of the tenor attached to this subject.

26 November 1979

MEMORANDUM FOR DIRECTOR, JOINT STAFF

Subject: Funding for Provisional Joint Task Force

1. Planning and preparation for operations, which may be conducted under the control of the provisional Joint Task Force, have not been without expense. Expenses to date include payment for civilian manpower, aircraft flying hours, supplies and equipment, and TDY of JTF members. All expenses incurred to date have been unprogrammed; TDY expenses have been paid by the individuals performing the TDY. In order to reimburse the individuals performing the TDY, preclude undue hardship on individuals required to travel as a result of Task Force duties, and to allow (the military) services to adequately track and recoup costs,

request fund cite and project codes be provided for the operation of the Task Force.

2. There is presently no funding expertise among the members of the (JTF) planning staff. Additional expenses will be incurred as the planning, preparation and rehearsals continue. It will also be necessary, at the conclusion of the mission, to provide an accounting for expenses by Service and appropriation. Request staff assistance be provided the (JTF) planning staff in the aggregation of costs and administration of such funding codes as are provided.

Signed/ James B. Vaught, Major General, USA, JTF RICE BOWL

The Director of the Joint Staff, Admiral Thor Hansen responded to the memo, on 30 November with hand written notation on memo. The Note read: "*Taken care of by having each service establish a fund source for TDY. Also by adding a Delta finance man.*"

The selection of the extraction mode (i.e., a helicopter lift-out) had involved a detailed analysis of the situation and the mission objective. The selection of the specific helicopter type was based on several pragmatic and technical factors. Selection of the aircrews to fly the machines was more subjective.

A survey of the capabilities of the American military helicopter fleet indicated that only the Sikorsky H-53, or one of its derivatives, had the lift and range potential to conduct the mission. The worst case extraction scenario required a minimum of four H-53s to conduct the Embassy extraction in a single lift (i.e., all hostages and the rescue force at one time). Given the fact that a launch situation could occur at any time, and no land-based, close-in launch site was politically confirmed, the helicopters would have to be able to operate from, and be maintained on-board, an aircraft carrier. This reduced the choice of models to those that had the ability to fold their 79-foot long rotor blades for movement and maintenance below decks. Overall, the H-53 took up as much deck and hangar space as the typical fighter aircraft. At some point, the addition of H-53s to the aviation inventory of any carrier would mean some fighters would have to be removed.

The choice of the 53 model came down to the RH-53D Navy Mine Countermeasures model or the Marine Heavy Assault model. The final selection fell to the Navy RH-53D because it was a better overall mission fit. It could carry extra internal fuel tanks and had external fuel tanks that the Marine version did not have. In addition, if spotted on the deck of the carrier by the Soviet tattletale surveillance ship, which normally shadowed U.S. Carrier Battle groups, it would not draw undue attention. The next question was selection of the aircrews. Given the lack of low-level nighttime, long haul and combat assault experience, an exclusive Navy crew was deemed unwise. A mixed Navy/Marine flight team was the option chosen. The Navy member would bring knowledge of that particular model helicopter and its operating characteristics, while the Marine crewmember would bring his combat-assault and overland-flight experience. The Navy pilots were selected from a Navy Mine Sweeper squadron stationed at Norfolk Air Station, while the Marine pilots came from several different units. A special instructor cadre was assembled from the Marine helicopter training school at Tustin, California, near Camp Pendleton, a major Marine training base. The Marines instructors were to assist in bringing the Navy pilots up to mission standards.

Off-line discussions had been held early-on which looked at the feasibility of using Army helicopter pilots who had extensive night flying and assault skills; however, none were multi-engine qualified, nor had any familiarity with the 53 in any configuration. The same discussions looked at using Air Force Air Rescue Service 53s and aircrews. The use of the Air Force 53s was quickly stymied. Their rotors and tail assemblies did not fold (as the Navy machines could), and thus could not be put below deck. If left on deck, their out-of-norm configuration would be quickly noticed by the Soviet surveillance ship (that shadowed the carrier) raising speculation as to their purpose. In addition, maintenance would be difficult and complicated because of different supply systems and flight components (USN versus USAF). Additionally, the possibility of USAF aircrews flying Navy birds did not sit well with the senior leadership of the Naval Aviation community.

This possibility also found disfavor with the senior Air Force Air Rescue Service hierarchy, who did not want their "white hat" aircrews and their humanitarian reputation tarred by being involved in a "black operation." In addition, the 1st Special Operations Wing, which would provide the C-130s, did not have any 53s in its inventory. Its projected fleet of twelve new MH-53J Pave Low helicopters would have been ideal for the helicopter role. These long range, heavy lift machines, an upgraded version of the basic 53, were designed and instrumented for such a long range night operation. However, budgeting and production had been repeatedly slipped by USAF in the previous years in favor of other programs. The first USAF SOF 53s were still in the early stages of production in November 1979. Similar types of pre-production delays were true for the Army's Blackhawk, the H-60, a good runner-up to the Pave Low. It, too, was in the very early stages of production.

The immediate "be prepared to execute on order" aspect of the JTF mission and the lack of a viable in-theater staging base and an unresolved refueling problem drove the near concurrent development of three force insertion concepts. The most immediate called for a quick reaction plan should the situation turn extremely critical (i.e., hostages were being killed). This was why the CH-53s had been pre-positioned on the *Nimitz*. The second involved seizing a remote, essentially inactive Iranian Air Force facility that was located in the refueling ellipse and using it as a refueling and possible personnel transfer site. This option was not favored, much less preferred, by anyone. However, it was necessary to develop and practice it until the preferred third option (the remote area refuel) could be validated and the bugs worked out. The third concept involved landing on a remote desert segment along the insertion flight corridor within the refueling ellipse and setting up a field refueling point. Although it was very complex, and demanding of men and machines, the third option offered the greatest possibility of overall success.

Marine Corps KC-130 tankers, which theoretically might have been able to provide in-flight airborne refueling support, were not themselves air refuelable. If the mission had to be launched from Diego Garcia, the KC-130s would be incapable of carrying enough fuel to refuel the helicopters and complete their own return flight. This was an absolute certainty if the launch had to be from Diego Garcia, and almost as probable if the tanker force were able to launch from Oman, a closer launch possibility.

By late November, the JTF operations staff was temporarily divided into two distinct focus cells. One cell was responsible for continued option and plan refinement, while the other cell was heavily involved in planning and developing a training program to be conducted in the western United States where the terrain and weather conditions resembled the Iranian deserts. The U.S. southwest did not have exactly the same, extremely hostile ground conditions, but the flying conditions, distances, and general barren nature of the real estate were very similar.

By the 28th of November, a written version of the rescue plan had been prepared in OPERATIONS ORDER format. It laid out responsibilities, functions and a mission sequence. This version was the central baseline and point of departure for all ongoing and future plan refinements and alternatives, several of which had to worked on, developed, and pursued (trained-to) until all the elements of the preferred option fell into place. This was no easy task for an in-being organization and much harder for an organization that had not existed two weeks earlier, and whose principle components had never trained together.

Colonel Beckwith, who was right in the middle of the field training with Delta, the Rangers and the balance of the force, routinely provided General Vaught with his opinions, regularly and usually in a very candid manner. Toward the end of November, Colonel Beckwith sent the following message to General Vaught summarizing his view of preparations to-date.

MSG 080
O 292200R NOV 79
FM CDR DELTA//BECKWITH//
TO COM JTF//MG VAUGHT//
SUBJECT: SITREP

1. NIGHT TNG (Training) CONTINUES FOR OUR HUNTER-KILLER TMS (Teams). THE AIM OF THE TNG IS TO REHEARSE THE SKILLFUL TAKING-OUT OF PERS(*ONS*) AT CHECK POINTS AND SENTRY POSTS IN AND AROUND EMBASSY COMPOUND. ASSET *(XXXX)* CONTINUES TO PROVIDE ADVICE AND ASSISTANCE TO THE ABOVE EFFORT. DUE TO THE PAUCITY OF HARD INTELLIGENCE AT THIS TIME, I ENVISION WE WILL STUMBLE INTO CHECKPOINTS AND SENTRIES AS WE APPROACH TEHRAN VIA TRUCK.
2. THE PLANNING CONFERENCE CONDUCTED AT THIS LOCATION THIS AFTERNOON BY YOU AND YOUR STAFF WAS VALUABLE, AND VITAL PARTS OF THE PLAN ARE FALLING INTO PLACE; HOWEVER, WE STILL HAVE A LONG WAY TO GO BEFORE WE CAN ACTUALLY MOUNT A RESCUE OPN TO RECOVER OUR HOSTAGES. WE MUST NOT ALLOW MISSION SUPPORT, SUCH AS HELOS, MC130 COMBAT TALONS AND SPECTRE GUNSHIPS, TO DICTATE THE PHASING OF THE GROUND TACTICAL PLAN INSTEAD OF SUPPORTING THE PLAN.
3. THE INTELLIGENCE COMMUNITY HAS PROVIDED US WITH A VAST AMOUNT OF INFORMATION AND I RECOGNIZE THAT THERE ARE NO CHOKE POINTS IN THE FLOW OF INTELLIGENCE; HOWEVER, MY MOST CRITICAL EEI'S *(ESSENTIAL ELEMENTS OF INFORMATION*) REMAIN UNANSWERED. THESE ARE THE VITAL QUESTIONS WHICH MUST BE ANSWERED TO REDUCE THE CURRENT RISK AND ACCOMPLISH OUR RESCUE MISSION: A. ARE ALL THE HOSTAGES ACTUALLY IN THE EMBASSY COMPOUND DURING THE HOURS OF DARKNESS? B. WHERE AND IN WHAT STRENGTH ARE CHECK POINTS ALONG MAJOR ROUTES, IN TEHRAN, WHICH LEAD TO THE EMBASSY COMPOUND? C. WHAT ASSISTANCE AND SUPPORT CAN BE PROVIDED TO DELTA BY IN-PLACE ASSETS? D. WHO WILL DRIVE THE TRUCKS IF AND WHEN *(ASSET ZZZZ)* OBTAINS THEM? E. ARE THERE ANY SAFE HOUSES VICINITY OF THE COMPOUND WHICH DELTA COULD USE PRIOR TO THE ACTUAL RESCUE? F. WHAT IS THE NIGHT TIME MO (*MODUS OPERANDI*) OF ROVING PATROLS AND SENTRY POSTS IN AND AROUND THE COMPOUND? (AGAIN, WE CANNOT AFFORD TO STUMBLE INTO THE ENEMY.) G. WHAT IS THE STRENGTH OF THE ENEMY INSIDE THE COMPOUND DURING THE HOURS OF DARKNESS? CAN THE ENEMY REINFORCE THE COMPOUND? IF SO, IN WHAT STRENGTH?
4. FROM THE OUTSET, I HAVE STATED THAT ANY PLAN DESIGNED TO RESCUE OUR HOSTAGES HAS TO BE SIMPLE, AND PERMIT DELTA TO ACHIEVE THE ELEMENT OF SURPRISE AS IT ENTERS THE COMPOUND. WE BELIEVE THE TROJAN HORSE CONCEPT UP TO THE WALL IS VITAL IN ORDER TO ACCOMPLISH OUR MISSION. WITHOUT THE SUPPORT AND ASSISTANCE OF IN-PLACE ASSETS,

WHO CAN HELP ME AS WE TRANSIT THE CITY TO THE EMBASSY COMPOUND, THE RISK REMAINS HIGH. AGAIN, HARD INTELLIGENCE IS THE KEY TO OUR SUCCESS. I ALSO REALIZE I AM PREACHING TO THE CHOIR, HOWEVER, OTHERS MAY NOT HAVE BEEN WHERE THE RUBBER MEETS THE ROAD IN THIS TYPE OF SPECIAL OPN (*OPERATION*).
REVW 30 NOV 2009
BT

It soon became apparent to General Vaught and the JTF planners that the President and the State Department, and many others were still hopeful that somehow the Iranians would, as a humanitarian gesture, release the captives if a dialogue was continued and reason could be achieved. This was a logical and rational assumption, but one that usually only works if one side is willing to give and the other willing to accept. In this case, those fundamental rules did not apply. The militants demanded the return of the Shah for trial and the United States was justifiably not willing to accede to this demand. Although the United States stood on the high ground of international diplomacy, our embassy staff remained imprisoned and cut off from the outside world, and the JTF knew a diplomatic solution was not in the cards. There was too much contention for power within Iran and "the" sole arbitrator, Ayatollah Khomeini, was not willing to surrender the hostages to the "Great Satan."

CHAPTER THREE
Serious Actions

During the last week of November, both the JTF J-2 and the Delta S-2 conducted independent analyses of the more than 200 foreign HUMINT reports provided by CIA. The goal was to identify the most credible reporting, and focus these resources on the information essential to support mission planning. Regrettably, both analyses showed the vast majority of the reporting to be a circulation of street rumors, diplomatic speculation and a regurgitation of foreign media coverage. One particular foreign agency showed a definite nationality bias, and its reporting bore indications that its sources may have been, more than any other, the unwitting conduit of Iranian disinformation. No reliable data on the hostages was forthcoming from any of these reports, nor was there any information of operational or planning significance, such as the guard posture and lighting conditions in and around the Embassy compound. The CIA was informed of the results. They were not happy with the two assessments. They had provided plenty of paper, but very little substance.

In the wake of these assessments, and accepting the CIA assertions that no residual CIA HUMINT capability existed in Iran, but also knowing thousands of westerners still lived in Teheran and air travel had not been interrupted, the JTF considered other options. Several individuals, from both the JTF and Delta, volunteered to run the risk of going in and checking out the environment. The CIA was against inserting any of these "amateurs" and finally admitted it was asking a retired operative, who had begun his service in the OSS during World War II, if he would accept the mission. He did, and, with the assistance of two Iranians whose families had suffered at the hands of the new Islamic regime, began to make plans to enter Iran.

His primary mission was to assess the feasibility of setting up an in-country support apparatus. General Vaught quickly recognized that this small team (none of whom were willing to be on the ground if a rescue attempt were to be conducted) was inadequate to provide the logistics and final support required. With this limitation in mind, and with the backing of the Chairman, he began the long and tedious process of requesting CIA assess a string of DOD volunteers to augment and eventually replace the CIA survey team.

During the same time frame, the JTF created a DOD HUMINT coordinating team that included HUMINT representatives from each of the services. The purpose was to determine what DOD information assets were available that could be brought to bear on the hostage problem. Determination of the actual environment in Teheran was the focus. TV and news coverage gave the impression of massive demonstrations, turmoil, and roadblocks throughout the city. However, reconnaissance imagery indicated that the demonstrations were confined to the area immediately in front of the Embassy compound and were largely waged for the TV cameras. Everywhere else in the city, activity seemed normal, including cars, buses and trucks stopping at traffic lights, and there was no massive network of roadblocks evident in photography, although rumors of these abounded.

During the first meeting of the service representatives, the Navy attendee indicated that they did not have any assets that were in a position to help, but that they might be able to develop one source. (This never came about). The Air Force had several non-Iranian business contacts who were long-term residents of Teheran. These sources were in a position to provide on-the-ground observations as to the general tempo of events in the city and assess the ease (or difficulty) with which non-Iranians could move about the city; however, they had no potential for providing reliable information regarding activities inside the compound.

The Army had some potential Iranian sources who (due to claimed placement) might be able to obtain information on the hostage detention situation through carefully directed elicitation. Both the Air Force and Army sources were utilized in their respective roles. Eventually, none of the Army sources proved to be reliable and no information of value were obtained. In addition, at least one of these (rent-a-spies) sources proved to be "professional fabricator" and quite capable of defeating a lie detector.

However in the early days, all of these possibilities were pursued as well as several private commercial contacts that volunteered their resources. These included among others, several individuals who had been involved in the escape from Iran of two employees of Ross Perot's EDS corporation eleven months earlier.

All of these various human sources provided environmental (i.e. situational) data to varying degrees of utility, but none were in a position to provide reliable data on the hostages, their precise location, or the conditions of their detention.*

***

* See On Wings of Eagles, by Ken Follett (New York: SIGNET Publications, 1984). Colonel Arthur "Bull" Simons, U.S. Army (Ret), who led the successful EDS operation, had also been the ground forces commander of the American raid on a North Vietnamese POW camp near the village of Son Tay in 1970. Although the Son Tay raid turned out to be a "dry hole" (the North Vietnamese had moved the American POWs less than three weeks earlier), the bold American action so shocked and stunned the North Vietnamese that the "lifestyle" of the American POWs improved substantially.

On the 28th of November, the DIA completed a comprehensive intelligence analysis of the total Iranian Air Defense structure. The study compared the Iranian Air Defense posture before the Embassy takeover and the activity patterns during the three weeks since the takeover. This composite "picture" allowed detailed air route planning to begin. Another mission effort was the meticulous compilation of a radar coverage analysis of Iran by the 1st SOW intelligence analysts. The original hand-drawn prediction was quickly validated by DMA cartographers' sophisticated stereographic techniques. It was then turned into a specially prepared composite chart with a radar overprint. The chart covered the entire Area of Operations and showed Iranian radar coverage at several flight altitudes (low, medium and high). The composite presentation showed the areas where there was no direct coverage or where higher terrain masked an area from effective coverage. Copies of this chart were provided to all JTF components, including the newly created Navy/Marine helicopter detachment.

Another one of the tasks that the DIA analysts undertook, at the request of the JTF, was to document the location of all the oil drilling rigs in the Arabian Gulf. Another was to track (over a period of several weeks) the ebb and flow and routes of ships as they transited the Gulf. This product was used to assist in defining the projected flight routes of the mission aircraft to avoid concentrations of oil rigs and maritime navigation choke points. However, the decision as to where to penetrate the Iranian land mass was eventually based largely on gaps in Iranian radar coverage, the availability of terrain masking, and the lack of population centers.

By this time, Delta had worked out a variety of concepts for clearing the compound and its dozen buildings. The Rangers had developed procedures for the seizure of the two airheads --Manzariyeh, a solitary strip of concrete about 40 miles south of Teheran, and a small airfield in southern Iran that fell within the insertion refueling ellipse. An isolated desert track suitable for use as a landing and refueling site had not yet been found, although an extensive imagery and map analysis effort was underway. A search of old archives yielded a 1950s Strategic Air Command (SAC) document containing ground surveys of a half dozen SAC bomber recovery sites in northern Iran. The document included a listing of its authors. One of these men, a geologist who had conducted on-the-ground surveys and had helped select the recovery sites, was located in downtown Washington. He quickly lent his expertise to the search. Unfortunately, none of the SAC sites was found to be viable. In every case, the weather had changed the topography significantly during the intervening twenty-four years. More than half a dozen new candidate locations were put under surveillance and continuing analysis.

Crippled Eagle

As the various insertion options were being developed, all the JTF force elements intensified individual and team skill training and physical conditioning in preparation for the mission and the joint training efforts that lay ahead.

The first major integrated training effort was held on the 29th and 30th of November. The first part of the training was conducted at Fort Bragg, North Carolina, and included elements of Delta, the Rangers, and 1st SOW, along with a team of highly qualified parachute "riggers" from Fort Lee, Virginia. The function of the Fort Lee team, headed by an Army Colonel by the name of Foley, was to provide assistance in developing a technique to effectively parachute multi-ton fuel blivets (giant rubber donuts) into a refueling site without the rubber containers breaking apart upon impacting with the ground. This effort was one of the possible means of delivering additional fuel to the helicopters during the mission. The Fort Bragg test period was followed by a series of force movements to the southwest desert for the first of the many integrated exercises.

***

The "Book" was the single most valuable document we had on our side of the ocean. It was a three-ring binder, eight inches by eleven and two inches wide. It was a standard government blue. It was the brain trust of the rescue planning. In actuality, there are seven identical books, one each for the JTF Commander General Vaught, the JCS J-3 General Schulter, General Jones the Chairman, Dr. Brown the SECDEF and the President. Number six was held by the JTF Chief of Staff Jerry King, and number seven by the team that was responsible for maintaining its currency. All seven copies were updated twice a day, originally, and then once a day at 6:00 A.M. after things settled down.

The book was indexed with a separate narrative for each of the options complete with map and graphics, a weather update, resumé of each force available and its present status, plus all the intelligence known at the time. A list of the hostages and their backgrounds, a world/middle East news summary, ongoing initiatives, sequence of events to date, special items of interest, and the Execution Chart were also included.

The Execution Chart was a joint effort of several planners, mainly the two operations officers, Commander Mayard Weyers, SEAL and mission planner extraordinary and Lt. Colonel Bob Horton, possibly the thinnest and most persistent C-130 pilot in the Pentagon. The chart was designed to make sense out of chaos. It displayed all the forces involved, the flow of each from their deployment location to the objective and back out of Iran. The decisions or actions of each along that flow, and the time frame of each supporting action required to make execution possible, from the moment of the "move-out order" to execution at the Embassy, and full recovery of the force and the hostages was catalogued on the chart. In the middle of the chart was a bold red line marked OTW (Over-The-Wall), the moment Charlie and his people were to do their thing. Each separate action that required a decision was outlined in a decision diamond. Each action that was to be taken by subordinate and supporting units/elements as the force moved along the flow was outlined in a rectangle. The chart put the entire complex program on a single page foldout and provided a means for the decision-makers to evaluate and question the planning, the status of a preparation, and eventually to approve, intervene or monitor, as they desired. The chart was changed as the options evolved. Two of the more critical elements on the chart, in addition to Charlie's OTW, were BMNT and EENT. (Begin Mean Nautical Twilight and End Early Nautical Twilight -- the time when it begins to get light and when it gets dark.) The force must get in country under cover of darkness and leave before first light. Iran is a big country and the window of available darkness is constantly changing with each day. The last page in the Book contained a sixty-day chart that graphically depicted sunset, sunrise, and moonrise, percentage of illumination and moonset. These, together with the prevailing weather, were all the natural parameters within which the mission had to be planned and conducted.

As part of the process of keeping the SECDEF, the Chairman and the JCS-J-3 informed of the JTF progress, a Daily Status Report was included in the "Book." The following is a composite of the reports covering the period 30 November through 3 December 1979.

***

STATUS REPORT

(30 Nov - 3 Dec 79)

1. Preparation for the actual operation continues. The six RH-53 helicopters have been flown from Diego Garcia to the KITTY HAWK (which is enroute to a MODLOC position in the Indian Ocean). This movement was completed 28193Z Nov 79. Four AC-130s are prepared for further deployment on order. MC-130s at Hurlburt Field are prepared to deploy via intermediate base on order. Delta is continuing planning and rehearsing in accordance with available information. Ranger staff is planning for mission to secure Manzariyeh Airfield.

2. Additional training required includes a full rehearsal with Delta, helicopters, MC-130s, AC-130s and Rangers. Decision has been made to conduct this training and rehearsal at the Yuma Proving Grounds. Movement to the southwest exercise (site) was completed on 3 December 1979.

   a. JTF Forward, Delta and the helicopter crews are based at the Yuma Proving Grounds.
   b. Two MC-130's and one AC-130 are located at Davis Monthan AFB

    c. Rangers are conducting an air land airfield assault exercise at Fort Benning.
3. The training/rehearsal schedule is as follows:
    a. Monday - Unit functional training (3 Dec 79).
    b. Tuesday - Full rehearsal (4 Dec 79)
    c. Wednesday - Full rehearsal (5 Dec 79).
    d. Thursday - Full rehearsal (if required) (6 Dec 79).
4. Logistics preparation is continuing on schedule.
5. Impacts of variance from basic plan:
    - failure to conduct full rehearsal will impair task force efficiency
    - lack of designated recovery sites impairs medical support planning
    - the lack of in-country support assets continues to impose constraints on operations

***

On 4 December, the militants announced that eight of the hostages had been singled out for trial. This sparked speculation, and rampart assumptions in Washington, which quickly led to possible constructs of the list of "eight." It was assumed that the group would include those suspected of being CIA, possibly three individuals, and at least three of the more senior military officers, two Colonels and a Lieutenant Colonel, all of whom had served in Vietnam. This latter speculation was prompted when the "students" singled out the Lieutenant Colonel, an Air Force pilot, and labeled him as a "war criminal." The number could reach eight, following the same Vietnam service "war criminal" logic by including the two senior enlisted personnel both senior sergeants who had served in Vietnam. The threat of trials was a sword of Damocles to be periodically unsheathed by the militants.

On 6 December, Delta and the recently constituted Naval helicopter force moved to a remote training complex in the southwestern United States in the vicinity of Yuma, Arizona, for an extended period of unit training and collective rehearsals.

Meanwhile, the unit operators and logisticians set about determining their non-organic equipment requirements -- Night Vision Goggles (NVGs), silenced weapons, motorcycles, specialized camouflage, etcetera -- and submitted them to the JTF for procurement. All procurements were accomplished by the JTF J-4, Lt. Colonel John Barnett, an unflappable and exceptionally superb logistics officer who had joined the JTF on the 12th of November 1979. John and his two-man staff kept the JTF afloat despite monumental challenges. Always operating under a time crunch, John and his team managed to acquire the required material from a range of resources -- logistic depots, reserve units, commercial sources, and occasionally from a non-DOD government agency which always wanted to be paid before delivery. Official fund cites were non-existent, and the majority of government items, from motorcycles to silencers were procured on a hand receipt. Often the material was provided by people at commands whose only guidance was "recover all XYZs in XVIII Airborne Corps and deliver (sign out) all of them to a Major XYZ, who will be waiting at Pope AFB Base operations weather lounge at 07:00 Friday morning. Any questions or arguments are to be referred to Lt. General Tackaberry (CG, XVIII Airborne Corps)." The senior officer of the "lending" unit, or facility had usually received a secure call from an officer higher in his command chain clearing the request. In this case, LT. General Tackaberry had been called by the General Meyer, the Army Chief of Staff, who requested that Tackaberry "provide whatever he was asked to provide."

At no time were any of these JTF requests denied by DOD agencies, theater commands or service units, nor by the civil service support structure. One example of this support involved a woman at a small military depot where life was normally very staid and routine. The following vignette compiled by one of the JTF training support officers, LTC Keith Nightingale, tells the story.

One Saturday Night

Tucked away all over the country, quite often in small communities, are a range of military posts and stations ranging in missions from production of combat material to routine warehousing and distribution. At the heart of each facility is a body of civilians who keep the place going. Last night, we encountered such a place.

The requirement was for 60 Night Vision Goggles (NVGs). They cost about $8,000 apiece and are absolutely essential to the mission. The problem was that NVGs were a very scarce commodity and very tightly controlled. Normally, the requisition and shipping process, assuming approval, would take 45-90 days, with no guaranteed delivery date. The JTF staff got the requirement to dredge these things up in time to make a night mission rehearsal in 36 hours. The JTF J-4, LTC John Barnett, the logistics officer, researched the Army stock depot locations and finally found the place that had them. Naturally, it was the start of a weekend when all the hard-working little old ladies in tennis shoes are elsewhere, as they should be.

After weaving his way through a maze of people over the phone, Barnett found the person with the keys to the kingdom at 11 P.M. John talked to this person -- a genuine little old lady -- for some length of time and basically said, "We need 60 of your NVGs by tomorrow night. I can't tell you what for, but only that it is crucially important." He then gave her a telephone number in the Pentagon to verify his authority.

With that, he instructed her to take the NVGs to the airport and put them on the next plane to Tucson via counter-to-counter service. No paperwork, no messages, no approval from the boss.

We learned the next day that the woman personally went to the warehouse after the call and signed for all 60 sets. Then, with the help of the night watchman, put all of them in her station wagon and drove them to the airport. After processing the shipment papers, she helped load the units on the next puddle-jumper to Tucson.

***

The question of funding and how to pay for the myriad of "consumables," such as aviation fuel, raised its head again in early December as this memo of 7 December from General Vaught to the General Shutler reflects.

MEMORANDUM FOR J-3

Subject: Fund Cites **7 December 1979**

1. A problem has arisen due to the lack of a fund cite for resupply of JP-4 *(fuel)* for the helicopters at the training site at Yuma.

2. Previous arrangements for the Marine Air Station Yuma (MAS) to provide JP-4 was working satisfactorily until they requested a fund cite for reimbursement. The total required to date is approximately $35K. Individuals on the ground have attempted to alleviate the situation; however, all possible solutions require reimbursement of fuel to MAS.

3. The best solution is to continue with MAS providing fuel by tanker (trucks) to the Army airfield where the helicopters are located and providing a fund cite to MAS.

4. The alternate solution would be for someone in authority to contact the appropriate person in the MAS chain of command and direct continued support keeping cost data for future submission at a later date.

5. The lack of appropriate fund cites may continue to cause problems in day-to-day activities in procurement of supplies, rations, etc., as the exercise continues. We currently have a fund cite for small expenditures from the Task Force Comptroller for Delta housekeeping supplies.

6. Request guidance in overcoming this situation.

Signed: James B. Vaught, Major General, USA, JTF RICE BOWL

This memo was returned with the following handwritten note from the JCS J-3, Lt. General Philip D Shutler: "*Returned, Fund cites handled by Services on site.*"

***

As with most official actions there is a people story behind them. In this case, the following recollection, again by Keith Nightingale, provides the backdrop to the last comment in paragraph two, *individuals on the ground have attempted to alleviate the situation.*

A Small Problem

Our senior Marine and his Army partner in crime have just returned from our support base. The Comptroller, a Navy type, wants up-front funds or he shuts off the fuel. Our guys are in a small quandary. They have no funds and no fund cite. They can't tell the local folks what we are doing or why. They have messaged SOD daily but that has not helped the local situation. For some strange reason, there is resistance in the joint and the service staffs to cough up money.

The partners call back to the "building" and talk to our General. They draft up a message that everyone wants to retool. It is called the "there is no such thing as a free lunch" message. General Shutler and Colonel Pittman talk -- one Marine to another -- on the phone but the problem remains -- No fund cite. The Hellos burn fuel and the Navy is guarding the tap. Its lights out tomorrow.

We are informed the "Free Lunch" message was not well received. Eventually, the Navy, robbing Peter to pay Paul, covered this instance, but the problem of funding continues to plague us. Although few service people actually know what was afoot, most of the "troops" we deal with sense the urgency and respond positively with speed and the highest priority. Their "can-do attitude" prevailed over long ingrained bureaucracy.

***

During the first week of joint training in early December, it quickly became evident that the helicopter force needed a lot of work. Most of the Navy Flight personnel had come from a Navy fleet mine-sweeping squadron based in Norfolk, Virginia. The detachment was headed by a Navy commander, and totaled 35 personnel. This included seven Navy pilots, seven Marine Corps copilots and twenty enlisted personnel. The Navy pilots are used to flying relatively short, day time, open water, Point A to Point B type missions and were not prepared for the demanding nature of the training regime. The training syllabus included seven-day work weeks, eight to nine hour nighttime missions over unforgiving and undulating hard ground, wearing eight pound night vision goggles (NVGs).

In keeping with his concern for the mission, and the men of his unit, Colonel Beckwith pulled no punches in his messaged report to General Vaught at the end of the first major round of field activities:

MSG O94

O 081400R DEC 79
FM CDR Delta//BECKWITH
TO COMJTF //MG VAUGHT

1. I HAVE HAD SUFFICIENT TIME TO REEXAMINE OUR PAST ACTIVITIES AT YUMA DURING 03-06 DEC, AND PASS TO YOU MY JUDGMENT ON KEY ISSUES:

A. THE AIR DROPPING OF HELO FUEL MUST BE VIEWED AS A LAST RESORT EMERGENCY METHOD OF REFUELING HELLOS IN ANY PHASE OF OUR PROPOSED OPERATION. THE PROBABILITY OF RECOVERING USABLE FUEL IS NOT VERY GOOD COUPLED WITH THE MAMMOTH TASK OF RECOVERY OF AIR ITEMS/FUEL ETC.

B. YOU ARE WELL AWARE OF THE HELO PILOT PROBLEM. THEIR ABILITY TO FLY AT NIGHT DID NOT IMPROVE DURING YOUR ABSENCE. IN FACT, IT WAS FORTUNATE THAT WE DID NOT LOSE AN ELEMENT OF DELTA AS A RESULT OF A HELO CRASH. THERE ARE THREE STRAIGHT FORWARD IMPORTANT PRINCIPLES INVOLVED IN SELECTING PERSONNEL TO PERFORM EXTRAORDINARY HAZARD TASKS/SPECIAL OPERATIONS.

(1) THE INDIVIDUAL BEING CONSIDERED FOR THE ABOVE TASKS MUST UNDERSTAND THE RISKS, VOLUNTEER, AND BE CAREFULLY SELECTED, BASED ON AN APPROPRIATE ASSESSMENT PROCESS.

(2) TIME MUST BE ALLOTTED TO TRAIN AND EVALUATE EACH VOLUNTEER CANDIDATE.

(3) EACH CANDIDATE MUST BE PROVIDED WITH PRECISELY THE SAME TOOLS, MACHINES HE WILL USE ON AN ACTUAL OPERATION.

(4) THERE ARE NO SHORT CUTS TO THE ABOVE THREE PRINCIPLES. I ALSO REALIZE I AM PREACHING TO THE CHOIR. HOWEVER, IT HAS BEEN MADE OBVIOUS TO ME THAT THE ABOVE PRINCIPLES WERE NOT CONSIDERED IN SELECTING THE HELO CREWS TO INSERT AND EXTRACT DELTA FROM IRAN.

C. STRONGLY RECOMMEND THAT EVERY EFFORT BE MADE TO CONDUCT THE NEXT FTX *(FIELD TRAINING EXERCISE),* INVOLVING DELTA, HELLOS, TALONS, AND SPECTRE AT SITE 51 VICE YUMA. DELTA PERSONNEL REMAINED IN THEIR ISOLATED SITE DURING THIS ENTIRE PERIOD AT YUMA. ON THE OTHER HAND, OTHERS RESIDED IN SEPARATE LOCATIONS IN PLUSH BILLETS AND WERE EXPOSED TO OUTSIDE AGENCIES, USE OF COMMERCIAL TELEPHONES AND THE U.S. MAIL. IN MY VIEW, OUR LOW VISIBILITY APPROACH TO A NON-PERMISSIVE FORCE OPTION MAY QUICKLY BECOME HIGH VISIBILITY BASED ON OPSEC (OPERATIONAL SECURITY) CONSIDERATIONS. I WILL BRIEF YOU ON MY FUTURE PLANNED TRAINING PROGRAM TOMORROW. VERY RESPECTFULLY.

REVW 08 DEC 2009
BT

During these field-training periods, the population of the SOD spaces thinned out substantially, although the tempo of the work did not. The EUCOM and Pacific Command Liaison Officers (LNOs) returned to their commands to coordinate the accomplishment of their respective commands support actions. For the Pacific LNO, this involved both USAF Special Operations Forces in Guam, Okinawa and Hawaii, and the Navy's Indian Ocean Carrier Task Force which was home to the mission RH-53s, as well as support at Diego Garcia. For the EUCOM LNO, this involved requirements to establish a forward staging base in Egypt and coordinate reconnaissance, tanker, intelligence and medical support. The major task was the pre-planning associated with converting the largely inactive Egyptian airbase at Wadi Kena (near the Aswan Dam in southern Egypt) into a viable launch base that aside from Diego Garcia was the only other potential launch site politically available.

On 10 December, the JTF received the first of several reports from the now-fielded CIA survey team. The report's purpose was to provide a ground level assessment of the feasibility of two locations as possible insertion zones. After comparing the reports and descriptions provided with imagery, the JTF discovered that the survey team had not reached, nor surveyed, either of the requested locations. Had the reports been accepted at face value and without verification, several significant operational decisions would have been wrong.

On 14 December, the militants conducted a televised press conference where a few of the hostages were allowed to read some prepared comments. During one of these statements, a Marine hostage used a term which indicated where some of the hostages were being detained. This location had not been identified by any of the original 13 releasees; however, it had been placed very high on the list of suspected detention sites by the JTF J-2 through other analysis. The hostage's comment confirmed: the location, a time frame and by link association the number and type of hostages being held in this location. This in turn required a modification in the ground force's operational concepts. The Mushroom would be a hard nut to crack.

On 23 December 1979, the JTF sent two supplemental messages to the normal Daily Intelligence Summary. The second supplement summarized the state of international affairs regarding the continued detention of the American hostages. Key elements of that message follow:

MSG 182
23101OR DEC 79
FM: JTF
TO: DELTA
SUBJECT:SUPPLEMENT NUMBER 2

1. AMBASSADOR MC HENRY SENT FOLLOWING LETTER TO PRESIDENT OF UN SECURITY COUNCIL DECEMBER 22.
2. BEGIN TEXT:
DEAR MR. PRESIDENT;
- ON NOVEMBER 4, 1979, 63 AMERICANS AS WELL AS PERSONNEL OF OTHER NATIONALITIES WERE SEIZED WHEN A DISCIPLINED, ARMED GROUP OF DEMONSTRATORS INVADED THE UNITED STATES EMBASSY IN TEHRAN. WHILE THIRTEEN OF THOSE CAPTURED HAVE BEEN RELEASED, AT THE PRESENT MOMENT, SEVEN WEEKS LATER, 50 AMERICANS REMAIN CAPTIVE.
- ON NOVEMBER 25, 1979, SECRETARY GENERAL WALDHEIM, INVOKING ARTICLE 99 OF THE UNITED NATIONS CHARTER TO REQUEST AN URGENT MEETING OF THE SECURITY COUNCIL, DECLARED THE PRESENT CRISIS A SERIOUS THREAT TO INTERNATIONAL PEACE AND SECURITY.
- ON DECEMBER 4, 1979, THE SECURITY COUNCIL ADOPTED RESOLUTION 457 URGENTLY CALLING UPON THE GOVERNMENT OF IRAN IMMEDIATELY TO RELEASE THE PERSONNEL OF THE AMERICAN EMBASSY BEING HELD IN TEHRAN, PROVIDE THEM PROTECTION AND ALLOW THEM TO LEAVE IRAN. THIS RESOLUTION ALSO CALLED ON THE SECRETARY GENERAL TO USE HIS GOOD OFFICES TO SEEK A PEACEFUL RESOLUTION OF THE CRISIS.
- ON DECEMBER 15, 1979, THE INTERNATIONAL COURT OF JUSTICE ISSUED AN ORDER CALLING FOR "THE IMMEDIATE RELEASE, WITHOUT ANY EXCEPTION," BY IRAN OF ALL AMERICANS HELD IN IRAN AND FOR THEIR SAFE DEPARTURE FROM IRAN.

This international call for the release of the hostages was ignored by the Iranian power brokers.

On Christmas Eve, the militants allowed a group of international clergy to meet with the majority of the hostages. The meetings were conducted in small groups and held at several locations within the compound. Forty-three hostages were seen, and notes from two others were given to the clerics for delivery to the hostage families. Five hostages (not counting the invisible Canadian six) were unaccounted for. These five were the same individuals that, for all practical purposes, had been held incommunicado since shortly after the takeover. Analysis of the data from this visit and other earlier indications showed that hostages were being held in several groups at different detention locations, and under different guard conditions. A composite analysis of all data available indicated (with a high probability) the location of four individual detention sites within the compound. However, the JTF staff and the leaders of the operational forces knew this fragile equation could change unexpectedly at the whim of the militants, their advisors, or key members of the Islamic clergy.

As the JTF continued planning, practicing and desperately pursuing hard, reliable on-the-ground intelligence, both the State Department and CIA maintained an ongoing belief that a negotiated release of the hostages was possible by the end of the year. The State Department was still pinning its hopes on the Iranian "moderates," (civil government officials) having enough influence to convince the "revolutionary fundamentalists" that a peaceful release held more benefits for Iran than a prolonged detention. The U.S. press grasped this hope and received substantial play on television and print media. Regrettably, the "moderates," labeled as western sympathizers by the fundamentalists, had very little influence and that modicum was in decline. In addition, the two leading moderate personalities, President Bani Sadr and Foreign Minister Ghotbazadeh, frequently expressed opposing views regarding the potential for release.

The JTF had no information to substantiate the early release theory and quickly came to view the situation as a protracted political standoff with extensive public posturing engineered by the Islamic fundamentalists to serve as a focal point of world attention. The intent was to hold the United States up to ridicule and at the same time purge Iran of western thoughts and attitudes, particularly American. A succession of purges of former government employees, technical schools, and military structures (the Iranian institutions most affected by western influence), had been ongoing periodically since shortly after the arrival of Ayatollah Khomeini nine months earlier. The only political solution available to the United States was capitulation, and this was not acceptable.

Throughout this period of questionable hopes, the JTF forces conducted intensive specialized training at their home stations, and nearby training sites, to perfect their specific mission skills and capabilities. At the same time, detailed three-dimensional models of the American Embassy compound and the surrounding city blocks began arriving at Delta. Models of the Ministry of Foreign Affairs (MFA) compound and several other key facilities followed as various options were developed and rehearsed. The flow and reliability of intelligence began to increase with each passing day, providing an ever widening and deepening basis of fact upon which to draw conclusions. Desk blotter-sized stacks of reconnaissance imagery arrived on an almost daily basis. Coupled with the periodic reports from the in-country CIA survey team, the meager DOD HUMINT assets, and backgrounded by international media and TV coverage, the JTF began to put together a more vibrant picture of the tempo of life in Teheran.

Except for a short Christmas-New Year's stand down of the tactical forces (Delta, the Rangers, and the USN/USMC helicopter team) to give the troops a small respite and maintain operational security, the JTF did not cease functioning. The JTF staff had continued to work the fourteen to sixteen hour days that had become routine. Christmas dinner was eaten off paper plates in the SOD/JTF workspaces. The meal was delicious, and the second of many periodic repasts prepared by the de facto personnel chief and morale officer, Navy Chief Collins and his very gracious wife. The first had been Thanksgiving dinner, served in the same manner and eaten at conference tables and work desks.

During the brief stand-down, it was decided that the majority of the Navy helicopter pilots were not making sufficient progress and some did not have their heart in the mission. After consultation between General Vaught and General Schulter, the JCS J-3, a change in personnel was deemed necessary. The mission was then given to the Marine aviation community to field a new helicopter force. Within a few days, six of the seven Navy pilots were relieved and replaced by a cross section of H-53 qualified Marine pilots and copilots from several different units and one USAF H-53 instructor pilot.

The last week in December also brought with it a major international and regional event. The Soviet Union invaded neighboring Afghanistan, bringing an increase in Soviet surveillance and added American concern to the region. With this event, a new set of questions arose. Was Iran to be next? Would the Soviet Union try to gain their long-sought, southern warm-water port? The Soviet move, combined with the instability in Iran, prompted the Chairman to create the Rapid Deployment Joint Task Force (RDJTF). The initial force was composed of most of the DOD's quick reaction forces conventional forces, including the XVIII Airborne Corps, the East Coast 9th Air Force, and afloat rotational Navy/Marine forces.*

***

JTF option refinements and specialized training had continued unabated throughout December. One of the key actions during the holiday period was making arrangements to conduct additional field training and a full-scale rehearsal of the various options in mid-January. However, not all government agencies had seen the need for the rescue planning nor military preparations. It was not until the last few days of 1979 that one of the recalcitrants, a CIA representative to the JTF, finally acknowledged that we (the U.S.) might have to execute the military option.

On 29 December, the JTF issued the fourth in a series of periodic intelligence assessments and 30-60 day projections. These assessments and projections were sent to all the operational components and served to update

* The RDJTF structure eventually gave way to the creation of the United States Central Command (USCENTCOM) which ten years later won its spurs in Desert Storm against the forces of Saddam Hussein of Iraq.

the Intelligence Annex to the JTF Operations Order which had been prepared 30 days earlier.

As New Year's Day faded into history, the self-generated State Department euphoria of a potential release of the hostages (during the Christmas holidays) was dashed by the cold realization that nothing within the Iranian equation indicated a near-term release of the hostages. Overall, there was a mood change within DOD, also. The hectic rush of catch-up and get-ready-to-go that characterized November and December was replaced by the steadier and more sober view of the marathoner in training.

The New Year also brought an increase in force resources. A group of Delta candidates who had just completed final screening and initial training shortly before Christmas were now available for integration into the ground force planning. Two additional RH-53s were added to the six already repositioned on the *USS Nimitz* (*CV-68*, the carrier now on station in the Indian Ocean and the inheritor of the original 6 RH-53Ds). These additions increased the margin of available lift from the 50 percent built into the original deployment of six RH-53s, to 100 percent of the essential four-ship simultaneous extraction capability. The Navy also advised the JTF that the addition of any more helicopters would warrant the withdrawal of equivalent fighter aircraft, thus decreasing the air strike and air defense capability of the Carrier Battle Group.

A major JTF planning review, the first of many, was held on 4 January 1980. It included a complete review of the situation and the status of intelligence efforts to date and projected. It also included a review of the logistic and communications status, the projected weather for both the operational and exercise areas. It concluded with a review of training and force proficiency status, discussions of operational concepts, and the development of a training and support schedule for the next 30 to forty days. JTF personnel also reviewed possible staging and launch sites in Egypt and Oman, in recognition of the need to be prepared to conduct any of the current contingency options.

During this formative period, the CIA informed General Vaught very quietly that "Bob," the recalled OSS man, had succeeded in acquiring a small fleet of vehicles, trucks, vans and a sedan to be used to transport Delta from their hide-site to the embassy. The vehicles were stored in a small warehouse complex south of the city, mid-way between the projected helicopter drop-off area and the urban buildup of the outskirts of the city. This was good news and indicative that things could be done if the right people were given the job.

Training still had to accommodate the two major options -- airfield seizure, which was not the preferred but, at the time, the only feasible option, and desert refueling. The latter had two variations that were being tested. One was landing tanker C-130s, refueling the helicopters, and transferring the assault force from the C-130 to the helicopters for the second leg of the mission. Another was airdropping fuel bladders, setting up a transfer site, and refueling the helicopters that would already have the strike force on-board. The latter option was definitely not preferred, but could not be discarded.

The imagery interpreters had been told to search for a smooth area at least a mile long, preferably two, and a half a mile wide in a remote, non-radar coverage area, within the refueling ellipse to support the airland option. A smaller area, but equally smooth and level to allow the parachute landing and movement of the round, 2,000 pound containers called "blivets," was required for the airdrop option. In early January, the DIA geographers and imagery interpreters concluded their analysis that had encompassed forty percent of Iran. They identified two areas within the refueling ellipse that met the JTF requirements and one, the larger site, held a strong potential to serve as a desert landing site. The team had reviewed eight years of imagery coverage of the site and found the broad flat area to be highly stable throughout the entire period. Based on his knowledge of the terrain and the landforms and the imagery record, the geologist assessed that the soil would support the weight of the C-130s. This site, nicknamed Desert One, became the focus of the ground refueling possibility.

After departing Desert One, the force would have to laager overnight somewhere short of Teheran and conduct the final reconnaissance and planning. This required places to hide the helos and to drop Delta where they could be in good position to launch the operation. The location had to be close enough to Teheran to allow easy access and far enough away to be isolated from casual observation. A map and imagery search narrowed the location down to a large mountain mass in the desert south of the city. One of the sub-locales was an ancient "caravansary," (caravan stop) with an earthen walled corral in close proximity to an abandoned mine, with an unused but serviceable dirt road that provided access to the main highway to Teheran. The imagery coverage indicated that the mine was abandoned and unattended, and that there was a reasonable good site up in the higher elevations, approximately six minutes flying time away, where the helos could land, be concealed, and a security screen set up. The proximity of the two sites would allow the Delta force to be dropped within hiking distance of the mine and the helos to hide relatively nearby. The remaining requirement was to check out the two sites on the ground.

All the candidate sites were put under photographic surveillance, as were several other key locations, such as the extraction airhead -- Manzariyeh and several other area airfields. The surveillance had two purposes: first, to determine the activity pattern in the areas of interest and, second, to maintain OPSEC concerning the primary sites by not focusing exclusively on them. Some discarded locations were carried on the reconnaissance menu specifically for the latter purpose.

Although there was a high degree of confidence that the Desert One Site (as it came to be called) was suitable, COMJTF and the component commanders deemed it unwise to commit to Desert One and abandon training on all other options until someone had "walked the ground." The CIA support team was not in a position to conduct the ground survey desired. In addition, they were not trained in taking soil core samples, calibrating penetrometer readings, navigating and taking measurements at night, nor installing landing instrumentation devices. These tasks required someone knowledgeable, experienced and competent in these skills. The final survey had to be done by a set of qualified "American eyes." This translated to a special operations combat controller. A proposal to conduct a field survey was initiated within a few days, but the request was denied. This and other requests were funneled through the CIA liaison who presented them to the State Department for concurrence before proceeding or forwarding them to the White House. If either the CIA or State non-concurred (or perceived the White House would not approve the request), it never reached the White House.

On the 18th of January, letters from 17 of the hostages were received by their families and loved ones. Some families chose to provide these to the Task Force through service or departmental representatives; others chose not to. Still others chose only to share specific portions with specific officials.

Whenever an original letter or note, and its envelope or shipping package was obtained, it yielded valuable data. Although a time difference was always encountered from the date the letter was written until received, which ranged from less than 36 hours to three weeks, a detailed analysis of the correspondence often verified, clarified and confirmed other indicators and analysis or prompted a reexamination of a previously held supposition. The value of this type of information and its periodic re-analysis proved its value over and over again. JTF analysis of this type of data indicated that the "5 percent" insurance group had been moved back into the compound and amalgamated into the other hostage groupings prior to Christmas. This reduced the number of hostage locations to two principle sites: the Ministry of Foreign Affairs, where the Chargé and two other Americans were being held, and four possible locations within the Embassy compound.

A few days later, it became evident to the JTF that the MFA trio of Lainqen, Howland, and Tomseth, the three American diplomats being held in the MFA for "their own protection," had totally lost their freedom of movement and would soon be officially added to the "to-be-extracted" list.

For the first time since their detention, the trio was referred to by the Iranian Ministry of Foreign Affairs officials as "hostages." This eliminated any question regarding the status of the trio and the JTF embarked on the identification of an appropriate force and course of action to free them simultaneously with the fifty held in the Embassy.

The State Department had previously accepted the claim of the secular side of the Iranian government that the three American diplomats were being detained for their protection. Statements by Iranian Prime Minister Ghotzebedah in early January radically changed this perception. In public pronouncements, the three diplomats were categorized as being equal to the Americans being held by the militants at the Embassy compound and would be judged similarly. This put the MFA trio on the rescue list.

As far back as 7 November, the JTF planning staff had been concerned that the "protective" detention of the Chargé D'Affaires (Mr. Bruce Laingen), and his two companions, was another rescue requirement just waiting to be added to the JTF's plate. However, it was not until after the Christmas season that the bubble burst and this requirement was officially added to the rescue mission.

Delta was fully committed to the Embassy compound. Given the probability of having to take down the fortress-like Chancellery building steadily increasing, and the need to clear more than a half dozen other buildings in the compound still persistent, General Vaught determined that an additional force would have to be added to the JTF equation to handle the MFA requirement.

As the MFA mission was officially thrust upon the DOD and the JTF after much of the detailed planning for the Embassy compound assault had been completed and rehearsals were underway, an additional sense of urgency surrounded the MFA effort. At the time, the JTF was envisioning the possible execution of the rescue option in early February. It was decided that a small, specially trained group be constituted from within the EUCOM community of Special Operations Forces. The EUCOM LNO was given the task to begin development of the MFA mission concept and tasked to recommend force assignment options.

Unfortunately, very little in the way of intelligence other than some old city maps and photographs was available of the MFA. The information provided by the CIA support team was marginal, often questionable, and most dangerous of all, unconfirmable. Details left unanswered included: the status of night time lighting in and around the Ministry, how was it guarded, which gates were manned, how was the area patrolled, and whether there were any military or militia forces in the local area that could interfere with the American rescue effort. However, the JTF did have precise information on where in the building the three hostages were sequestered and the status of the immediate guard force. The three hostages were being detained in a reception room on the top floor in the west-end of the center wing, known as the Ballroom. The Chargé was able to receive telephone calls from the State Department occasionally and periodic visits from a few members of the local diplomatic community. These limited insights, when combined with the data gained from the scheduled collection efforts, began to create a fuzzy but recognizable picture of the MFA environment.

All the HUMINT information available at the time (most of which was either dated or came from the CIA survey team) indicated the MFA was a "soft" target by comparison to the Embassy compound. Instead of surprise, shock and firepower as envisioned for the Embassy takedown, a quiet, low visibility operation conducted by a small team was deemed more appropriate.

In addition to the general concept of a covert operation, two other factors were paramount. First, the MFA rescue would have to be conducted in concert with the effort at the Embassy, and second, the extraction of both forces and all the hostages from Iran would have to occur simultaneously. Other than these basic considerations, planning options were open. Fortunately, one of the JTF intelligence officers, the former S-2 of Blue Light, had trained in Iran prior to the fall of the Shah and had visited many of the museum buildings located on the grounds of the MFA. Working with reconnaissance photography and several different maps (both U.S. military and Iranian civilian), plus a scattering of hand-held photographs (screened from the earlier massive printing of the historical files), the young Captain fleshed out additional details, including identifying some of the more obscure features of the complex including walkways, interior lighting and guard posts.

His input was extremely valuable to both the tactical planners and the model builders of the National Photographic Interpretation Center (NPIC), who were requested to produce another detailed three dimensional, properly scaled model. Again, this team of civilian government artists and imagery interpreters came through. They provided the new force a comprehensive representation of the MFA building, grounds and surrounding area within days.

The EUCOM - Berlin Brigade - Detachment A Special Forces Unit commander, Lieutenant Colonel Stan Oleshevic, a highly experienced, behind-the-lines operative with multi-linguist skills, was asked to immediately screen his entire force, select and assemble a team, and develop a tactical plan and begin training and rehearsals. Drawing on the model and the continuing flow of imagery, the EUCOM LNO developed a basic operational concept. Initial planning envisioned the use of a two-person "scout" team of Special Forces soldiers from the Berlin-based Special Forces Detachment A to be inserted into Teheran. They would conduct an on-the-ground reconnaissance of the MFA compound, and then recover to the mission-training site where their new knowledge would be used to develop the mission scheme.

The initial MFA force estimate concept called for a rescue force consisting of three to eight Detachment A Special Forces personnel, including the two-man scout team, plus Major Magee, the EUCOM LNO who would serve as the Officer-in-Charge. When it came time to execute, the two members of the force who made the ground survey reconnaissance would precede the balance of the rescue team into Iran by a few days to reassess the situation.

LTC Oleshevic quickly screened and nominated five personnel for consideration as the two-person reconnaissance team. All candidates had foreign language skills and could blend into several ethnic backgrounds. After evaluation by the JTF and the CIA, two of the five were selected for further area orientation and training. In the meantime, the other members of the MFA team began special skills training and familiarization with the target complex. This included building a full-size replica of the appropriate segments of the mission building and the detention location. All training was done at night and under conditions that resembled those to be found in Teheran.

Simultaneous with these initial actions, the operational concept and an execution timetable was briefed to General Vaught in Washington in mid-January. The EUCOM plan was approved for training and equipment procurement with modifications to be based upon the observations of the two SF advance scouts and any additional intelligence acquired by the JTF.

Flexibility in the tactical plan was allowed for, should the target environment not be quite as soft as initially painted by the in-country CIA survey team. Useful intelligence from CIA HUMINT sources was still essentially non-existent, and all other data concerning the day-to-day environment in downtown Teheran was very limited.*

* Fortunately, the small group of Americans lucky enough to have found refuge with the Canadian Ambassador remained undetected by the Iranians and theoretically invisible to the JTF planners. Eventually, the Canadian seven, as they were later referred to, were able to leave Iran undetected with Canadian assistance on 29th January. They exited Iran on a commercial airliner through Teheran's Mehrabad airport. This story was made into a made-for-TV movie starring Richard Crenna, who also starred in the TV movie about the earlier Bull Simons/Ross Perot rescue of the four EDS employees.

CHAPTER FOUR
Preparation

In spite of the continuing funding challenges and band-aid solutions that were applied to the funding problem, the machinery of the JTF kept right on running at 110 percent in most departments. However, not without an occasional hiccup, such as the big "I owe you" that had been run up for helicopter fuel at Yuma. One of the miracle workers that kept the JTF afloat and steaming forward was the JTF J-4, the logistics officer, LTC John Barnett, and his two-man staff, of which he constituted fifty percent. To look at John, he was an ordinary guy with none of the visible marks of the smooth executive or a rising political star. But inside the slightly rumpled exterior, he had the brains, dedication and experience worthy of a true shade tree genius and the "Star" material General Vaught thought he had.

JTF logistic requirements routinely had to be met on a short-notice basis. This took a special inter-personal finesse and highly developed skills in long-distance telephone patience. The standard items were always that -- standard -- but in large quantities and required immediate action. They included such divergent items as survival vests and radios, desert and snow camouflage clothing and netting. The more exotic items included a wide variety of reflective and absorbent paints, mobile fuel bladders capable of sustaining the impact of a parachute landing, specially ruggedized dirt bikes, advanced Night Vision Goggles (NVGs), and specially constructed and laminated navigation and landing aids.

Acquisition of the most essential equipment meant dealing with the supply systems and knowing the procurement procedures (and idiosyncrasies) of all four of the military services and the U.S. Coast Guard. Many times, the military cupboard was bare, and satisfaction of many of the unique or climatological requirements involved canvassing commercial sources and soliciting their cooperation in design and fabrication or modification of existing R&D prototypes that held promise as being mission-supportive.

As with the majority of the efforts of the JTF, many of these actions were continually ongoing and overlapping, with new ones surfacing every day. The "Logies" routinely worked the standard fifteen-hour JTF staff day, with seven-day workweeks being the norm throughout the period of the JTF's existence.

Much of overseas pre-positioning logistic work lay in the lap of the European Command, with the Pacific Command's responsibility largely discharged with the pre-positioning of the RH-53s on-board the Indian Ocean carrier. AWACS aircraft and their supporting flying gas stations,

KC-135s, and an occasional giant KC-10 from the Strategic Air Command, were establishing an operational footprint at Cairo West. Coincident with this operational signature, which was very reassuring to many of the Arabian peninsula countries, was the rotational build up and frequency of Military Airlift Command (MAC) C- 141 Starlifters, and the shorter-legged C-130 Hercules flights into and out of Wadi Kena.

At General Vaught's direction, the EUCOM liaison officer coordinated the deployment of two MC-130s Special Operations transports from the 7th Special Operations Squadron (7th SOS) at Rhein Main airbase near Frankfurt, Germany, to Wadi Kena. The purpose of this deployment was to provide the Soviet intelligence and surveillance system with the beginning of indications of SOF aircraft usage of Wadi Kena for routine training. A parallel mission was to provide Jim Magee, the EUCOM JTF liaison officer, with an opportunity to quietly conduct a ground survey of the existing facilities and the force dispersal potential of the airfield and its surrounding environments. Magee, normally the epitome of the posterboard Marine, conducted the survey in a worn and sweaty USAF flight suit (under the nom-de-guerre of Major McGreedy, USAF). He posed as a member of the Air Force Special Operations Combat Control team that was attached to the 7th SOS.

The site survey confirmed JTF impressions that the base was indeed austere and enhancements would be required to support the mission buildup, staging and recovery; however, it had the runway, the hangars and the basic ingredients for a JTF bull pen, and it was remote! The Egyptian Air Force considered Wadi Kena such a hardship tour that it rotated personnel every 30 days. Augmentation of its runway lighting, fuel storage and ground transport capabilities, and a major upgrade of its electric power capability would be required, but all of these were do-able. The greatest challenge was how to unobtrusively pre-stock enough fuel to meet the airlift-refueling requirements, which far exceeded the normal stock level of 400,000 gallons. The second challenge was how to move the large quantities of fuel required to more than a score of aircraft scattered all over the airdrome, and do this in a compressed time window with a limited fleet of trucks and without attracting attention or creating an unwarranted ground safety hazard. Additionally, the hangars (originally, Soviet-designed fighter hangarettes) allocated to the JTF numbered only four. The remaining 12 were filled with old, broken and inoperable Egyptian Air Force/Army vehicles, pallets, litter and garbage. The JTF would need to use all sixteen during the pre-launch buildup as well as all of the adjacent support bunkers, buildings, and parking spots, and have unobstructed use of the entire road network.

Each of the hangars and the associated buildings was inspected. A notional base loading and requirements plan was drawn up and briefed to the senior EUCOM flag officers, General Jim Allen, USAF (DCINCEUR) and Admiral Sam Packer, EUCOM J-3. The briefing focused on the enhancements required to bring Wadi Kena up to a state of operational readiness. Once this was accomplished, the load plan and the list of required support actions were sent back to the JTF in Washington for review and approval. The loading plan specified the use of each of the 16 hangars and the precise locations of each of the aircraft that constituted the rescue armada and where they would be positioned for maintenance and pre-mission launch checks. The recommendations for enhancing the austere desert complex were approved immediately, with little revision. A small EUCOM planning cell composed of logistics and operations personnel was tasked to manage and monitor the upgrade. They were to do this under the cover of upgrading the facility to serve as a general-purpose contingency support base.

The initial U.S. presence at Wadi Kena was the establishment of USAF logistics and maintenance facilities to support three possible uses. The EUCOM planning cell knew the three force requirements as: a Surveillance Task Force consisting of AWACS and KC-135 Tanker aircraft; a Fighter Task Force consisting of up to a wing (80 plus) F-4/F-15 tactical fighters; a heavy lift Transport Task Force. The initial USAF presence supported the first contingency, the rotating deployment of Airborne Warning and Control System (AWACS) and KC-135 refueler aircraft. The AWACS aircraft, flying radar platforms, extended America's eyes in the area. The long 12-16 hour mission of the AWACS required a fleet of twelve SAC KC-135 aerial refueling tankers in support. The combined number of aircraft and the high tempo of flight activity, essentially 24 hours a day, justified the base support build-up. The fighter deployment was planned by the Tactical Air Command, but never executed. It was part of one of the larger Iranian-related rapid deployment options. The heavy lift Task Force was the baseline for the rescue force option. This was further masked by the normal logistics flow of transport and SOF aircraft that began to frequent Wadi Kena.

Preparations at Wadi Kena accelerated in mid-January and continued at a deliberate pace throughout February. Concurrently, the cover plan was implemented. The fighter and tanker basing requirements were the mainstay of this rationale and the explanation for the upgrade effort at Wadi Kena. The base came to be referred to as "Site Alfa" by the planners in EUCOM and the JTF.

Throughout January, February, and March, the JTF training focus continued to be diluted by the need to practice for three different refueling scenarios in addition to the six basic operational phases. The three refueling options were: the remote airfield seizure (largely a Ranger mission); the blivet-drop refueling (helicopter crews and Delta); and the airland refueling option (helicopter and C-130 crews and the refueling teams). The six operational phases were: the Delta drop-off and transfer; the helicopter camouflage and hide requirement; the approach and assault at the Embassy and the MFA; and the helicopter extraction from both of these sites; plus the extraction airfield seizure; and force transfer and evacuation.

The seizure of the Manzariyeh extraction airhead south of Teheran, a major Ranger mission, was a challenge due to its vast size (an equivalent of two square miles) and the lack of any eyes-on-the-ground reconnaissance. The airfield had been identified very early in November by EUCOM's hostage recovery planning cell, and had been put under imagery surveillance by the JTF on the same high priority that had been accorded the Embassy compound. This surveillance was the only source of reliable and recurring observations. During one of the few times the Director of Central Intelligence (DCI), retired Admiral Stansfield Turner, visited the JTF planning spaces, he was given an update briefing by General Vaught which concluded with a request for an on-the-ground survey of the Manzariyeh. The DCI responded, "Well you know, I only have one asset [referring to the retired OSS operative], and besides I gave you a picture" (a general reference to the periodic reconnaissance photography). This type of uneducated comment would have set most of the JTF staff at the DCI's throat, or generated an outburst against the stupidity implied by the comment. Not so, General Vaught. He put a reign on his feelings, and quietly and politely explained that the type of information that was needed was not obtainable from of a picture taken during the day. The JTF needed to know the nighttime environment -- where their guards were posted, whether there were roving animals, whether activities on the runway could be seen from the nearby road, etcetera. The message was not received. No CIA effort was expended on these questions.

Whereas the extraction airfield at Manzariyeh was essentially non-operational and did not have an active Iranian military presence, the same was not true of the small remote Iranian Air Force training facility on the inbound flight route, which was the pivot point of insertion option two. This site, if used as a transfer point for Delta and the driver-monitors (and as a refueling point for the helicopters), posed a different set of challenges. It was an active installation with a persistent human presence. This site had also been under photo surveillance since mid-November. This extended period of surveillance allowed the development of the facility's operational and security profile. This included the approximate number of personnel assigned by day of the week, the functionality of all the buildings within the complex, even the day and time the water truck arrived and which way gates swung open. The Rangers and the Air Force Combat Control Teams (CCT) were the primary consumers of this information. The seizure of this site would be complicated by the need to not reflect any outward change in its appearance or routine while in American hands. This latter requirement introduced the need for linguists and role-players to maintain the essential cloak of secrecy and normalcy. A plan was developed, practiced and rehearsed. Meanwhile, the search continued for a remote landing site suitable to support insertion option three.

The periodic change in hostage locations, the possibility of last minute hostage movements, and the introduction of new members of Delta as they came out of the training pipeline, all combined to create a major planning and proficiency challenge. Virtually every man in Delta had to be familiar with every aspect of the ground operation and every building in the compound. He had to possess a detailed knowledge of the most likely and most difficult buildings, such as the three-story, sixty-room plus Chancery. The Chancery was not one of Charlie's favorite targets, due to the difficulty associated with its size and construction.

The extended night hours and a thousand miles of low level night flying, most of it wearing the cumbersome and tedious NVGs, probably placed the most extended stress on the helicopter crews who were trying desperately to achieve a modicum of mission competence and reliability. This second helicopter team, composed largely of Marines, a few sailors and one USAF copilot, had to do better than their predecessors.

Although the flight hours were not quite as long or tedious for the MC and EC-130 aircrews (because of their aircraft's capabilities and the aircrews' previous experience), they continued to practice countless numbers of blackout landings and blackout airborne refueling missions with KC-135 and KC-10 tankers. The AC-130 gunships practiced by conducting live fire range missions at the end of a 1,300 mile, eight hour flight transit, then recovering the same distance nonstop.

The mission requirements of the USAF Combat Control Team (CCT), who had to plan and rehearse control of the airflow for all the transfer options, also made for a strenuous training schedule. The airflow involved the phased airlanding, ground movement, refueling, personnel transfer, and rapid departure of upwards of twenty aircraft under blackout conditions. The CCT had to develop four different schemes of maneuver: one for the small but active IAF military installation (with its abbreviated runway); a second for the desert refueling "blivet drop" option; a third for the desert airland, C-130 to Helicopter transfer-refueling option; and lastly for the large extraction airfield. All of this was grueling, dirty, sweaty work. There was no glory in any of these training drills, just hot, dusty air, long hours and endless repetition, striving for perfection.

Most of the JTF operations planning staff and the command section deployed to support the training exercises and monitor the progress of the force, while the logistics and intelligence personnel kept the home fires burning and the supplied the deployed forces with food, gas, and information. They also began the preparation of Escape and Evasion (E&E) kits. The term E&E dates back to World War II when hundreds of RAF and USAF aircrews were flying into hostile airspace on a daily basis. Essentially all of continental Europe, from the coasts of Normandy to the factories of Romania, was hostile airspace. Approximately half of the allied aircrews who had a plane shot out from under them were able to bail out. Many were able to evade capture and were assisted by the allied underground. JTF 1-79 did not have any underground in Iran, so a good E&E package was essential.

The composition of the typical E&E kit has not changed much since WW II because the needs of the downed aircrew have not changed: avoid capture, stay alive, and get to friendly forces. An E&E kit is tailored the area of operation, and supplements the normal first aid, compass, rescue radio, signal flares, and personal weapons that combat aircrews carry. The JTF E&E packages were put together with the support of three national agencies. The CIA provided money in several currencies. The Defense Mapping Agency (DMA) provided several types and scales of maps designed by the JTF on plastic material. The Defense Intelligence Agency (DIA), working with the JTF, prepared a multi-lingual language guide containing key phrases, questions, and likely responses. The E&E plan itself laid out procedures for each segment of the insertion, execution, and extraction route. The procedures spelled out the direction and route, guidelines for movement and concealment, rendezvous locations, and identification procedures. The E&E plans and options were coordinated with each of the operational commanders to ensure that the JTF procedures were complementary to the normal service E&E guidelines.

***

THE WEATHER FACTOR

Weather was recognized as being one of the most critical information needs of the JTF from the beginning of the crisis. One of the initial actions of the J-2 on 5 November 1979 was to request the assignment of a weather officer. A young Captain by the name of Don Buchanan was assigned by the Air Weather Service as the JTF Staff Weather Officer (SWO).

In addition to the challenge of forecasting the weather for Iran and the possible approaches, the young Captain was called upon, often unexpectedly, to provide weather support for the major exercises. He was faced with this "domestic" challenge five times. The first was in early December, when a weekend call requested data to support the first major training exercise. Data was needed for most of the southern United States, with Yuma Proving Grounds being the focal point. Early in January, the young SWO was tasked by the J-2 to prepare plans to deploy a weather detachment to the Middle East to support the rescue force, should it deploy. The SWO began his communication resource planning with the JTF J-6, LTC Peter Dieck, an Army Signal officer with tremendous deployment expertise. Pete Dieck had been a member of the REDCOM CT JTF cadre and also had served a tour as Commander of the Joint Communication Support Element (JCSE), a fully deployable joint communication capability under JCS control. Just as the young weather Captain thought he had this task under control, he was directed to prepare a paper describing the current status of the weather support he was receiving in the Pentagon, and how he would envision weather support flowing to the Middle East Forward Operating Location (FOL).

The second exercise followed close on the heels of the paper, and was less of a surprise to the young SWO. This time he received a few days warning but the exercise area was now Nevada and the time was the cold middle period of January. Less than two weeks went by before his skills were tested again with exercise Number three, also in Nevada. This exercise was delayed several times due to extremely bad weather that was effecting the entire southern half of the U.S.A. The twice-daily weather forecast briefing now included both west and east coasts launch locations, and forecasts for the mid-continent aerial refueling areas, as well as ground level forecasts for the helicopter transfer site and the embassy objective area.

In late January, (after attending a JTF planning conference at Fort Bragg), during which accurate weather forecasting was again highlighted as extremely critical, the SWO was tasked to prepare a detailed Fact Sheet describing the weather capabilities and procedures planned for the Forward Operating Location (FOL). The requirement was to have a capability robust enough to accurately predict clear weather over a 500-mile flight route that had only one weather station reporting and that intermittently. Although the procedures and capabilities were deemed "adequate," if provided "finished" weather data, the capability was not deemed robust enough to provide the most current and comprehensive weather picture possible. The decision was made shortly thereafter to substantially upgrade the capability of the deployment element to receive "raw" weather data directly from the processing sites as well as "finished" assessments from Air Force Global Weather Central (GWC) at Offutt Air Force Base, Nebraska. At this point, several other weather officers were brought into the weather equation to accompany and operate the additional equipment. The introduction of this additional equipment added another communication requirement. The JTF J-6 again worked with the SWO. Together they accomplished this minor miracle.

Exercise number four took place during the last week of February and it was back to Yuma. The weather procedures developed and refined in the previous months and field exercises were again employed. This included twice daily weather forecasts for the next 24 then 48 hours, plus a ten-day outlook. Field units received daily, by secure teletype, the formatted weather forecast along with a narrative discussion. Another Weather officer was read-in and added to the weather support effort in early March. This officer supported Exercise Five, which took place in the third week of March. Exercise Five was at a new location -- Indian Springs Air Force Station in Nevada.

***

As training progressed, the various option rehearsals were conducted using not only the same techniques, but also distances equivalent to those envisioned for the actual operation. The confidence of the JTF and the JTF Commander was steadily but slowly rising, as problems were overcome, procedures worked out, and capabilities developed. In a unique effort to further hone the different force and staff elements' awareness of their capabilities and shortfalls, General Vaught instituted a program to measure their mission confidence and effectiveness. This included support functions such as communications, logistics and intelligence. Each element was to divide the total mission sequence into distinct segments, identify the requirements essential to ensure success in each segment within their area of responsibility, and apply a confidence factor to each. This process of self-examination, the results of which were briefed weekly to COMJTF, quickly identified the weak links and unsatisfied or overlooked requirements. Priorities were identified, solutions found, and procedures or capabilities enhanced.

As part of the overall evaluation process that was used to develop the assessment, each of the staff sections had earlier been directed by General Vaught to conduct a periodic evaluation of their function's ability to meet the needs of the mission forces. As an example of these functional assessments, the J-2 team chose to identify nine elements of the mission profile and evaluate the availability and reliability of the key information required to support each element. The nine mission segments chosen were: Air Route Planning; Helicopter Refuel Point; Delta Transfer/Drop-Off Point; Teheran Environment; External Security at the Compound; Internal Security at the Compound; Hostage Location Data; Iranian Irregular Reaction Forces; and

Regular Reaction Forces. The benchmark dates for these snap-shot evaluations were 4-7 November, 19 December, 14 January, and 1 February. In addition to a percentage estimate, a succinct statement defining the missing information was created. These statements were the critical Essential Elements of Information (EEI), and given consistent collection and analytical attention by the JTF, DIA and NSA. Similar attention was focused on the operational, logistics and communications areas.

Air route planning was the first to hit the 90 percent mark, followed by data on the regular Iranian reaction forces, with the irregular reaction forces next. These were followed in short order by data on the general environmental in Teheran, then the external security at the compound, then several refueling point options, and the Delta transfer point. The precise location of the hostages was next to hit an acceptable level. The last to be achieved was the status of the security inside the compound. At the initial onset of formal planning (7 November), none of the factors were assessed above 20 percent. By 19 December the average was 60 percent. By January the average for the nine factors was approaching 75 percent, and by the 1st of February the overall average was above 80 percent on all counts except the status of security inside the compound, and the precise location of the hostages. During the next two and half months, all of the percentages continued to climb in small increments. All climbed above the 90 -95 percentile level, but none reached 100 percent.

On 28 January 1980, the JCS J-3, Lt. General Philip Shutler, sent a memorandum to General Jones, forwarding a paper prepared by the JTF that explored the factors affecting a decision to launch a rescue effort.

Paragraph three of the J-3 memo that summarized the JTF assessment is presented below:

> 3. The odds on success (60-70% in execution tempered by 15-30 % possibility of disruption) do not appear to be high enough to warrant an attempt under current conditions. If we wait until hostages have been injured or killed, the pressure to act will be so high, and the situation in Iran so uncertain that the odds for success would certainly be drastically reduced. The hard part will be to recognize a time of increased danger and to act accordingly. The team is continuing to refine plans to deploy, in particular to get to the shortest response time consistent with operational security. Because the movement of the helo crews to the carrier takes the longest time and also because their stateside activity is the most likely OPSEC give away, we may want to move the crews forward in increments as the next step to reduce response time.
>
> Very respectfully,
> Philip D. Shutler
> Lieutenant General, USMC
> Director for Operations

The lead and closing paragraphs (Assessment and Summary) of the basic JTF paper from which General Shutler drew his assessment are presented below for additional clarity:

1. **FACTOR ASSESSMENT:**

a. The US Team: A team of personnel has been formed and trained to perform well. The machines have been modified and enhanced and the men have developed techniques to perform at a far greater capability than has existed previously. An adequate Command Control Communications system has been developed to support the mission. With the exception of Search and Rescue, events to be performed during the mission have been accomplished satisfactorily during functional training and two rehearsals. There are unknowns at this time to include the conditions at the currently selected helicopter drop off point for Delta and arrangements for a holding area for Delta in Tehran and the precise hostage location. We have good confidence that the team has the ability to perform each segment of the mission. However, due (to) the fact that each segment of the mission is interdependent on others, our assessment for total mission profile will be limited to the range of 60-70 % even after we receive satisfactory information on the drop off point and Tehran holding area.

b. Iranian Forces: [Remains classified]

6. **SUMMARY:**

The US team of man and machine is capable of performing the mission. Two important facilities remain undetermined: the drop-off point for Delta and a holding area for Delta in Tehran. Assuming satisfactory determined of these facilities, we assess the probability of the team's mechanical capability to complete the mission at 60-70%. We assess the capability of Iran to frustrate the mission at 15-30%. Although the future threat to the hostages is unpredictable, we believe that certain indicators and event would enable the US to ascertain when the safety of the hostages becomes seriously jeopardized. The useful life of the US team cannot be protracted indefinitely. The existence of the force could be compromised and operational security lost at anytime. We are unable to predict how long OPSEC can be maintained, but judge it to be in the range of an additional two to six weeks. Effective strategic and tactical deception should enable the mission to be conducted without prior knowledge of Iran or Russia. ***(End of paragraph/JTF paper).***

***

The circumstances of the still unresolved insertion option continued to have a substantial impact on the logistics, communications, operational and intelligence staffs as well as the operational forces. This opened-ended situation required the development of three logistics support profiles and an equal number of variations in command and control and communications procedures. This was hampered (or aided) by the fact that the force had a total of only three tactical SATCOM radios (all that existed in the armed forces at the time). Intelligence collection and analysis efforts were equally broad. It had to monitor all three of the insertion locations as well as the Iranian Air Defense posture, the activities of the Iranian military, clergy and the paramilitary Revolution Guard. This was in addition to tracking activities at the Embassy and the MFA; and the Delta unload and hide-sites, plus the helicopter hide location; and the extraction airfield and a dozen other contingency locations.

During February, and carrying on into early March, several hostage-related events occurred which reflected the psychological ups and downs of the period. On 6 February, fifty private American citizens of various backgrounds left the United States on a self-appointed mission to conduct a "people-to-people" dialogue with the Iranian authorities on behalf of the hostages. Three days later, the militants made a public announcement that there were no plans to release the hostages. The fifty came back to the States without visiting the hostages, or achieving any positive results, except filling the media void of the week. However, on 12 March, the leader of the American Indian Movement (AIM), Russell Means (a representative of one of the groups classified by the Iranians as oppressed), returned to the States with 136 letters from the hostages.

In mid February, the JTF again initiated a request through the CIA (and the Department of State) to the White House to conduct a ground survey of Desert One. Seventy-two hours later, the request was disapproved. Less than a week later, on 22 February, Khomeini announced that the fate of the hostages would be decided by the Majilas (the Revolutionary Parliament) when it convened, and said it would not be convened any earlier than April or May. The JTF staff wondered if the State Department would buy into this extended delay.

On 23 February, a United Nations fact-finding commission arrived in Teheran to evaluate the situation. On the arrival day, Bani Sadar, the Iranian President, speaking for the civil government, authorized the UN team to visit with the hostages. The same day, the militants denied any visit would occur. After eight days of dialogue and several false anticipations, the Revolutionary Council announced on 3 March that the Commission would be given permission to visit the hostages in a few days. Nothing happened during the next 72 hours.

On 6 March, the militants made an announcement that an agreement had been reached to turn the hostages over to government control "tomorrow or the next day." Some in Washington read this action as a prelude to a release. Forty-eight hours later, on the 8th, the transfer had yet to occur and the militants announced that none was planned. In addition, they stated that they had been instructed by Khomeini to retain control of the hostages. Frustrated and annoyed by the numerous false starts, recurring delays, and contradictory actions and claims, the United Nations Commission departed Teheran on the 8th (thirteen days after their arrival). They made their formal report in New York on the 11th of March. The events of the previous six weeks fully illustrated the conflict and contradiction that was played on the public stage by the Iranian participants.

PART II

CHAPTER FIVE
Visits to Iran

During an initial meeting with the service HUMINT representatives in mid-November, the Air Force representative revealed they had contact with a long-term resident of Teheran. This potential source was in a position to provide accurate and objective reporting on the tempo of everyday life in the vicinity of the Embassy and a few other neighborhoods in Teheran. Subsequently and privately, the USAF representative advised the J-2 that the individual would be traveling to Europe in the near future and was willing to meet for "business" discussions. With the approval of COMJTF and the USAF HUMINT office, Major Magee, the EUCOM LNO was tasked to return to Europe to meet the potential source. The meeting took place in one of Paris's finer hotels. The individual proved to be cooperative and knowledgeable, and properly placed to perform a key support role, as well as provide periodic data on the "environment" in Teheran.

Although not advised of the true intention of the assistance or anything about the rescue mission, the source was presented with a number of assistance requests to determine the extent of his capability and willingness to provide support. The individual was able to comply with all but one of the requests (which had been predetermined to be questionable in any regard). The caliber of his reporting was judged to be pertinent and current, and, as it proved out, to also be very reliable. This was particularly true on the daily situation within Teheran, on the activation and deactivation of local Revolutionary Guard militia groups called Komitehs, and on the tempo of life and the ability to travel in the vicinity of the Embassy.

After the vetting process was completed and the test information verified, procedures were finalized to permit future contact with the source during his periodic visits to Europe and, in an extreme emergency, in Tehran. Provisions were made to provide the source with an emergency means of communicating via telephone to Germany and via a TELEX terminal to a commercial firm in the United States. The company had done business in Iran for many years, and still had property and business interests in the country. The company was one of several private American firms which quietly offered its services to the DOD/JTF in the early days of the hostage situation. Its support was often invaluable, and offered without thought of compensation or public recognition. Ross Perot's EDS was the first to offer such assistance, and the first to deliver results.

In the meantime, preparation of two individuals selected to be the MFA "scouts" was progressing quickly. Both individuals were smart, nondescript in appearance, spoke a foreign language, had traveled and lived extensively in their respective countries, and could pass for natives. Occupational skills training and the associated documentary support, as well as a ten day submersion into the society of their "native" countries, which included total role-playing, the acquisition of native clothing and toiletry accessories was conducted. The scouts would travel separately, stay in different hotels, and make legitimate office calls on various Iranian businesses, seeking to present their product lines. They would also visit various government offices and initiate the process of applying for the permits and licenses required to conduct business in Iran.

During the period of the MFA plan refinement (Feb-Mar 1980), detailed planning and training continued for the Embassy assault, while various aspects of the infiltration options were repeatedly rehearsed. The original para-drop refueling option, while still the prevailing option, was rapidly losing favor. It became more and more apparent with each drill that the task of moving the oversized, extremely heavy, unwieldy bladders from wherever they landed on the desert floor to the helicopters was not only difficult, but unpredictably time-consuming, introducing a degree of unreliably that was progressively becoming unacceptable.

Meanwhile, Wadi Kena continued to be meticulously and quietly upgraded to support the rescue operation, while simultaneously meeting the real needs of the three overt options: AWACS/tanker support, fighter wing operations, and transport staging. Various aspects of all three options supported the rescue potential, although it was the transport option that most closely covered (reflected) the unique requirements of the rescue effort. During periodic reviews of JTF requirements, certain aspects of the enhancement program were modified. This was frustrating to the EUCOM logistic planners who were unaware of the rescue option, but the changes were explained by message direction from the JCS and associated with the overt options.

During this same period, intelligence on the ground situation in and around the Embassy compound was gradually improving. This was due to the USAF source, the CIA support Team, and an Iranian employee of an American firm who had left Teheran a few months after Khomeini and the Islamic movement took control. This individual volunteered to return to the city and, under the guise of disposing of the firm's remaining office assets, solicited information about the hostage situation from members of the Pasdaran and student community that he had known previously.

In addition to the unresolved refueling option, the issue of the exact launch sites was still open. The possibilities included various mixes: a helicopter launch from the Indian Ocean aircraft carrier, and a C-130 tanker launch from either Wadi Kena or Diego Garcia. A helicopter launch from the duty carrier, with Delta force on-board, would not only make for a long and arduous flight for the aircrew, but a muscle-numbing, tiring experience for the assault force as well. (This possibility was not looked at favorably by anyone who was marked to participate.) The question of overflying Saudi Arabia was still open and unbroached with the Saudi authorities. The same was true of the possible use of a small remote Omani airfield on the island of Masirah. The topic had not yet been raised with the Sultan of that nation. There were legitimate concerns for security, and the policy decision was made to not broach these topics directly until mission execution was imminent, and then only with the most senior officials of the concerned governments.

By the middle of March (after more than four months of dialogue with a host of shifting Iranian "power" centers), it became apparent to many senior American officials, particularly the President, a peaceful solution that would effect the release of the hostages was not at hand.

Similarly, the JTF was acutely aware that, with the approach of spring and summer, two environmental factors would shift against the mission-planners and force changes in the mission profile. By May, there would not be enough hours of darkness to mask the insertion on Night One and by June the desert air, even at night would be so hot that it would decrease the lift capacity of the helicopters, increasing both airframe and fuel requirements. All of these factors were known to General Jones, the Chairman of the JCS, and included in a memo to the National Command Authority (NCA, i.e., the President and the Secretary of Defense). The memo requested permission to conduct an on-the-ground survey of the Desert One site that had been first identified in January.

On 17 March, the CIA and State Department finally concurred with the need to conduct the survey mission after non-concurring with two earlier JTF requests. Presidential approval came five days later, on the 22nd of March. The Desert One survey mission was scheduled for 30-31 March, presuming the weather cooperated. The President also granted DOD authority to send the two MFA "scouts" into Teheran.

For the actual rescue operation, two advance teams would enter Iran via commercial modes of travel. One team, consisting of the two EUCOM Special Forces soldiers, would focus on the MFA. The second team, consisting of a representative from Delta Force (a former Special Forces officer and Son Tay raider, Mr. Dick Meadows) and a young American-Iranian airman, would focus on the Embassy, the approach routes, the potential hide-sites, and the Delta drop-off location.

A few days later, General Vaught advised the Chairman and Secretary Brown that the force had reached a seventeen-day launch window, and probably could shorten that time once the use of Desert One and the forward launch sites were confirmed. At this point, the JTF had only the Indian

Ocean carrier and Wadi Kena as confirmed launch sites. It would be a long way to Teheran from either location.

On the 19th of March the JTF Commander, Major General Vaught, released the following assessment.

19123OZ Mar 80
FM: JTF
TO: (FORCES)
SUBJECT: POLITICAL FORECAST MESSAGE
1. THE EMBASSY TEHRAN HOSTAGE SITUATION REMAINS A POLITICAL PROBLEM WITHOUT A NEGOTIABLE SOLUTION. HOWEVER DUE TO THE INTERNAL ISOLATION OF IRAN, INCREASED THREATS ON ITS WESTERN AND NORTH, AND A WORSENING OF THE MEDICAL CONDITION OF KHOMEINI, THE SITUATION COULD BE PARTIALLY RESOLVED (WITHIN) THE NEXT 12-14 DAYS.
2. THIS POSSIBILITY EXISTS ONLY IF BANI SADR IS ABLE TO CONVINCE KHOMEINI THAT IN FACT THE HOSTAGE SITUATION IS HAVING A NEGATIVE EFFECT ON THE STABILITY OF THE GOVERNMENT, AND THE ECONOMY OF THE NATION. IF SADR SUCCEEDS IT IS POSSIBLE THAT KHOMEINI COULD, IN HIS 22 MARCH NEW YEARS ADDRESS, DIRECT THE TRANSFER OF THE HOSTAGES TO A HOSPITAL UNDER GOVERNMENT CONTROL; REQUEST THE UN COMMISSION TO RETURN TO TEHRAN AND RESUME HEARINGS, WITH THE ULTIMATE GOAL OF NEGOTIATING THE RELEASE OF THE HOSTAGES IN EXCHANGE FOR A PUBLIC PRONOUNCEMENT OF ITS FINDINGS.
3. IF HOWEVER, A PRINCIPLE SADR RIVAL SUCH AS BEHESTI (WHO COVETS KHOMEINI'S ROLE AND) WHO IS EXTREMELY INFLUENTIAL IN THE REVOLUTIONARY COUNCIL AND WHOSE POLITICAL PARTY (THE ISLAMIC REVOLUTIONARY PARTY) APPEARS TO HOLD A MAJORITY IN THE NEW PARLIAMENT SUCCEEDS IN GAINING KHOMENI'S EAR AND CONVINCING HIM THE RELIGIOUS FERVOR OF THE ISLAMIC REVOLUTION WILL NOT BE SERVED BY THE RELEASE OF THE HOSTAGES WITHOUT EXTRACTING A FORMAL STATEMENT OF APOLOGY FROM THE US GOVERNMENT, THE SITUATION IS LIKELY TO DRAG ON INDETERMINABLY.
4. THE VIEWS EXPRESSED ABOVE REFLECT TWO EXTREMES, OPTIMISTIC AND PESSIMISTIC. THE REALITY OF THE FUTURE LIES SOMEWHERE IN BETWEEN, AND SOME INDICATION AS TO THE MOST PROBABLE COURSE HOPEFULLY WILL BE FORTH COMING ON THE 22 OF MARCH. IN EITHER CASE IT WOULD BE PREMATURE FOR ANY ELEMENTS OF THIS TASK FORCE TO STACK ARMS. EVERY EFFORT MUST BE MADE TO FURTHER REFINE OUR INDIVIDUAL AND COLLECTIVE SKILLS AND BE PREPARED TO ACCOMPLISH OUR ASSIGNED MISSION UNTIL ALL THE HOSTAGES ARE FREE.
VAUGHT SENDS.
REVW 19 MAR 20 1 0
BT.

The 22nd of March came and went without Khomeini making any reference to the hostage situation. On 24 March 1980, Major Magee, the EUCOM LNO, received a message providing formal authorization from JCS to insert the MFA scout team. After obtaining the concurrence of General Rogers USCINCEUR, and his Stuttgart-based Deputy General Allen, and the Director of Operations, Admiral Packer, Magee contacted the Detachment A Special Forces Commander in Berlin. Major Magee requested that the scout team be dispatched to meet with him no later than noon the next day in Frankfurt.

At noon on the 25th, the three men met in a nondescript hotel near Frankfurt International Airport. They reviewed the mission objectives and the procedures to be used during the mission, emergency contact protocols, and arrangements for debriefing upon the conclusion of the mission. At the end of the meeting, the three went their separate ways, the two scouts to make final travel and hotel arrangements and business appointments. The EUCOM LNO proceeded to take the autobahn south to Heidelberg to the headquarters compound of U.S. Army Europe (USAREUR). The purpose was to privately brief the CINC-USAREUR, General Fritz Kroesen. Magee had been directed by the EUCOM Deputy Commander, General Allen, to accomplish this critical mission since USAREUR soldiers (the MFA SF scout team) were about to be put in harm's way.

The briefing lasted about an hour and laid out the preferred options at the time, and other options under development, as well as the general time line for the rescue mission should it be executed in April. At the conclusion of the presentation, General Kroesen said that he appreciated the brief and understood why the mission planning and preparation had been so closely held. "You need anything or anyone from USAREUR, they're yours. Good Luck."*

The next day, 26 March 1980, EUCOM received another message from JCS directing the positioning of a USAFE/SOF MC-130 with a Search and Recovery capability at Muskat, Oman, to support the Desert One survey mission. After being repeatedly pressured by the JTF of the need to conduct an on-the-ground survey of Desert One, and reluctant to send any of its Teheran support team to conduct the survey, the CIA had offered to fly a qualified military specialist into Iran to conduct the ground survey. The JCS message and the MC-130 mission did not come as a surprise to Magee. The possibility of such a contingency mission had been discussed with the JTF in Washington ten days earlier. The discussion was part of the planning

---

* In his previous job as the Commanding General of Army forces in the United States, General Kroesen had been briefed on the REDCOM CTJTF and the Ranger involvement in the REDCOM CT training program, and subsequently authorized the creation of Blue Light and concurred with the formation of Delta.

done to support the DOD request for Presidential permission to conduct the Teheran scouting and Desert One survey missions.

Subsequently, Magee had a heads-up discussion with Lt. Colonel Ron Jones, the Operations Officer of the 7th Special Operations Squadron (SOS), the unit tasked to provide the MC-130. The discussions covered the sensitivity and the one-shot nature of the mission, and the need to ensure that the aircrew was very proficient with the use of the Fulton Personnel Recovery System. (The system, named after its designer, was parachuted to the potential extractee and involved a tethered balloon, a lift line and an extraction suit. The extractee donned the suit, inflated the balloon which rose to an altitude where the recovery aircraft would fly-by, snare the tether cable and reel the extraction suit and its occupant into the aircraft.)*

In early March, the JTF Staff Weather Officer (SWO) and the new expanded weather capability and additional personnel deployed to an overseas Forward Operating Location. The deployment had several purposes. One was to setup and test the equipment and procedures. The second was to be ready to support the MC-130 Emergency Recovery mission that was in a stand-by mode for the Desert One Ground Survey mission. The third reason was to establish a "weather signature" in the area that would remain employed and operational and its significance fade overtime. This would decrease the potential of the deployed weather element being a tactical indicator of an impending "special mission."

Upon receipt of the official tasking message at EUCOM, the USAFE recovery squadron (7th SOS) operations officer (Lt. Col. Ron Jones) was again contacted by secure phone and asked to immediately proceed to EUCOM headquarters. Upon his arrival, he was fully briefed by Major Magee on the mission and the requirements to have two MC-130 aircraft (primary and backup) on ground alert in Oman, and ready to launch within 20 minutes beginning at dusk on 30 March. Magee then initiated procedures to ensure that the MC-130 crews and their extraction passengers had a way to evade capture if the MC went down inside Iran. Then Magee arranged for two 3-man Special Forces (SF) teams to be assigned to support an overland escape if needed. One member of each SF team was to be a medic, and the other two would be infantry weapons specialists skilled in land navigation.

This tasking was laid on the EUCOM-USAREUR 10th Special Forces Group based at Bad Tolz, Germany, on the 26th, by special communications from EUCOM SOTFE. This was the same day the 7th SOS received its official mission order. The Bad Tolz SF unit, a veteran of numerous close-hold, need-to-know dealings with EUCOM SOTFE,

---

* This recovery technique was developed in the mid-sixties and was dramatically portrayed in the closing scenes of a James Bond movie where Bond and his traditional femme fatale were lifted out of the blue waters of the Caribbean.

responded in outstanding fashion. They assembled and positioned the E&E team with all the essential equipment for themselves, the aircrew, and the potential extractees within 36 hours. In the meantime, a JTF intelligence officer, Major Rod Toth of the 1st Special Operations Wing in Florida, fully conversant with the rescue mission, flew to Germany and rendezvoused with the MC aircrews and the Special Forces team. He brought with him detailed information, maps and photographs concerning Desert One and the Iranian air surveillance system, and was prepared to lay it all out and brief the emergency recovery force should they have to launch.

The two 7th SOS MCs departed Germany on the 29th, and were in position in Oman prior to the CIA aircraft departing its launch location.

On 30 March, the field survey of Desert One was conducted by Major John Carney, a USAF Special Operations Combat Controller Team (CCT) leader. He was delivered to the site in a small civilian STOL-type aircraft operated by the CIA. The aircraft was flown by a superb team of pilots. Between them, they had decades of clandestine aviation experience, much of it in similar circumstances. The flight to Desert One was uneventful, as was the landing. After a short landing rollout, the CIA flight crew cut the engine, and their single passenger muscled his three-wheeled dune buggy out of the aircraft and headed off into the darkness to conduct the survey. He had studied numerous reconnaissance pictures of the area as well as a specially constructed map and photo-product prepared by DMA based on JTF specifications.

Even with the use of his night vision equipment and the dune buggy, the task took him almost 90 minutes. The survey included two potential landing areas (two miles long and 800 feet wide) on either side of the bisecting, unpaved, unmarked track that ran through the area. Carney took penetrometer readings and core samples of the soil at predetermined distances, particularly in the two touchdown locations. He then implanted and concealed a grid of infrared beacons marking the touch down zones and the direction of the two-rollout strips. During this time he stopped once and watched a truck pass by. He could see the face of the driver as he lit a cigarette. The driver's eyes remained riveted on the dark road ahead of him and the small tunnel of light made by the headlights of the truck. Neither the CCT officer, his dirt bike, nor the CIA aircraft, all located some distance off the flanks of the dusty track, were visible in the darkness surrounding them.

With his portion of the mission complete, Carney made his way back to the tiny aircraft, roused the dozing crew, loaded his equipment and himself back into the aircraft, and surrendered his body and his collection of core samples to their care. The samples were important. They would verify the penetrometer readings he had taken and indicate the compactness of the ground under the lose covering of fine desert sand. In addition, when subjected to laboratory tests, the samples would reveal what would happen to the soil in the unlikely, but possible, chance that an errant squall line dumped a half-inch or so of rain on the landing site.

The flight out of Iran was tranquil until the aircraft approached the southern coastline. The aircraft was equipped with various electronic sensors to alert the aircrew if they were flying into radar coverage. Just prior to reaching the safety of international airspace, one of these sensors briefly picked up an emission from an unidentified search radar in a specific quadrant. The pilot gently nudged the aircraft in the alternate direction and continued outbound. There were no additional emission detections. The aircraft continued outbound another two minutes and was over the Gulf. The initial mission report, filed upon landing, included a notation about the technical parameters of the signal. Once the report had been filed, the Langley aircrew headed for some rest, and then a more leisurely flight to their "home" field. Their part of the mission was complete. Not so for the one-man survey party. He trundled onto another aircraft and began the long trip back to the States, reaching the East Coast of the United States less than 21 hours after he had departed Iranian soil. He was met at Washington and taken to brief General Vaught, while his collection of core samples were delivered to a topographic and soil analysis team at Fort Belvoir. A series of pressure compaction and hydrographic tests were performed. These would take 36 hours to complete.

Meanwhile the standby 7th SOS MC-130 emergency extraction aircrews and Special Forces E&E team, feeling somewhat disappointed and relieved at the same time, climbed on-board the fully fueled MC- 130s and headed back to their respective nests in Europe, and Magee and Toth back to their home stations.

Subsequent technical analysis of the radar signal pickup by the CIA "Fuzz Buster" revealed that the source of the signal was a civilian maritime radar from one of the hundreds of tankers and freighters that plied the Gulf. The analysis quickly put to bed JTF concerns about the possible detection of the reconnaissance aircraft and the possibility that the rescue mission aircraft might be subject to being "painted" by Iranian surveillance radars.

The Desert One Survey Mission was also used to test and exercise several aspects of the actual mission support structure. The intelligence network that was to track the mission movements and monitor the Iranian detection and reaction infrastructure was tested. No reactions were noted, and all physical signs of the landing and takeoff vanished within two days and were essentially undetectable at ground level, anyway.

Earlier a composite team of imagery analysts drawn from DIA and the National Photographic Interpretation Center (NPIC) had been created with the intent of being able to move into the European theater several days in advance of the rescue force deployment. The imagery team would establish a temporary operating site at a USAF imagery analysis and processing site in Germany. They would review all the data collected since they left their light tables back in Washington, and then combine and compare this data with the accumulated knowledge they had acquired since November, and then resume their daily monitoring function. Immediately after receiving the latest data collected on launch day, they would fly to the principal mission launch site and update the mission forces just prior to their departure. This procedure was tested during the survey mission and employed during the actual mission.

At the same time the middle desert of Iran was being visited by the CIA/USAF team, the two Army Special Forces scouts had penetrated the Iranian capital. The SF scouts conducted more than a dozen reconnaissance sorties against the MFA. During one of these probes, a member of the scout team actually gained access to the interior of the MFA building where the three American diplomats were being detained. This access allowed him to assess the type of guard force they might be up against. In another venture, one of the pair talked one of the Iranian guards into posing for a picture with him, capturing in the background a key section of the building they were interested in. They successfully completed their mission and were soon en route to the States for detailed debriefings.

Although the details of the Desert One survey were totally positive, the MFA scouts reported some disturbing facts about their objective. Contrary to the information provided by the CIA support team and other Americans who had left Teheran before the Embassy takeover, the scout team reported security in and around the MFA complex was persistent and, although not particularly strong, was sufficient to warrant a revision of the MFA plan. The information the scouts reported included the fact that all the external gates were closed and guarded, and the complex was lit throughout the night, but not all that well. Undetected ground movement was possible if carefully timed and planned to take advantage of shrubbery, shadows and areas devoid of light. Care would have to be taken to avoid an unplanned encounter with the two-man guard patrols that walked the southern section of the grounds adjacent to the museums and the proposed helicopter touchdown site.

A major factor bearing on the absolute need for an undetected closure with the MFA and the successful liberation of the three hostages, without creating any noise or clamor, was the fact that a major police station was located across the street from the southern perimeter of the grounds. The scouts noted police cars, and police on foot moved in and out of the station on a random basis throughout the night. There also was a potential for intervention by the local Pasdaran (i.e., Revolution Guard), which were sighted at the old Iranian Air Force Officers Club located along another adjoining street. The Club had been reported as burned out and closed. Although the facility may not have been functional, the American scouts learned that its surrounding grounds were being used by the revolutionary militia as a gathering point.

Collectively, these individual pieces of information prompted a re-evaluation of the MFA rescue plan. The Commander of the Special Forces unit tasked with the mission, Lieutenant Colonel Stan Oleshevic, was requested to fly to Washington, formulate the details of a revised plan and present it to General Vaught.

In the meantime, a detailed debriefing of the scout mission was conducted and the results presented to the JCS Director of Operations and the Chairman. Subsequently, Colonel Oleshevic received the same briefing and, together with the two scouts, Major Magee, and his own unit operations officer (who had accompanied him on the trip to Washington), developed a revised Concept of Operations. The force size would have to be increased, the approach plan modified, the hostage release tactics revised, and on-call supporting fire from the extraction helicopter and an AC-130 gunship added to the equation.

It was now judged that a force of 10 to 14 personnel would be required to accomplish the MFA mission. The new approach had to be practiced, rehearsed and perfected quickly. After receiving COMJTF approval for the revised MFA plan, the EUCOM team returned to Europe to close that training gap. This was accomplished in less than five days with the force leaders returning to the States immediately thereafter to attend a final planning conference scheduled for the 10th.

Although the information obtained during the reconnaissance mission was operationally invaluable, the greater value lay in the fact that it proved conclusively that such reconnaissance missions were not only essential, but could be accomplished with minimum risk if conducted by carefully selected and trained military personnel. It also supported the long-held JTF opinion that other military personnel could also be infiltrated into Teheran safely, if early and proper orientation and supporting and training actions were accomplished.

During the course of the previous five months (Nov 79-Mar 80), the structure of the medical and airlift support effort had gone through a half dozen evolutions as the scope of the situation and the operation came into focus. By 27 March, the medical requirements and the strategic airlift position were finalized.

The following is the Executive Summary, as submitted to the Commander in Chief of the Military Airlift Command (CINCMAC) of how MAC would support the rescue effort.

The following summarizes how MAC will move to position two employment C-141 aircraft, three medical evacuation, three redeployment aircraft and associated aircrews and equipment; the location of essential MAC mission coordinators and the minimum notification times for home station launch without revealing mission purpose; Iranian Hostage Extraction.

Six C-141 aircraft are primary to support the employment and medical evacuation phase. These aircraft are . . .

a. Three (3) employment C-141s, two primary and one backup. All crews (are) Special Operations Low Level (SOLL) (and NVG) qualified. Two additional MAC Medical technicians on each aircraft plus one Combat photographer from AAVS (Air Force Audio Visual Service). Aircraft configured with sidewall seats, centerline stanchions and litters: 72 sidewall seats, 28 litters.

b. Two primary MEDEVAC C-141s with Medical crew augmented with intensive care nurses and two physicians positioned at [classified site]. These missions arrive (forward support base) as routine cargo missions and are converted to MEDEVAC configuration by crews enroute (to extraction airhead).

c. MEDEVAC aircraft will be backed up by passenger configured force redeployment aircraft with comfort pallet and seats . . . End of Summary

CHAPTER SIX
Moving Out
(April 1980)

On the 1st of April, the Iranian President, Bani Sadr proposed that the National "Revolutionary Council" assume control of (and responsibility for) the hostages. At the same time, the United States government (USG) was poised to impose additional economic sanctions on Iran, but deferred them pending the outcome of this "transfer" possibility.

On the 3rd of April 1980, the JTF released the following message providing its assessment of the possible transfer of control of the hostages, which was the subject of extensive media and political speculation.

> 1. The assumption of control by the Revolutionary Council (if it does occur) does not mean a full nor near time release of the hostages. This office believes that the internal factionalism between the various competing groups in and out of the Iranian government limits complete resolution (of the situation).
> 2. The recent March press interview with the religious hard liner Mohammed Behesti probably provides the clearest indication of the view of the majority of [the] members of the Revolutionary Council. [Interview text follows]:
>
> > Ayatollah Dr Mohammed Behesti, Chief Justice of the Supreme Court and member of the Islamic Revolution Court, announced that the former Shah's flight to Egypt not only made his extradition more difficult, but also complicated the issue of the hostages. In a press conference Dr Behesti added that up to now, he could not offer any suggestion to the Consultative Assembly. What is important, he said, is that Iran wants to achieve its total political and economic independence, but the U.S. administration does not want to respect Iran's independence or the independence of similar countries. Dr. Behesti said that when the United States stops practicing such policies, we can find a basis for reconciliation with it. Dr Behesti added that the hostages trial should help us and the people to arrive at complete independence. As the IMAM once said: After that, we might forgive them. [End of Interview Text].
>
> 3. Even if control of the hostages occurs this does not mean movement will transpire, and in fact does not even guarantee that the militants will relinquish complete physical control.
> 4. Assuming control is transferred, the militants will, at a minimum, retain control of the compound and if the hostages are relocated, they will probably be moved to a military facility, a commandeered hotel or a foreign ministry building.
>
> BT

Meanwhile back in the States, in the JTF training and testing regime, the fuel blivet drop option was formally revised on the 2nd of April. It was decided after extensive field testing to include two stretched, "B" model versions of the MAC C-141, as drop birds with the MC-130's acting as pathfinders and drop leads. The C-141 aircrews were part of a select group of C-141 flight crews that were undergoing an intensive low-level flight training program to achieve SOLL (Special Operations Low Level) qualification.

On the 6th of April, Khomeini announced that the hostages would remain under the control of the militants, who themselves were under the influence of the Islamic fundamentalist clergy. Also on the 6th, the militants allowed a small group of "revolutionary" Christian clerics, including a noted Palestine Liberation Organization (PLO) supporter, to hold Easter services for the hostages. An Iranian television crew taped the services and some visits to the hostage rooms. Portions of the coverage were broadcast for international consumption. JTF analysis of the TV coverage gave strong indications that most of the hostages had been consolidated in the Chancery. This assessment meshed with other indicators that most of the hostages had been relocated from the scattered detention sites of the previous months. However, timely and definitive data on the five hostages who had not been seen or heard of since the takeover was still elusive.

On the 7th, the results of the Desert One soil sample analysis were received, and briefed to General Vaught. The results were positive, confirming the imagery analysis of 90 days earlier and the recent on-the ground CCT survey. The soil could support the weight of the C-130s.

This confirmation enabled the official abandonment of both the "blivet drop" and airfield-seizure options, and allowed all training efforts to be focused on option three -- the airland, ground refuel, and force-transfer process, and the timing of the subsequent mission events.

The combined success of the two reconnaissance missions, Desert One and the MFA, prompted the JTF, with the concurrence and support of the Chairman, to prepare and forward to the White House a mission assessment summarizing the results and benefits of the "visits to Iran."

Collectively, the two missions proved that the JTF could infiltrate an advance team into Teheran, and deliver the main force to a useable transfer site deep inside Iranian territory undetected. Desert One was now "the" option. All planning, training and rehearsal actions focused on perfecting the Desert One airland (and refueling-transfer procedures), with a continued focus by Delta on the compound assault, and the Rangers on seizing the extraction airhead, with the Berlin Based SF team focusing on the revised MFA plan. The helicopter contingent now knew the full extent of their mission and critical role they would be called upon to play. They were the crucial linchpin to mission success.

On the same day (7 April), the United States, frustrated by Khomeini's decision that the militants would retain control of the hostages and their fate would not be decided until possibly May or June, broke diplomatic relations with Iran and imposed new economic sanctions.

Seventy-two hours later, on the 10th, the militants again threatened to kill the hostages if the United States or one of its puppets (Iraq was cited) intervened in Iran. The next day, several thousand demonstrators were assembled outside of the Embassy compound. Standing in front of the Chancery building, they chanted the now-familiar litany of anti-American slogans for the benefit of the battery of TV cameras that maintained a daylight vigil at the main gate to the compound.

The news from Teheran served to set the tone for a full-scale JTF planning and situation review conducted the same day, the 10th of April. This all-day meeting, which included all of the principle members of the JTF staff and the five force commanders and their key mission leaders, was devoted entirely to a detailed and methodical review of the entire mission. It began with a review of all the intelligence held on all the mission sites to be used in Iran, then followed the sequence of all the actions, and sub-actions and supporting events that constituted the mission, beginning with the pre-mission logistic, communications, medical, weather and intelligence preparations. Next to be examined was the individual force deployment sequences, the launch timing and preparations at the half dozen overseas sites, and the command and control for the deployment, launch, execution, extraction and recovery phases.

During the review, the recurring question in the mind of most attendees was whether "we" would soon get the "go ahead" to execute. To some members of the JTF staff, the question was not if, but when, and they knew it was very soon. To a man, the force commanders and primary staff were convinced that they were ready and had a good chance at pulling it off. An insertion date of 24 April and an execution/extraction date of 25 April were used to validate and synchronize the nearly 400 major actions that constituted the entire mission sequence.

The 24/25 April time frame was one of eleven time frames that the JTF had identified in mid-November as being the most beneficial window to execute the mission. The time windows began with Thanksgiving 1979 and ran through 7 May 1980. Subsequent to the review, General Vaught apprised General Jones of the results of the review and his opinion that the force was prepared to accomplish the mission.

***

Following the review, the JTF J-2 staff prepared a composite mission threat assessment that laid out all the essential information that was to be provided to the combat forces. The assessment (essentially Annex B to the Operations Order) was sent to DIA, NSA and CIA with a request for comments and opinions prior to the assessment being released to the mission forces. Written responses were received from DIA and NSA.

Neither organization disagreed with the assessment, or provided any new information. No response was received from CIA.

Separately, the JTF J-2 had arranged for the Strategic Air Command's Penetrations Analysis team at Offutt Air Force Base in Omaha, Nebraska, to examine the proposed JTF flight routes for detection flaws. A set of maps depicting the flight routes was flown to Offutt by two members of the JTF, examined by the SAC analysts and flown back within 36 hours. One very minor turnpoint adjustment of three miles was recommended by the SAC team.

During the evening of the 11 April, General Jones briefed President Carter and several other senior government officials on the status of the rescue planning, the condition of the force and that a major rehearsal was scheduled to be held in the next 72 hours. General Jones outlined the mission sequence and the key precursor actions which called for the forward deployment and positioning of the force in Egypt and Oman (and requesting over-flight clearances from Saudi Arabia for operations on Night Two). The cabinet room discussions closed with the President approving the overall Desert One option and the deployment preparations for planning purposes, pending the conclusion of the imminent rehearsal and the events of the next few days.

Deployment planning was finalized the next day (the 12th), and the seventh large scale "exercise" (rehearsal) was scheduled for the 14th and 15th. The operational aspects of the cover plans that had been drawn up earlier were initiated, along with selected logistics actions for the real mission. The litany of the deception measures were designed not only to cover a specific mission preparation event, but to project continuity beyond the mission execution dates should a delay occur or rescheduling be necessary. Intelligence indicators to gauge the effectiveness of the cover and deception measures were communicated to elements of the SIGINT and PHOTINT structure that were monitoring the Teheran situation.

***

In addition to the daily (nightly) training that had been conducted by each of the individual force elements, six major training (rehearsal) exercises had been conducted during the preceding five months. Since the final mission profile to be executed (Desert One) was not approved as the preferred option until early in April 1980, the previous rehearsals were not identical. Aside from the Embassy takedown aspect, each had varied to a degree and reflected the effort to work out the kinks in whichever option was under development at the time. Each aspect of each option was tested individually and then tested in the operational sequence as part of the whole. However, the assault package (Embassy Takedown) was rehearsed in its entirety every time using real time and distance factors. In addition, as part of the individual unit training preparations Delta had practiced the "takedown" 72 times. The joint training exercises were typically conducted at two-week intervals. They varied in length, from an initial period of twelve days down to a normal of three.

The following table provides the basic data and focus of each of these proficiency exercises:

Event	Date	Duration	Location	Focus
1.	3-6 Dec	3 nights	Yuma PG	Helo Ops & Blivet Drops
2.	16-28 Dec	12 nights	Yuma PG	Helo Ops & Blivet drops
3.	16-18 Jan	3 nights	Yuma PG	DS #1 & Helo Ops
4.	29-31 Jan	3 nights	Nevada PG	**
5.	26-27 Feb	2 nights	Yuma PG	**
6.	25-27 Mar	3 nights	Indian Springs	Airfield Seizure

The final rehearsal, number 7, was conducted on schedule on the 14th and 15th of April and in accordance with the full mission sequence without any mishaps. The bulk of the force redeployed to their home stations on the 16th, while the JTF continued preparations for the mission deployment, under the initial cover of an OCONUS staging exercise.

***

On 14 April, representatives of the International Red Cross were allowed to visit the Embassy compound. They saw most, but not all, of the Americans, and snippets of the visit were broadcast on Iranian TV the next day, the 15th. The scenes suggested that most of the hostages were being detained in the Chancery building, but on different floors. There was a high locational correlation between the 6 April Easter visit by the clerics and the 14 April Red Cross visit. Together, the visits indicated that most, if not all, of the hostages were being held in the Chancery. However, lacking hard evidence, the assault plan also had to accommodate the previously scattered disposition of the hostages.

Early on the 16th, the American Chargé, Bruce Laingen, informed the State Department that he and his two hostage companions had been moved to a different room in the Ministry of Foreign Affairs building. This information was immediately communicated to the JTF and then to the Det A rescue team in Berlin. Fortunately, the change required only minor modifications in the MFA rescue plan.

On 16 April 1980, General Vaught distilled the overall Concept of Operations down to a four-page point paper for use in briefing the President. Although the Joint Chiefs had been privy to most all aspects of the plan as it evolved, it was deemed critical that the "Chiefs" be briefed on the mission sequence as it was to be executed.

The contents of that point paper are presented below:

(Page One)

<u>INTRODUCTION</u>:
Mr. President,
- Task Force Formed Mid-November
- Military options (last) discussed with you on 8 December
- Ability then (was considered) too low
- Since then capability has been strengthened significantly.
<u>INTELL</u>[igence] - Much better in all respects. Big ....
<u>PLANNING</u> - A sound mechanically achievable plan has been devised.
<u>TRAINING</u> - Four full scale rehearsals have been conducted in the US.
<u>EQUIPMENT</u> - Night vision devices, precise navigation aids, air landed rapid refueling system, satellite como, (and) silent landing techniques developed.
<u>SUPPORT</u> - Eight RH-53's on Nimitz
In sum, the Joint Chiefs agree that we have a sound achievable plan.
Next, I'd like to outline briefly the current situation and then follow with the plan.

(Page Two)

<u>CURRENT SITUATION</u>:
<u>HOSTAGES</u>
50 at Emb(assy)
3 at FM(A)
- Reasonably sure we know where they are.
- Kept by 125-150 persons at least a third armed with rifles and pistols.
- Embassy is 27 acres - fence 10 - 12 ft high.
- <u>LIKELY REINFORCEMENTS</u>
- Up to 100 armed persons from nearby stations could arrive within 10-15 minutes after rescue has begun.
- 200 + more in the next 15 minutes.
- Several hundred could be expected within 45 minutes.
- Organized elements of the regular armed forces are not expected during the first hour.
- There is a low probability that regular armed forces will discover or interfere.

(Page Three)

OVERALL CONCEPT OF OPERATIONS

- The operation will be accomplished during a nine-day period (7 days for warning and positioning the force and 2 days for execution and recovery). Heavy lift helicopters (RH-53s), AC and MC-130 aircraft, refuelable C-130Es, C-141 airlifters and KC-135 tankers will be used. The helicopters will launch from the Nimitz. Other air operations will be conducted from [xxxx remains classified].

- The operation in Iran takes two nights and one day. It is divided into three phases - Insertion, Hostage release and extraction.

- Upon last light of the insertion day, SFOD-Delta (with other JTF rescue force elements) will be airlifted by 3 MC-130s to an isolated desert LZ in Iran.

- The first MC-130 will land on the desert LZ and Delta forces will immediately set up blocking positions on the road in order to control any vehicular traffic transiting the area.

- The second and third MC-130 land desert LZ where number one has secured the area.

- The MC-130 aircraft will be followed by three EC-130s. Each of these aircraft will have two fuel bladders for a total of 18,000 gallons of fuel available for refueling purposes. Once the EC-130s have landed and are in position, the 3 MC-130s will depart.

- Concurrently, 7 RH-53s will depart the USS Nimitz to marry up with the forces at the LZ. While at the LZ, the helos will refuel from the EC-130s and load the Delta personnel (and the other rescue force elements).

- Once refueled and loaded, the helos will fly to a hideout area which is located approximately 100 KM from Tehran.

- The MC & EC-130s at the desert LZ will depart (after the helos have relaunched).

- Once the helos reach the hideout area, they will be camouflaged and defensive positions set up. This evolution will be completed prior to sunrise.

- Delta force will travel (by truck) from the hideout area to a warehouse, which is, located approximately 15 KM from Tehran.

- While at the warehouse, final preparations will be made for the hostage release phase.

--

(Page 4)

- That night, Delta will be moved by road into Tehran and enter the compound early the next morning.

- The hostage release can be completed in less than one hour - most will be out in 30 minutes or less.

- Two AC-130s will fly to the compound (and orbit) to provide on-call fire support if required.

- Concurrently, 4 MC-130s with Rangers (75 personnel) and fuel blivets will secure Manzariyeh (the extraction airhead). Two C-141s will land immediately thereafter and prepare for the arrival of the helos from Tehran.
- A third AC-130 will be available to provide on-call fire support at Manzariyeh.
- Once Delta has initiated the hostage release entering the Embassy Compound and initiated, the helos will be called in for extraction and transportation of the hostages and Delta (and other force elements) to Manzariyeh.
- A separate fully coordinated, concurrently executed plan will be used to free Mr. Laingen + 2 from the Foreign Ministry.
- At Manzariyeh the former hostages (and any wounded JTF personnel) will be loaded on the C-141 which will be staffed with an emergency medical team. This aircraft will fly to a US military hospital in Europe.
- Other personnel (Delta & Helo crews, etc.) will board the second C-141 and fly to Europe for further transportation to CONUS.
- The AC and MC-130s (with 75 Rangers) will return to the launch airfield or another as the situation requires.
- All MC/AC-130 flights will require air refueling on the outbound mission leg.
TO SUM UP --
- The mission can be done.
- It is highly dependent upon surprise.
- The next best time is 24-26 April
Sir, we await your orders.

General Vaught's Point Papers were, in essence, a distillation of a larger set of FACT SHEETS. Most of these were prepared on the 12th of April, reviewed daily and updated as new information became available. The two papers dealing with the hostage guard force and the estimated reaction times of the various Iranian forces were updated on the 22nd, the 23rd and the 24th. The following paragraphs are extracts from these two papers:

GUARD FORCE DISPOSITION

- Security of the hostage areas is maintained by personnel made up of several factions in the following proportions:
- Actual students//60 percent of total//
- Fatah trained militants//10 percent//
- Pasdaran militia//15 percent//
- Student leadership cadre (including university/religious leaders)//5 percent//
- PLO advisors//3-5 percent//

- Guard Force distribution is estimated to have a day/night duty ratio of 60/40.*

EXTERNAL FORCES REACTION TIMES

Reinforcements for the student guards and Pasdaran are available from several locations and organizations. Principal forces and their estimated reaction times, once they have received notification or heard a major disturbance in the vicinity of the (Embassy) compound, are shown below:

- Within 0-5 minutes - fire from within the compound and possibly, from a limited number of weapons positioned in surrounding buildings.
- Within 10-15 minutes reinforcements from student headquarters and Pasdaran Komiteh strength 75-100 from nearby Komiteh stations.
- Within 15-30 minutes Pasdaran reinforcements of up to 200 plus.
- Within 45-60 minutes IRG residual forces and mobs of 2,000-3,000 could form. AC-130 fire and Riot control agents could frustrate this potential threat.
- Within 60 minutes, it is possible that an Iranian Air Force fighter could react and attempt a launch against any orbiting aircraft.
- Within one hour it is possible that helicopters from nearby Army airfield or fighters from other IAF airbases could launch and attempt to interdict the force.

***

During the late morning of the 16th, General Vaught briefed the overall mission sequence to the Joint Chiefs of Staff who, after asking a few questions, concurred with the plan and its order of execution. This was not the first time the Joint Chiefs had seen the plan. They had received update briefings from the JTF periodically in the preceding five months and had seen the plan evolve. Later that afternoon, General Jones advised General Vaught that he and Colonel Beckwith were to accompany General Jones to the White House situation room that evening where they would brief the President.

Without being told, the small core of the JTF staff that were aware of the impending White House briefing (slightly more than a half dozen officers), assumed that this was "the" decision brief. General Jones would make introductory comments, provide an overview of the mission concept and the force composition, and then turn the presentation over to General

* PLO advisors are probably only present during the day and in the evenings when strategy meetings are held. The actual students function as personal guards of the hostages and as propagandists and ideologues trying to indoctrinate the hostages. The PLO (personnel) function as observers, advisors, and propagandists. The Fatah trained militants supervise security, interrogation and document exploitation. The Pasdaran, besides providing external security, maintain a presence within the compound, primarily providing sentries. Within the buildings, the students typically carry pistols. Those on duty outside typically are armed with G-3 rifles. Guards carrying rifles have not been observed carrying spare magazines for their weapons.

Vaught. General Vaught would present the mission flow, and the Command & Control arrangements, with Charlie presenting an overview of the ground closure plan and Delta's actions within the Embassy compound.

The JTF team returned to the Pentagon about ten o'clock that night. They were totally non-committal about the events of the evening. They did not make any announcement nor hold any "hot wash" discussions with the rest of the staff. There were no "how-did-it-go" questions from the remnants of the staff that included the EUCOM LNO, the JTF Chief of Staff, and two of the Task Force intelligence officers, plus the JCSE Communication team. General Vaught soon departed for his residence and Charlie headed for Fort Bragg. The JTF closed shop at about eleven.

The next morning, the wheels were very quietly set in motion to conduct an OCONUS move to the staging bases "to test the flow." All forces were told that they should treat the deployment just the same as if it were the real thing. The next few days at the JTF headquarters were measured to the beat of the deployment drum, slow and steady, beating away at a deliberate muffled cadence twenty-four hours a day.

Concurrent with preparations for the final rehearsal, the JTF operations team and the supporting airflow planners, mostly Air Force and some Navy, began an intense review of the airflow schedule. In addition to the main force, deploying to Egypt and Oman, the helicopter crews had to be flown to the *USS Nimitz* (a moving speck of Navy floating metal in the middle of the Indian Ocean a thousand miles from the nearest allied airbase). The air planners worked intensely throughout the period of the 14th and 15th and into the early morning hours of the 16th to have the flow ready to begin moving on the 17th.

This meant refining and revalidating the airflow timing, and deconflicting and blending it into the "normal" flow of MAC heavy weight aluminum that routinely made holes in the sky around the world. Part of this effort was to ensure that the space and weight of the personnel that had been added to the MFA force was accommodated on the inbound Desert One C-130s and the RH-53 insertion/extraction helicopters. There was no problem on the long haul outbound leg, as the evacuation C-141s had the capability to easily accommodate the extra personnel, although the CCT personnel handling the transfer loading at Desert One and the evacuation airhead had to include them in the ground movement and accountability plans.

The formal SECDEF order was issued without fanfare on a very close-hold basis on the 17th. This was only ten days after the Belvoir lab had confirmed that the soil at Desert One was strong enough to use as an expediency runway. Preliminary deployment movements were now less than three days away and execution only seven.

Under the guise of the OCONUS training exercise, the initial deployment sequence was begun. Some of the early actions included: the movement of a support weather team to a weather satellite downlink site which had been set-up earlier as a contingency support and signature buildup measure; the staging of the combined DIA-NPIC imagery analysis team to Europe; the quiet activation of three extended JTF communications networks; the blending of the command network into the collective radio background; the timing of aircraft movements to avoid unique or unusual signatures, including avoiding any foreign (Soviet/Iranian) surveillance possibilities at staging and transit sites; and reactivation of the intelligence monitoring network that had been used during the Desert One Survey.

Early in the deployment sequence, both the European Command and the Pacific Command Liaison officers departed Washington and returned to their respective headquarters in Germany and Hawaii to brief the Theater Commanders before proceeding on to their JTF duty stations. The LNOs briefed the top levels of the two command elements (two general/flag officers) on the projected launch sequence and the execution windows. The primary window was 24-26 April, with 1-3 May as the immediate alternate if weather conditions forced a delay. The LNOs also relayed General Vaught's gratitude for the tremendous support already provided and his most recent security concerns and guidance.

This guidance stemmed from his concern that any unusual U.S. military activity, particularly in the European theater, might generate undue speculation and result in a mission compromise. The LNOs relayed General Vaught's concern that any unauthorized actions, regardless how well intended, might cause a leak, and would most likely originate with support staffs and elements, such as medical personnel and MAC aircrews. The LNOs relayed COMJTF's emphatic message that he wanted no anticipatory actions at any headquarters or units; no convening of Crisis Action Teams (CATs); no unit status checks or personnel recalls; no hospital alerts; no change in communications or security procedures. The LNOs also relayed General Vaught's half-joking and half-serious threat that he was considering "locking up" the MAC C-5 and C-141 crews that would deploy the force if he got any hint of speculation or gossip concerning the mission. The LNOs concluded the brief by again expressing General Vaught's gratitude for all that had been done, and closing with General Vaught's bottom line: at this time the force had what it needed and he would call if anything else was needed. The briefings were received well by both command elements, with the EUCOM officers taking General Vaught's mention of "locking-up" the flight crews particularly serious. The EUCOM LNO was directed to advise General Vaught that taking such action would in itself be unprecedented and could auger a greater potential for a leak as the aircrews' non-availability for other missions already scheduled could engender uncontrollable speculation.

At the conclusion of his briefing at EUCOM headquarters, the EUCOM LNO, Major Jim Magee, was directed to travel to SHAPE headquarters (Supreme Headquarters Allied Powers Europe) in Belgium and personally brief General Rogers, who was dual-headed as the Supreme Allied Commander European, NATO and Commander U.S. Forces Europe.

Upon reaching SHAPE, Major Magee repeated the briefing for General Rogers and, at the conclusion, requested a letter from General Rogers directing any recipient of the letter to provide whatever support the LNO deemed necessary, and to consider the LNO's request for support as a direct order from General Rogers. Magee explained that he had been tasked by General Vaught to accompany the medical evacuation aircraft that would be carrying any injured hostages or force directly out of Iran to the nearest U.S. military hospital (which could be Incirlik, Turkey). Incirlik would be the preferred option, if the medical condition of the injured indicated they could not survive the longer trip to Germany. The letter would allow him to obtain immediate and unquestionable support from both U.S. and NATO commanders, if the need arose. General Rogers concurred with the utility of the letter and promptly had one prepared.

With the letter in hand, Magee again expressed General Vaught's gratitude for all the support General Roger's staff at EUCOM had provided, and also General Vaught's concern about the risk of anticipatory preparations at EUCOM. General Rogers asked the LNO to assure General Vaught no additional preparatory actions would take place in the European theater unless he directed them, and "that EUCOM would do its part; that there would be no leak in Europe; and he fully supported the rescue as being his highest priority." General Rogers closed the meeting with the admonition to Major Magee that, if he or General Vaught ever noted a lack of support from any U.S. European Command element, subordinate command or resource, they were to advise him personally and he would take immediate action to correct the situation.

Magee then proceeded back to EUCOM headquarters at Stuttgart. There he back-briefed the Deputy Commander, General Allen, and received a mission situation update via secure phone from the JTF staff in Washington. He then gathered his field gear and headed for Ramstein Airbase, where he linked up with the MFA rescue team and climbed on a C-141 bound for Egypt and the deployed JTF Headquarters.

Several months earlier, Delta (and the seven Farsi-speaking Americans who would monitor the Iranian truck drivers and were prepared to take over as drivers) had been provided photo books of the land route from the hide-site to the Embassy. The helicopter crews had been provided similar route books. Both sets of books included annotated maps and photography. The ground movement books contained photography of the full route with narrative descriptions of key landmarks and turn points. The helicopter air route books contained complete route maps and imagery of all navigation check and turn points. To enhance the navigation accuracy of the air route turn points and check points, all the points had been "data reduced" (by DMA cartographers using reconnaissance imagery) to precise coordinates to be plugged into the various navigation systems on-board the helicopters. None of these computer navigation systems were very robust or reliable, and none were integrated into the aircraft's overall control systems. The route maps and supporting picture book were the navigation baseline reference material. All of these materials were to be deployed with the force. Nothing relating to mission execution was to be "left" behind.

Shortly after the results of the Desert One survey were known earlier in April, the JTF had prepared a listing of personnel who would be exposed to direct Iranian retaliation during the course of the rescue mission. The listing was compiled by unit and function, and is presented below:

- Delta Force
- MFA Rescue Team
- JTF Scout Teams
- Driver/Monitor element
- Helicopter Crews
- Ranger Teams
- Combat Control elements
- Medical Trauma Team
- MC/EC/AC-130 Aircrews
- SOLL C-141 Aircrews

The total came to 389 mission personnel that would be operating on Iranian territory or in Iranian airspace, more than half of whom would be exposed throughout the duration of the mission, with the balance being exposed for approximately 12 hours.

A second listing was also compiled which reflected the scope, size and composition of the support structure that was committed to the mission. This tally sheet is shown below:

JTF Headquarters (Main)................. 31
JTF HQS (Alternate)...................... 02
JTF LNO (Afloat)......................... 04
JCSE (Dispersed)......................... 20
KC-135 Tanker Aircrews................ 48
RH-53 Maintenance (Afloat)...........130
AC-130 Maintenance (Forward)........ 93
MC-130 Maintenance (Forward)....... 45

KC-135 Maintenance (Forward)........ 68
C-141 Maintenance (Forward).......... 75
MAC Air Control Element (Fwd)..... 28
Fuels Support Element (Fwd).......... 20
Weather Support Team (Fwd) 05

This listing, which totaled 569, was not all-encompassing. It did not include the JTF coordination team that remained in the Pentagon, nor the Photo Intelligence team that was forward deployed to Europe (and then moved to Wadi Kena to brief the force on launch day). Neither did the list include the National Security Agency (NSA) communicators and analysts that maintained a vigilant overwatch of the Iranian national command and control structure. The combined number of military personnel directly involved in the rescue mission exceeded 1,000 (389 who entered Iran and 569 that provided direct support, plus another 100 or more intelligence, cartographic and communications personnel that supported off stage).

Around the world, at bases and posts throughout nine states and three continents, the different segments of the total package, including more than a thousand non-JTF support personnel, began to march to the same drummer without knowing the true reason for their actions. They had all done their jobs a hundred or thousand times before. It was through their efforts and professional dedication, extra sweat and long hours, that the rescue force was able to flow and assemble at their prescribed locations on time and without being detected. All of this was done in accordance with the master time-sequenced "spider-board" that the JTF J-3 section had been laboring on and modifying as the options changed, and capabilities were developed, tested and incorporated into the prevailing scenario.

A companion "spider-board" had been prepared and refined, and the foundation laid, tested, flexed and measured by the deception planners and the intelligence cells which monitored the effect of these protective measures. The deception blanket was fluffed up and began falling in place in advance of the actual force movement. It concealed the movement and activity wherever possible, or disguised its nature and purpose in those instances where it could not be made invisible.

Although the bulk of the JTF staff moved to the main staging base at Wadi Kena with the JTF command element, a seven-person coordination element remained in the Pentagon to act as an information relay from General Vaught to the Chairman. Their additional function was to advise the Chairman and the SECDEF as necessary, and to ensure that any critical information that surfaced in Washington was immediately forwarded to the JTF.

Separately, another small, invisible element prepared the letters from President Carter to the American Ambassadors and Chiefs of State of the countries through which the force would flow, once launched on the mission. In some cases, where the force would overfly but not land on the territory of another nation, the letters were to be delivered directly to the appropriate Chiefs of State the day of the over-flight. In some cases, this would be the 24th and, in others, it would be the 25th. In addition, it was time to make the crucial formal, but very secretive, diplomatic approaches to the Chiefs of State of such launch sights as Oman and Egypt. Earlier in the crisis, the Egyptian President had shown his support by granting the United States the use of several Egyptian airfields, but neither he nor any of his staff were specifically informed of the rescue preparations. Similarly, the Sultan of Oman had approved the earlier MC-130 use of the Seeb airfield for the survey mission. Now, it was time to obtain his concurrence for the MC-130s and the rescue force to launch from the island of Masirah.

Nearly thirty days earlier, in mid-March, the JTF had requested that the Navy position three additional RH-53s on-board the *USS Eisenhower*, the carrier due to replace the *Nimitz* on the Indian Ocean patrol. The turnover between the two carriers was still nearly a week away in April. The three additional airframes were intended to augment the eight-ship helicopter force already on-board the *Nimitz* at the turnover date. This action was another of the plan-ahead contingencies that the JTF had initiated should the rescue mission be delayed until sometime after May. This was a hedge against the upcoming seasonal change to hotter weather that was expected as summer arrived. In addition to the hotter weather, which would decrease the lift capacity of each helicopter, the season also brought a climatic probability of a general shift in the wind patterns. This shift would put the helicopters in a situation where they would be fighting a headwind, not the neutral to tailwind situation of the fading winter months. The headwinds would further increase the fuel requirements as well as consume valuable flight time in the reducing hours of darkness.

Upon being advised on the 17th of April that the mission was a "go," the JTF Operations Staff presented an expediency recommendation to General Vaught. The recommendation was that he seek the Chairman's concurrence to direct CINCPAC (with Navy concurrence) to order the *Eisenhower* to increase its steaming speed by three knots an hour during daytime hours and to full speed during nighttime hours. If this recommendation were acted upon quickly, it would position the *Eisenhower* and the additional three choppers at the top of the patrol path in close proximity to the *Nimitz* 36 hours prior to the launch date, 24 April. The staff rationale was based on the fact that this closure would provide the force with an added margin of backup helicopters should, during the final day of inspections, any of the mission helicopters become non-mission capable.

The recommendation also included the consideration that at least two, possible three, additional flight crews be assembled if the mission was delayed and weather conditions changed earlier than anticipated. The additional crews could be assembled by transferring a few of the fully qualified flight crews to the new choppers, and backfilling their vacancies with the best pilots from among those who had trained for the mission in November and December. During the intervening months (January-April), this latter group had been flying and maintaining the original eight aircraft on the *Nimitz*. In addition, there were some night-qualified CH-53 Marine pilots on-board the *USS Okinawa*, which was the floating home to a Marine Amphibious Unit that was part of the Navy's Indian Ocean Task Force.

General Vaught considered the recommendation seriously, and discussed the feasibility and merit of the action with the Chairman and a senior naval officer. Based on an assessment of the training proficiency of the eight primary crews, and assurances from the Navy of the mission worthiness of the eight helicopters already on-board the *Nimitz*, and with no adverse change in the prevailing climatic conditions predicted, the order was not issued.

Meanwhile, preparations were underway in Europe and the States to insert the four-man DOD scout/reception party into Iran several days prior to mission launch. The combined team was composed of the two SF scouts who had previously visited Teheran and scouted the MFA, and two additional DOD personnel who had been in training since mid-January for the Embassy/Delta support role. One was Dick Meadows, a former Special Forces soldier and Son Tay raider, now a Department of the Army civilian trainer with Delta. The other, a USAF flight mechanic, subsequently nicknamed Trooper Sam, was a naturalized American citizen of Iranian descendent. He had volunteered his services to the JTF shortly after the Embassy was taken over. The concept, which the CIA wholeheartedly supported, was that the DOD team would replace the CIA support team that would leave Iran 24 hours before the mission launch. The DOD team was to conduct last-minute reconnaissance of the objectives and the overland approach routes to be used by the two assault forces. In addition, they were to prepare the vehicles to be used by the assault forces, meet the force at the helicopter drop off site (some 40 miles outside of Teheran), and guide the force to the hide-site at the old mine while the helicopters moved to their own laager site. The following day, working with the driver teams, the advance scouts would shuttle the infiltration vehicles to the mine site and pick up the assault forces.

Prior to their separate departures from Europe, these four personnel were provided with a description and information on how to contact the USAF Iranian business contact that had met with the EUCOM LNO several months earlier. They were not provided his real name, but a pre-coordinated cover name. They were individually to conduct a standoff surveillance of the contact's normal luncheon location, until they had a positive image of what he looked like. They were instructed not to attempt any kind of contact prior to the rescue attempt, and make contact after the mission only if they were unable to exfiltrate the country on their own. Contact was to be a measure of last resort.

While the various forces, teams and flight crews were making their deployment preparations, the JTF staff was busy assembling individual Evasion & Escape packages for all personnel (except the four man advance team) that would enter Iranian territory. The basic ingredients of the kits were the same for everyone. In addition to a preset amount of Iranian and other foreign currency, each kit contained a waterproof set of maps specifically made by DMA for the mission according to JTF guidelines. The kit also contained a specially created multi-lingual language guide, called a "pointy-talky." The guide was designed by the JTF, the languages edited by DIA, and the booklet printed by DMA. Also included was a "blood chit" in English, Arabic and Farsi (the Iranian language). The "chit" was a letter, written in English and Farsi, which requested aid be given the bearer of the letter on behalf of Allah, and pledged that any such aid would be greatly appreciated and that the provider of assistance would be compensated by the United States government. The kits were issued to the soldiers, sailors, airmen and marines at their respective launch bases by their unit intelligence teams. As time to mount out came closer, one of the three Iranians who had volunteered to accompany the force (a former Iranian secret police operative that had been providing situational advise to Charlie Beckwith courtesy of the CIA) declined to go on the mission. However, two other Iranians, both former senior Iranian military officers, deployed with the force. They had been recruited earlier to provide an extra degree of "on-the-ground" geographic and sociological knowledge and a native ability to "work" the unexpected situation which, according to Murphy's Law, was bound to happen.

Beginning on the 17th, the forward flow began in accordance with the "spider chart." The security blanket of OPSEC, COMSEC and deception made the movement essentially invisible. In addition, NSA was monitoring the entire movement sequence to detect any unsuppressed indicators and advise the JTF. At the request of the JTF, the NSA had performed the same monitoring function for each of the seven previous rehearsals and major training exercises. By the second rehearsal, all indicators had been suppressed, but, since new people and new forces were involved in many of the follow-on exercises and rehearsals, NSA monitoring continued with a private report delivered directly to General Vaught at the conclusion of each activity. He then immediately directed whatever corrective or precautionary measure he determined was needed.

Between the 17th and the 19th of April, the bulk of the JTF staff and the various force elements had dispersed to the four winds and begun their deployment journey, each by circuitous routing. For example, the MC-130s to be used to carry the assault force into Desert One originated their movement from the mid-Pacific and came in from the east, while the JTF, Delta and the Rangers came in on different aircraft originating at different locations in the States and transiting different refueling stops en route. The arrivals were spread out over a 36-hour window, most arriving under cover of darkness. No two force elements followed the same route. No two major elements of the JTF deployed on a coincidental timetable. No two arrived at the same point on the ground within a few hours of each other, and no aircraft were on the ground during daylight hours when Soviet surveillance or hostile HUMINT might detect their presence.

The JTF STAFF at Wadi Kena eventually totaled 31 persons plus 15 communicators from the JCSE. The weather detachment numbered five and the Air Force Communication team that was supporting both the weather flow and interface with some of the strategic links consisted of 30 personnel. The aircraft maintenance and ground servicing teams (KC-135, MC-130, AC-130) constituted the single largest group, totaling 364.

Although the majority of the force staged through Wadi Kena, others never saw Egypt. The helicopter crews, their support team, and the Marine Corps intelligence officer assigned to support them flew west to go east. They traveled through the Pacific more than half way around the world to reach Diego Garcia, a joint-use British-American airbase in the middle of the Indian Ocean south of India. From there they were flown on-board the *Nimitz* under the cover of darkness by small Navy transport COD (Carrier On-board Delivery) aircraft capable of operating from the short flight deck of a carrier.

Early on the 20th, the residual JTF cell (JTF-Rear) that had remained in the Pentagon discharged one of its information functions. They alerted the Chairman and the SECDEF to a number of possible events that could occur during the mission period, and, if taken out of context, could be misinterpreted to read that the Iranian authorities had detected the force when this was not necessarily true. During the previous four months, the JTF had compiled a "Cry Wolf" book containing 22 such circumstances that periodically occurred.* Subsequent to the JTF deployment and after providing the "Cry Wolf" data to the Chairman and the SECDEF, the J-2 sent a message to General Vaught who was on the ground in southern Egypt at Site Alpha (Wadi Kena). A portion of this message is presented below.

MSG 004
DTG 201100Z APR 80
FM JCS/RC-J2
TO SITE ALPHA/J2
INFO SFOD/S2
1 SOW/A2
SUBJECT: CRY WOLF LIST
SITE ALPHA/J2 PASS TO COMJTF
(1) THIS MESSAGE CONTAINS COPY OF MEMO PROVIDED TO CJCS ON 20 APRIL 80 PER COMJTF DIRECTION.
(2) THE FOLLOWING IS A LIST OF ACTIVITY THAT MAY BE REPORTED DURING THE COURSE OF THE RICE BOWL OPERATION THAT IF TAKEN OUT OF CONTEXT COULD CAUSE UNDUE CONCERN AND POSSIBLY A PRECIPITOUS DECISION.
A. DETECTION OF AN IRANIAN C130 OR P3 ON A MARITIME SURVEILLANCE MISSION OVER THE PERSIAN GULF. THE IRANIANS HAVE BEEN CONDUCTING MISSIONS OF THIS TYPE FOR SEVERAL MONTHS ON A ROUTINE BASIS.
B. DETECTION OF AN IRANIAN NAVAL UNIT IN THE STRAITS OF HORMUZ. THE IRANIANS HAVE BEEN ATTEMPTING TO MAINTAIN A NAVAL PATROL IN THE STRAITS FOR MORE THAN TWO MONTHS AND MORE RECENTLY HAVE INCREASED THEIR PATROLLING OF THE NORTHERN PERSIAN GULF.†
(3) CJCS HAS BEEN INFORMED THAT THERE MAY BE A NEED TO ADD TO LIST AS TIME GOES BY. WILL PROVIDE INFO TO COMJTF SIMULTANEOUSLY//
REVW 20 APR 2010
BT

By the evening of the 20th, the residual JTF staff at the Pentagon (JTF-Rear) numbered less than nine. This team would monitor the operation from launch through recovery, and relay information from JTF-Main at Wadi Kena to the National Command Authority (NCA) in Washington. Officially, the National Command Authority includes the President, the Secretary of State (SECSTATE) and the Secretary of Defense (SECDEF), with the Chairman of the JCS (CJCS) serving in an advisory role. For this operation, the President and the Secretary of Defense constituted the NCA,

---

* Two of the events listed in the "Cry Wolf" book did occur early in the mission sequence, and were reported by NSA, but neither was a reflection that the force had been detected.

† The other nine examples of activity included in the message remain classified.

with the Chairman performing in his advisory role. Cyrus Vance, the Secretary of State, was opposed to a rescue effort and had quietly resigned when President Carter elected to proceed. By mutual agreement, announcement of the Vance resignation was held in abeyance until after the mission.

Command and Control (C2) of the rescue effort required the establishment of a highly reliable, secure communication network from the National Command Authority (President and SECDEF) in Washington to the Joint Task Force Headquarters (and alternates) and from that location to the deployed elements.

The JTF deployed with three distinct but inter-connectable communications paths. All were secure and had a degree of redundancy built in. One, the JTF network was a DOD circuit and ran from the Pentagon through satellite connectivity to Europe and into the JTF Command bunker at Wadi Kena, and from the bunker (JTF-Main) to the various force elements, including the advance team in Teheran. This network in and of itself was robust and included satellite, UHF and HF radio paths plus telephone connectivity back to the JTF-Rear in Washington. Another was an NSA network which ran from Fort Meade through land-line connectivity to the JTF spaces in the Pentagon and satellite links to a NSA-operated regional relay site in the Mediterranean area, and then via automatic relay to the JTF Headquarters at Wadi Kena. The NSA relay site was also the location of the regional monitoring site, primarily focused on Iran. One team of NSA analysts would monitor various Iranian communications networks for unusual Iranian activity, and signs the rescue mission had been discovered or compromised, while another team would monitor all the JTF radio frequencies to be used or available to the JTF. The regional site would report all these transmissions back to NSA and to the forward deployed JTF HQS at Wadi Kena, and the residual JTF-Rear at the Pentagon.

This "overwatch" system was designed to maximize communications continuity between the scattered JTF forces, particularly during the delicate Day One insertion operations when a wide range of differing and interoperable communications means were to be used. This was particularly crucial regarding the helicopter force, as some of the communications systems they were to employ were not satellite and were subject to the propagation anomalies caused by weather and flight attitude of the helicopter. The third communication path was operated by the CIA. This network was fed by inputs from the CIA regional coordination center. It ran from CIA Headquarters in Virginia to the CIA Liaison team at the JTF Headquarters at Wadi Kena, and to another CIA liaison team on-board the *Nimitz*, as well as to the JTF staff in the Pentagon.

Only the JTF command network, with its own redundancy built in, extended to the deploying force; however, the same messages could be broadcast by the NSA regional site, if the need arose. In addition, the JTF forward sites at Masirah, Oman and on-board the *Nimitz* were geared to monitor (and relay) all communications received from the deploying force (to JTF-Main) to ensure that critical information flowed in spite of communications anomalies. This ensured continuity of command, and provided a redundant listening and reporting mechanism. In addition, provisions and procedures also had been worked out to permit each of the three systems to pass traffic on another system, should a part of its network go down.

The JTF communication path ran directly from the deploying force elements back to JTF-Main at Wadi Kena, then to JTF-Rear in the Pentagon. The Chairman, operating from General Vaught's COMJTF desk in the SOD spaces in the Pentagon, was connected by secure phone directly to Secretary Brown, who in turn was linked directly to President Carter. The phone system was installed during the deployment phase through the joint efforts of JTF/JCSE communicators, the Defense Communications Agency, the White House Communications Agency and NSA. The time of receipt of a JTF radio call from Egypt to the Chairman was less than 30 seconds, and a minute and a half to the President, sometimes less.

The communications system was tailored to the unique operational requirements of the mission and exercised extensively. A basic command and control structure was in place by the third week of November 1979 and could have been used had a rescue effort been ordered at the time. The fact mission execution did not occur for several months, and allowed the testing of the various networks in a realistic environment. By April 1980, a high degree of confidence had been achieved. The overall system was considered reliable and responsive, although it was not as robust from an equipment perspective as desired, but nothing could be done in this regard. The force had all the technology and tactical satellite equipment that was available at the time.

The communication systems were, in every case, secure and redundant. Reliance was ensured by the use of satellite relays backed up by HF/SSB broadcasts. Code words were provided for personnel, events, and locations for use in both secure and non-secure modes and to reduce broadcast time. All equipment was mobile and portable; however, these smaller units had significantly reduced transmission capability that dictated the development of a highly disciplined communication system relying on the UHF satellites as the principle backbone.

In mid-April, the JTF J-6, LTC Peter Dieck, issued the final version of the communications instructions for the mission. The CEOI

(Communications-Electronics Operating Instructions) ran 14 pages. Only eight, highly controlled copies were disseminated. It laid out the procedures for all aspects of the mission and all the forces involved. Various segments were extracted and issued to individual sub-elements as required. The CEOI was organized into five major parts: General Instructions; Call Signs/Identifiers; Suffixes, Radio Nets and Frequencies/NAVIDS; Code Words; and the force Telephone Listing.

Thirty-six hours prior to mission execution, the JTF established four communications networks specifically for command and control purposes:

- Command Net Alpha: Provided the link from the NCA/CJCS in Washington to JTF Headquarters at Wadi Kena and to the alternate location at Masirah.
- Command Net Bravo: Provided command and control from JTF Headquarters to the various force elements, regardless of where they were.
- Command Net Charlie: Provided intra-theater command and control, and served as a key link between those force elements not possessing the UHF satellite capability.
- Command Net Delta: Provided the basic redundant capability and could serve as a primary path when desired.

Paragraph 2 of the CEOI message, the General Instructions, is presented below:

2. ITEM # 2 GENERAL INSTRUCTIONS
A. THIS CEOI IS EFFECTIVE 24/0001Z APR 80
B. PRIOR TO D-1 ALL COMMUNICATIONS WILL BE BY SECURE MEANS
EXCEPT ROUTINE AIR TRAFFIC CONTROL AND DECEPTION TRAFFIC.
C. FROM D-1 UNTIL COMPLETION OF OPERATION, LISTENING SILENCE IS IMPOSED ON ALL ELEMENTS. THIS SILENCE MAY BE BROKEN ONLY UNDER THE FOLLOWING CONDITIONS:
(1) REPORTING AS LISTED IN ITEM # 6 REQUIRED REPORTS.
(2) AS REQUIRED USING SECURED WSC-3 AND PT-25 RADIOS.
(3) TO TRANSMIT EMERGENCY/DISTRESS TRAFFIC.
(4) TO TRANSIT COMMAND AND CONTROL;/COORDINATION TRAFFIC
DURING THE ASSAULT AND EXTRACTION PHASE.
(5) ABSOLUTELY MINIMUM ESSENTIAL AIR TO AIR TRAFFIC EN ROUTE (E.G. BETWEEN TANKERS AND MC-130S) USING KY28 SECURED UHF.
D. ALL HF, VHF, FM VHF/AM, AND UHF SYSTEMS WILL BE NON-SECURE FROM D-1 (LAUNCH OF Delta AND Helo FORCES) UNTIL END

OF OPERATION, EXCEPT FOR AIRCRAFT UHF RADIOS, WHICH WILL BE KY 28 SECURED WHEN OUTSIDE THE TEHERAN MANZARIYEH AREA. UHF GUARD CHANNEL (243.00 MHZ) WILL BE MONITORED AT ALL TIMES.

E. COMSEC MATERIAL TO BE USED.

(1) ORESTES (KW-7) FOR WSC-3 TTY NETS

(2) PARKHILL (KY 65/75)

(3) NESTOR (KY 28/38)

(4) XXXXXXXXXXXXXXXXXXXXXXX [REMAINS CLASSIFIED]

(5) CRYPTO KEY WILL BE DAY 24. EVERYONE WILL STAY ON THE SAME KEY UNTIL OPERATION TERMINATION.

F. COMMUNICATION PROCEDURES.

(1) ALL TRANSMISSIONS WILL BE MADE IN THE FOLLOWING MANNER WITH TIME INTERVAL BETWEEN REPETITIONS STRICTLY OBSERVED.

(A) ALL RADIOS - TRANSMIT BY VOICE. WAIT FOR ACKNOWLEDGMENT. IF NO RESPONSE HEARD WITHIN 30 SECONDS REPEAT TRANSMISSION AND WAIT 30 SECONDS. ON THIRD TRANSMISSION REQUEST ANY STATION HEARING CALL TO RELAY TO ADDRESSEE.

(B) ON HF COMMAND NET - IF THERE IS STILL NO CONTACT AFTER REQUEST FOR RELAY BY ANY STATION IS MADE. SEND MESSAGE IN INTERNATIONAL MORSE CODE.

(2) TELETYPE TRANSMISSION ON THE WSC-3 UHF TACSAT JTF NET (COMMAND NET CHARLIE) IS NOT PERMITTED AFTER LAUNCH OF FORCES SO THAT NET REMAINS CLEAR FOR VOICE TRANSMISSIONS.

During the crucial time frame, the stepmother of the youngest Marine hostage (Kevin Hermiage) had traveled to Teheran as a private citizen (against the advice of the State Department). On 22 April, she managed to gain access to the compound and visit with her son. At the conclusion of their visit, the stepmother, with the young Marine standing at her side, made a short, televised announcement expressing her gratitude for being allowed to visit. The announcement was shown on TV around the world. The site of the visit was the Chancery building.

The last part of the JTF force to close was the AC-130 gunship element from the Pacific. The rescue force was at Wadi Kena or on-board the *Nimitz* by the 22nd, and preparations were made for a final detail-by-detail, minute-by-minute review of the events of the impending 72 hours. The only element of the force not directly involved in this face-to-face review was the helicopter flight detachment. However, radio communication was continuous between the small JTF LNO detachment that had accompanied the helicopter crews and JTF-Main at Wadi Kena. The *Nimitz* team included: the Pacific Command LNO, Lt. Colonel Jim Keating, Major Bob Mattingly (a Marine intelligence officer who had been working with the helicopter flight crews for the previous 90 days), and a senior Marine aviator from the CJCS staff, Colonel Chuck Pittman. Colonel Pittman had been extensively involved as a key coordinator between the JCS and the Navy on all matters involving the selection and training of the Marine helicopter crews. As a result of the transition from the Navy to the Marine aircrew mix, Colonel Pittman's involvement had evolved from that of a staff role to that of being the senior Marine and "de facto" Commander of the helicopter force. He would participate in the mission as an extra crew member on helicopter # 7.

Approximately 48 hours before mission launch, General Vaught requested a full accounting of the total weight to be carried on-board the helicopters. After receiving the information from Delta and being aware of the potential for an overload condition, he sent the following message to the helicopter force commander on-board the *Nimitz*:

SUBJ: HELO LOADS AT DESERT

1. DELTA HAS 97 MEN, 270 LBS PER MAN. 97 DELTA PLUS 2 DELTA RTOS ABOARD SHIP, 3 MONITORS, PLUS 2 RED EYE GUNNERS (FOUR WEAPONS), 5 DRIVERS, 7 EUCOM SF (MFA TM) FOR A TOTAL OF 116 PERS. WITH THE NUMBER OF PAX, WEAPONS, AND AMMO DELTA WILL WEIGHT 5200 LBS PER HELO (6 HELOS). RECOGNIZE THAT THIS IS 400 LBS OVER YOUR MAX.
REQUEST YOU REDUCE (EACH HELO) TO ONE 50 CAL AND ONE GUNNER (VICE TWO & TWO). PUT ALL SECOND 50 CALS AND SECOND GUNNERS ON SEVENTH RH 53. IF ONLY SIX A/C MAKE REFUEL SITE THEN SECOND 50 CALS AND GUNNERS PLUS CREW FROM SEVENTH A/C WILL COME BACK VIA C-130. IF SEVEN AIRCRAFT (HELOS) DEPART DESERT AND ONE GOES DOWN ENROUTE THEN SECOND 50 CALS WILL HAVE TO BE LEFT AT P/U SITE. IF SEVEN AIRCRAFT MAKE IT TO HIDE OUT THEN SECOND 50 CAL AND GUNNER WILL BE PUT BACK ON 6 RH-53S.
2. REQUEST THAT YOU PERSONALLY INSPECT ALL HELO TO ENSURE NO EXTRA WEIGHT IS TAKEN.
3. DETAILED WT. AND COMPOSITION OF EACH LOAD FOR SIX RH-53S WILL BE SENT IN APPROX 8 HOURS.
4. IF EIGHTH RH-53 IS OP READY, FLY IT, EMPTY LOAD, AS FAR INTO MISSION AS POSSIBLE. COL KYLE HAS ASSURED ME THAT SUFFICIENT FUEL IS ON HAND TO FUEL EIGHT HELO. DETAILS ON REFUEL FOR EIGHT HELO WILL BE TRANSMITTED BY SEP(separate) MSG. UNDERSTAND PROBABILITY OF 8 HELOS LAUNCHING IS NOT GOOD BUT TRY YOUR BEST.
5. GEN VAUGHT SENDS

BT

***

The air was stifling. Bunker 13 was hot and getting hotter, aided by the body heat of more than a hundred occupants. Sitting side by side, along the somewhat cooler concrete walls, were Delta assault personnel, the Ranger road-block teams, and the Driver monitors. Some slept halfheartedly, others read paperbacks or indulged in small group conversations. All had checked and double-checked their weapons, their communication gear and the other things that constituted their mission kits. Time was moving slowly and the atmosphere was laden with a quiet sense of commitment. As hot as the temperature was, the weight on each man's mind was heavier.

Inside each man is the same organic composition and systemic plumbing, yet each is markedly different. While each has a theoretically equal distribution of chemical elements, valences and similar molecular ingredients and electronic connectivity, each person uses them in a different way, with a different result. That is what makes these humans distinct but similar. Each sends and receives and processes messages thousands of times a minute. How well those messages are sent, received and processed is reflected in how well that person accomplishes his individual and team responsibilities.

Up to this point, various people from commanders, instructors, comrades and doctors had worked very hard to make sure these humans performed in a flawless manner. Although a total guarantee was impossible to provide, particularly given the lethal potentiality of the dynamics they faced, a measure of their commitment and preparation could be seen in their eyes. In each pupil could be seen, no could be felt, a certain hard, flinty aspect called determination. Among themselves nothing is said, but a great deal is understood.

In mid-afternoon, they were roused from their thoughts by the entrance of General Vaught. He reviewed the mission sequence and its purpose -- to recover Americans. He closed by telling them that he would see them on the ground at Manzariyeh, the extraction airhead. He wished them well, God Speed and safe return. They joined in singing "God Bless America," and then "saddle up and move out" to board the waiting C-141s that would take them south to the mission jump off point, Misarah airfield, on a tiny island off the coast of Oman. The C-141 flight was fast and relatively short, something approximating two hours. At Oman, they went through the checklists one more time, washed up, grabbed some chow, put on their mission uniforms, and settled in to wait for the call to board the black MC-130s that would take them to Desert One and the rendezvous with the helicopter fleet.

The MCs, their aircrews, armament and maintenance personnel had arrived the night before and set up a miniature tent city on the hard-packed, windswept desert soil, along one side of the single 8,000 foot runway.

They found that their temporary home had an interesting persona which included a small RAF detachment at the other end of the runway and, in the distance, a scattering of native villages and free-roaming camels. At night, the sounds included the beat of distant natives drums. In the morning, some of the crews woke to the smiling faces and nasty smell of curious camels. In addition to two rows of tents that constituted the American village, the airmen had created two semi-permanent facilities. Both were constructed of plywood and yellow pine 2x4 studs and both were essential to the transient aircrews. The first was a desert-style outhouse with a curved moon cut in the door. Its interior architectural portions were larger than normal. Everything was higher than normal and raised off the ground, making its use somewhat of a climbing and balancing challenge to anyone shorter than six foot four. Once situated, the long gaps in the plywood converted the ever-present sea breeze to a howling wind, reminiscent of the cry of a lonely wolf.

The other structure, a cross between a Vietnam-era "hooch" and a Coney Island Hot Dog stand, was likewise constructed of 2x4s and 4x8 plywood sheets. It served three critical functions, first as the map and E& E issue point, second as the pre-mission planning center, and lastly as the sole source of "cold drinks." However, the ice ran out in the first twelve hours, so the "cold drinks" quickly became warm, verging on hot, but no one complained; they were wet. During the "map sessions," some local culture, in the form of dried camel droppings, became the standard paper weighs. Part of the final mission preparations involved several walkthroughs of the taxi and takeoff plan. This was crucial, as the takeoff would be in total blackout conditions on an unlit runway. Further complicating the situation was the fact that there was no taxiway and barely enough room at either end of the runway for one C-130 to turn around. The lead aircraft, departing 45 minutes before the balance of the fleet, would have no problem; however, it would take special care and precise timing, and careful ground maneuvers to ensure that the remaining five aircraft launched safely and in close succession. As the launch afternoon dragged on, some of the aircrews took "field showers" to cool down. The showers consisted of two canteens of water, a slow soap, and four more canteens of water.

Numerous checks and final inspections of the aircraft and their myriad subsystems and the hybrid ground refueling systems began one last time ninety minutes before launch. Forty-five minutes later, the boarding sequence began and, within 30 minutes, the lead aircraft lifted off for Desert One. The others followed 30-45 minutes later. A paragraph from the diary of Major Jerry Utarro, one of the first two aircraft commanders involved in the mission from the beginning (the previous November) and who had been charged with the task of perfecting blackout landing techniques, reflects the feeling of the pre-launch hours: "When we aren't planning or talking through the mission, we are checking out the aircraft. We are ready and we want to go and bring our folks back home. This might sound corny, but that's how we feel. I do not think about what could happen, I think about what should happen."

Meanwhile, back in Washington, in mid-afternoon on the 23rd, one of the non-JTF planners, from the retaliatory options OPG (who had access to the rescue JTF), suggested to the JCS J-3 that the nickname for the planning effort, "RICEBOWL," be superseded in the execution phase by a more virulent term. This suggestion was included as item two of a short, two-paragraph message to General Vaught as presented below:

DTG 231805Z APR 80
FM: OJCS
TO: JTF CDR/SITE "A"
1. EUCOM HAS VERBALLY CHOPPED THEIR FORCE INVOLVED IN RICE BOWL TO JTF EFFECTIVE 1800Z TODAY. WAS AGREED TO BY GENERAL ROGERS, CINCEUR. HE HAS SO INSTRUCTED GEN ALLEN, DCINCEUR AT EUCOM. GENERAL HUYSER, CINCMAC, HAS INSTRUCTED HIS PEOPLE TO COMPLY WITH YOUR OPERATIONAL ORDERS ON USE OF C-141 DURING EXECUTION PHASE.
2. WOULD YOU SEE ANY PROBLEM IN OUR CALLING THE EXECUTION PHASE EAGLE CLAW. THIS WOULD DIFFERENTIATE EARLIER PHASES FROM EXECUTION. ALSO EAGLE CLAW WILL CONNOTE A STRONGER IMAGE IN THE AFTERMATH THAN RICE BOWL. IF ANY PROBLEM WITH THIS, WE WILL LEAVE ALONE.
BT.

The term Eagle Claw was reminiscent of the operational nickname (Eagle Pull) given to the earlier emergency evacuation of Phom Phenh, Cambodia. Although some members of the residual JTF Washington staff did not support the suggestion, it was deemed too trivial a topic to make an issue and the suggestion was dispatched without comment.

About four hours later, General Vaught officially advised the force that fighter aircraft from the *USS Nimitz* Battle Group -- Carrier Task Force 70 (CTF 70) -- would provide fighter support on Day (night) Two. The message providing the coordination instructions follows:

O 232250Z APR 80
FM JTF ALPHA
TO USS NIMITZ
JTF/SITE BRAVO
JCS/RC
SUBJ: CTF 70 CAP SUPPORT

1. CTF 70 WILL SUPPLY CAP (COMBAT AIR PATROL) SUPPORT TO GROUND/AIR UNITS REQUIRING ASSISTANCE. UNITS MUST HAVE UHF COMM ON 341.4 MHZ (PRI) AND 240,5 MHZ (SEC) BEFORE CAP UNITS CAN COMMIT. USE UNIT CALL SIGNS LISTED IN CEOI AND GIVE POSITION USING ECAP POINT CODE WORD. GROUND UNITS USE SMOKE TO ASSIST IF POSSIBLE.

ECAP POINT	DESCRIPTION	COORDINATES
ALPHA	REFUEL AREA	33-04-25N/55-52-55E
BRAVO	HELO HIDE	35-12-03N/52-09-00E
CHARLIE	WAREHOUSE	35-33-00N/51-33-00E
DELTA	EMBASSY	35-42-40N/51-25-30E
ECHO	MANZARIYEH	34-59-00N/50-48-10E
FOXTROT	KHARIZAN	35-27-15N/50-15-20E
GOLF	KARAJ A/F	35-40-25N/50-15-20E
HOTEL	SEMNAN NEW A/F	35-23-50N/53-40-15E
INDIA	RAILROAD JUNCTION	35-15-00N/52-45-00E

2. CAP A/C WILL MONITOR TACAN CHAN 99. GIVE POSIT IN RANGE AND BEARING FROM NEAREST EXCAP POINT. IF NOT POSSIBLE PROVIDE LAT LONG COORDINATES.
3. PASS THIS INFO TO ALL UNITS PRIOR TO START OF MSN.
4. REQUEST CTF 70 PUBLISH CAP CALL SIGN TO ALCON ASAP. (All Concerned - As Soon As Possible).

BT

***

Less than 24 hours before launch, a media incident occurred which could have generated "undue concern and possibly a precipitous decision" throughout the American rescue structure. During the early hours of the 23rd of April, the TEHERAN INTERNATIONAL NEWS SERVICE headlined, "A CIA plan to kidnap the U.S. hostages in Teheran has been revealed." The immediate question was: Did the Iranians know the mission was to be launched? Had a leak or security breach occurred? Had our earlier in-country preparations been discovered?

After quickly checking on the fuller details of the story, it was revealed there were none, and the story consisted of only the lead headline. A message was immediately dispatched to Site Alpha advising them of the following.

FM: JCS/RC-J2
TO: SITE ALPHA/J2
SUBJ: TEHRAN INTERNATIONAL SERVICE REPORTING
REFERENCE: OUR MSG 201332Z APR 80

1. The credibility of reporting from the Tehran International service has proved to be particularly low in the past. The report of today's date, concerning a "CIA plan to kidnap the US hostages", must be viewed with considerable skepticism.

2. For example, in item 10 of reference, Tehran International service (also) reported "without elaboration" that the U.S. was in the process of mining Iran's southern border waters.
3. Without more complete details and corroboration, all such reports from Tehran International Service should be view(ed) with a very high degree of skepticism, and considered a tool of Iranian propaganda.
BT

One of the most unusual and unpredictable events regarding the hostages occurred the night before mission launch. This was the last-minute receipt of some "fortuitous" CIA reporting. The reports allegedly came from a husband and wife who had been detained in the Embassy compound since the takeover. The husband, according to the reports, was a cook and had been preparing food for the hostages throughout the entire period of their detention. After an "accidental" meeting with a deep-cover CIA officer, who was on the same flight departing Teheran the couple was debriefed in Europe. This apparent coincidence seemed a little too fortuitous to some in the JTF, particularly the J-2 in the Pentagon. There was a danger that the "eleventh hour" nature of the information could precipitate its acceptance without any evaluation, thus putting the entire mission on questionable grounds.

The two debriefing summaries, one based on conversations with the husband, and the other on talks with the wife, inferred none of the hostages were detained in the Chancery, but were scattered throughout the compound. An immediate comparison of the reports (by the JTF J-2) with all other data available indicated the reports were old opinions and speculations, not a reflection of current situation. In addition, the two reports contradicted each other and failed to mention any of the previously confirmed detention sites, such as the Mushroom Inn or the Chancery. The opinions appeared to be based on the situation as it had existed in the first few days of the takeover, not as it had evolved during the intervening months or as it was now.

The J-2 sent an immediate message to Wadi Kena outlining the discrepancies and citing the multiple recent indicators that most of the hostages, if not all, were probably being held in the Chancery. Although some public speculation has surrounded this incident in the print media after the rescue attempt, Colonel Beckwith did adjust the ground tactical plan and focus more force on the Chancery.

***

At 241230Z April 1980, General Vaught issued the following execute order by message to all JTF forces:

FM: COMJTF (VAUGHT)
TO: DEPCOMJTF (GAST)
DEPCOMJTF/FIXED WING AIR OPS (KYLE)
CDR 1ST SFOD DELTA (BECKWITH)
DEPCOM Helo OPS (PITTMAN)
INFO: JTF/REAR (Washington)
SUBJ: EXECUTE ORDER
EXECUTE MISSION AS BRIEFED.
WE ARE READY AND ABLE. GOD SPEED.BT

General Vaught released the execute order after receiving confirmation from Colonel Pittman and the Helicopter detachment aboard the *Nimitz* and General Gast, Colonel Kyle and Colonel Beckwith at Oman that their respective forces were ready to go. He also received three other key inputs. One input was from the weather detachment forecasting clear weather for the mission. A second came from NSA indicating no change or unusual activity within the Iranian military or police infrastructure. The last came from the leader of the JTF advance team in Teheran, Dick Meadows. Dick and the other members of the team had conducted surveys of both the Embassy and the MFA, the Delta transfer point and hidesite during the morning and afternoon. Meadows had reported the codeword for "all in readiness" via his satellite radio.

Meanwhile, in Washington, the back room of the JTF spaces had once again undergone a transformation. It had been converted from a working and briefing area with dozens of people coming and going (as the need presented itself) to a subdued 24 hour watch and monitoring operation with access limited to less than a dozen personnel. As in the forward command post in Egypt, the full mission sequence for Day One, the insertion and hide segments of the mission, was posted in a time sequenced narrative form, event by event. A map presentation highlighting the routes and timing marks was posted in a parallel manner. A third listing showed the times "status" reports were to be transmitted, by whom and the meaning of the cover terms. These cryptic terms, normally less than three words, conveyed success or failure without much explanation.

If all was going well, there was no need for amplification. The monitors in the Pentagon and at the JTF bunker in Egypt knew what a positive message meant. A negative message could raise the ambiguity and apprehension level immediately, with the word "why" quickly coming to the forefront in the mind of the monitors. Although all the communications were secure, they did emit an electronic signal that was detectable if an observer was on that frequency at that time. Thus, even positive messages were short. If a negative message was transmitted, the monitors knew the next transmission would include a brief bit of explanation as to why (or a fuller description of the situation). The monitors would have to exercise extreme patience and wait for the follow-up report. They knew that the people on the originating end of the transmission were, for the most part, very busy trying to solve the problem or come up with workable alternatives. This realization, combined with the fact that the longer any transmission the greater the chance of detection, reinforced the patience of the monitors (JTF-Main and JTF-Rear).

The tracking maps and mission time-table had also been produced in smaller form for use by the Chairman, who was maintaining his presence in the SOD outer space, General Vaught's office. In addition to these references, the Chairman, the Secretary, and General Vaught each had been provided a "Cry Wolf" book. Waiting in reserve, for the events of Night Two, were three thick binders. The first was called the "Critical Facilities" book. It contained photography, descriptions and maps of Iranian facilities that might have to be shelled by the AC-130 gunships. The second was the "Trip Ticket" book. It contained maps, photography and a description of the route that Delta would take to the Embassy, and the MFA force to their target. The last binder contained maps and imagery showing the location of more than a dozen emergency pick-up sites known as "Bus Stops." Hopefully, books one and three would not have to be used.

In the meantime, the deception and security blanket was being stretched and extended by various actions to mask the intended operational dates and to provide cover, should the mission be delayed to the second planning window or beyond to another window of opportunity. The deception-coordinating team had presented their plan and the various measures to the Chairman, General Vaught, the JTF Chief of Staff, and the JTF J-2 three weeks earlier. Approval was immediately forthcoming, with minor reinforcing actions added and timing adjusted. Although most of the work of the deception team was put in motion prior to the beginning of the deployment phase, some "tactical," (i.e., contemporary) measures would be conducted during and after the mission execution on an "as-needed" basis. Because of these potential follow-on requirements, a representative of the deception team would monitor the mission progress as part of the JTF Washington cadre.

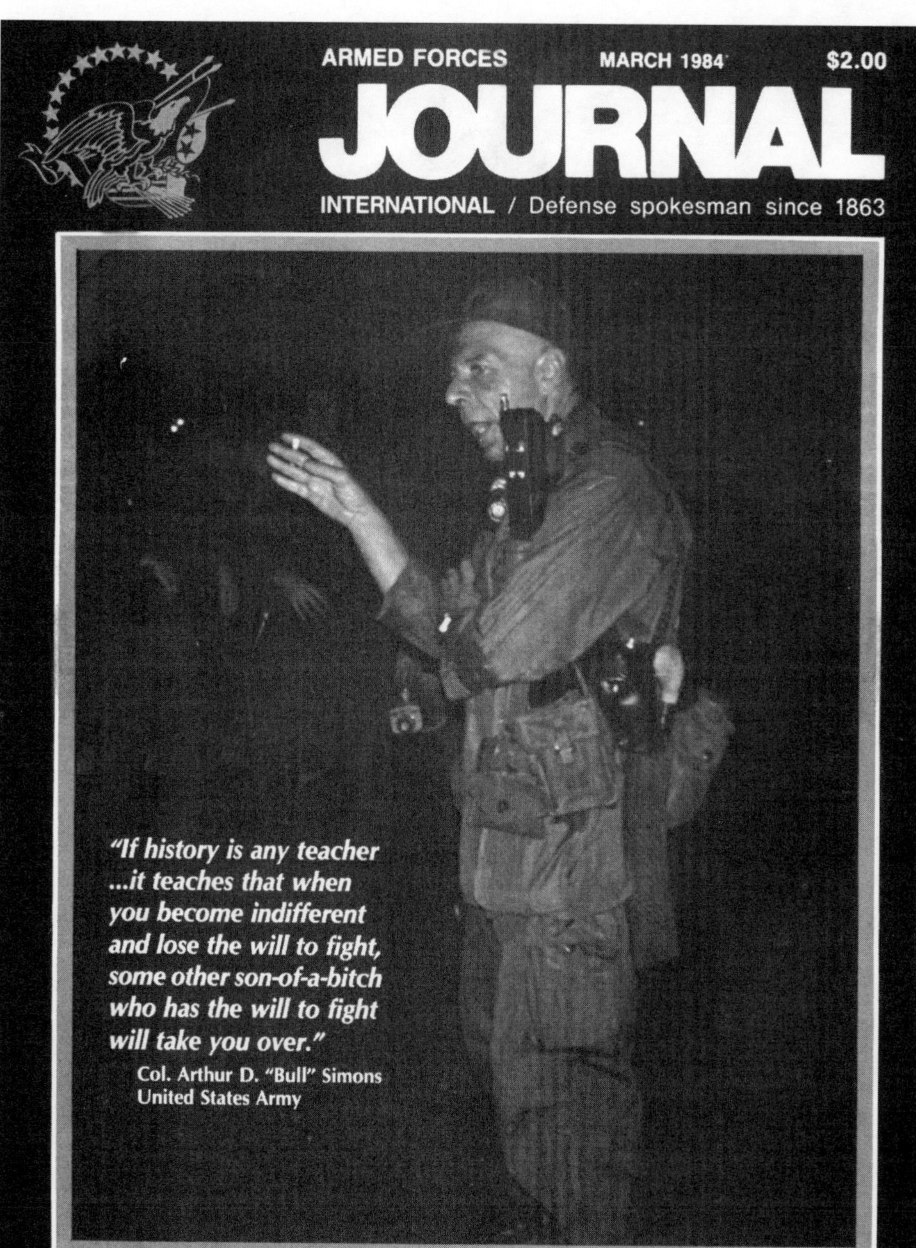

ARMED FORCES
MARCH 1984
$2.00
JOURNAL
INTERNATIONAL / Defense spokesman since 1863
"If history is any teacher
...it teaches that when
you become indifferent
and lose the will to fight,
some other son-of-a-bitch
who has the will to fight
will take you over."
Col. Arthur D. "Bull" Simons
United States Army
DoD's FY85 Budget

Cover, *Armed Forces Journa International*, March 1984. Photo of Colonel Bull Simons, U.S. Army, in battlegear just prior to launch of the Son Tay Prisoner of War Camp Rescue attempt in North Vietnam in 1970. The details of the story are told in the book *THE RAID*, by Ben Schemmer. Simons also led a highly successful, unarmed rescue of three American businessmen imprisoned in Iran in early 1978. Printed with permission of *AFJI*.

View of one section of the wall surrounding the U.S. Embassy Compound in Teheran where the American hostages were initially held captive. The mural tells the story from the Iranian fundamentalist viewpoint beginning with the return of the Alytollah Ruhollah Khomeni through the takeover of the Embassy.

The Embassy Motor Pool as viewed from outside the vehicle access gate.

Excerpt of 1970 Iranian street map of the center of Teheran, showing the location of the American Embassy Compound (A), the adjacent Iranian Military Garrison and Supply Depot, and the nearby Amjadieh Stadium and sports complex. The Ministry of Foreign Affairs (MFA), the collocated Archaeological Museum and the adjacent Police Headquarters are located some 25 blocks south (B). The Iranian Parliament complex is shown at (C), and several military compounds are identified by (D).

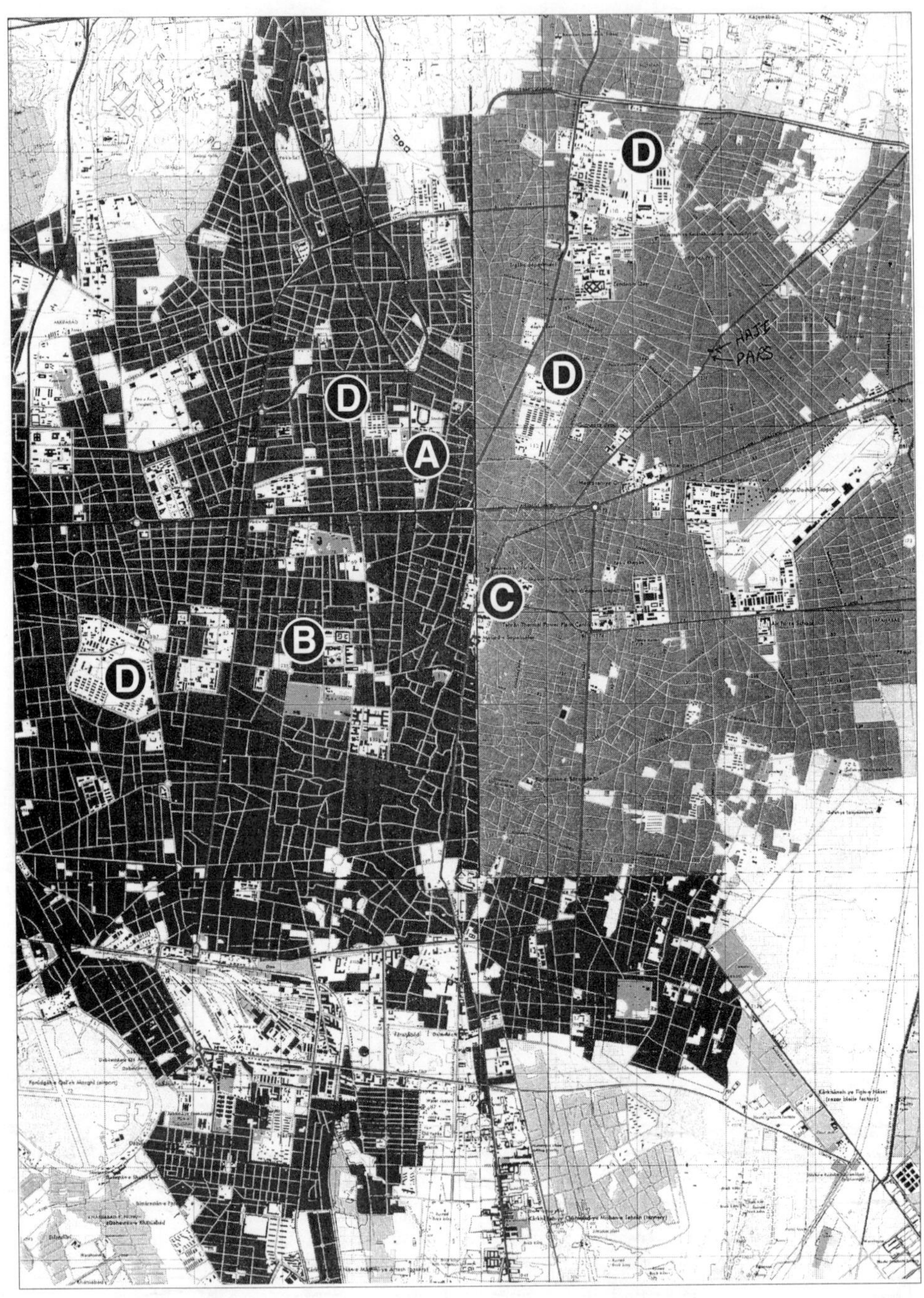

Copy of composite of four 1:50,000 scale U.S. Military maps showing the majority of the denser sections of Teheran in 1978. This map provides greater detail and positional accuracy; the previous street map had its value in street names and identifiying non-government facilities. The north-south distance shown is approximately eight miles. The Embassy area is shown at (A), the MFA at (B), the Iranian Parliament complex is shown at (C), and several military compounds are identified by (D).

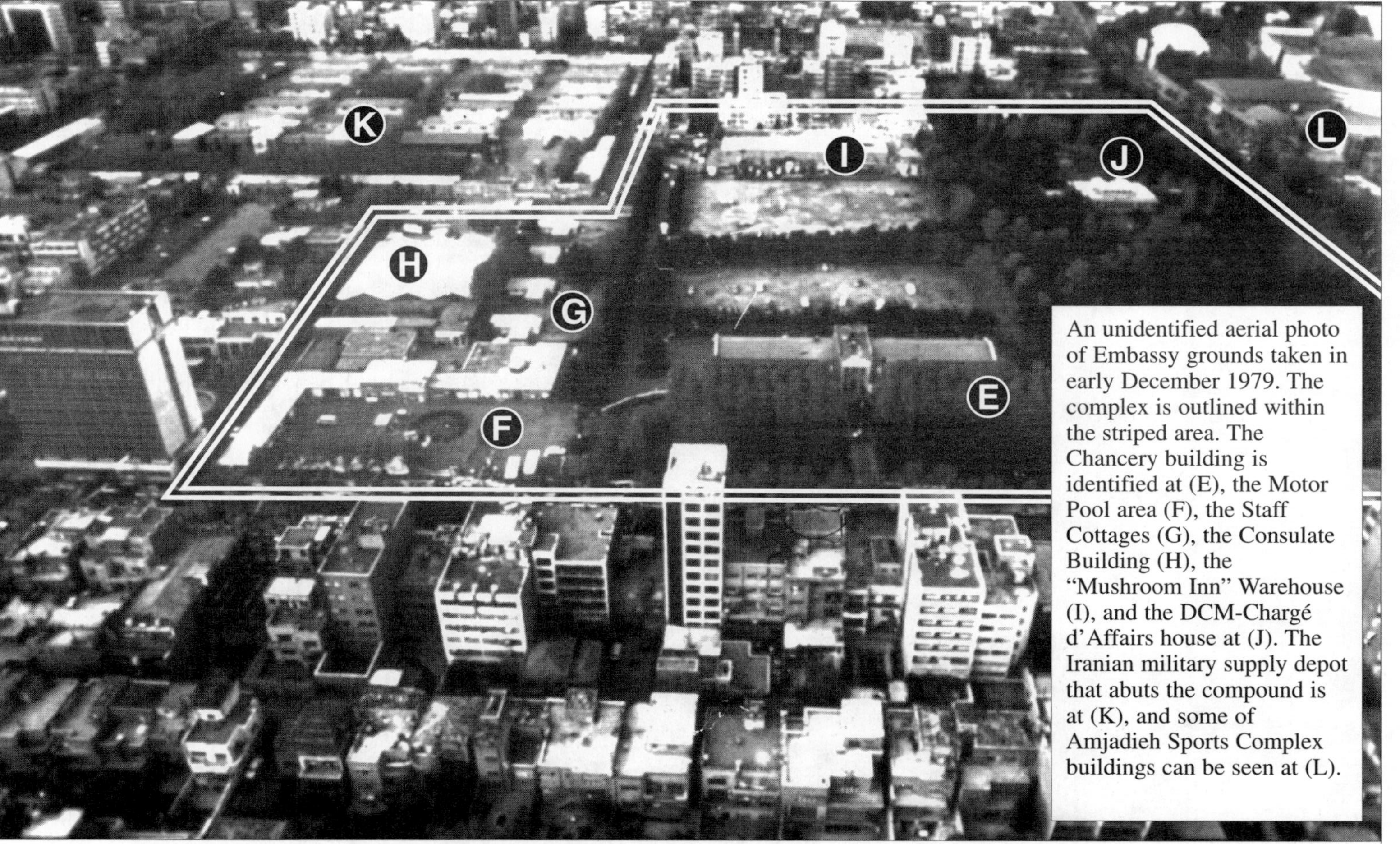

An unidentified aerial photo of Embassy grounds taken in early December 1979. The complex is outlined within the striped area. The Chancery building is identified at (E), the Motor Pool area (F), the Staff Cottages (G), the Consulate Building (H), the "Mushroom Inn" Warehouse (I), and the DCM-Chargé d'Affairs house at (J). The Iranian military supply depot that abuts the compound is at (K), and some of Amjadieh Sports Complex buildings can be seen at (L).

This is an Iranian copy of an American reconnaissance photo found by the Iranians when they searched one of the abandoned helicopters. The photo shows the Ajadieh Stadium and adjacent sports facilities, including a public soccer field, tennis courts, and swimming pool on the left, with the main entrance and smaller facilities on the right. The embassy compound is located further to the right across the very traffic-congested street.

BREVITY CODES

LOCATIONS	CODEWORD
ALTERNATE LANDING ZONE	ICEBOX
AMBASSADORS RESIDENCE	FOAMY
ARDALAN ST	GODPARENT
CHANCERY BUILDING	FOX HUNTER
COMMISSARY BUILDING	FULLBACK
CONSULATE BUILDING	FROG LEG
COTTAGES (A THRU D SUFFIX)	GAS TUBE
DCM RESIDENCE	FOG HORN
DELTA SAFEHAVEN DESERT LAND	FILIBUSTER
DESERT LAND	WATCHBAND
EMBASSY	FIRE BRICK
FISHERABAD QM DEPOT	GOODRICH
GHALE MAGHRI A/F	HIP BONE
HELO HIDE SITE	FIG BAR
INCIRLIK	ELECTION
IRAN	EMPLOYEE
JASK	HONEY DEW
JHAHROK A5F	HUPMOBILE
KARAZ	HOPALONG
MANZARIYEH	ESCORI DUTY
MEHRABAD A/F	HOCKSHOP
MINISTRY OF FOREIGN AFFAIRS (MFA)	EQUALITY
NAM JU ST	GOLD RUSH
NEA MAKRI	FARM
NIMITZ	DOMINO
OLD GUARD QUARTERS	GAYLORD
PRIMARY LANDING ZONE	HYPNOTIZE
QUOM	HEDGE ROW
ROOSEVELT BLVD	GLASSWARE
SAUDI ARABIA	ELGIN WATCH
SEMNAN A/F	GRAY MARE
SHIRAZ	HEARTLAND
STADIUM	GRAPEVINE
TEHERAN	ENVELOPE
TURKEY	INHABIT
VAHDATI A/F	HOT HOUSE
WADI KENA	EAR GUARD

A copy of the Brevity Code recovered by the Iranians and used in conjunction with more than a dozen or more other papers, photos and maps, to reconstruct their version of the mission. A booklet presenting the reconstruction was put on sale in Teheran in Farsi within weeks of the 24 April mission abort. This Brevity Code lists the names of key mission locations and provides the Cover Term (Codeword) to be used in any radio communications between the forces.

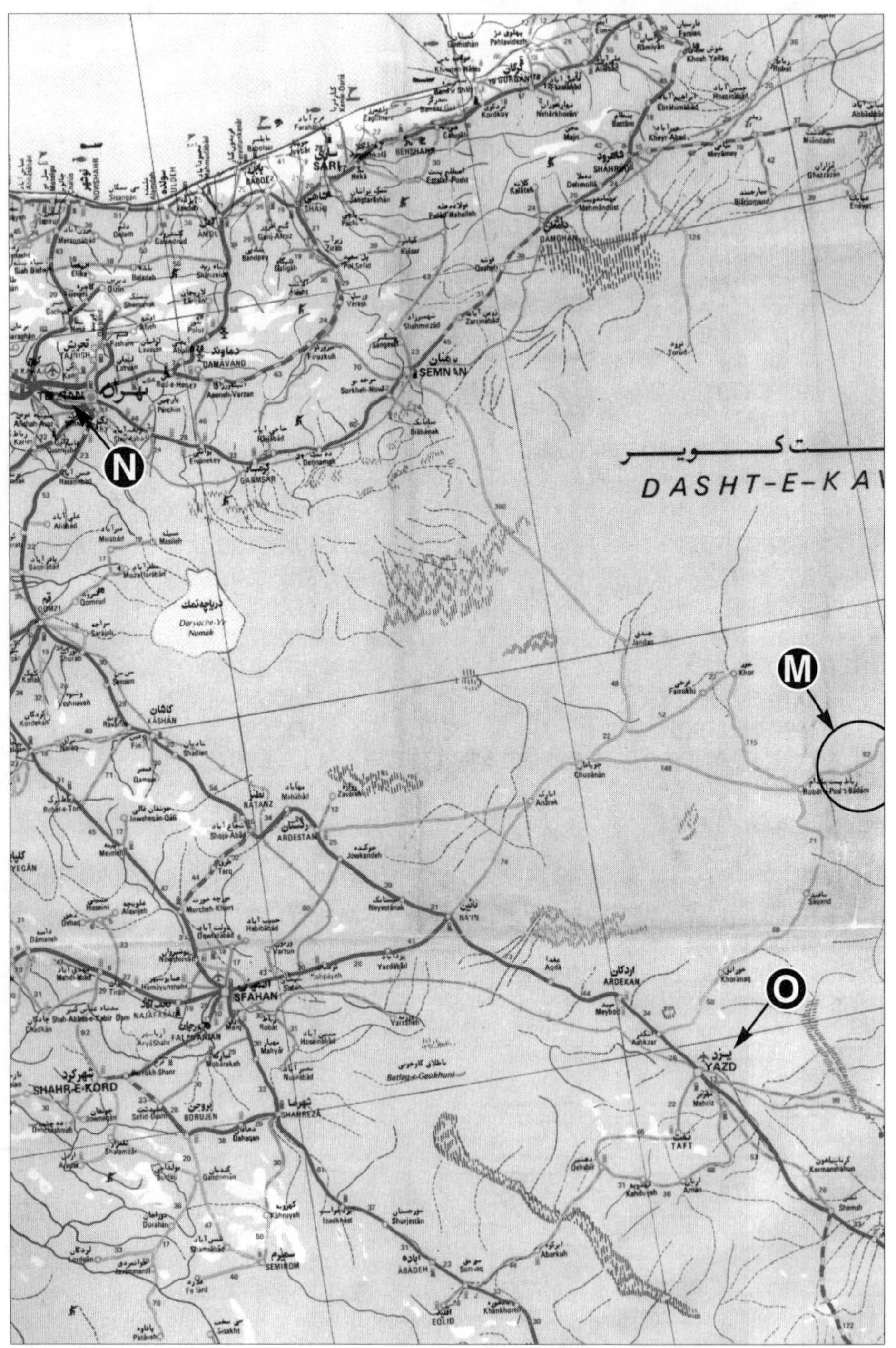

An excerpt from an Iranian National roadmap showing the road network in central Iran. The Desert One site is located at (M) along a route classified by the Iranians as "under construction," which translated to unimproved, non-surfaced dirt track. Teheran is located at (N) and the city of Yazd at (O).

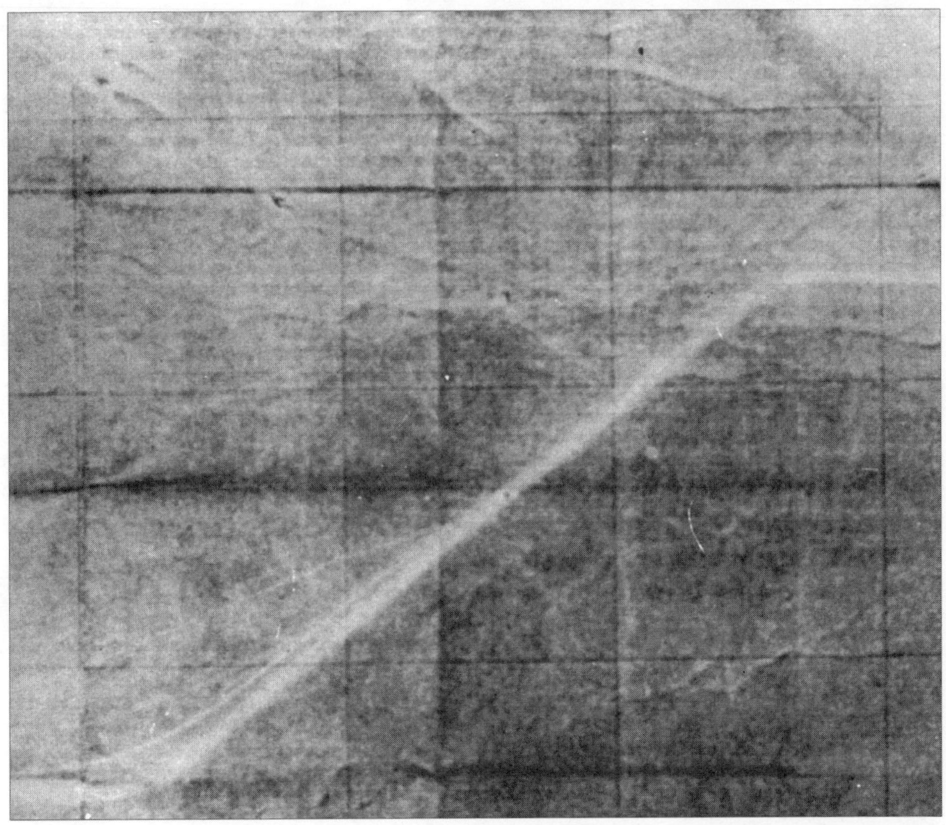

A copy of a reconnaissance photo recovered and published by the Iranians. It shows the segment of the road that identifies the area of Desert One. A landing zone was laid out on either side of the strait portion of the road. The dot seen at the mid-point in the straightaway is a vehicle, the only one seen that day for more than 10 miles in either direction. During the course of the more than ninety days of surveillance, no more than two vehicles were ever sighted. However, it was sometimes possible to gauge their speed, which typically exceeded 35 miles an hour. In addition, on several occasions, vehicles were noted to "short-cut" the lower curve by leaving the road and heading out straight across the desert floor without any noticeable reduction in speed. The combination of straightness of the road, the measured vehicle speeds, and the numerous signs of short-cutting, together with the long term (8 years) stability of the topography, indicated to imagery analysts that the area was flat and potentially suitable as a landing area.

منطقهٔ سوخت گیری ــ دشت طبس

روز ۲٤ آوریل

1 305.7
2 322.6
3 361.7
4 341.4

*FORM LITES – OFF FOR FUEL
* PISTT LITES – ON 15 SEC a/c.

[55]

123456 ++ ++

24th

1330Z A/C READY
1345Z POS FLT DK – HOLD APU TIL SIGNAL
1445Z START ✓ LIST
1500-1505Z T/O #6 → TAC 305.7
1525 – C-130 X CIP
1530 – HELOS X CIP
1805 – C-130 LANDS REFUEL
1910-1930 5 MC/AC LAND REFUEL
1933 * HELOS LAND REFUEL
DELTA LOADS – HEAD COUNT
2030 * T/O REFUEL
2245 LAND DZ – DROP RAMP
2250 T/O DZ
2306 LAND LAAGER
2040Z (25TH) T/O LAAGER

سند فوق، زمان عبور هواپیماهای سی ــ ۱۳۰ و هلیکوپترهای سیکورسکی را نشان می دهد، به فاصلهٔ ۵ دقیقه پس از عبور هواپیماها از مرز خشکی ایران، هلیکوپترها یکی پس از دیگری وارد ایران می‌شدند.

A copy of an aviator's "knee-pad" found by the Iranians at Desert One. It gives the projected mission timeline for the helicopters on Night One (April 24). The projected flight schedule began with take-off (T/O) from the Nimitz at 15:00 Zulu (London/Greenwich time), refuel at Desert One four and half-hours later (1930Z), and land at overnight laager site some 3:36 minutes later at 2306Z. Launch for the Night Two segment of the mission was projected to begin at 2040Z the night of the 25th.

Ground level photo of the Desert One Crash site, published in the Iranian booklet showing the remains of the C-130 transport on the left and the RH-53 helicopter on the right. The mountains in the background are more than ten miles distant.

Another ground-level photo looking the opposite direction with part of the C-130 in the foreground and one of less severely damaged helicopters in the background. This photo and the next comfirm the flatness and unobstructed nature of the landing area.

This photo shows one of the other helicopters destroyed beyond recovery. The fire that consumed this aircraft was probably a result of exploding ordnance from the C-130/RH-53 conflagration.

President Carter speaking to the JTF staff and the Air Force flight crews in May 1980 in the Pentagon reception room of Dr. Brown, the Secretary of Defense (seated to the President's left). Several of the JTF leadership are seated in the front row. From the far end, they include: Colonel Jerry King (Chief of Staff), Colonel Jim Kyle (C-130 Air Planner), Colonel Wickam (1st SOW), General Jim Vaught (JTF 1-79 Commander), General Phillip Gast (Deputy Commander), Colonel Roland Guidry (ISOW).

Major General James Vaught, US Army, Commander JTF-79 (12 Nov 79-20 Sep 1980) in Washington, D.C., as shown on national television after the hostages were released in January 1981.

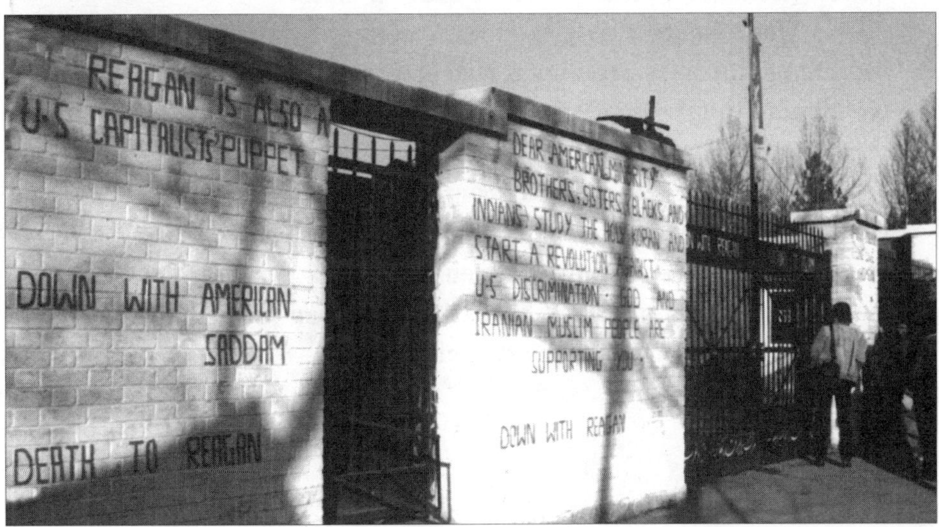

View of the embassy compound gate through which the Militants gained entrance during the 4 November 1979 takeover. This photo, taken after the release of the hostages, captures the continued targeting, for propaganda purposes, of the American presidency.

Though it is the duty of the soldier to serve, we, and our country, are honored that you serve so well. Our association with you and our insight into your character, integrity and strength of purpose lend far greater meaning to the words "Duty, Honor, Country" than a chiseled motto on a wall.

It has been our personal privilege and honor to serve you as you served the Commander-in Chief on an assignment coveted by many but worthy of few. The wisdom of this selection has been brought home to each of us in many ways:

Your strength of character in dealing with difficult decisions.

Your foresight and total involvement in all aspects of the operation have been an inspiration to all.

Your loyalty, understanding and support of subordinates who sometimes did things in unorthodox ways.

Your honest concern for a trooper who carried burdens far less than yours.

Your recognition that in spite of all the rank, pomp, circumstance, privilege, and priority associated with the mission: It was the ordinary Soldier, Sailor, Airman and Marine that had to sweat and possibly bleed to make it work.

Your unique ability to invent, encourage, devise and develop solutions to previously unaddressed problems and your willingness to take suggestions, change plans and battle elders if you thought it would enhance mission accomplishment.

For these reasons and many more we can't articulate, we would like to thank you for the opportunity you have given us to serve you and Our Nation and on behalf of a number of American Citizens who can't be here - thank you for getting us all much closer than we have ever been.

Copy of the scroll prepared by the staff of JTF-79 (12 Nov 79-20 Sep 1980) presented to General Vaught after the completion and submission of the JTF Capabilities Review to the Service Chiefs in May 1981.

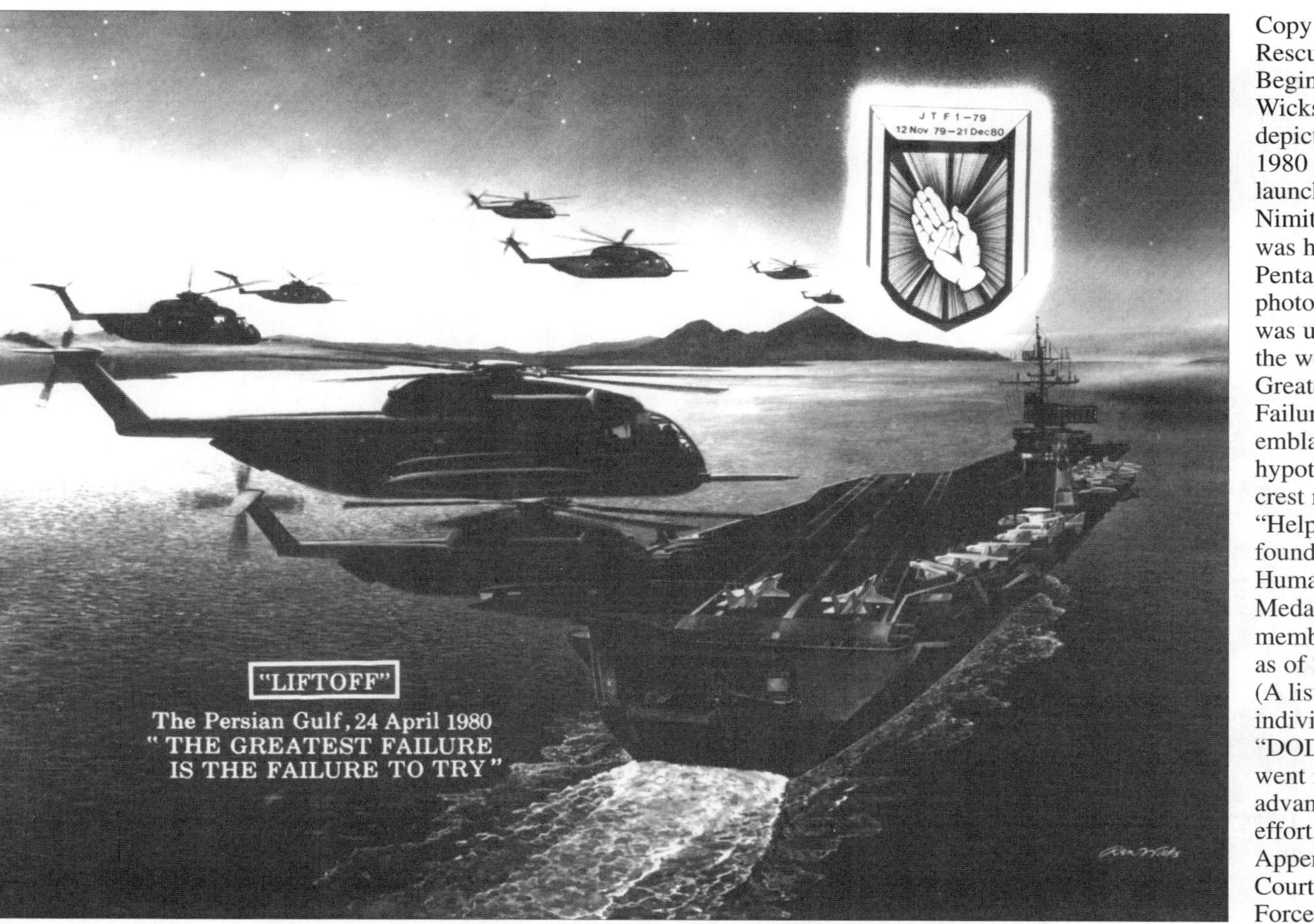

Copy of "The Iranian Rescue Mission Begins," by Ren Wicks, an oil painting depicting the 24 April 1980 helicopter launch from the Nimitz. The original was hung in the Pentagon. The JTF photographic copy was underscored by the words "The Greatest Failure is the Failure to Try," and emblazoned with a hypothetical JTF 1-79 crest reflecting the "Helping Hand" found on the Humanitarian Service Medal awarded to all members of the JTF as of 24 April 1980. (A list of these individuals, less the "DOD Scouts" that went into Tehran in advance of the rescue effort, can be found in Appendix 3.) Courtesy U.S. Air Force Art Collection.

Photo of front and back of Humanitarian Service Medal which was awarded to the members of the JTF 1-79 who participated in the rescue attempt of 24 April 1980.

Credible Sport: One of two specially modified C-130s developed by a team of Lockheed, Navy and Air Force aviation and rocket propulsion engineers, in mid 1980, in response to a JTF 1-79 requirement to create an extremely short field landing and take-off capability (less than 100 yards), to support a possible second rescue effort.

CHAPTER SEVEN
Committed

Just as darkness fell on the 24th, the C-130s lifted off from Masirah with the ground forces securely nestled in their bellies. All eight helicopters had launched from the *Nimitz* just prior to last light to make landfall along the Iranian coastline just after dark at a desolate point midway between the towns of Jask and Konarak. The two approach routes were different and the penetration of the Iranian airspace was timed to be minutes and miles apart.

Both flight groups flew different routes and altitudes within the broad corridor that had been defined as being void of any Iranian radar coverage. The precise routes had been selected by the aircrews to avoid overflying any population centers, military installations or police stations. The C-130s would operate under blackout and instrument-flying conditions at a nominal altitude of 1,000 feet, using their sophisticated on-board navigation systems and terrain avoidance gear to maintain their flight profile. The helicopter crews had chosen to fly at a lower altitude and maintain visual contact with the ground, checking for pre-selected landmarks and checkpoints to validate their timing and positioning.

There was one random Iranian sighting of a C-130 along the coastline about the time of the American penetration, but the sighting was categorized by Iranian officials (after a query from one Iranian station to another) as an Iranian aircraft and was disregarded.

The successful launch of all eight helicopters partially relieved the anxiety of the JTF, which was caused by earlier revelations that the *Nimitz* aviation detachment had not been flying the mission birds on the flight profiles or the mission duration that the JTF had requested months earlier. This came to light only after the helicopter force arrived on-board the *Nimitz*. The Navy had denied an earlier JTF request to put an inspection team on-board the *Nimitz* in early April, immediately following the Desert One survey. The JTF anxiety was further heightened by a mishap on the *Nimitz* hangar deck that coated all the helicopters with a fire retardant foam. The foam was immediately washed off, but concern lingered as to the possible gremlins it may have turned lose on the inner wiring, plastics and rubber that abounded in the assemblages of 25,000 parts that constituted each of the eight heavier-than-air flying machines called RH-53s.

The successful helicopter liftoff was considered a good start, after an auspicious preparation, and did much to make many members of the JTF believe that maybe, just maybe, the perennial weak leak might have been forged strong enough to make it last. Everyone sure hoped so!

In accordance with the mission "go-no-go" rules that had been hammered out and examined over and over again in planning sessions, exercises, rehearsals, and the more onerous, but essential, day-long "what if" sessions, it had been unanimously determined that a minimum of five choppers had to be operational at Desert One to continue the mission. The general odds were seven off the deck, six out of Desert One, and five operational out of the helicopter hide-site on Night-two. The word of "Eight off the deck!" was well received all around. Then everybody -- Washington, Wadi Kena, *Nimitz*, and Delta airborne in the C-130s -- relaxed somewhat and went into a subdued period of neutral buoyancy awaiting the next report.

Aside from the receipt of the code words indicating that the two forces had crossed the Iran coastline and the one stray Iranian spot report, the radio waves were quiet for more than 90 minutes. A radio report at 9:45 advised that helicopter Number Six was "down in the desert in board of the coast with a blade problem." The follow up report amplified the first. Number Six's instrument panel had shown a possible failure in the structural framework of one of the rotor blades. The crew, along with their flying partner (Number Eight), landed to check it out. The on-the-ground inspection showed that it was a true structural failure, not merely a bad warning light. Number Six was stripped of all mission-related and classified material and abandoned. It had gone down in an extremely desolate area immediately adjacent to a salt marsh; the odds against it being discovered by anyone with the means to communicate their find were astronomical. The crew of Number Six piled into Number Eight and continued on toward Desert One. Two hours into the mission, down to seven choppers, and still pressing on.

Fifty minutes later (10:40), the radio net announced the touch down of the first MC-130 at Desert One. Several miles out, the chief of the CCT element, Major John Carney, the man who had conducted the ground survey and implanted the spotting lights, activated his plantings from the cockpit of the lead MC-130. The pilot made a surveillance pass over the intended landing zone, scanning the area with the on-board Forward Looking Infrared (FLIR) system.

They spotted a small truck barreling along the road kicking up a plume of fine dust as he went. The pilot pulled off short of the truck and made a go-around for a second surveillance pass. This time the area was devoid of activity and he took the big machine around in a wide sweeping turn and lined up for the approach and touch down. Due to the physical placement of the FLIR, he had to retract it in order to lower the landing gear. Everybody in the cockpit had their eyes glued to thcir instruments or focused immediately ahead searching for details in the approaching touch down square, then shifting their eyes forward, scanning the desert floor ahead as the aircraft continued its roll-out after the touch down. The aircraft loadmaster began lowering the tail ramp a few seconds after the aircraft settled on the desert floor.

It was fully open by the time the aircraft came to a stop. The first to exit was the CCT element that was to control the landing and ground movement of the follow-on aircraft. Next came the two SF/Ranger roadblock teams, which headed in opposite directions toward their appointed locations at the northern and southern extremes of the two-mile-long straight stretch of desert road that divided the two parallel landing zones. No more than seven minutes had passed since the FLIR system had shown the area to be devoid of human activity, long enough for a vehicle traveling at 45 miles an hour to close with the intended roadblock checkpoints from more than four miles away.

Just as the southern roadblock team reached the road, a giant Mercedes passenger bus with its lights blinking between high and low beams came into sight in the darkness. One of the roadblock team raked the lower front end of the bus with M-16 fire while another launched a 40mm grenade. With these measures of persuasion, the driver quickly brought the vehicle to a shuddering stop. As soon as the vehicle had stopped, it was surrounded and an American soldier (one of driver/monitors) boarded the bus and, speaking Farsi, warned all the passengers to remain seated and calm and advised them that no harm would come to them if their obeyed. After a few minutes, the 44 passengers were led off the bus and seated on the side of the road, where all their actions could be observed.

Although the incident was unfortunate, it was not unexpected or unplanned for. In the event of such a situation, the JTF had made provisions to fly the detainees out of Iran to Wadi Kena and hold them there until the next night, when they would be returned to Iran and released at Manzariyeh, the extraction airfield southwest of Teheran. The plan called for any vehicles that were encountered to be moved off the road, hauled away, or burned as if involved in a nighttime accident. There was a general agreement that it would take in excess of 18-36 hours for the incident to be investigated, much less linked to a possible rescue effort. In any case, we would know of any investigation.

Only minutes behind the bus incident at the southern checkpoint, another vehicle with its headlights blazing came racing into the American security zone from the north. This dark mass was a medium-sized gasoline tanker truck. The same stopping tactic was employed, but the M-40 round ruptured the undercarriage of the truck and ignited the fuel. A giant flame quickly lit up the darkness around the northern checkpoint. The driver was not injured and quickly jumped from the truck cab, ran back up the road and scrambled into a small pickup truck, whose driver wasted no time in both flooring the little vehicle and doing a 180-degree turn, rapidly disappearing into the darkness. The JTF knew that gasoline smugglers used the road and, given the presence of the pickup truck and the quick action of the truck driver, the incident had the earmarks of this illegal activity, which meant that the driver and his associate were not likely to report their "loss" to the police.

The initial report of the incidents to reach the JTF staff at Wadi Kena was brief: "Have a bus and another vehicle and a truck. . . . The truck was a fuel truck and is burning." The report immediately caused great concern and it seemed that things were going from bad to worse with the "burning truck." However, once the follow-up report came in with a fuller picture of the circumstances, the level of concern diminished. The same reactions occurred in Washington as the JTF informed the Chairman, showing him the locations of the nearest towns and villages and police stations north and south along the road. The nearest village, which had neither a police station nor telephone lines, lay more than twelve miles away, too far for anyone to see the flames from the fuel truck since hills blocked the northern and southern approaches to the low lying terrain of Desert One.

Just as the situation at Desert One was being put to bed, the JTF (callsign Red Barn) received a message from the helicopter flight lead (Blue Beard One) relayed by Gravel Pit (Masirah): "[V]isibility markedly reduced. . . . unable to see the ground." This flight report was followed within five minutes by another relayed message: "Red Barn from Bluebeard One, two helicopters have landed in desert . . . zero visibility."

These messages again raised the level of concern in the bunker and prompted a review of the weather forecast. The JTF weatherman could not find anything in the weather data to indicate anything except clear conditions. After an agonizing 20-minute-plus wait, the JTF received a third message from Bluebeard One, "Red Barn Number One and Two airborne, proceeding Desert One." The JTF commander, anxious to obtain a fuller status of the helicopter force queried the flight leader, "Bluebeard One, this is Foreman (COMJTF), how many helicopters en route Desert One?" The response came back immediately, "Six for sure." The JTF believed there was an outside chance that there were actually seven helicopters en route to Desert One.

Where was the unaccounted helicopter? Twenty-minutes later, the JTF received another relayed message from Gravel Pit. This message, relayed from Bluebeard Five, reported he had "instrument problems" and was returning to the *Nimitz*.* The JTF Commander and staff accepted the report with resolution. Due to a lack of secure communications between the

---

* Number Five helicopter made it back to the *Nimitz* safely nearly eight hours after it took off. The helicopter maintenance team did not locate a specific mechanical problem and speculated that a temporary overheating situation had caused the foreboding problem indicators.

helicopters, Number Five did not know that Number Six was already out of the game. The JTF knew. Definitely down to six flyables. Mathematically, that was still enough to carry on, presuming all the remaining choppers reached Desert One in operational condition. Recognizing that time was slipping away, and that at least some of the remaining helicopters were very far behind schedule, General Vaught directed the staff to search for ways to make up the lost time.

It was now nearly midnight at Desert One and the CCT had finished laying out additional runway markers and had activated the mobile TACAN, a homing beacon, which the rest of the C-130 and follow-on RH-53s could use to locate Desert One. A few minutes before midnight, the sound of the approaching C-130s could be heard. The five aircraft -- one MC-130 acting as pathfinder and flight leader plus four EC-130s fully configured as fuelers -- began to stretch out for the approach and landing with a three to five-minute flight separation landing alternately on the two parallel landing zones. Both landing areas were now rigged with a touch down square and a directional marker. The road split the two areas and also was home to the Mercedes bus and its passengers, the CCT TACAN and the on-scene commander, Colonel Jim Kyle, who had been responsible for C-130 operations since November 1979. A mile north and south, the two road block teams were still in place, under the command of Lieutenant Colonel Jesse Johnson and Captain Wade Ishimoto, both Delta staff officers.

Shortly after midnight, a Delta force radio operator advised Red Barn, "C-130s on the ground, on schedule." Shortly after completing this transmission, Colonel Beckwith, the Delta Commander, asked Red Barn, JTF-Main, "What is status of Choppers?" Before Red Barn could reply, Gravel Pit (Misirah) responded with the information that Bluebeard One had requested a weather report at Desert One. Colonel Kyle responded, "Visibility five miles with negative surface winds." Bluebeard One responded, "Fifty minutes out and low on fuel." The news from the helicopters was a relief to the Desert One Command Post and the JTF HQs at Wadi Kena, who in turn relayed the information to Washington. The mission was still possible, although some calculated risks might have to be taken. The loss of the cover of darkness for the helicopter flight from the Delta drop-off point to the helicopter hide-site was the most significant. However, both locations were remote, it still would be extremely early in the morning, and the RH-53s bore no markings that would distinguish them from Iranian 53s.

By 12:30 A.M. on the 25th, the two Pathfinder MC-130s had departed Desert One so they could rendezvous with the two KC-135 tankers that would refuel them, and then recover at Masirah and ready themselves for the events of Night Two. The remaining four EC-130s (the helicopter gas stations) were positioned two on either side of the road with the refueling pumps ready, fuel lines extended, and the refueling personnel ready and waiting.

The original schedule had called for all of the choppers to be closing on Desert One now, but the choppers were nowhere in sight or hearing range. The best guess was at least another 30 minutes before the first one would arrive. There was no real word on the force status, except everyone knew that there was one helicopter down and abandoned in the south, one heading back to the *Nimitz*, and two some 40 miles out, with a big question mark on the remaining four. Hope had not expired -- if two could make it, the other four could, also.

Just before 1:00 A.M., the first two choppers arrived and were positioned for refueling. After the dust settled and Red Barn had been informed of the arrival, both Colonel Kyle and Colonel Beckwith headed to the lead chopper. They and the pilot with them moved away from the noise of the rotors of the choppers and the turbines of the 130s to a spot where they could hear each other talk. The pilot began by telling the two colonels that the flying conditions he just came through were the worst he had ever experienced. He described the flight through two "clouds." The fine powdery dust had robbed them of almost all visibility, reducing their vision to a small cone measuring less than the tips of the rotor blades, raising the temperature in the helicopters to the upward extremes, and forcing them to reduce speed from 120-130 knots to 80-90.

Charlie Beckwith, not being an aviator, did not fully relate to the information being imparted. However, Kyle, who had twice been called to the MC cockpit when they were flying through the clouds of dust, immediately understood the Marine's comments. The lead MC crew used its FLIR to see the ground below the aircraft, although their visibility in all horizontal directions was severely restricted. Although the MC-130 almost blithely flew through the two stacks of reduced visibility, Kyle recalled the sudden increase in the temperature and began to understand the stress and tension the helicopter crews had experienced. For the MC and EC crews, it was the insufferable heat that they associated with the two clouds, but navigation and flight positioning were not a problem. As the Marine pilot told the story, Kyle remembered "suspended dust," a phenomenon called a "Haboob." It was discussed in the initial JTF J-2 weather analysis issued in November. According to the historical climatological data, the phenomenon was not supposed to occur at this time of year, and, if it did, it was supposed to dissipate by nine to ten P.M. as the night air cooled.

However, it had occurred. It had not dissipated and it had trapped the helicopter crews in its disorientating vise for more than two hours. The first smaller cloud extended 45 miles across and took approximately a half an hour to penetrate. The helicopter crews had a small breather of about 30 minutes before they were swallowed by the second cloud. Although somewhat prepared for the effects of the second, based on their experience in the first, they were unprepared for the size of the second cloud. The second cloud extended more than a hundred miles across and required flying more than an hour and half. This was somewhat akin to driving a car in a blinding snowstorm on a dark, unlit, single-lane country road without the benefit of a yellow centerline or flanking white stripes to warn you of the cliff on one side.

As the pilot concluded his story, Kyle told him that contact had been made with the reception party waiting at the drop-off point south of Teheran and the weather there was clear and the winds calm. This news had a positive effect on the pilot and he headed off to converse with the other helo crew and compare notes while the refuelers began their job. When Kyle got back to the Command Post location, he learned that the balance of the helicopters were inbound with an expected arrival time of about 1:25 A.M. This was almost an hour and half behind the original schedule, but there were six choppers, enough to go!

By 1:30 A.M., all six choppers were on the ground at Desert One, and all but two were in the process of being refueled. Red Barn was pleased to receive the report, and directed Colonel Kyle to "consult with other element leaders and advise on the feasibility of launching with four helicopters now and the other two (the last arrivals) catching up later." Kyle was against splitting up the force and advised Red Barn, "Have six, will press on in forty minutes." Timing was going to be close, but the refueling and ground force transfer process was in process. Kyle estimated that he could have all six helos on their way shortly after 2:00 A.M. This would put them at the Delta drop-off site at 4:20 A.M., still under the cover of darkness, ten minutes to unload, fifteen to twenty minutes flight time to reach the helicopter laager site. The first rays of the morning sun would still be twenty minutes away. It was still possible, if there were no more "Murphies." There had been far more than were allowed, were normal, or were expected, but accomplishment of Night One's mission, "force insertion," was still possible.

Kyle headed towards the helicopter flight leader's RH-53, one of the last to land, to get his story and discuss the next leg of the mission. Beckwith had already closed with the pilot, Lt. Colonel Ed Sieffert, and asked the crucial question. He relayed the pilot's response to Kyle as they passed: "The skipper says the helicopter crews will be ready to go just as soon as the refueling and loading is completed." Acknowledging Charlie's words with a thumbs-up signal, Kyle climbed into the flight leader's helicopter and briefly reviewed the situation with Ed Seiffert, the flight lead and now helicopter mission commander. Seiffert told Kyle that the flight through the suspended dust had really drained the helicopter crews both physically and mentally, but their batteries were recharging fast and they would be ready to go as soon as the birds were gassed and the ground force on-board.

Back at Wadi Kena and in Washington, the situation looked better than it had in the previous several hours, and most were expecting the next message from Desert One to arrive in a half an hour or so, announcing the launch of the six helicopters for Teheran. Everyone was aware that the delay had cost valuable hours of darkness, and the helicopter crews and their security team might still be pulling their camouflage netting over the RH-53s and settling into their burrows as the sun came up, but this was not the time to quit.

All of these hopes and plans were frozen when the radios crackled in less than five minutes with the word from Desert One that Number Two chopper had a burned-out hydraulic pump, there was no spare available, and it was unsafe to fly the machine. Machines do not have hearts, but it had flown the previous two hours with the warning light on and had reached the failure point shortly after landing. Helicopter strength was down to five and, according to the "Go-No-Go" checklist, an abort situation, almost a final blow.

Long before this moment, they had reached a decision. There had to be six fit helicopters at Desert One or the mission could not go on. It would take five flyable aircraft to extricate everyone, hostages and rescuers alike, from the Embassy and Foreign Ministry in a single lift. It would be unthinkable to intentionally leave some people behind for a second lift -- not with the potential for several hundred, or several thousand, emotionally charged Persians surging toward the compound with hate in their hearts and guns in their hands.

Based on the exercise experience in the American deserts, it was assumed that one helo would break down at the hide-site, leaving five operational. To ensure this minimum number, six helicopters had to lift off from Desert One. If six had to be able to depart Desert One, then seven should be launched from the Carrier as one would probably not survive the first long leg from the carrier to Desert One. But Generals are paid to be prudent, so eight were launched from the carrier.

In spite of the data from the "what if" sessions and the logical conclusion that it was not prudent to go with just five machines (which would allow no leeway in tactics or no margin of flexibility in flight loads), the immediate question that came to mind, up and down the chain of command was, "Is there any way to continue?" On the desert floor, in the middle of blowing sand generated by the sixteen engines of the 130s and the downwash from the rotors of the five twin-engine operational helicopters, overlaid by the incessant noise from twenty-six turbines, this one question immediately subdivided into three more specific questions. Could the five helicopters carry a load intended for six? Could the size of the ground force be reduced to meet the weigh limitations of the remaining five machines? Were there any other options not previously examined?

Colonel Beckwith, who had carefully nurtured Delta force to maximize its capability against a still precisely undefined objective, quickly said no! The Marine flight lead knew the RH-53s were already overloaded even with six machines, and there was no way they could accept the weight of another 1,200 to 1,500 pounds each, which in turn would increase fuel consumption. Plus, there was the physical problem of space. It was already going to be crowded with 20 to 30 ground troops and their equipment in each machine. Without a decrease in the size of the ground force, four more bodies and equipment would have to be squeezed into each helicopter.

Even if the helicopter machine guns were removed and the driver-monitor force reduced to half its strength, the tradeoffs would not meet the necessary weight-fuel balance and also would deprive the force of these critical capabilities. In addition, there was the purpose of the mission: extract 53 American citizens from the hands of their captors and bring them home alive. Even with the machine guns removed, the driver-monitors cut in half, and Delta shedding non-essential equipment for the ride out, the four Embassy evacuation birds would have to lift a total of 38 personnel each, some of whom were likely to be wounded and require additional space. This was a questionable equation. A shuttle run between the soccer stadium and one of several emergency landing zones (Bus Stops) that had been selected from reconnaissance imagery was possible. This was an extreme alternative to a single shuttle run to the extraction airhead 35 miles south. Shuttles would consume valuable time and precious fuel. In addition, they would expose anyone left in the stadium to the wrath of the Pasdaran, the neighborhood militia, and the regular military as well as the fundamentalist elements of the population, all of whom would have a hour or more to react and marshal their strength against the stadium. The stadium had been selected as a temporary safe haven, not a second Alamo.

The JTF knew that they needed four fully-mission-capable birds out of the laager site the next night. Leaving Desert One with five, then shutting them down for 15 to 16 hours, as would have to be done, would increase the probably that no more than four, perhaps only three, would crank up for the next night's flights. Going into the mission objective area, the middle of an urban complex of eight million people, with anything else than the ability to lift the entire force and the freed hostages out simultaneously, was an invitation to disaster and widespread blood shed on both sides. Killing people was not the mission of the rescue force. B-52s, F-111s and the XVIII Airborne Corps could be very effective at doing that, but that was not the United States' national objective.

If the force had been faced with the same circumstances on Night Two, five choppers dropping to four (when the force was in Teheran), the gamble probably would have been taken; but, on Night One, the gamble was unwise and unnecessary. The hostages were not in imminent danger, the force had not been detected nor the plan compromised, and a withdrawal now would allow a relaunch at a later date. The three mission commanders agreed that it was an abort situation. The decision was communicated to Red Barn, who had voiced the question that everyone was thinking, "Is there any way to press on?" General Vaught did not second-guess the subsequent recommendation from the desert. He recognized, as did the field commanders, that going ahead with less extraction lift than required was not like clearing a field obstacle that, once overcome, is left behind and has no further impact on mission success. To go on without the required capability would be akin to carrying a millstone that was bound to get heavier. With a saddened but realistic feeling in his gut, General Vaught concurred with the field commanders and communicated his abort recommendation to General Jones. The CJCS accepted it sadly and immediately relayed the information to the Secretary of Defense and the President for concurrence and approval. The bottom line was that three separate mechanical breakdowns, totally unrelated to the helicopter crew proficiency or dedication, or to the unforecastable Hoboobs, had forced the termination of the mission.*

The National Command Authority accepted the decision of their field commander, who was already preparing to give the recovery order. The sick helicopter would be destroyed and left on the desert. The bus passengers were to be loaded onto the Mercedes and left for the next passing vehicle. The entire American ground force would come out on the four EC-130s after the tankers had topped off the five flyable helicopters. The helicopter flight crews would retrace their inbound route, hopefully without having to again endure the ordeal of the two Hoboobs. When the RH-53s got close to the coast, the *Nimitz* would steam north to meet them. Search aircraft would be launched to guide the weary crews to the *Nimitz* flight deck, while carrier-based fighters waited with crews poised to launch should an Iranian intervention action manifest itself. Now, to execute the extraction.

---

* Additional details of the events at Desert One are contained in two first-party books written by Charlie Beckwith (*Delta Force*) and Jim Kyle (*Guts to Try*). See Bibliography.

CHAPTER EIGHT
Extraction

As soon as the instructions from Red Barn reached the desert site, the wheels started turning. Delta began transferring themselves and their gear back to the C-130s. The helicopter crews checked their machines, laid out a reverse course and flight formation. The CCT began policing up the various runway markers, the TACAN, and the implanted beacons. The bus guard team and the two road block teams were to remain in place until the helos had launched and all other departure preparations had been made.

At this time, the JTF staff still considered the possibility that the ground force could be recovered to Oman, await the arrival of the three helicopters on-board the *Eisenhower*, reconstitute the helicopter force, and be prepared to relaunch in less than a week with an initial helo force of nine. It was about this time that the JTF radio came alive again with the word, "We have a crash. A helo crashed into one of the C-130s. We have some dead, some wounded, and some trapped. The crash site is ablaze; ammunition is cooking off."

The communiqué stunned the staff and started a whole different set of thought patterns and reactions. Alert the medical teams, standby to launch them to Wadi Kena, prepare for other extreme measures. Although momentary panic occurred among the occupants of the burning C-130, order at the desert site was quickly restored, and the evacuation orders given less than 10 minutes earlier were drastically changed. Leave all the choppers, leave the bus passengers, recover all the injured, get the wounded out on the first plane, account for all personnel and double check, and conduct a thorough search of the area for the unaccounted before the last plane leaves. Mentally salute those consumed in the flames.

After issuing these orders, General Vaught left the musty JTF command post, now, steaming with renewed energies, and went to his sleeping shelter to talk to General Jones privately and advise him of this latest event -- a true calamity. Twenty minutes after the initial report of the crash, the Desert One on-scene commander, Colonel Kyle, reported that the force was prepared for withdrawal and had all but eight personnel on-board. The eight included five members of the USAF C-130 flight deck crew and three Marines from RH-53 Bluebeard Three.

As reconstructed later, the crash occurred when Bluebeard Three was attempting to reposition out of the turnaround path of a C-130 that was preparing to depart. The RH-53 pilot became disoriented in the dust bowl created by the down wash from his rotors. As he lifted off, the chopper drifted to the right toward the invisible C-130. The tips of RH's 76-foot rotors blades hit the 38-foot-high tail of the C-130. The impact and torque of the rotors threw the RH-53, with rotors still flailing, forward and down, impacting the top of the C-130. The impact area was just above the rear of the forward crew compartment where the C-130's mid-air refueling plumbing was located. The combination of fuel fumes and electrical sparks from severed wiring in the same area created an immediate wall of flames that quickly trapped five of the C-130 flight crew in their small work area. The same wall of fire climbed up and back, feeding off the RH-53 fuel tanks which had ruptured upon impact with the C-130, turning the rear cabin of the helicopter into an incinerator. In spite of the rapidity of the conflagration, the helicopter pilot and his copilot, although severely burned, managed to get out the cockpit windows and slide to the ground. Similarly, the C-130 safety pilot, who was not in his seat and was positioned just at the break point, jumped down the stairs from the flight deck to the cargo area and escaped just as part of the bulkhead collapsed from the intense heat, blocking the stairway exit.

Another of the C-130 crewmembers, the radio operator, whose work position on the forward bulkhead of lower deck was in the area flooded by flames, was immediately enveloped. His call for help was heard by one of the Detachment A-SF troopers. Partially shielding himself from the flames with a field jacket, the SF soldier ran back and dragged the burning airman out of the flames to the rear of the plane. Another Det A trooper, witnessing the two struggling men, came back into the plane and pulled them both out of the dying airframe. In the meantime, the remainder of the USAF flight crew and the Delta and Det A troopers who had been in cargo compartment when the crash occurred had managed to evacuate the burning aircraft. The situation was soon made worse by the hundreds of rounds of ammunition and anti-tank rockets that began cooking off as the fire spread to the cargo area. The fumes and fuel fed the fire (and the potential for a larger explosion) from the nearly empty fuel bladders that occupied the full length and breadth of the cargo compartment.

Projectiles from the exploding munitions ripped holes in the three nearest helicopters leaving only two untouched. One of these was Number Two, the bird with the hydraulic failure. Fortunately, the flight crew of the C-130 parked immediately next to the burning RH-53/C-130 inferno had immediately taxied the aircraft away from the disaster site. Several of the Marine helicopter crews wanted to return to the helicopters to retrieve classified material. Because of the danger from the exploding munitions, the request was denied by the on-scene commander, Colonel Kyle. He judged the material not worth the risk of additional lives being lost. The Marines were ordered to assemble and account for their flight mates and then board the C-130s. The American force at Desert One was down to three flyable C-130s and one RH-53.

At 03:05 A.M., just prior to departing Desert One, Colonel Kyle radioed Red Barn and requested an air strike from the *Nimitz* be conducted on the helicopters to deny the machines and the classified material they contained from falling into the hands of the Iranians. The JTF staff had also been considering this possibility, and initially considered a similar option. The message from Kyle was acknowledged. After a review of the possible implications, COMJTF and General Jones judged that there was nothing to be gained, and the act of conducting "bombing" missions in Iran and the danger to the stranded bus passengers at Desert One and to the American hostages in Teheran did not warrant such a measure.

In the meantime, two MEDEVAC C-141 Starlifters that had been on radio alert via a SATCOM link in Saudi Arabia were given mission orders by the JTF to proceed to Masirah to receive casualties. Simultaneously, EUCOM was ordered to launch a MAC C-9 Nightingale "flying hospital" with a medical burn team from Germany to Wadi Kena to pick up the injured and move them to Germany for intensive care.

Jesse Johnson and Wade Ishimoto, the road block officers, were the last members of Delta to climb on aircraft number six, Jerry Uttaro's aircraft, the last American plane to leave Desert One. The two Special Forces soldiers were followed by John Carney, the CCT leader who had planted the infrared landing lights thirty days earlier. John had recovered all of the lights except one. This last light was purposefully left to serve as a take-off direction beacon for Uttaro's aircraft. The human cargo of C-130, tail number 1818, included many of the burn victims, the last of the road block teams, and the CCT personnel, which included several trained as Paramedics. They and several of the Delta troopers, also with medical training, administered to the wounded.

Throughout the situation, while everything seemed to be coming apart at the seams, General Vaught maintained a very cool, professional, and in-charge manner. He gave concise guidance to the JTF staff and precise orders to the on-scene commander at Desert One. As soon as the last JTF C-130 was airborne and the medical aircraft moving, he directed the two officers maintaining the Delta and the JTF communications logs to develop an integrated sequence of events. He also directed the NSA team to immediately report anything that indicated that the Iranians knew of the mission effort or were attempting to intervene with the flight of the C-130s out of Iranian airspace.

According to the flight projections, the C-130s would still be in Iranian airspace when the sun rose. The relatively slow-moving, unarmed transports would be easy targets for any Iranian fighter pilot. General Vaught reaffirmed that the Commander, Carrier Task Force (CTF 70), the *Nimitz*, was prepared to intercept any Iranian aircraft that attempted to interfere with the exfiltration of the 130s. Shortly before sunrise, the lead C-130 reported that they all were out of Iranian airspace, with one of the three aircraft dropping slightly behind because of the loss of one engine, and that all three aircraft had enough fuel to make the Masirah recovery site.

The three C-130s carrying their precious human cargo, some burned, most resolutely dejected, landed at Masirah at about 6:00 A.M. local in the full light of the new day. It was after dawn when the last C-130 touched down at Misarah. The two medical-configured C-141 Starlifters were waiting at the end of the runway, poised to depart once the injured were transferred. This did not take long, and then the process of double and triple accounting for all others members of the force that had departed Misarah fifteen hours earlier began. General Gast, the Deputy COMJTF, conducted a direct, face-to-face head count and identification check to confirm the correct physical status of the force. The results were grim -- eight dead, all aircrew (five USAF, three USMC, all consumed in the fire). Their bodies were unrecoverable at the time. Four others, severely injured with major burn damage, would require extensive treatment at the stateside DOD Burn Centers in San Antonio, Texas. All except the eight Americans consumed in the fire at Desert One were accounted for.

Upon receiving the head count, General Vaught initially directed that the force refuel and depart Masirah as soon as possible, destination Wadi Kena. Shortly thereafter, it was decided to fly all the ground force and the uninjured helicopter crews to Wadi on the second Medical Evacuation C-141s. Unlike everyone in the ground force, the C-130 crews had not had any opportunity to catch any sleep since they began their pre-mission preparations 16 hours ago. It was judged that it was an unwarranted safety risk to require them to fly another three-hour-plus mission. The C-130 crews were debriefed at Masirah and returned to their tent village to await staggered departures during the next 36 hours. The recovery at Wadi would allow the helicopter pilots to be interviewed concerning their flight through the Haboobs and to permit a reconstruction of the full sequence of helicopter events from carrier liftoff to refueling at Desert One. The four individuals who were severely burned were excluded from the debriefing process. After they were stabilized in Germany or Texas, as their medical condition dictated, they would be debriefed thoroughly.

Shortly after the last of the rescue force lifted off from Desert One, a small group of JTF cadre, in concert with a JCS General Officer, began drafting a statement for public release. The rule was that there would be no announcement until the force was clear of Iranian airspace and the basic facts of the abort and the flight mishap would be the outer limit of the announcement. There was to be no identification of any of the forces involved, nor the size of the force, nor the fact that DOD personnel (the four-man JTF advance team) was still in Iran. Several drafts were prepared and disappeared with the JCS General Officer.

At 7:00 A.M. EST on 25 April 1980, President Carter went on national television and announced the cancellation of the mission, stressing that the mission was a rescue effort, not an attack on the Iranian people. This was the first public acknowledgment of the mission, and the fact that it was attempted came as a surprise to the majority of the world, including the Ayatollah Khomeini and the Soviet intelligence apparatus.

The text of the Oval Office announcement is presented below:

THE WHITE HOUSE
STATEMENT BY THE PRESIDENT
ON
HOSTAGE RESCUE ATTEMPT
The Oval Office
(7:00 A.M. EST)

THE PRESIDENT: Late yesterday, I canceled a carefully planned operation which was underway in Iran to position our rescue team for later withdrawal of American hostages who have been held captive there since November 4th.

Equipment failure in the rescue helicopter made it necessary to end the mission. As our team was withdrawing, after my order to do so, two of our American aircraft collided on the ground following a refueling operation in a remote desert location in Iran. Other information about this rescue mission will be made available to the American people when it is appropriate to do so.

There was no fighting; there was no combat. But to my deep regret, eight of the crewmen of the two aircraft which collided were killed, and several other Americans were hurt in the accident.

Our people were immediately airlifted from Iran. Those who were injured have gotten medical treatment and all of them are expected to recover.

No knowledge of this operation by any Iranian officials or authorities was evident to us until several hours after all Americans were withdrawn from Iran.

Our rescue team knew, and I knew, that the operation was certain to be difficult and it was certain to be dangerous. We were all convinced that if and when the rescue operation had been commenced that it had an excellent chance of success. They were all volunteers; they were all highly trained. I met with their leaders before they went on this operation. They knew then what hopes of mine and of all Americans they carried with them.

To the families of those who died and who were wounded, I want to express the admiration I feel for the courage of their loved ones and the sorrow that I feel personally for their sacrifice. The mission on which this team embarked was a humanitarian effort and was not undertaken with any feeling of hostility toward Iran or its people. It has caused no Iranian casualties.

Planning for this rescue effort began shortly after the Embassy was seized. But, for a number of reasons, I waited until now to put those rescue plans into effect. To be feasible, this complex operation had to be the product of intensive planning and intensive training and repeated rehearsal.

However, a resolution of this crisis through negotiations and with voluntary action on the part of the Iranian officials was obviously then, has been and will be preferable.

This rescue attempt had to await my judgment that the Iranian authorities could not or would not resolve this crisis on their own initiative. With the steady unraveling of authority in Iran and the mounting dangers that were posed to the safety of the hostages themselves and the growing realization that their early release was highly unlikely, I made a decision to commence the rescue operations plans.

This attempt became a necessity and a duty. The readiness of our team to undertake the rescue made it completely practicable. Accordingly, I made the decision to set our long developed plans into operation. I ordered this rescue mission prepared in order to safeguard American lives, to protect America's national interest, and to reduce tensions in the world that have been caused among many nations as this crisis has continued. It was my decision to cancel it when problems developed in the placement of our rescue team for a future rescue operation. The responsibility is fully my own.

In the aftermath of the attempt, we continue to hold the government of Iran responsible for the safety and for the early release of the American hostages who have been held so long.

The United States remains determined to bring about their safe release at the earliest date possible. As President, I know that our entire nation feels the deep gratitude I feel for the brave men who were prepared to rescue their fellow Americans from captivity. And as President, I know that the nation shares not only my disappointment that the rescue effort could not be mounted because of mechanical difficulties, but also my determination to persevere and bring all of our hostages home to freedom.

We have been disappointed before. We will not give up in our efforts. Throughout this extraordinary difficult period, we have pursued and will continue to pursue every possible avenue to secure the release of the hostages. In these efforts, the support of the American people and of our friends throughout the world has been a most crucial element. That support of other nations is even more important now. We will seek to continue, along with other nations and with the officials of Iran, a prompt resolution of the crisis without any loss of life and through peaceful and diplomatic means.

Thank you very much.

END (7:07 A.M. EST)

Later that day, Secretary of Defense Harold Brown followed the President's lead with a similar statement, although with a decidedly different tenor. The concluding paragraphs of his statement are presented below:

[A]s you can see from this description, the mission was complex and difficult – but it was the judgment of the Joint Chiefs and myself that it was operationally feasible. This judgment was reached after a thorough assessment, which included many practice exercises. Our plan was carefully conceived and training exhaustive. The plan provided for the possibility of terminating the operation because of difficulties, such as mechanical failure or detection. The flight to the assembly point and the refueling (site) had been carried out successfully, but we concluded, based on established criteria, thoroughly considered earlier, that the number of helicopter failures reduced the chance of subsequent success to the point that dictated ending the mission.

I think you can understand why we felt that we had to try this difficult operation. In our opinion it represented the best course of action for getting our hostages out of Iran expeditiously. And it was also the course that raised the least risk of harming the Iranian people, and the least risk of causing instability in this troubled region.

We are disappointed that the mission failed, and saddened at the loss of our eight fellow Americans. But we will not rest until we have secured release of the hostages.

//Office of the Assistant Secretary of Defense (Public Affairs) April 25, 1980.//

***

Meanwhile, at Wadi Kena, the JTF staff was concerned with protecting the composition of the force from media exposure, an event that would have severely reduced the potential to launch another attempt in the near future with the same forces. The staff recommended to General Vaught that the various components of the force be dispersed as soon as feasible. This included Delta, the Rangers, the EUCOM Special Forces element, the driver-monitor teams, and all three of the C-130 elements.

General Vaught accepted the recommendation and directed that, after a quick debrief, Delta and the Rangers board the Night Two extraction C-141s that were standing by at Wadi Kena and begin retrograde back to America, but not directly to their home posts. Delta went back to one of the training sites for several days of decompression, which was normal after one of their type missions. The Rangers were swallowed up in the flow of a big Army exercise and rolled into their garrison post without any fanfare. The EUCOM Special Forces element also joined an ongoing field exercise and returned to their home post at its conclusion. After a brief rest, the air package was broken down into its individual mission specialties and the aircraft proceeded to their home stations via circuitous routing and several stopovers, recovering at irregular intervals within the normal training flow.

Within 36 hours, the JTF staff also departed Egypt, heading for Washington after a change of planes and uniforms in Europe. General Vaught, the force mission commanders, and the entire JTF staff knew that there would be boards of inquiry and a potential hunt for a scapegoat. They also knew that the mission was not over, had not been canceled, and that there was a tremendous need to get on with building a better and stronger capability for the next go around.

The C-141 lifted off the runway at Wadi Kena at 7:00 A.M. Egyptian time, climbed to a cruising height of 36,000 feet, attained a speed of Mach .7, and turned west toward North America. The aircraft was carrying the senior JTF Command Group and the rescue ground force. Each man was torn within himself. Each wanted to return and do it again and each wanted to put it far behind him.

The C-141 loadmasters passed out blankets, and people tried to sleep in the backward-facing coach class airline seats, without much success. The crew offered hot food, but no one wanted to eat. There was so much to think about and so little to say. The seven-hour flight was both too fast and too slow.

The aircraft touched down at Andrews Air Force Base, outside of Washington, at about 10:00 P.M. Eastern Standard Time, and rolled to a halt at a carefully isolated spot on the far side of the field. The site was normally reserved for dangerous or quarantined cargoes.

General Glenn Otis, a small man of tremendous intellect and big heart, the number two officer in the Army staff hierarchy, stood quietly outside the crew door and waited for it to open. Once it opened, he stepped briskly up the crew stairs and turned to the right, waiting for his eyes to adjust to the dim, artificial light. As his eyes focused in the semi-darkness, he was able to make out a dozen or more faces, eyes, arms, and detached forms. Some had eye patches, others had bandages visible on their arms and faces. These were the men closest to the carnage of the burning C-130 and RH-53. Several were those that went back into the inferno to carry others to safety. He went from man to man, shaking their hands, thanking them for trying. The entire visit took less than 20 minutes. General Otis and General Vaught then departed for the Pentagon. The balance of the C-141's human cargo quietly deplaned and walked to one of two C-130s waiting a short distance away to carry them to a small military post off the beaten track, where they would spend a few days before returning to their home stations and their families.

The JTF staff would arrive at Andrews in another aircraft some eight hours later. After a night with their families, they would be back in the Pentagon the next morning to begin the planning process again.

Meanwhile, the four-man advance party was still on the ground in Teheran. The plan had called for them to leave Iran with the rescue force on Night Two. This was no longer an option. However, they all had return airline tickets but no flight reservations. It was required that visiting foreigners possess round-trip tickets before being admitted to Iran, but the tickets held by the individual team members were "open," no departure date specified. Compounding their situation was the fact that the flight schedules were erratic,and it was the Iranian weekend, so the reservation offices were closed. Each made his own arrangements via his hotel. One of the four, the Iranian American airman, elected to remain behind to provide a safety net, should any of the other three be detained at the airport. Posing as a driver/luggage handler, he monitored the departures of the others from a distance in the crowded terminal until he had seen each of them successfully processed through customs and security. When the last of the three had departed safely, he called some family relatives, then took a bus to the small town where they lived. After visiting for a few days, he booked a flight out of Teheran, catching the plane a few days later.

Once the first member of the advance team reached a location with international phone access, he advised the JTF of the departure sequence and the fact that member number four had elected to stay behind. Based upon this information, the JTF coordinated with the EUCOM LNO to begin making plans for an emergency recovery mission similar to the one developed to support the Desert One Survey team.

The afternoon after the American force had withdrawn from Desert One (the 25th), officials from Teheran visited the landing site, accompanied by a mix of photographers and television crews. The Iranian official most prominent was Ayatollah Khakalki. He had earlier been categorized by HUMINT reports as being a particularly mean individual. Footage of the crash scene began to show up on Iranian TV that evening, and stills of the burned aircraft hulks and the charred remains of the U.S. servicemen consumed in the C-130/RH-53 crash began to flood the print media within days. Most, if not all, the classified material that had been left in helicopters seven and eight was removed under the direction of Khakalki and taken to Teheran for examination that afternoon.

Some of this information was used to locate the warehouse where the JTF's fleet of vehicles awaited the arrival of the rescue team. Other material, particularly the flight logs, maps and reconnaissance photography, was used by the militants to begin construction of their own version of the mission sequence. However, before going to "press" with their story, they added a set of questions, rife with hyperbole and innuendoes, in an effort to indict the Iranian secular political leadership and senior members of the Iranian military structure as co-conspirators in the American rescue effort. None of these accusations were true. However, one unilateral action, taken by the Iranian Government the day after the American attempt, aided the conspiracy theory. The Iranian Air Force was directed to destroy the remaining American aircraft and make the landing area unusable. This was intended to preclude a revisit by American forces. The Iranian Air Force conducted several bombing and strafing runs on the site. They succeeded in their mission. The site was so pitted with bomb craters that it would have been impossible to conduct any kind of fixed-wing flight operations. However, the IAF strikes also resulted in the death of at least one member of the Iranian Gendarme/Revolutionary Guards and the wounding of several others left to guard the desert site.

Back in the United States, the JTF was monitoring the news media coverage of the event; three situations arose from the focus and hunger for information and the proverbial scoop. One could have had dire consequences for the American advance team still in Iran. Less than 24 hours after the mission abort, a senior Pentagon official was detailed to provide a deep back-grounder to a reputable Washington print media journalist. Although the DOD spokesperson knew the plan in detail because of his administrative job, he apparently had no appreciation of the security implications of some of the material he disclosed. The backgrounder was printed in the *Washington Post* 48 hours after the abort and reprinted in the *Tehran Times* the next day. The JTF had not been privy to the fact that the backgrounder was to be given and, after discovering it in the *Washington Post*, was concerned about some of the revelations the article contained. None of the advance team had yet managed to leave the Iran, yet the article revealed the fact that the team had been inserted, how many there were, where they arrived from, and part of their cover information.

News of the *Washington Post/Tehran Times* article reached Colonel Beckwith on the 26th. He responded with a message to General Vaught:

O 262055Z APR 80
FM Delta/ADVANCE/BECKWITH
TO COMJTF//MG VAUGHT
SUBJECT: SAFE RECOVERY
1. MY MOST IMMEDIATE CONCERN AT THIS POINT IS TO ASSURE THE SAFE RECOVERY OF [LAST TEAM MEMBER OF SCOUT ELEMENT].
2. I WAS APPALLED TO LEARN THAT THE EXISTENCE OF [SCOUT TEAM] WAS DISCOVERED BY THE NEWS MEDIA AND REFLECTED IN WASHINGTON POST AND TEHRAN TIMES. THIS DISCLOSURE SERIOUSLY JEOPARDIZES THE MISSION AND EVERY EFFORT MUST BE MADE TO PREVENT FURTHER DISCLOSURE OF SUCH INFORMATION, AND TO SAFELY RECOVER [LAST MEMBER OF SCOUT TEAM].
3. RESPECTFULLY REQUEST THAT THE FOLLOWING BE DONE:
A. [REMAINS CLASSIFIED]
B. [REMAINS CLASSIFIED]
C. [REMAINS CLASSIFIED]
4. I AM PREPARED TO SUPPORT THE EFFORT TO SAFELY RECOVER [REMAINING SCOUT] WITH EVERY ASSET AVAILABLE TO DELTA.
RVW 26 APR 2010
BT

A replay of the preparatory actions that were implemented to support the emergency extraction of the Desert One Survey team was begun. However, without definite information from the remaining scout, actions could only proceed to a certain point. The JTF confirmed the *Tehran Times* side of the equation when one of the advance team members angrily threw a copy of the *Times* down on the J-2's desk, with the comment, "Who the hell is the idiot that tried to get us killed?" This was yet another example where an early rush to "tell the story" could have had disastrous consequences for the team and the United States. Fortunately, the Iranian security apparatus was less than efficient. The last of the four members of the DOD scout team, Trooper Sam, safely reached American soil under his own power ten days after the mission abort. The MC-130 emergency recovery capability was kept "on tap," ready to launch, until word was received of his successful exfiltration.

***

The decision to abort the mission and the subsequent helicopter/C-130 crash quickly labeled the entire mission a failure, with the net result of worldwide press speculation on the events at Desert One and the preparations that preceded it. The media focused on the scenes of the burned out hulks of the two aircraft and began their own re-creation of the mission. The Iranians also were busy trying to re-create the story from their own perspective. Both were aided in their efforts by the classified material left on-board the helicopters. The Iranians created a book with reproductions of some of the U.S. imagery and map products showing various key locations, which they put on sale on the streets of Teheran. One of the major U.S. news services managed to buy some of the original classified material within five days of the withdrawal including a map of Teheran that showed a series of "Bus Stops" and aerial photographs of these locations.

The "Bus Stop" locations were, in fact, emergency landing and recovery sites for the helicopters, should any of them run into mechanical problems or suffer weapons damage after they left the sports stadium and were forced to land short of the extraction airhead south of the city. By reference to the bus stop number, another helicopter (and, in a few cases, a C-130) would be able to land and pick up the stranded Americans, while an orbiting AC-130 Spectre gunship would employ its arsenal of highly accurate weapons systems to keep any hostile ground force at bay.

The media continued to exploit the death scenes from the desert, including several showing high-ranking Iranian religious leaders (who were also the Iranian political leadership) poking at the charred remains of the American aviators. Others pictures showed the same Clerical leader holding clear plastic bags containing the E&E money left on the helicopters and the

"Bus Stop" map. One of the most critical pieces of data found by the Iranians was a hand-drawn sketch prepared by one of the helicopter crewmembers. It showed the location of the warehouse where the vehicles that the ground force was to use in their approach to the Embassy and the Ministry of Foreign Affairs were stored. Fortunately, the advance party had sanitized the site of any information relating to them, the previous owner of the vehicles, or the unwitting agent who had leased the warehouse and its small compound to the CIA survey team months earlier.

Meanwhile, back in Washington, both the U.S. Senate and House of Representatives committees that deal with the affairs of the Armed Forces called the JCS Chairman, General Jones, General Vaught, Colonel Beckwith and others of the rescue force to testify before their committees.

Overseas, politicians from several of the allied nations publicly expressed their indignation and disappointment at not having been consulted beforehand. However, privately, the JTF received confidential communiqués from various military elements of these same countries expressing sorrow at the American losses and admiration for launching the attempt. One of these arrived only hours after the force recovered at Masirah. It came from some British airmen serving with the Sultan of Oman's tiny Air Force. Two members of the RAF detachment quietly drove a lorry near one end of the small row of American tents alongside the empty Misarah runway and deposited two cardboard boxes in the dirt. Both cases contained cold beer. Bass Ale! One of the cases had a hand printed message: "To you all from us all for having the guts to try." More formal messages arrived in the next three days from several of the European counter-terrorist forces, including Germany, France, Great Britain, and Italy. The most unique was in the form of an editorial in a Japanese-language newspaper addressed to the leaders of Japan. In essence, it respected the willingness and bravery of America to undertake such a venture alone, but warned that Japan should be wary of following such an American lead in other things too closely, lest Japan accept risks it was not prepared to pay for.

During the immediate post-mortem period, the JTF staff essentially divided into four elements. The public element was involved in presenting testimony as requested by the Senate and the House. A behind-the-scene team was busy compiling the information needed to support the public element and document the events. A third element, essentially the slightly expanded JTF intelligence team, was busy monitoring the situation in Iran and attempting to track the hostages who had been dispersed throughout Iran two days after the mission abort. The fourth element consisted of staff members who were emotionally drained by the impact of the abort and burned out by their non-stop commitment to mission preparation that had consumed most of their waking hours for the last five months. This small group moved on to other assignments, and over a period of two weeks were replaced with a largely new team of equally dedicated individuals. Of the original JTF cadre, only the Commander, General Vaught, the Chief of Staff, Colonel Jerry King, the EUCOM and PACOM LNOs, Major Magee and Lt. Col. Jim Keating, and the intelligence cadre continued into the subsequent mission-planning efforts.

In early June, as the Congressional hearings were winding down, the Chairman, with the concurrence of the SECDEF, convened a multi-service panel of senior military officers to examine the events of the mission and the preparations leading up to it. The fundamental guidelines given the panel were threefold:

1) Examine the events surrounding the abort and the mission failure, and determine if there was any gross negligence within the JTF;
2) Take a positive approach;
3) Identify areas needing improvement and make recommendations as to how the deficiencies might be corrected.

Named after its chairman, Admiral Holloway, a retired former Chief of Naval of Operations, the panel came to be called the Holloway Board. Its membership included six general/flag rank officers, three active duty and four retired. Its service composition included one Navy officer -- Admiral Holloway, a Navy aviator, and one Marine, Major General Al Gray, a well-rounded infantry officer with an extensive background in intelligence and raiding operations. Two members were USAF officers -- retired Major General Leroy Manor, the Commander of the Vietnam POW raid into Son Tay in North Vietnam in 1971, and Brigadier General Piotrowski who as a junior officer had served in Laos in the Air Commandos in the late 60s. The board was round out by two Army officers -- retired Lieutenant General Sam Wilson, former Director of DIA at the time of the tree-cutting incident at the UN compound on the Korean DMZ in 1976, and Major General James C. Smith, a U.S. Army Aviator.

The board interviewed virtually all the members of the JTF staff and reviewed all the records, and, after two months of investigation and analysis, submitted its report to General Jones in late August. In the meantime, JTF planning and preparations for a second effort continued, and were back on a 12 to 14-hour work schedule within three days of the April mission abort.

PART III

CHAPTER NINE
Planning Resumed

By the first week in May, the second-round planning effort was going full bore. However, some critical ingredients had changed for the better. Mainly, the services opened their checkbooks and their manpower pools. The events of April 24/25, 1980, had shown that, even with the best and most dedicated "can-do" attitude, a force could not always succeed with "make-do" capabilities. In addition, the ramp-up time expended in the first effort showed that a well-trained and standing capability was essential to gaining control of a situation quickly, rather than being manipulated by the adversary.

Behind the secured doors of the JCS-SOD spaces, the modestly reinforced JTF headquarters cadre, now numbering 32 souls, continued to exist, but were hidden behind a triple-reinforced wall of security. The immediate shield was a small group of staff officers that constituted the recently created Joint Test Directorate (JTD). The JTD became the window to the rest of the Joint staff and the Service staffs. Its mission was to coordinate the development of new capabilities and strengths that the JTF could draw upon. The JTD analyzed the options conceived by the JTF planners and developed capabilities which appeared to have both broad and special utility. This unfettered, somewhat open-ended approach was essential. Due to the dispersion of the hostages, the rescue challenge was more complicated now than it had been during the first go around, and it was much too early to decide on a specific set of requirements or solutions, or, conversely, to discard any idea that provided an increased capability.

Within the JTF, responsibility for operational planning passed to a team of "not quite new" planners. The leader of this group was one of the officers that had constituted the nefarious "what if" team that had challenged many of the JTF planning and tactical assumptions. Thus, the knowledge of the previous months of operational preparation was available without having to defend any previous assumptions or actions. The former Devil's Advocates now had the responsibilities their predecessors had borne for so long.

In early May, General Vaught called the JTF and the newly formed Joint Test Directorate (JTD) staff together in the operational setting of the Delta compound. He outlined the new organizational structure and stressed that the JTF was in business, as long as the hostages were still being held. What he did not tell the assembled leaders and planners was just as significant. Less than three days after the force left the charred remains of eight Americans on the bleak and windswept Iranian desert, a grateful and honorable President (after thanking the members of the ground forces for their dedicated efforts on behalf of all Americans) passed on a few quiet commands. His words were directed to a small cluster of men gathered on the tarmac at the Delta recovery site. To General Vaught, he said, "Get ready to go again." To the senior member of the State Department that was part of this small knot of men, the President said, "You do everything you can to resolve this situation via diplomacy." He then turned to the third man among the inner circle, standing there on the gray-black tarmac, a senior civilian intelligence official, and said, "And you provide them the intelligence they need to do their jobs."

General Vaught did not relay the details of this event to the men standing before him. He did not need to. His audience knew that the need for a rescue capability would exist as long as the fifty-three Americans remained hostages. General Vaught then reviewed the broad options that he felt were available to the Joint Chiefs, should DOD be called upon to go again. Many were a larger variation of the earlier options, with some substitution or addition of forces as the potential level of anticipated Iranian resistance grew. In all the scenarios examined, it was clear that, if the United States was to recover the American captives alive, the operational forces of JTF 1-79 would be tasked to accomplish the surgical aspects of the mission. However, there were key deficiencies that needed attention: a better helicopter capability, better ground intelligence, and an improved secure communications capability.

In mid-May 1980, less than three weeks after the tragedy at Desert One and within two weeks of the Presidential directive to prepare the force to go again, the majority of JTF Air Force flight crews and the JTF staff were assembled in Washington. The setting was the fourth floor of the E-Ring in the Pentagon, in a large, multi-purpose reception room adjacent to the office of the Secretary of Defense (SECDEF). The room was normally reserved for high-level Secretary of Defense Protocol functions. For most of the attendees, this would be their only visit to the well-appointed room, the outer wall of which was punctuated by four windows providing an unobstructed view of the Potomac, the Tidal Basin, and the Jefferson Memorial. None of the 120 uniformed attendees had the opportunity to take in the view, but the bright morning sunlight gave the room a pleasant, open feeling, substantially different from the dust and flame of Desert One. Although the impending event was somewhat anticlimactic, given the events of the last three weeks, the atmosphere was one of a new beginning and better sailing.

A simple, unadorned podium was positioned in one corner, with a small four-inch high platform behind it. The door to the SECDEF's office was immediately behind and only a few feet distant. The five rows of chairs were the straightback, concert type that could become uncomfortable, but the pending event would not last long. Next door, in the SECDEF's office, a smaller meeting was underway. There were less than nine people in that room: Harold Brown, the SECDEF; General Jones, the Chairman; General Vaught; two Army SF sergeants; one USAF Airman; one Department of the Army Civilian; the President of the United States and Commander-In-Chief, Jimmy Carter; and the Presidential photographer. President Carter was congenial and warm to the four men who had risked all without seeking gain. Some small talk ensued, but the primary function was the presentation by the President of the highest intelligence award the nation could bestow to each of the four "scouts." The ironic part of this recognition was that it would, for security reasons, go no further than this room until after the four men had left the service, some years later. Most of those waiting in the adjacent reception room did not know the four, or their names, and it would remain that way for a long time.

After shaking hands and offering his thanks to each of the four, President Carter followed General Vaught into the adjoining reception room, where General Vaught announced his entry with the words: "Gentlemen, the President of the United States." The sea of uniforms, mostly Air Force Blue with a smattering of Army and Marine Green and a handful of Navy, arose in unison, coming to rigid attention. Reflecting his Navy experience, the Commander-In-Chief responded to their show of respect with a hardy "As you were!" He moved to the podium, taking the one step up provided by the small platform while the assemblage resumed their seats, although with a marked degree of attentiveness. The President was smaller in stature than most had envisioned him, but his radiant smile and quiet composure identified him as a unique person. His brief talk reinforced the perception that he was an unassuming, quietly religious person sincerely concerned with the well being of his "flock" and deeply grateful to this particular group for their contributions to the nation. There was regret for the loss of the eight lives at Desert One, but none for launching the effort to recover fifty-three others. He expressed his admiration and thanks to the force for having the guts to try.

At the conclusion of his talk, the President stepped down from the podium and came forward to shake hands with General Vaught and some of the senior officers sitting in the front row. General Vaught moved more quickly. He gently but firmly guided the President to the first person seated in the first row, and then propelled the Commander-in-Chief along the first row, the second, the third, forth and fifth, introducing each person by name and role. Mr. Carter shook hands with each until reaching the last person in the last row, who was also guarding the exit door. Mr. Carter turned as he reached the door, quietly waved to the standing figures, and softly said,

"God Bless you all." He exited, surrendering himself to his Secret Service escort who were waiting on the other side of the door.

***

JTD efforts in May and June 1980 were directed toward reviewing and cataloging all the basic skills and capabilities that might be required. The requirements were based on the new picture that the JTF Intelligence team was assembling about the scattered hostage-detention sites. These sites ranged from private homes to religious schools and former consulate locations. However, there were some common characteristics about each which led the JTF to develop and test several sets of capabilities and tactics that could be applied, regardless of the specific characteristics of each location. The scope of these capabilities ranged across virtually every area of support and operations. They extended from intelligence surveillance and communications, to new tracking techniques and weapons, special training and the fielding of a whole new set of aviation and scout capabilities that were non-existent in November 1979.

Most of the capability development and training operations were carried out under the project designator "Honey Badger." This was the unclassified term applied to the wide-ranging JTD capabilities-enhancement program. The Army and Air Force signed up to provide funds to cover the training and testing costs, a far cry from the "take-it-out-of-hind" era of 76-79, and the "trust me, the check's-in-the-mail" months of November 79 through May 80.

Many of these capabilities were developed and tested without regard to a specific rescue option. The effort was capabilities-focused and accomplished as part of the layered approach to maintain security. The basic goal was to develop a much broader and substantially more robust set of capabilities than existed on either 4 November 1979 or 24 April 1980. A wide range of capabilities and material were developed, refined, modified and tested. These resources included a range of aircraft modifications, different types of helicopters, vehicles, radios, night-vision equipment, breaching techniques, clothing, batteries, power sources, parachutes, extraction techniques, and emergency medical capabilities. The effort even entered into the world of shipboard helicopter loading and launching techniques. Waterproof maps and charts designed to provide survival and land navigation information in addition to the basic map presentation were designed and re-created.

However, the basic JTF mission responsibilities remained essentially the same. Delta was focused on any ground missions dealing with the Embassy or other high value target complexes. The EUCOM Special Forces continued to focus on the MFA and several smaller, isolated targets in the urban areas. The Rangers had responsibility for seizure and security operations at all major target complexes, including more than a half dozen airfields and military installations. All aviation planning was in the hands of the 1st SOW and a new Army aviation team that was being formed.

These training enhancements primarily involved Army and Air Force elements, although the Navy had begun creating its own version of Delta with a strong maritime bent. Eventually, SEAL Team Six was the outgrowth of this Navy effort. The catalyst for this Navy initiative was a Navy Commander by the name of Richard Marchinko. Commander Marchinko had been the principal Navy Special Warfare (SPECWAR) liaison officer to the JTF during the first attempt, and had played a key role in developing and perfecting some of the tactical deception techniques to be used on Night Two.

Actual military planning for specific rescue options was extremely tightly controlled. Information on capabilities flowed from Honey Badger and its smaller cousins inward through the JTD to the JTF. The JTF was now closeted in an expanded work area carved out of real estate commandeered from an unsuspecting JCS staff element that had been located behind the back wall of the original JTF/SOD spaces. In turn, direction flowed outward via several channels, depending on the need, function and activity. It might go to a specific coordinating element in the Army or Air Force staff, and then out as an Army or Air Staff requirement. It might flow through the JCS J-3 to one of the Unified or Specified commanders (EUCOM, PACOM, SAC or MAC), or it might flow down the JTF communication structure, which remained intact and alive throughout the entire effort, including the turbulent period of the postmortem and inquiries. The JTF C-3I structure, among other responsibilities, continued to provide the JTF operational forces with a continuous intelligence flow and a secure means of coordinating specialized training.

On the 3rd of June, General Vaught briefed the JCS on the ongoing JTF mission-concept development and the force preparation measures. At the conclusion of the briefing, the attendees concurred with the need, and his recommendations, to substantially increase JTF aviation capabilities several fold. The most fundamental change was the addition of an Army helicopter force composed of 30 UH-60/Blackhawks and more than a dozen CH-47/Chinooks, plus the fielding of the Air Force MH-53 long range helicopter capability.

The Air Force action involved the creation of a new, nine-aircraft, long-range, night operations penetration squadron composed of the newly produced MH-53s (Pave Lows). The new unit would be part of the 1st Special Operations Wing at Hurlburt Field, Florida. There also was a requirement to improve and expand the USAF Combat Controller force, tactical weather support capability, and combat medical support. These capabilities already existed as separate entities, but were trained to different standards, equipped differently, and usually operated separately. In sum, there was a requirement to develop inter-operability between the various operational elements, raise the training standards, upgrade equipment, and ensure communications interoperability across the board. There was no quick fix. Action was begun on all fronts, simultaneously.

Immediately following the JCS decision of June 3rd, the Army began action to create its mid-range special operations helicopter force. The core elements of this capability were created by transferring helicopters, flight crews and maintenance crews out of the 101st Aviation Group of the 101st Airborne Division (Air Assault) which was just being equipped with the new UH-60 (Black Hawk) helicopter. Although not quite as capable in range or night navigation as the USAF Pave Low, the Blackhawk provided a substantially better organic capability to the Army Special Operations Forces than they had ever had. Together with the Pave Lows, they provided the nation an unsurpassed vertical lift insertion and extraction capability. Members of the 101st cadre were briefed into the ongoing JTF program at the Pentagon on the 29th of July, and the JTF C-3I secure communications-teletype network was extended to Fort Campbell the next day.

Another JTF effort revolved around an initiative to create a helicopter capability that could be rolled on and off a C-130 aircraft and be immediately flyable without any assembly. One of the earliest options was to modify the Army's OH-58 helicopter to meet the requirement. During a meeting in late July in Dallas, Texas, one of the JTF staff officers mentioned the requirement to Texas businessman Ross Perot, who had again come forward after the abort and offered to assist the JTF in any manner possible. Perot was familiar with a wide range of aviation industry officials. After a short telephone call and within 90 minutes, a Vice President from Bell Helicopter, a former Army aviation brigadier general, was in Perot's office. He listened to the JTF idea. The idea called for compensating for the height of the OH-58 by temporarily swapping out the regular skids for a shorter set, thereby dropping the overall height of the OH-58 by six to eight inches. This would allow an OH-58 to be loaded onto a C-130 or a C-141 without being dismantled. Without hesitation, the Bell VP asked to use Perot's phone. A brief call alerted a team of Bell engineers. Less than three hours later, a team of engineers and fabricators went to work and, in 48 hours, the JTF had a C-130 at the Bell plant where a load/unload test was accomplished under the supervision of a JTD Honey Badger officer. The test proved the feasibility of the short skid concept as an emergency expediency. Six sets of skids were fabricated and added to the growing stockpile of capabilities.

However, a better solution to the helicopter roll-on/roll-off requirement came out of General Vaught's Korean and Vietnam experiences. He recalled that the Hughes OH-6 helicopter, although relatively short-ranged, was small enough to meet the roll-on/roll-off requirement and had a tremendous power-to-weight lift ratio. The aircraft, nicknamed the Loach (Light Observation And Command Helicopter), had been retired from active service several years earlier. After a series of phone calls, General Vaught learned that a small Army National Guard depot in Pennsylvania still had six in storage. He and two other members of the JTF staff flew to the little airfield and were greeted by the civilian "custodian" of the aircraft, who took a personal and professional pride in ushering the JTF trio into the hangar and the presence of the robust "Little Birds." One look told the visitors that a true bonanza had been found. The machines were in almost mint condition. The custodian was quick to point out that he had one ready to fly right then. A brief test flight was conducted, with the custodian at the controls. The flight confirmed General Vaught's remembrance of the lift capability and maneuverability of the airplane. The JTF trio left shortly thereafter, heading back to the Pentagon. General Vaught left the custodian with his thanks and a request to prepare the miniature fleet for return to operational status. This was accomplished within five days, and Army Special Operations Aviation was born.

Subsequently, another dozen of the robust little machines were found at another National Guard unit and transferred to the active duty force and operational status. Eventually, a total of 20 OH-6 helicopters were transferred from the National Guard (NG). Eight NG instructor pilots, three other NG officers, and 19 NG enlisted personnel volunteered to support the aircraft transfer. The mission of the Guardsmen volunteers was threefold: train and qualify 25 active duty army aviators; train 18 crew chiefs; and provide organizational maintenance support during the initial training cycle.

At the same time, the Military Airlift Command (MAC) was tasked by JCS to train eight additional C-141B aircrews in low-level night operations and blackout landing techniques. The C-141B was a modification to the original C-141 airframe that increased the load capacity, extended the fuselage length from 145 feet to 168 feet, and added an in-flight refueling capability. MAC was given one month to have the aircrews qualified. In the meantime, the majority of the JTF aviation effort during July was directed at acquiring and training the new fleet of OH-6 "Little Birds."

The 101st Airborne Division (Air assault) was tasked to provide 20 volunteer aviators with certain skills. Five other aviators who met the qualifications were drawn from other units. During the initial training and screening, special emphasis was placed on the candidates obtaining maximum performance from the aircraft under maximum gross weight conditions. This initial flight qualification phase was completed on 9 July 1980. All twenty-five successfully completed the flight qualification phase.

Joint training was conducted on the 10th and the 11th using the range facilities at Fort Huachuca, Arizona. The training concentrated on developing skills in maximum performance operations under night-flying conditions. During this phase, the 1st SOW, other USAF elements, and Delta provided CCT and Pathfinder support and assistance in developing standardized procedures and night operations techniques.

The operational concept for the "graduation" exercise was conceived on 10 July and called for some intricate aerial and assault maneuvers under blackout and hostile-fire conditions supporting a rescue effort. Tasking was established on the 14th. On the 15th, permission was granted to use a quasi-inactive airfield in Texas as the exercise site. Ground and air reconnaissance of the complex was conducted on the 16th, and the final detailed Operation Order was published on the 18th. The "graduation" exercise was successfully conducted on 20-21 July, and the after-action "Hot Wash" confirmed the value of this new aviation asset.

***

While the JTF and the JTD were engaged in reconstituting a new rescue capability, factional in-fighting continued in Iran. Within weeks of the Desert abort, the Islamic fundamentalists won full control of the Parliament (Majlis) and Ayatollah Mohammed Behesti, a former Chief Justice and advocate of the continued retention of the hostages, was elected Speaker. Less than thirty days later, on the 22nd of June, Bani Sadr, the last vestige of secular rule and western influence, was declared unfit for office and was stripped of the Iranian Presidency. An order for his arrest on charges of treason followed. Sadr escaped to Paris and went into a self-imposed exile. However, factional turmoil continued in Teheran and a new round of executions began. A week after Sadr was deposed, Behesti and 70 other fundamentalists were killed when a massive explosion rocked the headquarters of the Islamic Party during a meeting of the party leadership. On 24 July, the former Prime Minister, Ali Mohammed Ali Rajai, was elected to the Presidency. His tenure was short. On August 30th, he and the new Prime Minister were both killed in another explosion. Akbar Hashemi Rafsanjani, the Speaker of the Majlis, came to be the next center of power, eventually rising to the position of President.

***

By the middle of August, the JTF/Joint Test Directorate had developed and refined a variety of capabilities to assault a wide spectrum of dispersed locations simultaneously. It was believed by every member of the JTF staff and most of the leadership of the operational forces, and confirmed by General Jones, that, should the Iranians begin killing hostages, the newly created Rapid Deployment Joint Task Force (RDJTF) would be the major instrument of U.S. military power. The RDJTF had been created in reaction to the Soviet invasion of Afghanistan the previous December, and to the possibility of a Soviet move south to the Gulf. The RDJTF included virtually all the American immediate reaction forces located in the continental United States, including the XVIII Airborne Corps and the aviation assets of Ninth Air Force. The JTF 1-79 staff believed that the RDJTF, with the assistance of the Navy/Marine Indian Ocean Task Force and SAC bombers, would be given the mission of neutralizing the Iranian armed forces, while JTF 1-79 would be given the mission of assaulting the known and suspect hostage locations.

Meanwhile, the JTF continued to build the numbers of executable (i.e. trained and rehearsed) rescue options. They were catalogued under a third security layer, nicknamed "Snowbird." Nearly a dozen "Snowbird" options were developed, refined, and rehearsed by early fall, 1980. They ranged in force size according to the intended target category and were designed in packages to be used in part or total, or combined to match a new or modified threat situation.

Inherent in the development of these force options was the underlying assumption that the intelligence picture would have matured enough to reliably identify where most, if not all, of the American hostages were located. The period from May through July was marked by an intense DOD/JTF effort to develop reliable and active intelligence on the hostage locations. Some of these initiatives were technical and supported by the National Security Agency. These technical initiatives were coordinated by an highly qualified, imaginative NSA engineer, Mr. Bob Spence, who had been teamed with the NSA Liaison officer, Commander Bud Fosset, to provide technical expertise to match Fossett's operational background. Spence was open-minded to investigating virtually any solution and, through his dedication, several unique communications collection techniques were developed, tested, and employed. Other collection efforts were more human-source focused and relied on the CIA. During this three-month period, the CIA vainly tried to obtain reliable HUMINT on the hostages from inside Iran, but to little avail. The military service HUMINT agencies attempted to do the same, essentially with similar negative results.

Operational DOD commands are normally restricted from performing this type of clandestine Human intelligence collection activity, except in direct support of ongoing military operations. However, based on the lack of reliable conventional HUMINT information, the JTF strove to develop a DOD operational support and reconnaissance capability similar to that employed in March and April (i.e., the EUCOM reconnaissance team and the Delta support team).

General Vaught had convinced the Army Chief of Staff and the Chairman of the need for this capability, and gained authority to quietly, but officially, create this very essential eyes-and-ears element. Initial efforts to build this capability began within the JTF in early May, but, by late May, the function was separated out and a compartmented program established. June and July were spent identifying and screening possible members of the force.

On 31 July, General Vaught sent a memorandum to General Jones (and the Secretary of the Army) requesting funding for the new DOD force. The essence of the memorandum is presented below:

Subject: Request for Funding **31 July 1980**

1. To assure an effective in-country support structure for the rescue force, I directed the formation of a small operations group (which would infiltrate) by various means, into Iran. This small, hand picked group is tasked to train, plan and be prepared to conduct a wide variety of operations to enhance mission success and permit the primary rescue force to focus on its primary mission rather than ancillary tasks.
2. The force has been assembled at a secure training site and is prepared to commence intensive training. However, the request for equipment, weapons, and ammunition submitted through Army channels has been deferred by the Army pending authorization of approximately [$ xxxxxxxxxx] to fund the expenditure.
3. [This paragraph remains classified.]
4. Recommend that [$ xxxxxxxxx] be made available to the Army as a matter of urgency to permit training to commence.

James B. Vaught
Major General, USA

The funds were approved within a week and field training of this crucial "support" force began in earnest. (Another sorely needed capability was being built.)

***

The Honey Badger Training (and test) Program had been developed by dissecting the major SNOWBIRD Option I-IX training tasks. These tasks were then assigned to specific mission units, training areas identified and dates assigned. The initial training programs were designed to perfect individual and unit skills and integrate these during joint-force training. Initially, JTF forces trained at Dugway Proving Grounds, Utah, White Sands Missile Range, New Mexico, and Fort Huachuca, Arizona.

Training Exercise PHOENIX was one of the first joint exercises. It was designed to provide a vehicle to consolidate all Honey Badger capabilities. It did not attempt to depict a given scenario. Rather, it served to bring the entire force together to exercise joint tasks and concepts. The major lessons learned served as the planning basis for the rapid seizure of (and immediate operation from) an active enemy airfield.

The PHOENIX scenario required the air assault and seizure of two airfields in Nevada by Rangers. Once the two airfields were seized, Pave Lows (MH-53s) and Blackhawks (MH-60s) (with ground assault forces on-board) would conduct the extraction-rescue of personnel from separate remote sites and then return to the two seized airfields. There the hostages and the rescue force would transfer to the waiting fixed-wing C-130 extraction transports and return to their base of origin. The helicopter forces launched and recovered at Dugway, Utah, while the C-130s launched from White Sands, New Mexico. This geographical dispersion provided realistic distances and climate conditions comparable to Iranian/Mideast conditions.

Several important sub-tasks were exercised within the overall program. Among them were: helicopter low-level, long-distance navigation; fixed-wing, low-level penetration; joint command and control; air-ground communications; and airfield extraction.

On the 5th of August, General Vaught signed out a Memorandum to the Director of the Joint Staff and the Service Operations Deputies, who reviewed and summarized the status of SNOWBIRD Program. The following is representative of the tenor of the ten page report:

> **Subject: SNOWBIRD Training and Preparation Program**
> General: Operation SNOWBIRD, the planning and preparation of a Joint Task Force to accomplish the rescue of the American hostages in Iran, was tasked to the undersigned by competent civil authority on 26 April 1980. . . . Since definitive intelligence has not been available, it was necessary for the Joint Task Force to design a number of possible options and train a wide spectrum of forces. To date, these forces included 2,477 personnel and 136 various aircraft. Most of these forces were incorporated into a July 1980 training program that was briefed to the Service OPSDEPS on 2 July. . . . The Honey Badger exercises incorporated many of the training and validation tasks that had to be accomplished to prepare the Joint Task Force to execute SNOWBIRD Options One through Eight. ICE BOX activity was to evaluate the feasibility of Option Nine.

In closing the report, General Vaught, although citing significant JTF achievements and growth in capabilities (all focused on the narrow scope of requirements associated with a forced-entry rescue scenario), concluded that the United States was ill-prepared to conduct any sort of Special Operation (on a broad scale). He cited the fact that the Army had reduced its Special Operations Force strength by 70 % from their pre-Vietnam level, and a further 10% cut was forecast for the next fiscal year. He also stated that the Air Force had reduced its Special Operations Force by 75% during the same period. He summed up his analysis with the following comment: "The JTF has accomplished much but the continued lack of an adequate national Special Operations capability may well plague the United States in the future."

There were 15 enclosures to the 5 August 1980 report. The last enclosure was a short list of five recommendations:

> a. Fund JTF SNOWBIRD [rescue mission preparations] activities through 30 September 1980.
> b. The intelligence community [CIA] be pressed to use all available resources to fulfill SNOWBIRD requirements.
> c. Grant authority to approach [Department of State & CIA] regarding the dispatch of site survey teams to validate/select launch and staging sites.
> d. JTF 1-79 to be dissolved between 1 and 15 November 1980.
> e. JSOC [Joint Special operations Command] be phased in beginning 15 August and SNOWBIRD mission passed to JSOC on 1 November 1980.

The last two recommendations were based on the impending recommendation by the Holloway Board that a standing Counterterrorist Force be established.

***

Throughout the month of August, the tempo of aviation planning and tactics development was extremely intense. It began on 1 August when the Joint Aviation Plans and Operation Division was established as part of the Joint Test Directorate under the Honey Badger rubric. The mission of the division was to develop and train to deployability standards a mission-capable force consisting of a variety of helicopter assets from Army, Air Force and Marine rotary wing resources. Another key part of the Division's mission was to develop and articulate doctrine and procedures for the conduct of "Joint Helicopter Special Operation Missions," and draft a requirements blueprint for future aviation force enhancements.

To this end, a three-day working conference, sponsored by the JTD/JTF was conducted on 6 - 8 August. Attendees included representatives from the JTD/JTF, the 101st Aviation Group, the USAF 1st Special Operations Wing, US Army Aviation Center, and the Marine Corps Aviation Weapons and Tactics Squadron One. The conference adjourned after compiling of a set of mutually agreed procedures that provided for a degree of force interoperability previously unheard of.

Upon completion of the conference, the attendees returned to their units and began the chore of converting the thoughts, ideas and agreements of the conference into detailed operational procedures. They had less than ten days to accomplish this task because, beginning on the 18th and continuing through the 31st, the procedures would be put into practice.

The operational training conducted during that two-week period was designed to wring out and perfect the procedures, and test and refine the operational doctrine. This was done in a series of mission-oriented exercises over realistic distances in an operational mission environment. In addition to the training, a key purpose of the effort was to evaluate the potential of these newly created special mission force packages to successfully conduct a series of Snowbird mission options.

Four different types of helicopters and flight crews were involved in this first major effort. Twenty different crews flew 25 aircraft. The four airframes included UH-60 Blackhawks and CH-47 Chinooks from the Army, HH-53H from the Air Force, and a mix of HH/CH-53C/Ds from the Air Force and Marines. The Little Birds, as the reclaimed OH-06s were now called, were held separately and trained very discretely, with knowledge of the unit's existence held very tightly.

Five days prior to the start of this integrated heavy-lift helicopter training period, the JTF J-2 issued a 60-90 Day Situation Projection. The message is reproduced below in its entirety:

0 132020Z AUG 80
FM JCS/SNOWBIRD/J-2
TO (ALL FORCES)
CITE J-3 0288
SUBJ: 60-90 DAY SITUATION PROJECTION
REF: A. JCS/SNOWBIRD /J-2 CITE 0274
B. JCS/SNOWBIRD/J-2 NBR 065

1. MESSAGES CITED ABOVE PROVIDE JTF ASSESSMENT OF HOSTAGE LOCATIONS BASED ON DATA DATELINED AS OF 18 JUN THROUGH 31 JULY 1980. RECENT POLITICAL EVENTS IN IRAN AND CONUS PLUS RENEWED REPORTS OF THE POSSIBILITY OF HOSTAGE TRIALS WARRANT A REEXAMINATION OF THE SITUATION AND THE DISSEMINATION OF AN 60-90 DAY EVENTS PROJECTION. THIS MESSAGE PROVIDES SUCH AN ASSESSMENT.

2. A MAJOR GOAL OF KHOMEINI IS TO ESTABLISH A PURE ISLAMIC GOVERNMENT DEVOID OF WESTERN INFLUENCE AND AT THE SAME TIME HUMILIATE THE UNITED STATES, OBTAIN U.S. ACKNOWLEDGMENT OF ITS "SINS" DURING THE REGIME OF THE SHAH, AND PUNISH THE U.S. PRESIDENT WHO PROTECTED THE SHAH [AN AVOWED TARGET OF KHOMEINI'S HATE]. THE

PROTRACTION OF THE HOSTAGE SITUATION ACHIEVES SOME OF THESE OBJECTIVES SPECIFICALLY; HUMILIATION OF USG, AND PUNISHMENT OF THE PRESIDENT BY THEORETICALLY REDUCING HIS POTENTIAL FOR REELECTION.

3. BASED UPON ONGOING EVENTS IN IRAN, SUCH AS THE CONTINUING PURGE OF MILITARY AND POLITICAL LEADERS WITH WESTERN BACKGROUND INCREASING CONTROL BY IRP, AND SELECTION OF IRP HARDLINER AS PRIME MINISTER IT IS CLEAR THAT SECULAR [MODERATE] INFLUENCE IS DECLINING AS THE POWER OF THE HARDLINER AND CLERICS RISES. THESE INFLUENCES ARE NOT LIKELY TO ASSIST IN OBTAINING A POLITICAL SOLUTION TO THE HOSTAGE SITUATION.

4. BASED UPON THE FOREGOING THE FOLLOWING PROJECTION OF EVENTS IS PROVIDED FOR PLANNING PURPOSES.

(A) NO HOSTAGES WILL BE RELEASED PRIOR TO THE U.S. PRESIDENTIAL ELECTION UNLESS USG MEETS IRANIAN DEMANDS OR ANOTHER HOSTAGE MEDICAL PROBLEM OCCURS.

(B) REPORTING ON POSSIBLE TRIALS WILL INCREASE, BUT ACTUAL TRIALS OF INDIVIDUALS IS UNLIKELY ALTHOUGH A "GRAND JURY STYLE" OF INDICTMENT PROCEEDINGS IS POSSIBLE.

(C) TEMPO OF ACTIVITY WILL PICKUP WITH THE APPROACH OF U.S. ELECTIONS, REACHING A PEAK IN MID-LATE OCTOBER.

(D) IF PRESIDENT CARTER LOSES THE ELECTION, KHOMEINI THRU THE MAJLIS MAY DIRECT THE INCREMENTAL RELEASE OF MOST OF THE HOSTAGES, RETAINING SOME NUMBER (5-10) AS SPIES AND WAR CRIMINALS, HOPING TO OBTAIN CONCESSIONS FROM THE NEW PRESIDENT IN JANUARY. HOWEVER, IF PRESIDENT CARTER WERE TO BE REELECTED IT IS EXTREMELY DOUBTFUL THAT ANY OF THE HOSTAGES WOULD BE RELEASED WITHOUT SIGNIFICANT CONCESSIONS BY THE USG.

5. IN SUMMARY, THE CURRENT JTF ANALYSIS IS THAT NO BREAKTHROUGH IS LIKELY PRIOR TO THE U.S. PRESIDENTIAL ELECTIONS AND KNOWLEDGE OF ACTUAL LOCATIONS WILL CONTINUE TO BE EXTREMELY RESTRICTED WHILE EXTENSIVE DECEPTION ACTIONS WILL CONTINUE TO BE EMPLOYED.

REVW 14 AUGUST 00

BT

Midway through the helicopter work-up program, at 10:30 A.M. on Saturday the 23rd of August, the Holloway board publicly released its findings and recommendations. The principle (and largely fore-ordained) recommendation was to create of a standing Joint Counter-Terrorist Task Force composed of those elements of the military services that possessed the unique capabilities required of the mission.

Less than 30 days after Admiral Holloway submitted this recommendation (and six years after General Hennessey had tried to create such a capability), the Secretary of Defense initiated action. He directed the Chairman of the Joint Chiefs of Staff to task the three military services

(Army, Navy and Air Force) to fund, man and equip such a force, and JCS to create a Joint Command and Control structure.

JCS moved fast, but there was some residual horse-trading and retention of service control by the services. Only a portion of the service capabilities was directly assigned to the new CTJTF and most of these on a rotational and on-call basis. The Command headquarters was headquartered on Fort Bragg, North Carolina, initially in some World War II barracks, a few miles from the original Delta compound. An Army general officer was selected to be the commander, and the services scrambled to provide him with a staff three times the size of JTF 1-79 in less than 60 days. The goal of the new staff was to assume planning and execution responsibility from JTF 1-79 as rapidly as possible, but all parties concerned recognized that this was not going to be an overnight event.

The new staff would have to be assembled, develop their own procedures, go through a learning and shakedown period, and become familiar with the capabilities and limitations of the combat forces they would employ. In the meantime, not only were the capabilities of the existing forces growing, but several new force elements were being created and maturing, many with a substantial head start on the "new headquarters." During the next several months, it became apparent to some observers that, in some areas, the maturity of the new CTJTF organization was being undermined to some degree by a "not-invented-here" syndrome. This was compounded in some quarters by an underlying assumption that if JTF 1-79 had done it, it was automatically wrong.

The unclassified mission of the new organization was to study special operations tactics. Its true mission as the DOD counter-terrorist reaction force remained classified until 1992, when its unclassified mission statement was modified to reflect more clearly the operational aspects of the force. That revised mission statement read, "Provide the Joint service expertise for a standing Joint Special Operations Task Force."

Simultaneous with the JSOC staff being assembled, the JTF/JTD team continued to develop capabilities and refine rescue options. Later options, such as SNOWBIRD OPTIONS VII and VIII, envisioned the use of various sea-going ships as expedient staging, launch and recovery platforms for helicopters. Possibilities included situations where a land base could not be obtained, or where a maritime launch platform provided a better strategic or tactical option for improving the probability of mission success. These capabilities were tested and perfected in late summer. SNOWBIRD Option IX (Operation ICE BOX) envisioned the close-quarters insertion of an assault force using OH-6 "Little Birds," rapid hostage release and immediate retrograde. The concept was conceived in June, with force training and preparation to take place in July. Option IX was used as a model for force structure and equipment decisions.

Option X was the most revolutionary option and the one the JTF believed, and the Chairman concurred, had the greatest potential for employment and mission success. Option X involved the simultaneous takedown of multiple, dispersed targets, and, depending on the availability of additional assets, could be applied with minimum adjustments in a range of circumstances. Option X was used as a refining force and decision model tool.

Option X, which was referred to by some as the "Godzilla" option, focused on the use of a totally air-refuelable fleet of heavy transports with specially trained aircrews to deliver assault forces to a number of locations simultaneously. The armada would be led by MC-130s acting as a combination pathfinder and weather reconnaissance. The collective force would launch from a host of bases around the world, including the United States, and fly directly into Iran via several different approach routes, seizing several landing areas simultaneously. The MC-130s would deliver the Ranger seizure forces and USAF Special Operations Combat Controller Teams (SOCCT) and/or Army special action ground support teams from the new "Scout" capability.

The concept called for the seizure forces to establish security and neutralize any Iranian forces found at the site(s). The CCT would set up the air traffic control and landing beacons for the follow-on heavy-lift transports. The heavy lifters would deliver a range of helicopters and other fast vehicles in two waves. Helicopters that required some assembly would be in the second wave. The transports carrying the rescue forces and smaller helicopters (which did not require any assembly) would be first. AC-130 gunships would be interspersed in the flow to provide an extended interdiction and security presence which would move with the rescue forces as they closed with the various rescue sites.

Not all of the assaults would come from the air; some would be carried out by select rescue teams in fast-moving armored vehicles. As the various forces (air, ground, and maritime) closed on their objectives, Command and Control (C&C) aircraft would climb to an altitude from which the movements of the American forces could be monitored via signals received from identification beacons carried by each force element. As the forces closed with their objectives, and the Command and Control platform assumed its position, another C & C aircraft would assume a second surveillance position where it could vector U.S. fighter planes against any Iranian aircraft that were launched in response to the American rescue forces. After a short period of time, KC-135 tankers launched from other locations would arrive near the fighter CAP area (Combat Air Patrol). The tankers would remain on orbit and refuel the fighter aircraft until the last of the rescue force was safely out of Iranian airspace.

At the time Godzilla was undergoing its first incremental field test and rehearsal in late August and early September, the JTF had identified where the majority of the hostages were being held. Reliability was 100 percent on 45 of the 52 remaining hostages. Three were still in the MFA. Forty-two were believed to be in an old World War II vintage prison in downtown Tehran, not far from the Ministry of Foreign Affairs (MFA) complex. The reliability as to the precise location of the remaining seven was far less. Four were assessed as being held within the Embassy compound; however, confirmation of the specific detention location within the compound was difficult to obtain. One hostage, Richard Queen, who had been released by the Iranians in mid-summer due to a serious medical condition, confirmed that he, along with two older men and the two remaining women hostages, had continued to be detained in the Embassy after the April rescue attempt. This left three Americans unlocated.

***

On 22 September 1980, after a long period of border bickering, Iraq invaded Iran, charging across the Iranian south eastern frontier in an effort to seize total control of the southern confluence of the Tigris-Euphrates river network in the area known as the Shatt al Arab waterway. The mid-point in this meandering river waterway had been considered by the international community to be the mutual border between the Iran and Iraq, with both countries using it as a joint-use international waterway. However, both claimed historical precedents dictating otherwise.

When Iraq made this bold military move, many observers, particularly some American intelligence analysts, presumed that the conflict would be over quickly with a lopsided victory going to the Iraqi war machine. This prediction was based upon their presumption that, without the American technical aid (which the Iranian military had been receiving for years), and given the Khomeni military purges plus the voluntary flight of many middle rank and senior officers , Iran could not muster a meaningful defense. The JTF did not concur with this assessment. Iran responded with religious furor against the Iraqi violation of its national sovereignty. The war took over the headlines in Teheran and, on the 23rd of September, the Speaker of the Majlis Rafsanjani said that the Iraq attacks were part of "a large U.S. plot and will have an impact on the destiny of the hostages." The same day, Teheran Radio announced that the Majlis had decided that the problem "of the hostage spies has been frozen indefinitely." Concurrently, the militants announced that the hostages in six cities were being transferred.

About the same time, a "new" CIA HUMINT source began to report that all the hostages had been returned to Teheran and were being held on the Embassy grounds. The source claimed that as of 16 September, upwards of 20 of the male hostages were being held in the compound in the Ambassador's residence. This information, which came to be called the "Eureka" briefing, was presented to the JTF staff by a senior CIA officer. It ran counter to data obtained from other sources and the JTF analysis of the potential detention sites. However, the CIA official claimed that the source had excellent placement, and was even able to see the hostages periodically and, upon occasion, had even spoken to several.

Although the flow of this "Eureka" reporting continued unabated, the JTF leadership had substantial doubts as to its validity, but the CIA official's claim that the source was totally reliable and had "access" could not be ignored. The "source" kept reporting sightings and meetings with the hostages, always citing the location as within the Embassy compound. Some of his reporting was echoed by a "new" Army source that emerged in the same time frame. The two independent HUMINT sources seemed to corroborate each other, although the JTF could not find any other information to support their claims.

The conflict between the HUMINT reporting and the JTF all-source analysis again raised the issue of pursuing several JTF initiatives targeted at locating the hostages. Several months earlier, in May, in parallel with increased surveillance measures and the "Scout" initiative, the JTF intelligence team, with the assistance of DIA, NSA and CIA, had initiated actions to determine the feasibility of employing some experimental technologies to assist in locating the hostages. Once the preliminary technical feasibility assessment was completed, the JTF-J-2, with General Vaught's concurrence and support, requested a meeting with DIA, NSA and CIA representatives to discuss the operational implications of implementing the technical options. The first of what became a long series of weekly meetings at CIA was held on 29 May.

During the subsequent two and a half months, discussions were conducted to no avail. None of the options, according to the CIA, were technically achievable or operationally feasible. In addition, the CIA attendees did not offer any alternatives and even arranged to have one conceptual option publicly compromised. However, both the JTF and NSA believed one specific option held substantially more promise than the others, although the CIA did not exhibit any enthusiasm for pursuing it, either. In mid-September, the JTF briefed the Director of DIA, Lt. General Eugene Tighe, on the proposal. He concurred that the program had merit, involved very little risk and, despite its initial cost, had a potential that extended beyond the present crisis. General Tighe recommended to the Chairman that the program receive full DOD support and funding. The option was presented to the JCS Operations Deputies (OPSDEPS) on 26 September 1980 and approved for development and funding. The funds were transferred to NSA within three days and, within a few weeks, a prototype capability was undergoing field testing.

On the 28th, two days after the OPSDEPS decision, General Vaught sent to the Chairman a memorandum reviewing the dual subjects of hostage location and intelligence collection. The memo laid out the suspected hostage locations at the time and identified the reliable information held by the JTF which indicated that the bulk of the hostages were being detained in an old prison in downtown Teheran, referred to as the Komiteh prison. The memo also stated that the information was somewhat dated. It closed with a paragraph stating that two HUMINT sources (one CIA and one Army) had recently claimed that upwards of twenty of the hostages were seen in the former Ambassador's residence within the Embassy compound as recently as 16 September. The JTF memo commented on these reports in the following sentence: "[*T*]*here is no way to validate* [*either of these sources*], *and one or both of the principal sources could be fabricators or deception agents. At the present time, we have no way to independently evaluate the reliability of either of these sources.*"

On 2 October, General Vaught prepared a follow-up memorandum addressed to the SECDEF requesting that the SECDEF raise the subject of hostage intelligence at the next National Security Council meeting. The thrust of the memo can be gleaned from its first two paragraphs, quoted below:

MEMORANDUM FOR THE SECRETARY OF DEFENSE 2 October 1980
Subject: SNOWBIRD Intelligence Status
1. Pursuant to NCA direction of 26 April 1980, Joint Task Force 1-79 began on 1 May to rebuild and prepare various military forces for another rescue effort. Since that time and continuing unabated to date, the men of JTF 79-1, and many elements of the military Services and DOD agencies have invested substantial time, effort, personnel, equipment, and funds to reconstitute the force and improve its capabilities. These goals have essentially been accomplished. DOD capabilities today are several fold more redundant and reliable than last April. However, this large investment does not appear to have been matched by a similar intelligence community effort. The basic charge given the DCI (Director of Central Intelligence) by the NCA (President) on 26 April remains unfulfilled.
2. While the safe return of the hostages through diplomatic negotiations is the preferred means, and we recognize military force is the option of last resort, it is imperative that intelligence keep abreast, if not ahead of operational planning, if we are to be able to effectively apply military force should the situation dictate.
3. . . . DOD proposals appear to have received only marginal CIA endorsement.

In accordance with normal JCS procedures, the memo was to be routed through the JCS J-3 to the Chairman, and then to the SECDEF under the Chairman's signature. Four days after submitting the memo to the new JCS J-3, it was returned (on the 6th) with the guidance to "restructure and process thru Joint Staff." The memo was revised the same day and resubmitted. Its intent was unchanged, but its flavor was much reduced. The lead paragraph now began:

> 1. During the past five months the JTF has proposed several initiatives (to locate the hostages). Regrettably most of these proposals have received only marginal CIA support and DOS rejection. . . .
> [The subsequent sub-paragraphs then outlined the status of several of the DOD initiatives. Paragraph Two began with the following recommendation.]
> 2. In light of the current instability in Iran and the potential threat such instability holds for the hostages, recommend SECDEF discuss with the DCI and the Secretary of State the need to pursue the initiatives . . .

***

Concern for the hostages was not limited to the White House, their families and the JTF. In addition to the immediate families of the hostages, other Americans quietly offered their support to the JTF through less timid intermediates. One was a well known sports figure, Tom Landry, then the coach of the Dallas Cowboys. Another was Mr. Merv Morrison, a successful businessman from California. Both reached the JTF via a mutual associate and fervent patriot, Ross Perot of Dallas, Texas. The JTF knew that occasionally some of the hostages were allowed to use the Embassy VCRs, and that the "tape library" was old and growing older. Landry and the Dallas Cowboys shipped a full collection of Dallas Cowboy football games from the previous season. Mr. Morrison's contribution came to be even more unique and representative of the true diversity of the American melting pot where all things come together and blend without recourse to identity or credit.

During a Tuesday visit to the East Coast, Mr. Morrison and his gracious wife met with two members of the JTF and asked what could he do to help the hostages and the JTF. The solution was a $ 10,000 bank account set up by Mr. Morrison to provide humanitarian assistance to the hostages. Some of the hostages had a need for new clothes and items such as socks and shoes. The account was put to immediate use. Two young JTF officers, both junior captains, one Marine and one Army, who had been assigned to the JTF after the April mission abort, came up with one solution. Send every hostage a jogging outfit, sneakers and socks. Their next challenge was to round up 52 sets of the same quality and style in the appropriate sizes.

They accomplished this minor miracle in three days with the cooperation of a very energetic middle-aged lady who was a cross between the picturesque grandmother and a first class dynamo. She managed to assemble the order according to their shopping list. They acquired fifty-two brown shopping bags from a local supermarket and marked each with a hostage name and the appropriate sizes, then began the sorting and matching process. Separately, a local Protestant minister, a friend of one of the hostage families, was contacted; he agreed to prepare a letter under his parish letterhead to accompany each individual set of clothes.

That Friday night, the two adventurers loaded all fifty-two sets of clothes and the minister's letters into the covered bed of a blue Ford F150 pickup truck and drove to the headquarters of the Defense Mapping Agency just north of the District of Columbia. There, they met Colonel John O'Meara, the DMA Liaison Officer. John, in his standard "wizard of the impossible role," had arranged for each of the fifty-two sets of personalized clothing and the minister's letter to be "shrink wrapped," just like they were a bundle of maps hot off the press. Early the next morning, the two Captains packed the individual packets into a half a dozen large boxes suitable for international mail. The boxes were sealed and addressed to: Guardians of American Hostages, U.S. Embassy, Teheran, Iran. The young duo loaded the boxes into the blue pickup and set off for a small village in the backwoods of the Virginia countryside.

The village was the home to a small congregation that the letter writing minister was affiliated with during the summer, and it was this letterhead he used on his missive to the "students." The local one-room post office and its staff of one was nearly overwhelmed by the boxes, but with some mutual assistance on both sides of the counter, all the parcels were weighed and stamped properly. Within an hour, all the boxes were in the custody of the U.S. Postal Service and were on their way to Tehran the next Monday. One of the junior captains paid the postage charges in cash and, with a receipt in hand, headed back to Washington. Upon reaching the JTF spaces and pronouncing that the shipment was "on its way," he turned the receipt in to the account custodian. The mailing charges were entered into the account record down to the penny. The account was closed out on 20 January and the residual funds were sent to Mr. Morrison with the grateful thanks of the JTF. During the subsequent debriefing of the hostages, it was confirmed that the Dallas Cowboy videos and the Minister's clothing packets had arrived at the Embassy and most, but not all, of the clothing packets reached the intended recipients. The debriefings also confirmed that a shipment of Bibles reached the hostages early in their detention and were put to good use, but many were confiscated by the "students" just before the hostages were released, as the students suspected some hostages were using the Bibles to maintain coded diaries. In another instance, a donation of several Polaroid Instamatic cameras, batteries and film packets sent by another minister along with a plea to the students to allow the hostages to send photos of themselves to their loved ones fell on deft ears. No snapshots were received in the States.

***

In early fall, Jack Anderson, an editorial columnist for the *Washington Post*, published a column which gave birth to the term "October Surprise." The thrust of the article intimated that the Carter administration was considering (i.e., planning) a massive military effort against Iran to secure the release of the hostages in time to favorably impact President Carter's reelection possibilities. From a DOD and JTF perspective, there was absolutely no truth in the allegation. However, as part of its security review, the JTF examined all ongoing events in both the JTF Honey Badger training program and the larger world of JCS exercises to determine a possible basis or triggering event which might have given rise to the speculation.

Two candidates emerged: one was an impending rehearsal of one of the larger scale rescue options; the other was a much larger and long scheduled JCS/REDCOM Joint Readiness Exercise (JRX). The JCS/REDCOM JRX had been developed as part of the JCS five-year exercise program. The scenario had been developed in the early spring and used the unrest in Iran and the Soviet invasion of Afghanistan as the political-military backdrop for the lead-in portion of the exercise. A summary of these scenario settings is routinely submitted up-the-chain about 60-90 days prior to the exercise start, for final approval. Part of this process involves providing a copy of the scenario to the State Department to ensure that the content of the scenario does not conflict with the prevailing State Department philosophy. Given the content of the Jack Anderson column, the JTF concluded that someone in the State Department had mistakenly taken the JRX scenario (and the impending REDCOM exercise) out of their intended context, and, due to the coincidence of time and geography, had put a political interpretation on the information and communicated this interpretation to Anderson.

***

The escalation of the Iraqi initiated conflict created additional challenges for the JTF. One of the results of the sporadic Iraqi airstrikes in Tehran was a heightened state of alert among the Iranian military and a rejuvenation of the Air Defense structure in and around Teheran. One of the more pronounced defensive measures taken by the Iranian Army was the emplacement of a wide variety of anti-aircraft guns throughout the city, with a sizeable number placed on the tops of the taller buildings in downtown Tehran. At the request of the JTF, an Army Imagery and Order of Battle team undertook the compilation of a detailed analysis and laydown of the total urban area defensive system. After reverifying the type of guns and the precise locations of each gun position, all of the locations were plotted on a high-detail map. The team then depicted the effective engagement radius of each site according to the caliber of its weapon system. A portrait of overlapping engagement circles and interlocking fields of fire emerged which, from the two-dimensional perspective of the planar map, was relatively impressive.

However, when examining the enlargements of the companion imagery, the JTF intelligence analysts noted that many of the rooftop weapons systems were positioned toward the center of the roof rather than close to the building edge. This finding prompted a request to DIA to prepare a follow-on, three-dimensional, vertical analysis. The rooftop center location severely limited the ability of the Iranian gun crews to depress the gun barrels below the horizontal, even if a given gun system had the mechanical ability to depress the barrels some 3-5 degrees below that. The rooftop height of each position was calculated and the results noted on both the original planar plot map and then a vertical cross-section profile. The resulting analysis revealed that the effectiveness of virtually all the rooftop systems could be negated by flying below their horizontal field of fire. Further work identified seven air corridors that would allow American helicopters to fly (if the need presented itself) into and out of the city with virtual impunity from the established anti-aircraft threat.

Meanwhile, the focus of JTF operational training had expanded again, and the month of October was focused on training and developing a combined Army/USAF heavy-lift helicopter assault capability. The program was nicknamed POTENT CHARGE. The objective of the program was to develop a joint USAF H-53 and Army CHINOOK/H-47 assault capability for use against SNOWBIRD targets. On 6 October, a Potent Charge training meeting was held with Delta planners presenting the proposed ground plan to the helicopter mission planners. On the 9th, the helicopter forces deployed to the field site and conducted procedural training with the ground force (Delta, Rangers and CCT). On the 10th, an orientation-reconnaissance mission was flown to the proposed exercise landing zone as a safety measure. Procedural and task training continued through the 12th. Combined assault training began on the 13th. The schedule called for afternoon and night training. During the afternoon segment, the aircrews flew five assault profiles. The forces performed the same sequence of five assaults at night. The 14th was a repeat of the 13th. By the end of this two-day training period, the Rangers had exercised their preferred ground plan eight times, the Air Force had conducted eight assault profiles, and the CH-47s had flown a dozen missions. These were evenly split between day and night missions. The POTENT CHARGE program was concluded on the 16th of October with a 16-hour night field training mission.

***

While the JTF forces and their new capabilities were being developed and perfected, another even more ambitious initiative had been undertaken by the Air Force at the request of the JTF. In early July, the Air Force had asked the Lockheed Martin Aircraft company to undertake a feasibility study and develop a technical concept to meet a unique aviation requirement on behalf of the Rescue Task Force. The JTF needed a C-130 type aircraft that could land in less than a hundred yards, inside an athletic stadium, and take-off in the same distance. This meant a steep rate of descent on a line almost parallel to the profile of the bleachers, a highly controlled and precise touchdown, and a very abrupt, level stop -- all of this without blowing tires, damaging the landing gear, or interfering with the ability of the crew and the aircraft to take off again in only a slightly less demanding profile. The takeoff role would have to be only a few yards with a near vertical jump into the air, at the same time gathering sufficient forward momentum (i.e., airspeed) to attain the necessary aerodynamics to remain airborne. The normal lift-off speed of a C-130 exceeded 100 miles an hour and regularly took in excess of 3, 000 feet to achieve.

The challenge was formidable, but not without some precedent. Transports and bombers had been using strap-on jet and rocket propulsion units to assist in achieving takeoff speed for more than thirty years, and retro-rockets had been used by several nations to retard the landing rollout of extreme heavyweight parachute cargoes for almost the same time. During the previous decade, American rocket specialists had developed other, more powerful rocket engines along with instrumented computers to control their "burn" time. Some of this knowledge came from the space program, other data and expertise from Navy rocket motor programs. Aerodynamic data came from designs and flight tests of large Short Take-Off and Landing (STOL) transport prototypes, such as the YC-14 and YC-15 built by Boeing and McDonnell Douglas, respectively, three years earlier, and the extensive Lockheed database on the numerous variants and models of the C-130 itself.

Following the tradition of the Lockheed "skunk works" in Burbank, California, the LockheedMartin team created an East Coast version at the Lockheed Martin facilities at Marietta, Georgia. The "works" had given birth to many things aeronautical, including the high-flying U-2 and the hypersonic SR-71 reconnaissance aircraft. Both had been created off-stage and in a remarkably short time frame. The Lockheed Martin Marietta team, working with Air force special operations flight crews and avionics system engineers and rocket propulsion experts from four Navy test centers, set to work and within three weeks had developed a technical concept, a production approach, an integration scheme, and a test program. The package was submitted to the Air Force for approval and, by 19 August, a formal contract was in place.

The program called for five simultaneous efforts to be brought together in two operational airframes within 90 days or less. The design phase called for two wind tunnel scaled-down models to be used for aerodynamic testing. A standard C-130 would be used to determine the effects of the rockets on the airframe and the aircraft engines and the burn conditions of each set of rockets to be used on the operational aircraft. This test-bed aircraft was dubbed the Iron Maiden, as the various sets of rockets were hard welded to the airframe. Five different sets of rockets were involved in creating the required Super-Stol capability. Two sets of quad-mounted, forward-facing Navy Mark-56 rocket motors were to be grafted into the fuselage, forward of the wings, to provide the deceleration required during the touchdown. Several sets of smaller Shrike missile motors were mounted externally and vertically on both sides of the fuselage in the mid-section of the aircraft. Their purpose was to cushion the impact of the mid-air drop that accompanied the ignition of the forward-firing (stopping) Mark-56 retrorockets. Another dual set of quad Mark-56 rocket motors were mounted on the inboard underwing pylons to provide the immediate acceleration and jump capability required during the takeoff. As a complement to the wing-mounted lift Mark -56 rockets, two additional sets of Shrike rockets were mounted on the outboard pylons, to selectively provide directional control and compensate for a lack of thrust, should one of the lift Mark-56s not function. If the Mark-56s performed as planned, the wing Shrikes would be fired to provide added boost in the critical lift phase. A fifth set of two-rocket motors, these being the much smaller ASROC, were mounted under the tail (just forward of the flat beaver tail segment) to provide pitch control during the initial phases of the take-off.

Other enhancements to the two H-Model operational C-130s included adding an air-refueling capability identical to that installed on the new stretched C-141Bs that were undergoing JTF SOLL training, and installing new precision navigation systems. In addition, a Terrain Following/Terrain Avoidance flight control system, and new improved Forward Looking very high resolution Infrared landing system and several self-defense measures were incorporated. The Government-Industry team of 20 Navy, 50 Air Force and more than a thousand civilians were closing in on the requirement. The two H-Model C-130s that had been flown into Marietta, Georgia, in mid-August emerged as very different aircraft on 18 September. One month after the formal contract award and less than ten weeks from the beginning of concept development, the first airworthiness test flight was conducted. Two days later, 20 September, the forward-firing Mark-56 retro-rockets were tested, inaugurating three weeks of incremental stair-step progressive testing and flight operations.

While the two mission aircraft were being modified, the aircrews piled up 400 hours of time in a specially designed flight simulator that focused on the most critical and demanding phases of flight -- the approach and landing sequences. The simulator, a converted R&D unit, used the advanced FLIR and new avionics and rocket control computers as the principal learning tools. From the aircrew perspective, the takeoff phase was a relatively straightforward operation, nothing more than zero launch rocket ride, so it was not built into the simulator sequence. On 17 October, the first fully modified aircraft was ready to enter the test phase of development. On the same day, during the taxi segment of its airworthy flight test, all the rocket systems were test fired just as they were to perform in a full flight profile. Only one minor revision in the flight control systems was required to correct an aileron buzz, and this was accomplished in less than two days. The flight test and crew proficiency training program continued without incident until 29 October. During the takeoff phase of the mission, the aircraft set several new records. The nose gear was six feet off the ground within ten feet of break release and the aircraft was fully airborne within 150 feet. By the time it had traveled 375 feet the aircraft had attained an altitude of 30 feet and an airspeed of 115 knots. The "Credible Sport" XXC-130 Super Stol was halfway to achieving mission-capable status.

However, prior to the flight, it was learned that the mission computer that was to fully integrate and control all firing events was not yet perfected. Given the experience of the previous flights, the flight crew elected to proceed with the mission on the belief that they had acquired enough experience to properly judge when to manually ignite the retro-rockets. This estimate proved to be incorrect. During the manual sequence, the bottom set of deceleration rockets, which were to be fired only after touchdown, were fired a few seconds prematurely. The rockets worked perfectly, but the aircraft was not yet on the ground and the resulting drop of some twelve feet turned the intended controlled quick-stop landing into an airframe-jarring pancake crash. One wing broke off upon impact and a fire resulted. Within eight seconds the fire was under control, none of the flight crew were injured, and the fuselage was largely intact, as was the majority of the new instrumentation. However, within a week, the cost of the miscalculation, combined with the results of the recent Presidential election, which foreshadowed the impending change in the White House, resulted in the "Credible Sport" program being terminated. It would not become part of the growing American rescue capability. However, some its components would.

***

Approximately a week later, on 14 November, the JTD released an Operations Order (OPORD) for a major exercise to be conducted during the last week of the month. The exercise, nicknamed Storm Cloud, involved the majority of the forces that now constituted the JTF family of capabilities. The force list included: TF 79.1 (Delta), a Ranger force, TF 160 (101st Aviation), 1st SOW, USAF CCT elements, Scouts teams, JCSE communications teams, and Air Defense Teams equipped with Stinger missiles. SOF aviation resources included: AC/MC/EC-130s, MH-53 Pave Low(s), UH-60 Blackhawks and AH-1G Cobra gunships. Non-Special Operations forces included: C-5/C-141 transports, KC-135 tankers, E3A-AWACS aircraft, and Navy F-14 fighters providing Fighter CAP.

The mission was to covertly penetrate the hostile territory (of the target country) and conduct simultaneous air assault operations to recover U.S. assets (hostages) being illegally held (at several geographically separate locations). Command and Control was exercised on three communication nets, two being satellite and one HF. All operated in the secure mode. The tactical nets included intra-air, air to ground, ground and fire support. The Command and Control structure operated from eight locations, including a dual set of JTF airborne command posts (AWACS & AC-130). General Vaught was the overall commander. The mission was successfully executed, on time, without any accidents and in accordance with the rehearsed plan during the night of 23-24 November 1980. The mission critique was conducted the next day at the Pentagon in the SOD/JTF planning room at 1:00 P.M. Another version of Godzilla had been perfected.

In the closing days of November, the reality and high probability that a different set of American rules would be operative after 20 January 1981, when Ronald Reagan assumed the Presidency, struck the Iranian leadership. By early December, the nature of the Iranian public and private rhetoric began to show a marked change. In the opinion of the JTF, this was the first real possibility of a political agreement between the Iranian power centers, led by Ali Akbar Rafsanjani, the speaker of the Majlis (National Assembly), and the American negotiating team. The JTF envisioned an undefined formula that could culminate with the release of the hostages just prior to or coincident with the swearing in of the new American President, Ronald Reagan. The President-Elect was characterized in Iran as a "John Wayne" hardliner, and a person likely to release the full might of the American military force on them.

In anticipation that the President-Elect, or key members of his transition team, would want to be brought up to date on the available military options, General Jones conducted a thorough review of all the options and capabilities. This included the rescue capability and its command and control structure, as well as a detailed review of the host of possible punitive actions. Most of these plans had been developed shortly after the Embassy takeover, then refined and put on hold. After the Desert One mission abort, these and other retaliatory options, and selective punitive strike plans, were revived and reviewed and, in turn, put on hold. In mid-November 1980, nearly a year after their creation, they were pulled out again, revisited, and prepared for presentation to the incoming administration. The call never came.

By early December, after three months of CIA drum-beating, the "Eureka" reporting was slowly and reluctantly being conditionally accepted by some of the JTF cadre. It was accepted not because it was believed or could be proven, but because it could not be disproved and because of the several week time-lag in receiving information from the single reliable, albeit irregular, JTF source. The principal disbelieving holdouts were Brigadier General Richard Secord, now the principal Air Advisor to General Vaught, General Vaught himself, and the author. The lack of CIA action to investigate the Komiteh prison site (or any of the other reported detention locations), coupled with the CIA delay in pursuing the earlier technical initiatives, had combined to create frustration and doubt within the JTF regarding the CIA's commitment and the general validity of "HUMINT." It was during this period of turbulent reporting that responsibility for the rescue mission was formally passed to the new DOD Counter-Terrorist Joint Task Force, the Joint Special Operations Command (JSOC) located at Fort Bragg.

The transfer of mission responsibility from JTF 1-79 to the new Joint Special Operations Command (JSOC) began in mid-December and was concluded on 22 December 1980. On that date, JTF 1-79 was formally deactivated, and JSOC assumed responsibility for rescue planning and command. However, select elements of the JTF 1-79 headquarters staff remained in existence and continued to be an information focal point within the Pentagon for the hostage situation. This residual cadre consisted mainly of the communication structure, which was being upgraded and transitioned for use by the new CTJTF and the intelligence team, which was maintaining situational and tracking continuity, and feeding the JSOC (and the expanded JTF force elements) with daily intelligence updates and assessments. The Command element, a small operations team and the EUCOM and PACOM

Liaison Officers also were busy closing out the files and preparing the results of the Honey Badger Project for release to all U.S. Special Operation Forces. Most of the other staff functions (funding and logistics) had been eliminated or absorbed by the newly created JSOC Washington Liaison Office that was being set up "down the hall."

Active negotiations were ongoing in December between representatives of the Carter administration, the State Department, and Government of Iran (with Algeria acting as an intermediary). However, the Iranians were bargaining hard, not only for relief from the international sanctions, but most strongly for the release of all of the Iranian funds and assets frozen by the American fiscal actions of early 1980. This was a fundamental Iranian pre-condition for the release of the hostages. The Carter administration was working feverishly to accommodate the Iranian demands, with the goal of obtaining the release of the hostages on their "watch."

The Iranian leadership had a different agenda. The Iranian agenda was geared to obtaining maximum concessions from the U.S. government under President Carter (before the Reagan team assumed the reins of government) while delaying the hostage release so that it would occur on the Reagan watch. Periodically, the JTF was queried by a member of the National Security Council staff as to the possibility of an early hostage release. In each case, the JTF reviewed the situation and came back to its basic judgment formulated in August 1980 and revalidated several times subsequently. This judgment was based on the fact that the Iranian fundamentalist religious-political leadership had the capability to unilaterally terminate the confrontation at any time of their choosing and had consistently chosen not to. The JTF held that, in the final analysis, it would be the fundamentalists that picked the day, the hour and the minute to release the American hostages, and this would not be any earlier than 20 January 1981.

As of late-December, the Iranian negotiators were holding firm on their demands and setting new conditions at each round of dialogue. From an external perspective, it appeared that even these negotiations might not secure the release of all of the hostages. With this possibility in mind, the JTF began developing a request to the NCA asking permission to conduct precautionary reconnaissance missions into Iran to survey the principal landing areas for "Godzilla," or a derivative. The request was stillborn, as the State Department was convinced the hostages would soon be released.

During the last week of 1980, the JTF Intelligence team reported that the bulk of the hostages had been moved in mid-December from their "prison" environment to a "hotel-type" detention facility in northern Teheran. At the same time, various statements by the Iranian government officials uniformly began to reflect a conciliatory tone and indicate a need to resolve the hostage situation. Also at this time, a flood of HUMINT reporting hit Washington. During the last ten days of December, a new stream of "street" and "walk-in" reporting flooded the HUMINT channels. More than a dozen HUMINT "rent-a-spy" reports were received indicating that the hostages were being held in more than half a dozen hotels in Teheran. Some of these reports claimed direct sightings and visits by such personages as "Doctors" that had visited the reported detention site.

On 6 January 1981, the JTF J-2 released a Special Assessment on the possibility of a hostage release. Its major segments are presented below:

Cite 0523
SUBJ: SPECIAL ASSESSMENT
1. . . . . RAJAI STATED ON IRANIAN TELEVISION THAT KHOMEINI HAD AGREED TO ACCEPT AN ALGERIAN OFFER OF ITS GOOD OFFICES TO RESOLVE THE REMAINING DIFFERENCES BETWEEN USG AND GOI.
2. [REMAINS CLASSIFIED]
3. [REMAINS CLASSIFIED]
4. ALTHOUGH ALL OF THE ABOVE IS PROBABLY TRUE, RECENT MEDIA REPORTS AND SPECULATION COULD JEOPARDIZE ANY TENTATIVE AGREEMENTS. IT MUST BE RECALLED THAT AT LEAST FOUR TIMES DURING THE PAST THIRTEEN MONTHS THE POSSIBILITY OF RELEASE WAS VIEWED, AT LEAST BY SOME OPTIMISTS, AS BEING IMMINENT. IN EACH CASE THE POSSIBILITY WAS STYMIED, MORE OR LESS AT THE LAST MINUTE AS A RESULT OF IN-FIGHTING BETWEEN CONTENDING FACTIONS WITHIN TEHRAN.
5. THE SPECULATION OF AN IMMINENT HOSTAGE RELEASE WILL CONTINUE TO PERSIST FOR THE NEAR TERM. THE POSSIBILITY OF RELEASE, HOWEVER, COULD BE THWARTED AT ANYTIME FOR ANY NUMBER OF REASONS RELATED TO POLITICAL FACTIONALISM. ADDITIONALLY, EVEN IF A HOSTAGE RELEASE IS ANNOUNCED, THE POSSIBILITY STILL EXISTS THAT SOME HOSTAGES COULD BE DETAINED AT THE LAST MOMENT WITHOUT ANY FOREWARNING TO USG.
6. COORDINATION WITH NSA, DIA AND CIA THIS DATE HAS CONFIRMED THAT ALL INTELLIGENCE ACTIVITIES RELATED TO THE HOSTAGES ARE CONTINUING, AND WILL CONTINUE UNTIL ALL 52 HOSTAGES ARE IN USG HANDS.
REVW 07 JAN 01
BT

CHAPTER TEN
Release and Reality
(An Analysis of the Facts)

The JTF assumed that any release would not be directly to American authorities, but would be through the Algerian negotiating representatives (or some other entity) who would coordinate the final transfer to American officials. For planning purposes, it was assumed that the Algerian intermediaries would accept responsibility for the hostages in Teheran and transfer them to U.S. control in Algeria. Subsequently, the hostages would be flown to a U.S. Military Hospital in Weisbaden, Germany, for medical examination and treatment and, if their physical and psychological condition permitted, an intelligence debriefing, before returning to the United States and reunions with their families.

The EUCOM staff had begun coordinating and preparing for the potential release in early January. Arrangements included the arrival, security, and medical preparations. This involved USAF and German officials at Rhein Main Airbase (near Frankfurt), the landing site of the USAF C-9 Nightingale Medical Evacuation aircraft that would bring the former hostages from Algeria. Security extended to their safe ground-transfer via bus from Rhein Main to the USAF hospital in downtown Wiesbaden for treatment, a distance of some twelve miles. As part of the pre-release preparations, the EUCOM LNO (Major Magee) was asked by the JTF J-2 to review the security situation along the ground-transfer route and in the immediate vicinity of the hospital.

The JTF was concerned that a small fanatical element within the local Iranian community in Frankfurt might attempt to ambush, bomb, rocket, or otherwise interfere with the movement from the airfield to the hospital. Magee coordinated with the local and Federal German police authorities that had the responsibility for security along the land route. The German authorities were likewise concerned about an attempt by radical elements to disrupt the ground transfer. They had already begun preparations to limit access along the bus route and to position GSG-9 elements along the segments of the route that were viewed as most vulnerable to attack.

Back in the United States, arrangements for the debriefing had to be handled much more delicately. Even though the use of DOD facilities, services and personnel was accepted as a matter of course in a situation such as this, State Department permission was specifically required for the Defense Department to interview the non-DOD hostages. After ten days of dialogue, the size and composition of the debriefing team was finally worked out between the Defense Intelligence Agency and State Department. Lt. Colonel Bob Morrel, who had evolved to be the principal DIA focal point for JTF support and the primary DIA contact with the Department of State, would serve as the Chief of the DOD Debriefing Team, with the JTF J-2 discretely functioning as his Number Two.

***

On 17 January, the JTF J-2 received a secure telephone call from a senior assistant to the National Security Advisor. During the course of the previous fourteen months, this official had periodically contacted the JTF for an opinion whenever there was a perceived or anticipated change in the hostage situation. The question this day was, "Do you expect them [the hostages] to be released soon? Within the next 48 hours?" The JTF response was, "No, not until noon on the 20th." This was not the answer desired by the questioner. Hoping for a pre-inauguration release, the State Department requested that the DOD debriefing team be pre-positioned at Andrews Air Force Base on the 18th. Pre-positioning occurred. Early release did not.

At noon Washington time, on 20 January 1981, the DOD debriefing team and a large State Department contingent numbering nearly 30 personnel were on-board a USAF passenger transport aircraft sitting outside the Andrews AFB Passenger Terminal. The aircraft and its occupants were waiting for Ambassador Cyrus Vance (the former Secretary of State who had opposed the rescue mission) to board the aircraft. President Carter had asked Ambassador Vance to head the State Department reception delegation. The Ambassador was inside the terminal in the VIP lounge watching Ronald Reagan take the Presidential oath of office on television.

The USAF transport, nicknamed by some "Air Force Three," was configured much like a standard civilian airliner with a small first class section and a large cramped coach section, with one critical exception. A radio center was positioned between the first class space and the coach area. The JTF J-2 was standing in this small area watching the transfer of power from Mr. Carter to Mr. Reagan on a 9-inch TV; however, he also had a radio receiver in one ear. It was through this receiver that, at 12:03 P.M., just as Mr. Reagan was concluding the Presidential Oath of Office, the JTF officer was advised that the two Algerian transports carrying the American hostages had been cleared to takeoff from Teheran. A few minutes later, Ambassador Vance boarded the aircraft and made an announcement that the Algerian aircraft were airborne with the hostages on-board. His announcement was met with tremendous cheers, clapping of hands, and shrieks of joy. The American public got their first view of the hostages when the hostages were deplaning at Rhein Main in Germany. The bus ride to the Weisbaden hospital was accomplished without incident. The first order of business for the newly freed Americans was food, showers, telephone calls to loved ones, a quick medical check, and then sleep. A more thorough medical and dental examination and psychological interview followed the next day. The next major event was measuring and fitting the hostages for new civilian clothes or military uniforms as the case might be.

*** The Debriefings ***

The hostage debriefings began on the 22nd of January. It took the better part of five days to interview all the hostages. The individual debriefings were correlated daily, and used to reconstruct a composite view of the full 444 days of captivity. The debriefings and the reconstruction confirmed much of the JTF earlier analyses, and revealed that several claims made by HUMINT sources and Iranian officials were intentional lies.

The debriefings revealed that the militants exercised direct physical control over the Americans from capture to release, and that the militants were controlled by and responded to direction from a hard-line faction of the Islamic religious hierarchy throughout the period. The continuing presence of Mullahs at the compound and various detention sites confirmed the extent of their involvement. The Mullahs in turn controlled revolutionary guard entities throughout the country. The rapid development, coordination and implementation of the 26th of April nighttime hostage dispersal plan were clear evidence of this interface. Most of the detention sites were guarded by local members of the Pasdaran Revolutionary Guard. None were guarded by the regular Army, and some detention sites were located within Pasdaran training sites. Others were Mullahs' homes, and one detention site was a former American Consulate building. The extended use of Komiteh Prison, which was run under the auspices of the Ministry of Justice and controlled by the Mullahs, was further evidence of their involvement.

Although the militants accomplished much of their own housekeeping chores, they received substantial support from various segments of the Iranian Government. This included news coverage, radio and TV broadcast time and support (all key events were videotaped by technical teams from the government-run TV). The "students" were also provided food, water, telephone service, heating, and electric power. The Revolutionary Guard maintained security around the Embassy Compound, but allowed free access to the militants. The militants were given small arms training and were provided very sound security advice by knowledgeable experts throughout the detention period. One example was the removal of the closed-circuit TV system from the Chancery and its installation in the Komiteh prison. In addition, the militants received substantial information and moral and psychological support from Iranian support and student groups in the United States.

The Americans hostages had been blindfolded and their hands tied upon seizure, and a no-talking rule was imposed. These restrictions remained in force for the majority of the first three months. Thereafter, the no-talking ban was lifted between roommates. However, the blindfold rule was applied on all movements out of a cell or room, and the hands-tied procedure was enforced on any out-of-building transfers. All external moves, even trips from the Chancery to the Mushroom Inn and the Ambassador's residence for showers, were accomplished in cars or vans and under guard. All off-compound transfers were accomplished in vans with the windows blacked out. Circuitous routing was often used to confuse the hostages as to location, distance and direction. Physical security was high throughout the 444 days of captivity, but varied with time, location and prisoner.

Hostage treatment during their captivity varied, but included beatings, long periods of solitary confinement, extended periods of being tied or handcuffed, mock firing squads, threats of being thrown to the crowd or shot and, in several cases, denial of medical attention or medication. Individuals receiving serious abuses fell into three categories: those who were known or suspected to be associated with the CIA and/or senior military officers, those who attempted escape, and those who antagonized their captors. If a hostage did not fall into one of these categories, treatment was generally benign after the first 45 days.

During the first few months, it was common for the hostages to have an armed militant guard present at all times. By March of 1980, this procedure had been dropped, with unarmed guards in the hostage hallways and armed guards at key entry and control points and external perimeters.

Other hostage control measures extended to censorship of both outgoing and incoming mail. The delivery or dispatch of mail was a function of several factors that fluctuated over time. The key factors were the individual hostage's behavior, the translation competency of the guard group, the volume of mail, and extent of conflicting militant duties.

*** Detention Locations and Assault Assessment ***

In chronological order, the debriefing confirmed that, during the first month to six weeks of captivity, a small group of hostages were rotated to two private homes outside of the Embassy compound and held there as insurance against an American rescue attempt. By mid-December 1979, this practice had been suspended and all the hostages, except the MFA trio and the Canadian seven, were being held on the Embassy compound. The debriefings also confirmed that, from mid-December 1979 through mid-March 1980, the hostages had been divided into groups and held in a variety of different buildings within the compound. These locations principally included the Ambassador's residence, the furniture warehouse (the Mushroom Inn), and the Chancery building. The debriefing also confirmed that, by mid-March 1980, all the hostages were being held in the Chancery, where they remained until the night after the April rescue attempt when all but five were relocated.

A detailed analysis of each debriefing allowed the JTF to confirm precisely where each hostage was on the night of the attempt. The hostages were locked in rooms in small groups, with one to two guards positioned in each hallway (cellblock style). The debriefing also confirmed the JTF estimate of guard locations and strengths. All of this information was laid out on a schematic of the Chancery building, floor by floor. As part of this independent evaluation, the tactical assault plan that had been developed and rehearsed by Delta, and would have been executed had Delta reached the compound, was overlaid on the hostage and guard locations.

The comparison indicated that, if the rescue team had reached the Embassy compound undetected, the subsequent breaching and clearing of the Chancery by Delta would have quickly neutralized all the militant guards with minimum casualties to the force and a high probability of no casualties to the hostages. If all the hostages were in their rooms at the projected time of the assault (as was normal at that time of night), the comparison indicated that there was no reason to think any hostage would have been injured during the assault. If by chance a hostage had been in the hallway or a rest room during the initial assault, there was a possibility that he/she may have become a casualty depending upon his/her action at the time. This possibility had always existed and was recognized and considered during the dozens of training drills conducted by Delta.

*** Dispersion & Consolidation ***

The debriefings confirmed that the dispersion of the hostages began the night *after* the Desert One abort was learned by the Iranian clerical leadership. Thirty-five of the male hostages were tied and blindfolded, and driven in small groups of two to three in closed vans in two three-vehicle convoys to the cities of Tabriz, Hamadan, Qom, Esfahan, Shiraz, Yazd, and eventually Jahrom. In some cases, this was a two-day process and, in a few, even longer. The JTF was able to track much of this activity through a combination of sources and methods, although at times the timeliness of the information was lacking. Ten other hostages were held in the Evin Prison Annex in northern Teheran for a few days, then divided and dispersed. One group was flown to Mashad in northeast Iran, and the other was driven to a small town a few hours drive northwest of Teheran. It was not until these groups reached their remote destinations that the JTF was able to resume tracking continuity.

Beginning in early June, the militants began to bring the various groups back to Teheran. This consolidation continued through July and was totally concluded in late August. Shortly after the mid-July release of Embassy Counselor Richard Queen by his captors (due to an undefined medical condition), the JTF learned that five hostages had remained in the Chancery throughout the dispersion period. This group consisted of two women and three men, including Queen. Similarly, the JTF confirmed that the MFA trio had never left the city and continued to be detained in the MFA.

By 1 September 1980, all of the American hostages were back in Teheran. The JTF had confirmed indications, received in early August, that the majority of the male hostages, at least 42, were being held in the Komiteh prison in the southern part of the city, relatively near the Ministry of Foreign Affairs. By mid-September, the JTF had very reliable locational and identification data on the hostages imprisoned in the Komiteh. And, in addition to the three diplomats detained in the MFA, the JTF believed that the remaining four members of the "Queen group" might still be in the Embassy, although there was no concrete proof of this. This left three Americans unaccounted for. These three individuals had essentially been held incommunicado throughout most of the period of captivity. Two of the trio were suspected by the Iranians of being CIA officers. The third individual consistently gave the militants a "hard time" whenever an opportunity showed itself, thus bringing his isolation upon himself.

During the last week of October 1980, approximately a dozen of the senior American hostages were transferred from the Komiteh site to the Evin Prison Annex. The remainder of the Komiteh population continued to be held there for another seven weeks. By the end of the first week of November, the American Embassy compound had been emptied of its last American occupants when the four Chancery detainees were relocated. The two women were moved to the Evin Annex and the two men transferred to the Komiteh prison.

The debriefings confirmed the subsequent December transfer of most of the American hostages from their long-term prison and prison-like detention locations to a pre-release site, an Iranian government guesthouse complex located in extreme northern Teheran. The transfer had begun in mid-December and was concluded by 24 December, with the exception of the MFA trio. During the evening of 24 December 1980, several of the hostages who had been at the pre-release site the longest (approximately a week) were blindfolded and their hands tied. They were then placed in a closed vehicle and driven around for approximately 20 minutes, apparently in an effort to disorient them. They were then brought back to a different wing of the building that had been their point of origin.

The militants attempted to transfer the MFA trio at the same time, but one of the American diplomats physically resisted the transfer (by slugging a guard), and the three Americans were returned to the MFA. They remained there until the 3rd of January, when they were forcibly relocated to the recently vacated Komiteh prison, presumably as punishment for their earlier resistance. The trio were held in the prison until the evening of 15/16 January, when they were taken to the pre-release guest house site.

*** The Release ***

Beginning on 19 January, the hostages were told individually that they were candidates for release and that their answers to questions about the conditions of their captivity would have an impact on their chance for release. They also were read an article, from an English language edition of an 18 January Teheran newspaper, which summarized the ongoing negotiations. Each hostage was interviewed briefly by a female militant. The interviews were filmed "for the student records." Following the interview, each American was given a general physical exam by the Algerian doctors and returned to his/her room.

Contrary to the public claims of the Iranian negotiators, the debriefings confirmed that the hostages had not been brought to Teheran-Mehrabad airport, in anticipation of an earlier release, and then returned to the detention site when a glitch in the money-transfer procedures occurred. The Americans were brought to the airport only once, and that was the night of their actual release, 20 January 1980.

At approximately 7:00 P.M. Teheran time (10:30 A.M. EST) on 20 January, the American hostages were told that they had an hour to pack. Within 15 minutes, the guards came back and told them that they were leaving "now." All but one of the hostages were blindfolded, placed on buses, and driven to Mehrabad Airport. One American, a State Department employee, was pulled off the bus before it left the pre-release site and beaten because he responded quite vocally to some profanities made by a militant about Americans. The dissenting American was later delivered to the airport in a sedan just in time to catch the "Freedom flight," although he was a little the worse for wear.

The bus trip to the airport took approximately thirty-five minutes. The drive was accomplished under blindfold and with the vehicles darkened, but the hostage's hands were not tied. The Americans waited on the buses between 15 and 45 minutes before being taken off one at a time and ushered through a human corridor of Iranians chanting fanatically "Down With America."

Much like some of the earlier events staged for international media consumption at the Embassy, this last militant "Hurrah" was staged to convey the impression to the TV viewer that the departure crowd was large and composed of irate Iranian civilians. Not true! A close examination of the video and the observations of the hostages indicated that the corridor was composed of approximately 40 militants.

Although the full 444 days of the American detention was not planned in detail beforehand by the captors and the fundamentalist clergy, virtually the entire Iranian side of the confrontation was stage-managed for political and physiological impact from the initial takeover until the final release. The *JTF Intelligence History* of the rescue attempt closed with the following statement:

> *In summary, the events of the fifteen months of the hostage situation bear the hallmarks of an orchestrated campaign of psychological warfare designed to enhance the influence of the Islamic revolutionary hard liners, humiliate the United States, and purge American influence and values from Iranian society.*

*** Intelligence Fallout ***

The hostage debriefings and the reconstruction of the events of their detention revealed that intelligence analysis was far more accurate than HUMINT reporting had been. Foreign-source HUMINT reporting proved to be almost always wrong, and often dangerously misleading. This disturbing revelation had been a constant concern of the JTF planners, particularly in the nine months following the mission abort at Desert One.

The hostage debriefings confirmed that they were never "regrouped" at the Embassy in the fall, as claimed by the "Eureka" reporting of September and October, but in fact most were detained at the Komiteh prison, as indicated by the JTF analysis. This finding underscored the consistent JTF concern as to the weakness of depending on uncontrolled, untested and unverifiable HUMINT sources for critical mission data. Of special note is the fact that, amid the flood of the foreign HUMINT reporting (and journalistic-diplomatic speculation which occurred in December 1980 and January 1981), as rumors of an imminent release abounded, nearly a score of "specific locations" where the hostages allegedly were being held were reported. None proved to be true, and, moreover, neither the Komiteh prison, which housed 80 % of the hostages for four months nor the final pre-release government "guest quarters" site, which held upwards of 49 hostages for more than a month, were ever reported.

PART IV

CHAPTER ELEVEN
Competing Perspectives

In November 1980, with six months of Honey Badger projects completed or near completion, General Vaught directed the JTD/JTF to catalogue all the capabilities that had been developed and compile them into a single document by functional area. This included the results of all tests and exercises (good or bad). His intent was to ensure the fruits of the JTD/Honey Badger effort (lessons learned, capabilities developed) were not lost but in fact passed on to the broader special operations community who could benefit from them. This corporate effort, called the *JTF Force Capabilities Review*, was completed on 11 May 1981, and included data on nearly 200 initiatives, ranging from sniper rifles and communications to advancements in aviation. It was disseminated to the services for review in early June. The JTF/JTD requested comments and distribution suggestions from all four of the Services. All of the Services concurred with its value, but their responses reflected differing tones and perspectives.

The Army response was the most positive. The Army recommended distribution of the document beyond the existing SOF community. The recommendation included the unified geographic theater Commands EUCOM, PACOM, SOUTHCOM, etcetera, as well as the Tactical Air Command (TAC) (then the owner of the 1st SOW), Strategic Air Command (SAC), and the Military Airlift Command (MAC). The Army further recommended that immediate action be taken on many of the recommendations and initiatives presented in the *Review*.

The Air Force also recommended an expanded distribution (similar to that suggested by the Army), to include all the Unified (theater) and Specified Commands as well as several internal Air Force commands. However, the Air Force response was a little less supportive than the Army reply and recommended that the document be more fully evaluated before proceeding with any of its recommendations.

The Navy response was couched in a different frame of reference. Its thrust began with the phrase: "With the Iranian Hostage Incident behind us, it is now time to take appropriate actions within the established service and joint channels." The Navy did not recommend widening the distribution, or taking any action.

The following comments extracted from the *JTF Operation Capabilities Review* provide a critical footnote to the history of JTF 1-79:

> Overall intelligence support for mission planning, training, and execution was responsive, professional and generally adequate with one major limitation . . .

> the lack of continuing reliable HUMINT reporting. . . . Throughout the entire period rescue planning was severely constrained by inadequate HUMINT collection. The composition and modus operandi of the Iranian elements holding the hostages was never (fully) known. The exact location of the hostages remained elusive throughout (much of) the crisis. On-scene reporting from reliable observers was almost nonexistent. These voids caused planners to make worst-case assumptions and extensively safe-sided plans. Prompt corrective action must be taken on both the HUMINT and complementing technical fields to correct this glaring deficiency.

At the time that the *JTF Capabilities Review* was undergoing service scrutiny, the Intelligence History of the operation was being compiled. This document laid out the twists and turns in this functional arena. Its most telling aspect was its effort to document the most crucial and persistent deficiency, the lack of adequate, reliable human-source intelligence.

Classic clandestine HUMINT, based on a network of foreign reporters, ranged from non-existent to potentially misleading. However, the in-country logistic support efforts conducted by the CIA advance team, and the reconnaissance surveys conducted by the JTF military scouts, were absolutely crucial to the operational equation.

Although SIGINT played a key and valuable role in gaining knowledge of the formal Iranian military and government structure, it could do little against the specific hostage-location problem. Imagery, the only source that was U.S.-controlled and had continuing access, became the foundation of much of the composite JTF analysis. When coupled with an extensive use of non-traditional, open-source information and the numerous comparative reevaluations conducted by the JTF J-2 staff, imagery proved to have far greater value than normally expected of "Target Materials."

The success of the overall intelligence analysis was rooted in the continuity, dedication and experience of the small coordinating staff that served both as a focal point for decentralized collection and production, as well as quality control and integrated analysis. This small staff was supported by more than 300 other intelligence and MC & G specialists from DIA, DMA, NSA, NPIC, and service HUMINT and Imagery elements. Intelligence support was also provided by SAC, which did a detailed analysis of the proposed penetration routes, validating all routes and turnpoints with one minor modification." The JTF Intelligence History reflected three enduring facts:

> **Fact One** -- Information considered sensitive by the adversary will always be tightly controlled and protected.
>
> **Fact Two** -- Street rumor, fabrication, purposeful deception and third-hand gossip can and will be used to confuse the situation, misdirect interest and conceivably set a trap. This last thought is particularly germane in a situation

where the adversary is a hostile government, or a relatively large or long-term organized entity, such as a criminal syndicate, a religious body, a political party or paramilitary rebel force intent on humiliating the government.

Fact Three -- Aside from the direct on-the-ground reconnaissance and survey missions conducted by the JTF itself, the most effective intelligence during both Ricebowl and Snowbird was the result of painstaking analysis of multiple details gleaned from a very wide range of information sources. It was not the product of a single technical media, nor the result of a flock of recently recruited HUMINT "rent-a-spies."

***

At the same time the Capabilities Review was being prepared, General Vaught had forwarded two JTF memos to the JCS J-3 for approval and release to the Director of Defense Intelligence Agency (DIA) for action. The first memo, dateed 8 December 1980, outlined and proposed a series of DOD pre-contingency intelligence actions that would substantially enhance operational planning in future situations, if implemented upon receipt of a warning or indications of a potential attack on a U.S. facility, such as an Embassy. Six months later, in mid-June 1981, after a period of extended coordination with State Department, the Director of the DIA responded:

S-2690/DI-2 18 JUN 1981
MEMORANDUM FOR THE DIRECTOR FOR OPERATIONS, JOINT STAFF
Subject: Pre-Incident Intelligence Preparations
Reference: J-3/JCS Memorandum of 8 December 1980, subject as above.

1. Pursuant to your referenced memorandum, DIA approached the Department of State with your suggestions for improving the security of high-risk embassies. As State is currently involved in a multi-million dollar program to improve the security at embassies and consulates, they demonstrated a lively interest in the proposals. They were, however, concerned about the additional costs involved and the possibility of certain measures.
2. While State is taking effective steps to improve the security posture of US diplomatic facilities worldwide, we have observed very little concrete action to implement any of your specific proposals. DIA therefore is developing a formal proposal to State's Office of Security to add impetus to the previous discussions.
3. DIA also is preparing a proposal to introduce your suggestions through the National Foreign Intelligence Board. This will serve to broaden the thrust behind actions for embassy security as well as involving the (other government agencies) in the development effort.
4. We at DIA appreciate your thoughtful suggestions and concur that implementation of the measures you have proposed would enhance the security of our embassies. We will keep you advised of our efforts to involve the Department of State in effecting the security enhancement measures you have proposed.

Director, DIA

***

Two days after the first JTF/J-3 memorandum was released, a second JTF-prepared memo was also released by the JCS J-3 to the Director DIA. This second memo, dated 10 December 1980, identified a key intelligence deficiency and proposed a solution.

Five months later, on 5 May 1981, the Director DIA responded to the second memo. Unclassified extracts from this set of correspondence are presented below:

JCS J-3 Memorandum
MEMORANDUM FOR DIRECTOR, DEFENSE INTELLIGENCE AGENCY
Subject: Intelligence Capability 10 DEC 1980

1. A review of the intelligence collected during the past year to support Iranian contingency planning revealed a serious and persistent information deficiency. This deficiency revolves around the need of military planners to have accurate and timely situation oriented operational and environment data.
2. Although technical systems can and did provide some of the information needed, the nature of the required data puts the burden of collection on reliable human observers.
3. The current DOD/Service HUMINT structure is not organized to satisfy these requirements. Recommend consideration be given to developing, (such a capability - seasoned human observers) within DOD.

Director for Operations
Joint Chiefs of Staff (J-3)

***

The DIA Response:
MEMORANDUM FOR DIRECTOR FOR OPERATIONS, JOINT STAFF
SUBJECT: Intelligence Capability 5 May 1981
Reference: J3-JCS Memorandum of 10 December 1980, subject as above.

1. As noted in your memorandum, planning for the Iranian crisis was hampered initially by a lack of operational intelligence. As you observed, much of the required data could be acquired only by human sources and technical collection systems had limited utility in satisfying the requirements. . . . Additional funds have been programmed and additional personnel have been dedicated to the type of problem you have noted. I am persuaded that our responsiveness will be enhanced as these measures take effect.
2. . . . (however), at this time limited resources, extensive and diverse threat environments, and other national-level initiatives militate against creation of such a (observer-scout) cadre.
3. The provision of timely and accurate intelligence support to both military planners, and operational commanders is a matter of utmost concern to this

Agency. Hence, methods are continually reviewed and improvements sought to enhance this key intelligence function. Your comments and thoughtful suggestions toward this end are appreciated.
Director, DIA

***

These memos, along with the tenor of the Navy comments on the Capabilities Review, were but the initial indications of institutional foot-dragging and a return to a "business-as-usual" attitude in many quarters that were to plague the further development of a national special operations capability. Fortunately, some "diehards" recognized that the capabilities embodied in JSOC and those created in the aftermath of JTF 1-79 and Desert One could easily wither away if not supported, matured, and integrated into a greater whole.

A handful of former members of the JTF were among those that were concerned. These officers drafted a "Statement of Operational Needs," which outlined what was required functionally and organizationally to create a meaningful special operations capability. Fortunately, some "heavies" in the senior Army staff, such as General Meyer and General Otis, had the foresight to take these recommendations to heart and move ahead. None knew how long the road would be, nor that it would bend so much, and take more than seven years to travel. U.S. Special Operations Forces had been part of the military growth throughout the 1960s, when they played prominent roles in Vietnam, Laos, and Cambodia. However, with the American pullout and force downsizing of the mid-to-late '70s, SOF wallowed at the bottom of the trough. Nearly nine active duty Army Special Forces group equivalents shrank to three, all under-strength, one of which was scheduled for imminent deactivation in 1980. SOF aircraft suffered similar reduction fates or were transferred to the Reserves. The Navy decommissioned its only special operations submarine. SOF manning levels in every Service dropped well below authorized strengths. Funding declined precipitously, amounting to about one-tenth of one percent of the U.S. defense budget by 1975.

The aborted attempt in April 1980 to rescue the U.S. hostages held in Teheran had provided an unwelcome, but essential, "wake up call." Immediate improvements followed the mission cancellation, but strong institutional resistance to change reasserted itself, once the hostages were home. Some service decision-makers consistently siphoned off special operations funds for conventional forces, and frustration began to mount in both the Senate and House Armed Services Committees. A major recommendation of the Holloway Board in its August 1980 report was that a standing Counter-Terrorist Joint Task Force (CTJTF) be established as a field agency of the Joint Chiefs of Staff with permanently assigned staff personnel and certain assigned forces. The CTJTF would plan, train for, and conduct operations to counter terrorist activities directed against U.S. interests, citizens, and/or property outside the United States as directed by the President. In the fall of 1980, this CTJTF was created under the name of the Joint Special Operations Command (JSOC), which came be known colloquially as Jay-Sock. Headquartered at Fort Bragg, the Joint Special Operations Command (JSOC) was a multi-service, sub-unified component of JCS. The prime directives of JSOC at its creation were: to study joint special operations requirements and techniques; to ensure interoperability and equipment standardization; to plan and conduct special operations exercises and training; to develop joint SOF tactics; and to provide the joint service expertise for a standing Joint Special Operations Task Force.

JSOC, its organization, assigned forces, capabilities, techniques, and activities generally are classified, but public statements and Congressional testimony in the intervening years have identified the Army's Delta Force and SEAL Team Six as permanently assigned Special Mission Units (SMUs). Other units associated with JSOC include AFSOC flight crews and Special Tactics personnel, the Ranger Regiment and elements of the Army Special Operations Aviation Regiment (SOAR).

One of the earliest operational missions received by the new command (and the remnants of the JTF 1-79 staff) as well as the field components (principally Delta, the Rangers and the 1st SOW) occurred in mid-1981. In a memo from the Chairman of the JCS, the JCS J-3 was tasked to activate a JTF and initiate contingency planning to raid a POW complex in Laos and recover any Americans being held there. The mission went to JSOC. The reconnaissance coverage of the complex left no question that the installation had been built to be a prison compound and was still serving that purpose. It consisted of a wooden stockade and a mixture of interior buildings used as the headquarters, guard quarters, prisoner cells, and a dining hall. The site was in an isolated rural setting, not near any city, town or village and accessible by only one secondary dirt road. Nearby land had been converted to vegetable plots and was attended by the compound occupants. A pattern of sorts in the midst of the vegetable plots was speculated to spell out "B-52," which raised the possibility of American airmen being among the prisoners. Mission planning was begun immediately and proceeded rapidly to a point within 24 hours of the forward deployment of the rescue force to a final training and rehearsal site in the western Pacific. A full-scale replica of the compound was about to be built at the training site when a termination order was received from the Chairman.

Although the site was definitely a military prison, a ground reconnaissance team sent in by another U.S. government agency could not confirm that any Americans were among the prison population. None of the handheld photographs or the tape recordings they brought back showed any indications of an American presence. The news was received with mixed emotions, and a small degree of skepticism by some members of the former JTF regarding the validity of the reconnaissance reporting. What the JTF did not know at the time was that, parallel to the planning and training efforts, the Chairman had tasked the Director of the DIA to convene a small group of analysts to review all the information available, including that provided by the ground reconnaissance team. After more than six weeks of reviewing and comparing all the data, the team chief, Lt. Colonel Bob Morrel, who had served as the principal DIA Liaison with the JTF 1-79 and continued in that role with JSOC, reported their findings to the Director and the Chairman. The team could not find any conclusive evidence of an American presence in the camp. It was this conclusion that prompted the Chairman's termination order.

***

The first major service initiative regarding a revitalization of SOF followed shortly thereafter in the fall of 1981. It was an Army proposal to create a joint "Strategic Services Command." The idea originated within the same small group of individuals that had fostered the creation of Delta and supported the establishment JTF 1-79. It was at least partially based on the JTF-generated "Statement of Need." Formally, it was a proposal by Army Chief of Staff, General Edward Meyer, to create a joint unified combatant command that would provide a coordinated focus and counterbalance to the persistent and increasing problems of terrorism and insurgency. The thrust of the proposition was to integrate the various service "special operations forces" into a cohesive national special operations force that was capable of operating anywhere in the world in a range of mission areas. The Army proposal, although initially supported by the Air Force, died quickly when the Navy and, in turn, the Marine Corps objected to the concept.

When General Meyer failed to convince the other service chiefs to support the creation of a national level joint "Strategic Services Command," he decided to take the lead and at least effect the restructuring of Army SOF into a more coherent capability. In 1982, the 1st U.S. Army Special Operations Command (1st SOCOM) was created at Fort Bragg. Its purpose was to amalgamate the Army Special Operations Forces, incorporating many of the capabilities created by JTF 1-79, and build on this foundation. The Army initiative included the fielding of a third Ranger Battalion and a Ranger Regimental headquarters. The regimental headquarters was to host a set of crucial support capabilities, including a logistic and movement coordination cell, an intelligence analysis team, and an advance reconnaissance capability. Task Force 160, the 160th Aviation Battalion, the 96th Civil Affairs and the 4th Psychological Operations Battalions, as well as the active duty Special Forces Groups were integrated into this "one-stop-shopping philosophy." These actions did not occur overnight, but most were in place and viable by 1984.

Within the Air Force, changes were occurring, also, but at a much slower pace. In March 1983, the USAF 1st Special Operations Wing was transferred from the Tactical Air Command (the Fighter Air Force) to the Military Airlift Command (MAC). This followed the earlier and larger transfer of TAC's tactical airlift C-130 squadrons to MAC, consolidating virtually all USAF airlift into one organization. Subsequently, MAC created the 2nd Air Division under 23rd Air Force, consolidating virtually all of the meager USAF SOF assets under one commander. The further rejuvenation of the aging SOF airlift program looked acceptable on paper, but, as the years passed, only minimal real growth occurred. The program began to look more and more like a series of unpaid promissory notes that disintegrated further at the end of every fiscal year.

At the operational planning and joint training level, the creation of these two service SOF commands (1st SOCOM- Army and 2nd AD/23AF-Air Force) was to pay many benefits in the years to come and contributed significantly to the development of a coordinated air and ground Special Operations (SO) capability. It was these two organizations, along with the 12th Air Force and the XVIII Airborne Corps, under the respective command of Lt. General Chuck Cunningham, USAF, and Lt. General James Lindsay, USA, that continued the traditions of JTF 1-79 and Honey Badger. This four-command community jointly pursued a program of integrated joint training exercises at the operational level designed to test and perfect a combined arms capability to meet a range of contingencies. One of the earliest and largest of these efforts occurred in the 1984-1986 time frame, and focused on Nicaragua and its growing military capability and penchant for exporting its revolution to other Central American countries. All of the lessons learned from Desert One and its aftermath were applied to the development and exercising of a fully integrated set of contingency options. One of the key underpinnings of these options was a wealth of reliable intelligence and operational data collected by military reconnaissance teams that periodically visited key locations in Nicaragua.

Meanwhile, the Navy hierarchy, with the possibility of a joint "Strategic Services" command, began a program of tremendous expansion and growth within its Special Warfare (SPECWAR) Community. The SPECWAR community included the SEALs and Special Boat Units (SBUs), as well as Swimmer Delivery Vehicle (SDVs) units. Priority attention was given to the creation of a maritime-oriented counter-terrorist capability (SEAL Team Six, a Navy version of the Army's 1st SFOD-Delta), and its supporting SBU, SDV, and aviation elements. The first Commander of Team Six was Commander Richard Marcinko, one of the original Navy Liaison Officers to JTF 1-79. The greatest expansion of manpower occurred in the two Special Warfare Groups (Group One on the West Coast and Group Two on the East Coast).

Although these collective forces had gained strength by 1983, and certain select elements had worked together in various counter-terrorist exercises, an integrated command and command-oriented structure outside of the JSOC did not exist. And the ability to effectively use the now-available advance reconnaissance and special support capabilities was lacking. As the planning for and the events of the U.S. intervention into Grenada in 1983 revealed, there were misperceptions and a lack of understanding, both among the "conventional" forces as to the capabilities and limitations of SOF forces, and within JSOC of the utility of the "reconnaissance and support teams." In addition, there was a distinct lack of integrated SOF conventional-force planning experience within some service operational staffs.

CHAPTER TWELVE
The Congressional Crusade

Both the suicide truck-bombing of the Marine barracks in Beirut and the coordination problems encountered during the Grenada operation in October of 1983 caused additional Congressional attention to be focused on terrorism and the whole spectrum of low-intensity conflict and the nation's capability to respond. As a key player in both areas, the role and capabilities of SOF were to take on more importance among an expanding group of concerned legislators.

By the middle of 1984, Congressional interest in DOD reorganization as well as SOF revitalization had increased. The House of Representatives established a special panel to track improvements in U.S. Special Operations Forces, signifying sharpened interest in that small but important branch of the military. Representative Earl Hutto (D-FL) was appointed chairman of the panel. Congressman Dan Daniel from Virginia told the House that his Readiness Subcommittee intended to provide recommendations to Hutto's panel for its consideration of the FY '86 Defense Authorization request.

By early 1985, Congressman Daniel, an "elder statesman" in the House of Representatives and a long-time supporter of DOD, openly took up the banner on behalf of SOF. Daniel had very little direct knowledge of, or experience with, special operations, but several years earlier, in the spring of 1980, Daniel had been involved in a study concerning the need and capabilities of the then-newly-created Rapid Deployment Joint Task Force (RDJTF, which subsequently became USCENTCOM). Although the study did not focus on special operations specifically, the issue of SOF employment and capabilities surfaced many times. Daniel began to develop a feeling that the DOD and the senior service staffs were neither interested in, nor very good at, employing special operations forces. He saw considerable inter-service parochialism standing in the way of progress. In 1985, as the Chairman of the Readiness Subcommittee of the House Armed Service Committee (HASC), Daniel convinced the HASC Chairman to place the responsibility for SOF in the hands of his readiness subcommittee.

Daniel then directed the sub-committee staff to look at the failed Iran rescue mission and identify for him the real problems with SOF. Although the seeds of concern and change had already been planted, they were given "Vigor-gro" when the sub-committee staff reported back that the root problem in SOF was the issue of diverse command and control. Daniel was also influenced by some unique personalities. One of the most influential was a fellow Virginian named Samuel V. Wilson, Lieutenant General U.S. Army, Ret.

Sam Wilson joined the Army in June 1940 after walking 12 miles from his farm in Rice, Virginia, to the recruiting station, in Farmville, Virginia. After two years of enlisted service, Wilson was commissioned in the infantry and joined the paramilitary ranks of the OSS. He served extensively, behind Japanese lines, in the China-Burma-India theater with Merrill's Marauders. His exploits are detailed in a book entitled *The Marauders*.

Through the subsequent years, he served in command and staff assignments in special operations units and the Central Intelligence Agency (CIA). He also became a Russian Foreign Area Officer (FAO) and spent several years in the Soviet Union, where he developed a reputation as one of the leading U.S. authorities on the Soviets. In Vietnam, he was accorded the rank of Minister in the U.S. Foreign Service while serving with USAID, and later as U.S. Mission Coordinator under Ambassador Lodge. Although he commanded special operations units at all levels, Wilson also commanded the 82nd Airborne Division for a short period, giving him credibility among his peers on the conventional side of the Army. General "Sam" was appointed Deputy Director, Central Intelligence Agency, under then-Director George Bush in 1974. In May 1976, he was selected to be the Director of the Defense Intelligence Agency. Sixteen months later, on the 1st of September 1977, with great reluctance, General Wilson left the Army earlier than planned for the sake of the one thing he loved more that the Army -- his wife, unfortunately stricken with cancer.

Daniel had visited Wilson in Vietnam and had come to respect him and his opinions as he did few other men. In October 1979, Sam Wilson was called back from retirement by General Meyer to participate in the impending evaluation of Delta Force in its November operational validation. In his report and critique prepared for General Meyer, Wilson had recommended the creation of a permanent joint task force to provide the command and control, and the support which Delta would require in the future. In the summer of 1980, General Wilson was called back again, this time to serve as a member of the Holloway Commission. As a contributor to its Report, he re-echoed his recommendation for the creation of a standing Joint Task Force. His recommendation corresponded to the need seen by General Jones, General Meyer, and General Vaught, as well as numerous others, and was seconded by the majority of the panel.

By August 1985, General Meyer was not the only public SOF proponent within DOD. Noel Koch, Principal Deputy Assistant Secretary of Defense for International Security Affairs was a very outspoken supporter of SOF enhancement. Koch regularly authored articles in *Armed Forces Journal International* (AFJI) and, in an interview with Ben Schemmer, the *AFJI* editor in August 1985, Koch stated, "If you look at the service programs historically, you'll see that they don't change very much or very fast in their emphasis. The traditional 'core' will get funded first and foremost, then the programs that are peripheral to the individual services' core interests, missions and traditions 'compete' for the resources that are left. For the services, SOF have [has] never been a core program."

Funding for SOF and SOF-related programs was probably the single most critical issue among legislators. In the perspective of many, the Pentagon, particularly the Air Force, was simply not funding SOF adequately.

In late 1985, a Senate Armed Services Committee staff group completed work on a two-year, detailed study entitled "Defense Organization: The Need For Change." The study was published in October 1985, and became the foundation upon which the Defense Reorganization Act (the Goldwater-Nichols Bill) was built. The group had spent two years conducting an extraordinarily detailed study of DOD and the National Command Structure.

Historical analyses dating back to the American Revolution provided a basis for a series of recommendations relative to the reorganization of the DOD. The staff looked at a number of special operations as part of its research. Vietnam, Mayaquez, Iran, and Grenada all served to show that America's special operations track record was none too impressive.

Regarding the threats posed by terrorists, insurgents, and other unconventional forces, the report pointed out, "*[T]he capabilities needed to respond to these threats are not the traditional ones of services; the services have a tendency in force planning to focus on high-intensity conflicts upon which resource programs are principally justified; there is a need to coordinate the activities of the services as they seek to develop required capabilities in order to avoid unnecessary duplication; there is a need for innovative thinking and new approaches to these threats. . . .*" The staff report proposed a "strong . . . multi-functional, organizational focus for low-intensity warfare and special operations." The study and its recommendations were taken very seriously by several members of the Senate Armed Services Committee.

By the November-December '85 time frame, Senator Bill Cohen of Maine had become convinced that change was required and began to establish his position on the SOF situation. In an article entitled "A Defense Special Operations Agency: Fix for a SOF Capability That is Most Assuredly Broken," which was published in the *AFJI* (January 1986), the Senator outlined his views and those of many of his colleagues on SOF. In the article he pointed out that:

> [T]he Congress expressed its views of where special operations ought to be in the Fiscal Year 1986 Defense Budget. The sense of the Congress is that: (1) The

> office of the Secretary of Defense should improve its management supervision; (2) Joint command and control should permit 'direct and immediate' access to SOF by the National Command Authorities; and (3) The Commanders-in-Chief of the regional commands should have sufficient SOF in-theater to execute their war plans and deal with contingencies.

The Senator went on to say, "[M]any conventional officers quite rightly point out that there are high costs involved in the maintenance and employment of SOF. The problem is that to date, the balance has been heavily tipped against SOF." In expressing his vision for the future, the Senator wrote, "[B]ut I am convinced that we can no longer temporize on the need to establish a clearer organizational focus for special operations and a clear line for their command and control. I intend to use the opportunities available to determine what changes are necessary, and to see that the necessary changes are made."

***

By early 1986, work was being done separately but concurrently on both the Senate and House Bills. The Senate Armed Services Committee staff team, working on the SOF Bill, was directed by Senator Barry Goldwater, the committee chairman, to devote their primary effort on the overarching Defense Reorganization Bill which had omnibus implications, and to wait until that was completed before refocusing attention on the SOF legislation. The Goldwater-Nichols proposal was introduced shortly thereafter and began the long process of dialogue and negotiation. (Senator Goldwater had been an advocate of greater cooperation and integrated-joint actions since at least 1958, when then-Major Barry Goldwater, USAF Reserve, had written a staff study to that effect as a student of the USAF Air University.)

The attitude among the sponsors of the SOF initiative was that the SOF legislation should rightly follow the Goldwater-Nichols Bill, and that its final form could be that of a "Sense of the Congress" resolution rather than directive legislation. On the 15th of May 1986, after the Goldwater-Nichols Bill was well on its way toward passage, Senator Cohen introduced his SOF proposal as Senate Bill (S2453), which was co-sponsored by Senator Nunn. The Bill outlined a new command structure which included a new four-star, joint-command for Special Operations Forces on a par with the unified geographic joint commands (EUCOM, PACOM, LANTCOM, SOUTHCOM and CENTCOM), and the functional "Specified" Commands (i.e., SAC and MAC).

In June, Representative Daniel submitted his SOF Bill to the House for consideration. It was entered into the legislative record as HR 5109. The Daniel Bill proposed the creation of a National Special Operations Agency

(NSOA) with a three-star director and a distinct budget for SOF. July and August of 1986 were taken up with hearings, testimony and debate.

Admiral Crowe, the Chairman of the JCS at the time, testified twice during this period. He was accompanied by Richard Armitage, Assistant Secretary of Defense for International Security Affairs (ISA). As the JCS Chairman, Admiral Crowe agreed that change was needed, but he maintained that it was a DOD responsibility to determine what form those changes should take and also to implement them. Admiral Crowe told the lawmakers that the DOD had also recognized the problems with SOF and was preparing to implement several changes in the SOF structure. He announced the DOD proposal during his appearance before the House Readiness Subcommittee on 16 July, and the Senate Sea Power and Force Projection Subcommittee on 5 August. Crowe said that the administrative mechanism was in motion to have the DOD plan for SOF reorganization in place and functioning in about six months. He explained that the DOD plan provided for a Special Operations Force Command (SOFC) commanded by a three-star officer who would report to the Secretary of Defense through the JCS in the same manner as a four-star unified or specified commander. The current JCS SOF staff organization (JSOA, the Joint Special Operations Agency, which had replaced the original JCS J-3 SOD) would be terminated and its personnel would be absorbed into the SOFC.

Three plans were now on the table: the Senate plan, proposed by Senators Cohen and Nunn; the House plan, proposed by Representative Daniel; and the DOD plan, proposed by the service chiefs. Neither body of Congress considered the DOD plan satisfactory and proceeded to develop their respective initiatives.

Senator Cohen's opening statement at the Senate hearing was lengthy and poignant. He spoke of a new form of warfare which had emerged in recent years: "[A] form of warfare that we have not properly understood, and that we have not effectively deterred." The Senator from Maine lauded the success of both the Israelis and the British in special operations while comparing their accomplishments to the failures of the U.S. forces. Using the Mayaguez incident, the failed Iran Rescue attempt, and the experience in Grenada as examples of U.S. SOF limitations, he expressed his view in the following statement:

> I do not believe that this record is attributable to persistent bad luck or an inadequate caliber of men in the armed services. In my view, we have not been effectively organized to fight the most likely battles of the present or the future.

Meanwhile, in the House of Representatives, Rep. Daniel's Bill had been introduced as binding legislation rather than in its original form as a

"Sense of Congress" resolution. The Daniel Bill, similar to the Cohen Bill, was picking up bipartisan support as testimony progressed. The Daniel Bill passed the House, then it and the Cohen amendment went to a joint Senate-House conference committee to find an accommodation between the two pieces of the proposed legislation.

The joint conference began in mid-September, 1986. There were many divergent goals among those who had worked so diligently to get the two pieces of legislation this far. Fortunately, the concerns overlapped and all attendees shared one common desire -- to see the United States develop a capable and credible special operations capability. Lawmakers on both sides of the aisle and in both houses looked closely at the Joint Low-Intensity Conflict Report of 1985 and found that even the DOD had acknowledged that there was a problem. The events of Vietnam, the Mayaguez, Iran, Beirut, Grenada, and several other less-publicized situations pushed lawmakers to the edge of their tolerance. Supporters in the Senate wanted to force the DOD and the Administration to begin taking a more comprehensive look at low-intensity conflict and military operations other than open warfare; House members wanted to see a new emphasis on SOF funding and procurement.

The adequacy or inadequacy of SOF airlift was a key issue that repeatedly surfaced during the hearings. The most recent incident cited occurred in October 1985 when the SOF quick reaction Special Mission elements ordered to the scene of the Achille Lauro highjacking in the Mediterranean could not initially get off the ground due to airlift problems. As Noel Koch had pointed out in his discussions with AFJ, the JCS/theater war plans called for five times more Combat Talons (MC-130s) than the Air Force had and, time after time, Congress had authorized funding for new Talons. However, every year, the Air Force re-programmed those funds and never bought the additional SOF aircraft. This frustrated members of the Armed Services Committees. Senator Nunn demonstrated this frustration on the Senate floor in 1986:

> For about three years, we have been waiting on the five-year defense plan to reflect the needs of the special operations forces . . . We had the Iranian hostage rescue mission and a woeful inadequacy of transportation for the forces at that stage. Sen. Goldwater and I had written letters, done everything we could to try and focus on the need for transportation for special operations forces. The regular forces were not interested . . . So we mandated that they include transportation for special operations forces in the five-year defense plan. And we held up certain aircraft programs until they did. Guess what happened? They finally decided they needed the aircraft so they . . . put the special operations forces in the plan. What happened then? They came back and now they have taken those special operations aircraft out of the plan. This is a sad commentary . . . This is what has happened over and over again with the forces.

After extended discussions and testimony by former SOF and Special Mission Force Commanders (including the first Commander of the Joint Special Operations Command Brigadier General Richard Scholtes, USA), the Joint Conference Committee drafted legislation that included the key elements of both the House and the Senate proposals.

The House had ceded on the National Special Operations Agency issue, in lieu of an operational command, but insisted on the inclusion of separate funding provisions embodied in the creation of a new Major Force Program (MFP) funding program (MFP-11) to be managed by the new SOF Command.

Less than a month earlier, the Goldwater-Nichols Act (PL-99-433) -- the DOD Reorganization Act -- had directed the DOD to "review" the "Missions, responsibilities, (including geographic boundaries), and force structure of the unified and specified combatant commands. . . ." It further directed consideration of several issues including the "creation of a unified combatant command for special operations missions which would combine the special operations missions, responsibilities, and forces of the armed forces."

The new SOF-focused composite bill was voted up in both houses of the Congress and was signed into law on 14 November 1986. Section 1311 of the Cohen-Nunn (Daniel) legislation (P.L. 99-661) preempted the terms "consideration" and "review" used in the Goldwater Bill and mandated the creation of a Joint Command for Special Operations. This was the first time Congress had taken this type of action regarding the creation of a military command. Normally, the creation and structure of combat commands had been a Department of Defense or JCS role, as appropriate.

Section 1311 also prescribed the organizational and budgetary innovations in fair amount of detail, to include the following:

- A Board for Low-Intensity Conflict within the National Security Council (NSC). It was the sense of Congress that the President should designate a Deputy Assistant to the President for National Security Affairs who would serve as the Deputy Assistant for Low-Intensity Conflict.
- An Assistant Secretary of Defense for Special Operations and Low-Intensity Conflict (ASD SO/LIC). The principal intended duty (of this official) was overall supervision of special operations activities, including oversight of policy and resources.
- A unified combatant command for special operations force to which all active duty and reserve SOF in the United States were to be assigned. Its Commander in Chief was to develop strategy, doctrine, and tactics; train assigned forces; conduct specialized courses of instruction for commissioned and noncommissioned officers; validate requirements; establish priorities; ensure combat readiness; prepare budget requests for special operations peculiar

weapons, equipment, supplies, and services; and otherwise promote SOF professionalism. Additionally, he was responsible for monitoring the preparedness of special operations forces assigned to other unified combatant commands.

- Major Force Program (MFP)-11. The Secretary of Defense was to create a new budgetary category that would integrate SOF requirements into DOD's Five-Year Defense Plan. The ASD SO/LIC was to oversee the preparation and submission of program recommendations and budget proposals by the Commander in Chief of United States Special Operations Command (CINCSOC). Only the Secretary of Defense may revise SOF programs and budgets approved by Congress, after consulting with CINCSOC.

***

The 1986 legislation had also included guidance regarding the theater sub-unified Special Operations Commands known as SOCs. Each of the theater-oriented, geographically focused Unified Commands: U.S. Atlantic Command (LANTCOM), European Command (EUCOM) Pacific Command (PACOM), Southern Command (SOUTHCOM) and Central Command (CENTCOM) included a small, subordinate-theater Special Operations Command (SOC). In Korea, a small standing Joint Special Operations Task Force supported U.S. Forces Korea and coordinated with the Republic of Korea SOF forces under the auspices of the UN Combined Forces Commander to conduct special operations. Each SOC cadre planned for a unique set of contingency missions in accordance with the theater war-plans. Congress originally decreed SOC commanders in EUCOM and PACOM be general or flag officer grade, but allowed the Secretary of Defense to designate the rank of the other three theater SOC commanders. Other specifics included in the Bill were: a timetable for the selection and nomination of the ASD SO/LIC and the Commanding General of the new United States Special Operations Command (USSOCOM).

A little more than a year later, on 4 December 1987, frustrated by slow DOD action, Congress enacted Section 1211, P.L. 100-180. The proponents of this new piece of SOF legislation felt compelled to do so by the continued bureaucratic resistance and protracted delays within the Department of Defense to take action on the DOD reorganization and reform of special operations capabilities, policies and programs. Specifically, Section 1211 of this "follow-up" law stated:

- Designated ASD SO/LIC as the principal civilian adviser to the Secretary of Defense on special operations and low-intensity conflict matters. The first incumbent was to report directly, without intervening review or approval, to the Secretary of Defense personally or, as designated by the Secretary, to the Deputy Secretary of Defense personally.

- Directed the Secretary of Defense to publish a charter for the ASD SO/LIC. Its contents were to include duties, responsibilities, and authority, relationships with other DOD officials, and miscellaneous matters.
- Designated the Secretary of the Army as acting ASD SO/LIC until the office was formally filled for the first time. He was to submit monthly progress reports to the Senate and House Armed Services Committees.
- Gave CINCSOC Head of Agency authority to facilitate the development and procurement of special operations peculiar hardware. His staff was to include an inspector general who would conduct internal audits, inspect contracting/purchasing arrangements, and otherwise facilitate the implementation of MFP-11, which was to be created not later than 30 days after P.L. 100-180 was enacted.

***

SOF programming and budgeting problems persisted, despite passage of the previous laws (PL 99-661 and PL 100-180) in 1986 and 1987. Congress therefore enacted a third piece of legislation (PL 100-456) on September 29, 1988, to further clarify segments of the earlier laws. This additional legislation provided that CINCSOC should prepare and submit to the Secretary of Defense SOF program recommendations and budget proposals. He was to exercise authority, direction, and control over the expenditure of funds for all forces under his command. Congress extended those powers to include Special Operations Forces assigned to the theater-unified commands.

In April 1987, two months after the Congressionally-prescribed nomination date, the Senate confirmed the delayed nomination of the first Commander in Chief of USSOCOM. General James Lindsay, U.S. Army, the Commander of the U.S. Readiness Command and former Commander of the XVII Airborne Corps, to be the new CINCSOC.

Concurrently, DOD planned to deactivate REDCOM, change the name on its MacDill headquarters building, and reassign the bulk of the REDCOM staff to the new SOF headquarters. Earlier SOF proposals, dating back to the days of the 1982 Strategic Services Command proposal, called for a low-visibility command located in proximity to the Washington area at a location such as Davidson Army Airfield, an Annex of Fort Belvoir. However, based on "cost and manpower considerations," DOD decided to deactivate the REDCOM Command which had been (along with its predecessor, the U.S. STRIKECOM) responsible for joint training and the deployment of contingency JTFs. Shortly after General Lindsay's confirmation and the conversion of REDCOM, command of all CONUS-based active and most reserve component special operations forces, including SEALs (which the Navy had hoped to withhold), passed to USSOCOM.

The new SOF command was, and is, unlike any other U.S. Unified command in several significant respects. The SOF Command/Commander, unlike the regionally-oriented unified commands/commanders, has no designated geographic Area of Responsibility (AOR), and only commands/conducts "selected special operations" on rare occasions when the President or Secretary of Defense so directs.

The responsibilities of CINCSOC somewhat resemble those of a military Service in that he prepares forces for use by regionally-oriented combatant commands, and normally only monitors the activities of the Special Operations Forces deployed in each theater. Also similar to a Service Chief, the Commander of USSOCOM has Research & Development responsibilities, and prepares fiscal program/budget proposals for activities/resources, although only those peculiar to special operations forces. However, unlike the services, USSOCOM does not have the authority to recruit personnel from civilian life or run a personnel accession program.

CHAPTER THIRTEEN
Maturing the Force
(1986-1996)

Special Operations capabilities and forces of the major services had been growing at different rates since the early investments of the Honey Badger program. Organizationally, the Army took the lead with the creation of the Army 1st Special Operation Command in 1982, activating additional SOF units soon thereafter. The Air Force took a similar step, transferring its SOF forces from the Tactical Air Command to the Military Airlift Command, and creating the 2nd Air Division to coordinate all USAF SOF elements.

Concurrent with activation of the new Congressionally-directed U.S. Special Operations Command in April 1987, the Air Force SOF structure was converted and upgraded from the air division level to a numbered Air Force level. The 23rd Air Force was created and designated as the USAF component of the new joint United States Special Operations Command. At the same time, the Navy, in the process of expanding its Special Operations (SPECWAR) force structure, created the Navy Special Warfare Command (NAVSPECWARCOM) at Coronado, California. By September 1987, the conversion from REDCOM to Special Operations Command was essentially complete, although the "new" staff was far from being a "mature, well-oiled machine" knowledgeable of Joint Special Operations.

On 16 December 1987, in accordance with the provisions of P.L. 99-661, President Reagan forwarded a report to Congress on *U.S. Capabilities to Engage in Low-Intensity Conflict and Conduct Special Operations.* Subsequent congressional hearings included critiques of the report. In the opinion of some, the relatively few accomplishments as of that date reflected minimum compliance with the letter of the law, rather than positive support of the intent of Congress.

The SOF force structure within the three service components began to thrive soon after congressional legislation. Each component added units and capabilities. The Army reflected the largest growth, the Navy next, and the Air Force last. This was due largely to the long lead-time required to manufacture aircraft, vice transfer and train personnel. The following pages are a synopsis of the evolution and capabilities of the various elements of the U.S. Special Operations Community.

ARMY SPECIAL OPERATIONS FORCES
Sine Pari -- Without Peer

The history of internal Army actions is replete with examples of the growth and the maturity of the Army SOF community and its recognition as a key player in both Army and joint operations. One of the earliest Army actions following the Congressional mandates of 1986 was focused on raising the status and ability of the Army Special Forces community to train and maintain itself within the Army personnel structure. On 9 April 1987, the Army designated the Special Forces career field a separate "Branch" of the combat arms team, analogous to infantry, armor, and artillery, with its own personnel management, training and acquisition structure.

On 1 December 1989, U.S. Army Special Operations Command (USASOC) was activated at Fort Bragg, NC, replacing its lower echelon predecessor, the 1st Special Operations Command. As an Army Major Command, USASOC controls all active Army and Army Reserve SOF in the continental United States and transmits policy guidance to National Guard units through the State Adjutants Generals. The Commanding General wears three stars, compared with the two permitted his predecessor in lst Special Operations Command. The USASOC subordinate elements include a new Civil Affairs and Psychological Operations Command, activated simultaneously, and an Integration Command that oversees the Ranger Regiment and Special Operations Aviation Regiment, and a Special Forces Command formed a year later.

On 16 May 1990, the 160th Special Operations Aviation Regiment (SOAR) was activated, replacing the lower-echeloned 160th Aviation Group, which had been the Army focal point for SOF aviation since 1981. The new Regiment included the Regimental headquarters and two active-duty aviation battalions; one stationed at Fort Campbell, KY, and the other at Hunter Army Airfield, GA. The force included MH-60 Black Hawks, MH-47 Chinooks, and *A/MH-6* "Little Birds." Mission capabilities ranged from infiltration, resupply, and exfiltration support for Special Forces and Rangers to armed attack, aerial security, medical evacuation, electronic warfare, mine dispersal, and command/control. The top Regimental priority was support to the JSOC Special Mission Units, followed by support to JCS and CINC-directed exercises, SOF selection and joint-force training, the National Training Center, the Joint Readiness Training Center, and the Combined Maneuver Training Center (in Germany). Authorized personnel strength approximated 1,400.

A month later, on 20 June 1990, command of the U.S. Army John F. Kennedy Special Warfare Center and School located at Fort Bragg was transferred from the Army Training and Doctrine Command (TRADOC) to the Army Special Operations Command.

On 27 November 1990, the Army created the Special Forces Command (SFC) to provide a single focal point for professional training and development of the Special Forces soldier, both enlisted and officer. The SFC is the largest Army SOC component, consisting of five active-duty Special Forces Groups, two Reserve Groups, and two Groups in the Army

National Guard (ARNG), plus a signal battalion, and a support battalion. The combined personnel strength is approximately 10,000.

SPECIAL FORCES

De Oppresso Liber

The Special Forces Command (SFC) consists of seven Special Forces Groups, geographically oriented and capable of executing the full range of Special Operations missions in support of the combatant commander. The 12-man SF Operational Detachment is the core of the force and is composed of specially selected commissioned and noncommissioned officers who have undergone intense medical, engineering, demolition, communications, and weapons training. SF detachments rely on their combined skills, language expertise, and area knowledge to conduct both host-nation training or small-unit combat operations, to include Direct Action and Strategic Reconnaissance missions.

RANGERS

Rangers Lead the Way

The 75th Ranger Regiment consists of three geographically separate battalions and a regimental headquarters. The third battalion (3/75) and the Regimental headquarters were created in the early 1980s as part of the Army SOF revitalization. The Regiment is capable of providing an exceptionally well-trained and highly responsive strike force ranging in size from 150 to more than 2,000 soldiers within 18 hours of alert. Rangers are capable of deploying rapidly by land, sea, or air to conduct direct action operations at the company, battalion, or regimental level. Primarily fighting at night, Rangers rely on the elements of surprise, teamwork, and basic soldiering skills to achieve success. Rangers have taken part in every major combat operation in which the U.S. has been involved since the end of the Vietnam War.

ARMY AVIATION (TF 160)

Night Stalkers

The 160th Special Operations Air Regiment (SOAR) includes three aviation battalions operating the MH-60K Black Hawk, the extended range, heavy lift MH-47E Chinook, and the AH/MH-6 "Little Bird." This select group of aviators employs state-of-the-art equipment, and, along with the airmen of the Air Force Special Operations Command, provides extremely accurate heliborne lift and attack capabilities in a wide range of mission profiles. These missions include force insertion and extraction, armed escort, target suppression and destruction, and resupply. Within the Army, they have been the forerunners in developing aided night-flight procedures, tactics, and equipment. These soldiers' ability and performance exemplify the fact that "Night Stalkers Don't Quit."

PSYOP

Verbum Vincet -- Win the Mind, Win the Day

The reach of the PSYOP soldier has few barriers. These Active and Reserve units support both conventional and unconventional military operations worldwide, influencing opinions, emotions, attitudes, and behaviors of foreign audiences to create conditions favorable to American or host-nation goals. One of the most important criteria for PSYOP personnel is their regional orientation, which is developed through intense cross-cultural and language training and education. The active-duty Army psychological warfare capability is composed of the 4th Psychological Operations Group (the 4th POG, located at Fort Bragg) and its five subordinate battalions, each affiliated with a specific geographic regional command.

CIVIL AFFAIRS

Seal the Victory

Civil Affairs (CA) forces assist the commanders in fulfilling both civil and military support requirements. The only active force component is the 96th Civil Affairs Battalion at Fort Bragg. Its authorized strength is 212 personnel. The Army Reserve is the principal repository of CA specialties and skills that the active duty 96th does not have. Twenty-four additional CA battalions are in the U.S. Army Reserve. Typical specialties include public administration, education, finance, health, safety, welfare, labor relations, legal matters, property control, transportation, food distribution, and public works. Civil Affairs reservists typically are employed in short-term peacetime contingency missions due to their limited availability (2-3 weeks) and the potential for disruption of their civilian careers. However, CA reserve units and selected individuals participated in Operations Desert SHIELD/STORM, and individual CA reservists volunteered and served in Operation Just Cause in Panama in 1989 and Haiti in 1992.

NAVY SPECIAL WARFARE FORCES

The Only Easy Day Was Yesterday

The Naval Special Warfare Command (NAVSPECWARCOM) was established on 16 April 1987 at Coronado, CA. Its mission, somewhat expanded since 1987, is to train, equip, organize, and provide naval SOF personnel skilled in maritime and riverine operations to the operating fleets and joint commands. Foreign Internal Defense (FID) training missions normally claim top priority in peacetime, while "Direct Action" missions are the main wartime functions.

The Admiral who commands NAVSPECWARCOM has exercised operational control over all U.S.- based Naval Special Warfare (NSW) forces since March 1988. This was shortly after then-Secretary of Defense Weinberger disapproved dissents by senior Navy officials who sought to retain operational control. The one exception to the SECDEF blanket assignment order is one SEAL team permanently assigned to JSOC's Special Mission Unit force. As of October 1988, the Commander of NAVSPECWARCOM also has been responsible for the administration, training, maintenance, support, and readiness of all active NSW forces, including those assigned to unified commands overseas. The Naval Surface Reserve Force administers and supports NSW reserves.

Between May and October of 1988, the NAVSPECWARCOM Commander negotiated four Memoranda of Agreement (MOA) with other Navy Commanders to ensure proper support for NSW-deployed forces and for the Naval Special Warfare Center. Other signatories were: CINCLANT Fleet; CINCPAC Fleet; Commander, Submarine Force Pacific and the Chief of Naval Education and Training. CINCSOC and the Chief of Naval Operations subsequently concluded a more comprehensive MOA.

The total active and reserve personnel strength of NAVSPECWARCOM approximates 5,500. Naval Special Warfare Group One is headquartered in Coronado, CA, and Group Two at Little Creek, VA. Each group contains three SEAL teams and a SEAL Delivery Vehicle (SDV) team. A Special Boat Squadron supports each group. SEAL platoons and supporting boat unit crews train together routinely throughout 18-month pre-deployment, deploying, and post-deployment cycles.

The Naval Special Warfare (Training) Center is co-located with NAVSPECWARCOM and is the "schoolhouse" and source of new doctrine. A Naval Special Warfare Development Group (Dev-Group) was activated at Little Creek, VA. in September 1989. The Dev-Group provides centralized management for the development, test, and evaluation of current and emerging technologies that might have NSW application and assists in devising new SPECWAR tactics.

SEA-AIR-LAND (SEAL) TEAMS

The SEAL force, which had been sharply reduced after the Vietnam War, has been substantially rejuvenated and expanded. Although, organizationally, only one new team has been activated since 1986, the number of operational 16-man platoons is now 60 compared to fewer than 20 in 1981, a 300 percent increase. The platoons rely largely on concealment and surprise to accomplish their missions, which include unconventional warfare, foreign internal defense, counter-terrorism, direct action, and special reconnaissance, as well as hydrographic/coastal reconnaissance and surveillance, underwater demolition, raids, combat swimming, and riverine operations.

SEAL detachments in the U.S. Naval Reserve (USNR) are manned exclusively with NSW veterans who have served at least four years on active duty. Their principal purpose is to augment the active-duty SEAL teams with individual ready reserves, when required. (Army and Air Force SOF reserve components, in contrast, are called up mainly as units.)

SEAL Teams are maritime, multi-purpose combat forces organized, trained, and equipped to conduct a variety of SO missions in all operational environments. SEAL teams combine underwater demolition skills with many of the scouting and direct abilities of the Army Special Forces. Operating mainly in 16-man platoons from sea-based platforms, SEALs primarily conduct clandestine ground and waterborne reconnaissance and Direct Action (DA) raid-type missions in a maritime, littoral, or riverine environment in support of joint and fleet operations. A wide variety of delivery and recovery techniques are available to insert and extract SEAL personnel. The three most notable are all strategic capabilities: parachute insertion by long range aircraft; deployment from ocean-going surface platforms; and submarines. Tactical insertion can be accomplished by a variety of smaller surface platforms.

SEALs most often rely on waterborne surface craft in mission situations that call for the delivery of sizable forces and fast reaction. A mix of coastal/interdiction and patrol boats, mini-barge assault troop carriers (MATCs), and combat rubber raiding craft (CRRC) with distinctively different characteristics provide a range of insertion flexibility. However, the nature of the threat, the environment, and the availability, endurance, draft, range, signatures, armament, and seaworthiness of the various platforms are factors that influence the choice of insertion platform. Cyclone class patrol ships, for example, have great range, endurance and can survive sea states with 10-foot waves, but cannot move long distances fast enough in situations requiring an extremely fast reaction time. Conversely, unarmed and slow rubber raiding craft can be air-dropped in close proximity to the insertion beachhead, often within hours of a mission order being received.

SEAL DELIVERY VEHICLE TEAMS

SEAL Delivery Vehicle (SDV) Teams, formerly called Swimmer Delivery Teams, are specially trained SEALs and support personnel responsible for operating and maintaining SDVs and Dry Deck Shelters (DDS). SDVs are wet submersibles designed to conduct clandestine reconnaissance, Direct Action, and passenger-delivery missions in maritime environments. Dry Deck Shelters, installed on submarines just before each mission and removed thereafter, allow the launch and recovery of SEAL Delivery Vehicles (SDV) while submerged. When teamed with their host submarines, SDV and DDS platoons provide the most clandestine maritime delivery capability in the world.

SPECIAL BOAT SQUADRONS

Special Boat Squadrons (SBS) and Units (SBU) are composed of specially trained naval personnel. They are responsible for operating and maintaining a variety of Special Operation ships and craft, such as High Speed Boats, Rigid Inflatable Boats, and Patrol Coastal ships which have been specially designed or configured to conduct coastal and riverine interdiction as well as support of naval and joint Special Operations. These units have great strategic mobility and can respond to crisis situations worldwide. They provide the Navy's only riverine patrol capability and SOF's best small craft support. The NAVSPECWAR Fleet includes the following surface delivery capabilities:

- The MARK V patrol boat is the newest craft in the fleet, exceeding 80 feet in length. It was designed to replace several types of aging Navy Patrol craft, some of which date back to the Vietnam era. The primary mission of the Mark V is medium-range insertion and extraction of special operations personnel. The boat can be forward deployed by airlift as well by sealift on-board larger surface ships. Depending on the mission location, it is also self-deployable. The Mark V is capable of speeds in excess of 50 knots and has a troop delivery capacity of a SEAL platoon (16 fully-equipped combatants).
- SEA SPECTRE is a 65-foot, four-hull seagoing coastal patrol unit officially designated the Mark 3 Patrol Boat (PB-Mk3). The Sea Spectre class is the most advanced "small" Patrol Boat in the Navy inventory, and was designed as a high-speed weapons platform for coastal patrol and maritime interdiction missions.
- SEAFOX is a high-speed, 36-foot, fiberglass-hull Special Warfare Craft, Light (SWCL) developed to fulfill the tactical support requirements of the Special Warfare Groups. It can be carried on most ships using standard ship davits and can be airlifted by the C-5, C-141, and C-17.
- The Mark Two PBR, at 31 feet LOA, is the smallest of the SPECWAR Patrol Boat Fleet. The Mark Two was designed for high-speed, shallow-water and riverine operations. Originally designed in 1966 for use in the Vietnam conflict, more than 500 units have been produced.

NAVAL SPECWAR HELICOPTER CAPABILITY

A Navy Reserve Helicopter squadron is designated to support each of the NAVSPEC WAR Groups, one on each coast. The two squadrons

(Helicopter Combat Support Squadrons -- HCS-4 and HCS-5) have a dual-mission responsibility. The missions are combat search and rescue for downed aircrews, and support to the NAVSPEC WAR Groups. Both squadrons operate the HH-60H Seahawk helicopter, a version of the Blackhawk.

AIR FORCE SPECIAL OPERATIONS FORCES

A Step Ahead

In March 1983, the 23rd Air Force was activated under MAC as the USAF Special Operation Air Force. It included: the entire USAF Special Operations air fleet (forty airframes); the worldwide assets of the Air Rescue Service; the full USAF Medical evacuation fleet; and the entire MAC Combat Controller and Combat Medical (PJ) force; and the majority of the Combat Weather teams.

Collectively, the force contained a tremendous breadth and depth not only of aircrew (helicopter and fixed wing) experience, but also a highly qualified and motivated pool of parachute-qualified, skilled volunteers to meet the expanding manpower and experience needs for new Air Force Special Tactics Teams. An expansion of the Special Tactics force was required to support the assault and reconnaissance forces of the growing Army and Navy SOF community.

Five years after Desert One, the total USAF SOF aircraft inventory included 13 MC-130 Combat Talons, 19 AC-130 Spectre Gunships (9 "H" models in the active force and 10 Vietnam vintage "A" models in the reserves), plus 7 MH-53 Pave Low helicopters. Except for the seven Pave Low Helicopters, this was the same force that was available for Desert One in 1980 and Grenada in 1983. In December 1985, all eleven of the 1st SOW C-130s ordered into the air, during an Operational Readiness Inspection at Hurlburt, failed to past the inspection. This was not from a want or lack of hard work or trying, but largely because of a lack of spare parts and maintenance dollars. This maintenance failure was a black eye that prompted immediate command support. Funds and parts began to flow to the SOF air fleet. Six months later, during the follow-up "retest exercise," the fleet operated at a near 98 percent in-commission rate.

In August 1987, five months after USSOCOM was activated and shortly after 23rd headquarters moved to Hurlburt Field in the Florida panhandle, General Patterson, the 23rd Commander, took it upon himself to unofficially subtitle the 23rd as the "Air Force Special Operations Command (AFSOC)." He solidified his action by having the new identity emblazoned on the entrance to the headquarters. This decision was made in deference to the impending visit of General Lindsay, the newly confirmed Commander In Chief (CINC) of U.S. Special Operations Command. The new CINC had already made it known that the presence of MAC in the command line of his Air Force forces did not sit well and "muddied the waters."

At the time, Major General Patterson projected the force structure to grow substantially within the next two years. The growth would be from one CONUS-based operational wing (the 1st SOW) at Hurlburt field, one training Wing at Albuquerque, NM, and the three small overseas squadrons in Europe and the Pacific to a combat force of three robust multi-functional Wings. One Wing was to be based in Europe and another in the Pacific, plus a third operational Wing, ("a second" 1st SOW) was to be based on the West Coast of the United States to support the West Coast-based SEALS, Rangers and Special Forces units. This growth would position four operational wings to support operations anywhere on the globe, plus a full-up composite year-round training wing centrally located at Albuquerque, NM. Together with the Air Rescue Service and the Medical Evacuation fleet, this structure would provide a worldwide capability and SOF global reach.

By October 1987, the Command had obtained Headquarters USAF and MAC concurrence to create a composite Special Tactics Group consisting of SO-qualified Combat Controllers and PJs to directly support the expanded Army and Navy Special Operations Forces. Work was also underway to create a Special Operations-qualified Combat Weather unit. Many of these goals were well on the way to full accomplishment by 1988, to include the creation of an operational wing in Europe and the Pacific. However, in early 1989, General Lindsay (who did not want anything that was not "pure" SOF in his command) requested headquarters USAF, (over the objections of Major General Patterson) to divest AFSOC of all "non-special operations units." The Air Staff took the request under advisement.

On 22 May 1990, Headquarters Air Force officially redesignated 23rd Air Force as the Air Force Special Operations Command (AFSOC), and raised its status to that of a Major Air Force Command reporting to the Chief of Staff, and terminated its subordination to MAC. At the same time, Headquarters USAF honored the earlier request of General Lindsey and reassigned the Air Rescue Service and the Aero-Medical Evacuation fleet back to MAC. These decisions later complicated combat search and rescue support in Operation Desert Storm in 1993 in Iraq.

In 1991, the total Air Force underwent an extensive force realignment, and along with the other military services began a major draw-down in force strength. AFSOC units were among the first to be organizationally reduced. The creation of the West Coast SOW was postponed indefinitely and the two overseas wings were downgraded to "Groups," although with their operational capabilities much improved from the pre-1986 time frame.

By 1993, six years after Congressional action, SOF long-range air and extraction capabilities were on the mend. Six Air Force SOF aircraft programs were in progress. The MC-130 Combat Talon and MH-53 Pave Low populations had grown to 28 and 41 airframes, respectively, and new AC-130U model Spectre gunships and improved munitions were in the mill. At the same time, the Army's Special Operations Aviation Regiment (SOAR) was receiving new model MH-60K Black Hawks and the extended range MH-47E Chinook helicopters.

SPECIAL OPERATIONS WINGS & GROUPS

Any Time, Any Place

These Active and Reserve units provide fixed-wing and specialized rotary-wing capabilities for SO missions. The crews and aircraft provide surgically precise, multi-target firepower and engage in a variety of missions, such as infiltration and exfiltration of SOF operational elements, armed escort, reconnaissance, interdiction, resupply/refueling, and combat search and rescue. Additionally, they perform psychological operations using video and radio broadcasting and conduct literature drops. The USAF Special Operations Airlift fleet includes five variants of the C-130 turbo-prop transport and two helicopters (MH-53J and MH-60G):

- **COMBAT TALON I/II - MC-130E/H:** The E Models were initially deployed in 1966; the lead H Model in 1991. The mission of the MC-130 is to provide a day/night, adverse weather capability to airdrop or airland personnel and equipment anywhere in the world. A secondary mission is to provide deep-penetration air refueling support to the SOF helicopter fleets. The 1996 inventory lists 14 of the older E models transports, of which nine are equipped with the Fulton air recovery system. Since the delivery of the lead H model in 1991, the H model fleet has grown to 24 platforms.
- **SPECTRE - AC-130 GUNSHIPS:** AC-130H and U-model Spectre gunships are armed with twin 20mm cannons, a 40mm cannon, and one 105 mm howitzer which make a formidable weapons suite for close air support, air interdiction, and armed reconnaissance. Electronic warfare and target acquisition suites are equally impressive. A searchlight, low light level television, and infrared sensors, together with hi-tech navigation and fire control systems, facilitate pinpoint accuracy during extended loiter periods at night and in adverse weather. The Air Force canceled plans to transfer the older H-model gunships to the Air Force Reserve in the early nineties based on the increase in mission requirements that evidenced themselves in the late eighties. The fleet now numbers 21 and is now twice as strong as it was in 1979.
- **COMBAT SHADOW - MC-130P TANKERS:** One MC-13OP/N tanker (aerial refueling) Combat Shadow squadron at Eglin AFB, FL, stands ready to refuel U.S.- based Army and Air Force SOF helicopters in flight. Two other SOF tanker squadrons at Alconbury, UK, and Kadena, Okiwawa, Japan, perform identical functions for SOCEUR and SOCPAC. Although

actions are underway to improve their survivability, the use of HC tankers is usually reserved for operations in relatively low-threat environments, because most of the tanker fleet lack terrain-following radars and state-of-the-art defensive countermeasures. However, a portion of the MC-130 Combat Talon long-range penetration fleet have been modified to accomplish the refueling function over hostile territory. There were no air-refuelable C-130 tankers available in 1979; now the fleet consists of 28 airframes.

- **COMMANDO SOLO - EC-130 PSYOPS:** The 193rd Special Operation Group (SOG) Pennsylvania Air National Guard at Harrisburg Airport, PA, operates two EC-130E Commando Solos, which are aircraft dedicated exclusively in PSYOP. They can broadcast over AM, FM, and HF radio bands and beam color television programs via HF/UHF. The 193rd SOG also operates two other EC-130s configured to perform electronic warfare functions such as electronic jamming, signals monitoring, analysis and reporting. Both of these capabilities were used very successfully in Panama in 1989 and the Gulf Conflict in 1990.
- **PAVE LOW - MH-53 Insertion/Extraction Helicopters:** In 1986, AFSOC possessed just seven long-range MH-53H Pave Low helicopters. By 1993, the force had grown to 35 of the much improved "J" models, which are among the world's most technologically advanced rotary wing aircraft. Most of the aircraft are now shipboard-capable with folding rotor blades. Their ability to penetrate deeply into hostile or denied air space during foul weather in the dead of night and return undetected was demonstrated at the start of the Allied air campaign against Iraq in 1993. Two USAF Pave Low MH-53s led a flight of Army Apache Attack helicopters to within missile strike range of two key Iraqi air defense radars, which the Apaches attacked and destroyed with Hellfire missiles. The MH-53 organic defenses include three 7.62mm mini-guns or three .50 caliber machine guns, armor plating, and assorted electronic countermeasures. The MH-53J fleet now numbers 40.
- **PAVE HAWK - MH-60 RESCUE Helicopters:** A Special Operations Squadron (SOS) at Hurlburt Field flies all of AFSOC's medium-range MH-60G Pave Hawk helicopters, which conduct missions similar to those of Pave Lows but carry fewer troops. Folding rotor blades and tail stabilators facilitate shipboard operations and transportability by C-5A and C-17 aircraft. Both the MH-60G and the MH-53J have the inherent capability to perform Combat Search and Rescue (CSAR) missions.

SPECIAL TACTICS SQUADRONS

First There That Others May Live

Special Tactics Squadrons consist of combat control and pararescue personnel, uniquely organized, trained, and equipped to establish and control the air-ground interface for SOF operating in austere and hostile environments. Fully interoperable with SEAL, Special Forces, and Ranger units, they select, assess, and mark assault zones; control air traffic; and provide casualty recovery, treatment, and evacuation staging. Special Tactics Teams also operate forward area rearming and refueling points; direct and position aircraft using visual and electronic signals, and designate targets. In addition, they assist in offensive attack and demolition operations; provide human intelligence and airfield reconnaissance; conduct personnel recovery; provide advanced trauma care; and coordinate evacuation operations and are trained to conduct selected aircrew duties.

SPECIAL OPERATIONS SCHOOL

The U.S. Air Force Special Operations School, unlike its Army and Navy counterparts, emphasizes education rather than training. Three thousand students from throughout the U.S. SOF community, all U.S. military Services, and foreign countries annually attend one of its 15 courses. The school offers courses of 3 to 10 days duration nominally five times per year. These courses cover a broad spectrum of subjects that include cross-cultural communications, revolutionary warfare, foreign internal defense, crisis response management, psychological operations, geographic area orientations, and special operations planning. One of the courses most in demand is the Special Operations Planning Workshop. The workshop was developed shortly after the deactivation of JTF 1-79 and constructed with inputs from staff of JTF 1-79. Several of the raid participants and senior officers of note, such as Lieutenant General Sam Wilson, present seminars and lead planning discussions. Another related course, titled Joint Special Operations Staff Officers Course, was created subsequently and conducted in a very interactive, pragmatic manner with guest speakers from throughout the Special Operations, Joint Staff and Intelligence Community.

MARINE CORPS SPECIAL OPERATIONS CAPABILITIES

Section 167, *Title 10, United States Code*, identifies Special Operations Forces "as core forces or as augmenting forces in the Joint Chiefs of Staff Joint Strategic Capabilities Plan, Annex E, dated December 1, 1985." It also acknowledges forces described in the Terms of Reference and Conceptual Operations Plan for the Joint Special Operations Command, in effect on April 1, 1986 as SOF, plus forces designated by the Secretary of Defense. The United States Marine Corps possesses no Special Operations Forces meeting any of these terms or definitions. However, beginning in 1985, selected Marine Expeditionary Units (MEU) have been trained for and designated as "Special Operations Capable" (SOC) prior to the normal overseas deployment. This capability rating is not a permanent matter. The longer the force is out on the deployment, the less SOC-capable it becomes in many areas. This is due to the lack of the ability to continue sustainment training in many of the SOF unique skills and proficiency areas.

SOF-associated skills, such as Close Quarter Battle (CBQ) training, specialized demolition operations, clandestine reconnaissance and surveillance skills, tactical recovery of aircraft and personnel, in-extremis hostage recovery capabilities, and the seizure/destruction of offshore oil production facilities receive concentrated attention during pre-deployment training. Each MEU must demonstrate a required degree of proficiency before it receives the SOC designation.

The MEU is essentially a conventional task force that includes a reinforced infantry battalion, a reinforced helicopter squadron, and a service support group. Total personnel strength approximates 1,800-2,000. Assigned forces function together for a year, then return to parent organizations. Each MEU relies on a Navy Amphibious Ready Group (ARG) for mobility, sustainability, and communications/intelligence support. One MEU is routinely deployed with Carrier Task Forces in the Persian Gulf, another in the Mediterranean Sea. A third MEU, based in Okinawa, Japan, embarks when the Commander in Chief, U.S. Pacific Fleet, so directs. It was an element of the Mediterranean MEU, a Marine TRAP (Tactical Recovery of Aircraft and Personnel) Team that was flown into Bosnia by Marine helicopters to provide ground security during the extraction of Captain Scott O'Grady, USAF, after his F-16 was shot down seven days earlier.

POSTSCRIPT
CONTINUING CONCERNS

Although the Eagle is no longer crippled,
and the talons have been sharpened,
The eagle's eye and the lift of his wings
still pose a potential Achilles heel.

In October and November 1980, there was a potential for the forces to conduct a second Iranian rescue attempt. If it had been focused on the Embassy grounds in Teheran, as indicated by the "Eureka Reporting," they may have been drawn into a deadly and devastating trap.

In 1983, the initial phases of military operations in Grenada (Urgent Fury) were hampered not only by time and tides, but by the lack of reliable "on-the-ground" military observers and a less than perfect information dissemination system.

In 1989, a principle objective of Operation Just Cause -- the capture of General Noreiga during the initial hours of U.S. intervention into Panama -- went unfulfilled for five days amid a plethora of false reporting until Noreiga independently accepted political asylum in the Papal Embassy.

In 1991, a lack of an on-the-ground and limited aerial tactical reconnaissance capability during the Allied campaign led to a prolonged hunt for Iraqi Scud missile launchers. These limitations contributed to the targeting of an Iraqi command facility that was also being used by the Iraqi government as a civilian "bomb" shelter.

Shortly after becoming Director of the CIA in May 1995, Dr. John M. Deutch, in an address to graduates of the National Defense University, made the following statement regarding CIA support to military operations:

> A singular purpose of this effort is to assure that we provide future military commanders with dominant battlefield awareness. . . . That means that imagery, signals, human intelligence must be integrated and distributed in a timely fashion to battlefield commanders. . . . All our efforts at analysis, at modeling and simulation point to the tremendous tactical advantage that comes when you understand where the enemy is and where the targets are. And if the enemy does not have similar information, it means that victory will come more rapidly, and therefore the casualties will be lower.

Dr. Deutch's statement is encouraging, but its fundamental premise is not a new revelation. History has repeatedly shown that the more you know about the enemy and the less he knows about you, the better the odds of military victory. True victory is measured in the achievement of national goals and political objectives with minimum loss of life. These objectives must be clear, positive and worthy of attainment, otherwise the cost in lives and suffering is a waste of our most precious national resources -- our citizens and our national stature. Hopefully, Dr. Deutch's statement is being honored by commitment, dedication and success rather than by neglect, as has often been the case in the past thirty years.

OTHER AREAS OF CONCERN

There are two other areas of strategic concern that warrant continuing and persistent attention. Both are directly related to the effectiveness and survivability of SOF forces. Both impact on the force's ability to meet the unexpected challenges and evolving capabilities of a host of emerging, extremely committed adversaries, declared and potential. The first area is concrete and specific; the second is fundamental, philosophic and enduring.

As a nation with global interests and responsibilities, the "lift" capability of the Eagle must always be maintained and improved, if we are to be able to respond to or preempt a crisis. Specifically, we need a modern fleet of long-range airborne SOF infiltration and extraction platforms, which possess greater speed than the C-130 and MH-53 fleets, incorporate stealth technologies, self-defense mechanisms and Low Probability of Detection (LPD) communications, while maintaining (or exceeding) the range and carrying capacity of the C-130.*

The other area of concern is the need to recognize that if we, as a nation, are to maintain a viable Special Operations Capability, we must continually seek improvements across the full array of capabilities. This is essential in an era where adversaries have easy access to advanced technologies and will always have the advantages of prior planning, choice of location, and time of execution. This potential will have increasing lethality as the interdependence of our national infra-structures increases. If we are to stay ahead of the potential adversary, SOF must continually seek improvements across the full spectrum of needs -- surveillance, communications, logistics, material, medical, training, movement, and insertion and extraction.

* The turbo prop blades of the C-130s, the rotor blades of the MH-53/MH-60 helicopter force and the soon-to-be-introduced V-22 Osprey Tilt Rotor provide a radar cross section signature that is larger than a B-52, making undetectable insertion or extraction more and more problematic. Fortunately, this deficiency and other limitations of the C-130 fleet were recognized in an "Air Force Executive Guidance" document dated 11 September 1995. Signed by General Ronald Fogelman, then Air Force Chief of Staff, and Dr. Shiela Widnall, Secretary of the Air Force, it called for a new SOF aviation platform. The target date was set at 2015, 17 to 18 years from now. It will be needed much earlier, or the Eagle may find itself crippled again.

PART V

APPENDIX ONE
SOF Deployments 1987-1996

In 1992, the ASD-SO/LIC, in conjunction with the United States Special Operations Command, published the first *SOF Posture Statement.* Subsequent editions were published in 1993 and 1996. This GPO-printed and distributed booklet was designed to educate and inform, and correct mis-impressions concerning SOF. It contained a review of SOF missions, programs, and budgetary data and was distributed to Congress, DOD, and made available to the general public. The following chronology was compiled from these three editions. The chronology reflects the breadth, scope, diversity and dedication of the current generation of United States Special Operations Forces, much of which was nurtured by the demands, requirements and contributions of JTF 1-79 and the subsequent Joint Special Operations Task Forces committed in Grenada, Panama, and Iraq.

1987

PERSIAN GULF -- OPERATION EARNEST WILL/PRIME CHANCE

The U.S.-Allied response to Iranian operations against international oil tankers transiting the Persian Gulf. Army SOF helicopters teamed with SEALs and Special Boat personnel to capture an Iranian mine-laying ship. They carried out assaults against offshore oil platforms used by the Iranians to harass international shipping, and Special Boat Units performed escort, patrol and interdiction duties.

1988

HONDURAS -- OPERATION GOLDEN PHEASANT

Special Operations Forces were deployed as part of a larger U.S. contingency force show-of-force deployment to Honduras in response to Nicaraguan border incursions.

AFGHANISTAN -- OPERATION SAFE PASSAGE

SOF were deployed to the northern Pakistan frontier to provide land mine clearance training and medical assistance to Afghanistan resistance groups and their families.

1989

PANAMA -- OPERATION JUST CAUSE

Although conducted in December of 1989, contingency planning had begun in March 1988, in the wake of threatening and harassing actions taken by the Panamanian Defense Forces against U.S. forces and their dependents. Special Operations Forces were involved in much of the joint planning throughout the subsequent eighteen months. More than 4,000 of the 27,000 troops involved in Operation JUST CAUSE were SOF personnel. Special Operations Forces had responsibility for more than a third of the 27 initial targets. The full range of special operations capabilities was employed during the initial six hours of operations and continued throughout the follow-on operations. Some of these actions are summarized below:

- To neutralize Panamanian naval capabilities, Navy SEALs engaged in a variety of missions. On one mission, four SEALs slipped into Balboa

Harbor and attached plastic explosives to the hull of the *Presidente Porras* to sink the 65-foot coastal patrol boat precluding its possible use as an escape means by General Noriega, the Commander of the Panamanian Defense Forces (PDF).

- Air Force SOF units in AC-130 SPECTRE gunships destroyed Panamanian Defense Force (PDF) command and control facilities with minimum damage to surrounding facilities. In addition, these gunships supported ground troops by suppressing enemy fire and protected the U.S. Embassy from retaliation. The SPECTRE gunships are powerful psychological weapons; when confronted by the threat of the AC-130's fire, numerous Panamanian garrisons chose to surrender.
- Army Rangers seized Torrijos/Tocumen and Rio Hato airfields, and Special Forces secured the Pacora River bridge. AFSOC Special Tactics Teams supported these operations. Collectively these operations neutralized PDF combat units, effectively preventing reinforcement of Panama City.

  PSYOP teams were assigned to conventional forces throughout the operation to help limit collateral damage and induce PDF units to surrender.

1990

PANAMA -- OPERATION PROMOTE LIBERTY

A follow-on, nation building assistance effort to reconstitute the Panamanian civil government and the new civil police force. SOF personnel, particularly Army Special Forces, PSYOP and CA specialists, played a key role in these activities utilizing their language and area skills extensively.

During Operation PROMOTE LIBERTY, SOF units were crucial to the rebuilding Panama's infrastructure. Army Special Forces assisted in stabilizing certain areas by establishing roadblocks, performing identification checks, hunting for arms caches, apprehending criminals, and helping local government agencies restore public services. SOF CA personnel also advised Panamanian agencies and acted as consultants to the Office of the President of Panama in financial, public works, health services, and judicial matters. One of the CA's most important functions was to ensure effective communications between U.S. Agencies and Panamanian ministries. Temporary shelters were constructed at Albrook Air Force Base for displaced civilians from the El Chorillo section of the capital. CA planners worked closely with Panamanian leaders to maintain order and reestablish essential services:

> We immediately transitioned from a fighting force to a nation-building force, restoring law and order, and self-determination for Panamanians. . . . This operation highlights for me the value of Special Forces language and cultural training and unique military skills. It also embodies the Special Forces motto "De Oppresso Liber" ("to liberate the oppressed)."
>
> Major, Army Special Forces

LIBERIA -- OPERATION SHARP EDGE

SOF elements were deployed to help relieve a Marine Fleet Anti-Terrorism Security Team (FAST) security augmentation team and the U.S. Embassy Marine Guard Forces protecting the U.S. Embassy and its staff. Subsequently these forces assisted a U.S. Marine Expeditionary Unit in executing the follow-on Emergency Evacuation Operation.

SAUDI ARABIA -- DESERT SHIELD

SOF were deployed early as part of the U.S. deterrent response to the Iraqi occupation of Kuwait. A particular challenge in the Gulf War was the coordination of the multinational Coalition Forces, most of which had neither worked together nor employed similar operating procedures. SOF was used to establish highly effective working relations with Arab and other Allied forces. General H. Norman Schwarzkopf, Commander in Chief, U. S. Central Command, described SOF as the "glue" that held the Coalition ground forces together.

1991

KUWAIT/IRAQ -- OPERATION DESERT STORM

U.S.-Coalition offensive operations to drive Iraqi forces from Kuwait. SOF from the Air Force, Navy, and Army played decisive roles throughout Operation DESERT STORM. SOF was among the first forces to deploy and, as demonstrated by Operation PROVIDE COMFORT, is frequently the last to leave.

- The opening gambit of the war, an offensive air attack, was a joint Air Force and Army effort designed to disable part of Iraq's early warning radar system. This opened a safe corridor through which allied air forces could begin Operation DESERT STORM's air campaign. On 17 January 1991, PAVE LOW helicopter teams crossed into Iraq, flying at 100 knots, at less than 100 feet off the desert floor providing pathfinder escort for Army attack helicopters. Both the Air Force and the Army were successful in their missions - the Iraqi radar sites were destroyed. Air Force SOF also assisted PSYOP units by dropping leaflets, followed by a 15,000 pound daisy-cutter bomb to breach Iraqi mine fields. Air Force SOF elements also conducted numerous insertion and extraction missions.
- SOF involvement ran the gamut of missions. Army Special forces conducted FID training operations with Royal Saudi Land Forces and, later, with the Pan-Arab forces comprised of troops from Egypt, Syria, Oman, Morocco, Bahrain, United Arab Emirates, and Qatar. SOF personnel conducted extensive training for these culturally and linguistically diverse troops. In addition, SOF personal carried out special and high-risk missions, from daytime surveillance to night reconnaissance to behind-enemy-lines infiltration to observe Iraqi troop movements.
- SOF provided command and control support to two Arab corps, and accompanied them into Kuwait to expel Iraqi forces. Then SOF assisted the Kuwait Army in operations to clear Iraqi snipers and rear guard forces, and conducted demolition of mines and booby traps. SOF forces also provided

forward area and long-range reconnaissance and target designation for air and ground attacks. SOF teams located targets and provided the terminal guidance to strike SCUD launchers. PSYOP units supported theater information campaigns to influence enemy behavior and effect early surrender. CA units controlled dislocated civilians and enemy prisoners, and supported USCENTCOM's immediate post-combat military assistance to Kuwait.

- Navy SOF played a pivotal role in the opening of the ground campaign with a deception operation. Timed to start with the ground war, Naval Special warfare forces simulated preparations for a large amphibious invasion on the Kuwaiti coast. SEALs planted shallow water demolition charges as high-speed boat units operated offshore. These activities drew elements of two Iraqi divisions to that area, while far to the west, coalition forces attacked across the Saudi-Iraqi border. SEALs also coordinated close air support and trained Saudi forces.

"The variety of missions that the Special Operations Forces provided over there was across the entire spectrum of what they are expected to do. . . . They were absolutely magnificent."
General H. Norman Schwarzkopf, USA
Commander in Chief, U.S. Central Command

TURKEY/NORTHERN IRAQ -- OPERATION PROVIDE COMFORT

In the aftermath of Operation DESERT STORM, the United Nations reported that the refugee survival situation in northern Iraq and Turkey was so severe that 2,000 Iraqi Kurds, mostly children and elderly, were dying in the mountains each day. Immediate action was taken by Air Force SOF personnel in MC-130E COMBAT TALON aircraft, which led conventional C-130s to the Kurdish refugees in the mountains, where bundles of emergency supplies were dropped.

When Operation PROVIDE COMFORT's Combined Task Force was organized, its main objective was to immediately stop the loss of life in the camps and to stabilize the population. The plan called for providing humanitarian assistance for up to 700,000 Kurdish refugees for a minimum of 30 days, then to resettle them at temporary sites where they could be more easily sustained and protected. SOF elements in conjunction with U.S. Marine forces, and supported by Air Force SOF MH-53J PAVE LOW helicopters, located suitable sites for refugee camps and then worked with refugee leaders to organize and train the population to be more self-sufficient. SOF Civil Affairs units developed plans for medical assistance, food distribution, and day-to-day camp operations and managed their implementation and execution:

> When we arrived in Camp Cucurka, we found approximately 130,000 Kurdish refugees crowded into a small valley with a death rate in the camp of over 125 people a day. In the first two weeks, we were able to reduce the death rate to less than 10 a day.
> Master Sergeant, Army Special Forces

KUWAIT -- CIVIL RECONSTRUCTION

Immediately after Iraq was driven from Kuwait, Civil Affairs units moved into the city to assist in restoring the Kuwaiti governmental and civilian structure as quickly as possible. The 63 CA people assigned to the Kuwaiti Task Force (KTF) included civil administration and basic government management experts, doctors, lawyers, a veterinarian, an agronomist, a fire chief, and a city planner. This group coordinated actions between the military and civilian population, managing scarce resources.

By the time the Kuwaiti Task Force (KTF) departed, the Kuwaiti medical community had regained 98 percent of its prewar capacity. And the Ministry of Health was fully operational; sanitation was improved and the sewer system was restored. Kuwaiti police forces had begun to assert control; public lighting was restored; television and telecommunications services were partially restored; more than 200 oil well fires were under control; transportation was reestablished; and public education began on schedule in the fall of 1991. The international airport was reopened, and the transition to civil control was accomplished by late April 1991. The major port of Ash Shuwaybah was opened; others were cleared of explosives and prepared for operations; and all major roads were cleared of debris and repaired.

SOMALIA -- OPERATION EASTERN EXIT

SOF personnel were deployed to evacuate U. S. Embassy staff and foreign diplomatic personnel from the embassy compound. The emergency evacuation was completed moments before hostile forces overran the Embassy compound.

BANGLADESH -- OPERATION SEA ANGEL

SOF was deployed, along with elements of a U.S. Marine Expeditionary Force, as part of a U.S. disaster assistance effort in the wake of a devastating typhoon, which caused extensive damage, and loss of life. Cyclone Marian took 139,000 lives, killed more than a million cattle, and wiped out rice, jute, salt pans, and other means of livelihood. During Operation SEA ANGEL, SOF assisted the U.S. Marine-led effort to stabilize the country by sending Special Forces disaster relief teams into remote areas to gather information and coordinate relief efforts. The SF teams identified each area's needs and ensured supplies were received and distributed quickly.

PHILIPPINES -- OPERATION FIERY VIGIL

SOF was deployed, as part of a large U.S. disaster assistance effort, in response to a series of devastating volcanic eruptions at Mount Pinatubo.

ZAIRE/CONGO -- OPERATION BADGER PACK

SOF was employed along with U.S. conventional forces as part of a major operation to evacuate U.S. and foreign personnel from riot-torn areas.

CAMEROON -- MEDICAL ASSISTANCE

A 12-person team from the 353rd Civil Affairs Command treated an outbreak of meningitis. The team, which include four doctors, three nurses, and one corpsman, vaccinated approximately 60,000 people, performed hundreds of medical consultations, and treated thousands of patients in just 10 days.

LATIN AMERICA -- ANDEAN COUNTER-DRUG SUPPORT

SOF was deployed in support of U.S. objectives for the Andean Ridge Counter-Drug Strategy. SOF trained host nation police and armed forces dedicated to counter narcotics, primarily through exercises and mobile training teams. SOF teams also supported the Drug Enforcement Administration, the U.S. Information Agency, and the State Department's Narcotics Assistance Staff. SOF's greater role in counter-drug missions was demonstrated when SOF deployed to BOLIVIA to train the 16th Bolivian Battalion in counter-drug operations. The training included a leader's course, a light infantry course, advanced individual courses, and a battalion staff course. SOF concluded its training effort with a 15-day exercise involving all Bolivian military services, the UMOPAR (Bolivian Drug Enforcement Administration), and the U.S. DEA.

1992

EXPANDING MISSIONS FOR THE 1990S AND BEYOND

"Even the definition of combat is changing. While traditional concepts are still valid, we are finding new definitions of combat embodies in new kinds of military operations, such as humanitarian and disaster assistance, a whole range of peace operations, counter-proliferation, and even protecting the environment."

General Wayne A. Downing, USA
Commander in Chief, USSOCOM

CUBA -- OPERATION GITMO

During Operation GITMO, both CA and PSYOP units contributed to the assistance efforts for more than 30,000 Haitian refugees at temporary facilities at Guantanamo Bay Naval Base, Cuba. Virtually the entire active component 96th CA Battalion and more than 200 U.S. Army Reserve volunteers served as camp administrators and CA advisors to the Commander of Army Forces and the Commander, Joint Task Force GITMO. Civil Affairs Personnel assisted in screening the refugees and establishing internal camp operations. These efforts were essential for maintaining order among the Haitians, whose frustration with being detained in the camps for months often manifested itself in outbreaks of civil disturbance. PSYOP personnel used their equipment and interpersonal communications skills to provide current information to the camp populations to neutralize misinformation and rumors, to enhance law and order within the camps, and to create a more positive atmosphere.

ECUADOR -- AVIATION SUPPORT OPERATIONS

Aviation support (and training) operations, an old and proven concept dating back to World War II was reinstated by AFSOF and demonstrated anew when a joint Army-Air Force SOF element deployed to Ecuador to work with Ecuadoran Armed Special Forces and Air Force Special Purpose Units.

FLORIDA -- DISASTER ASSISTANCE

Along with other members of the United States Armed Forces, SOF PSYOP personnel provided assistance in the wake of Hurricane Andrew. PSYOPS Teams employed their communications and foreign language skills to provide immediate aid to Floridians in the aftermath of Hurricane Andrew. During a three-week blitz, active duty and reserve component PSYOP specialists from the 4th and 5th PSYOP Groups were instrumental in providing critical public service information via print, radio broadcasts, and loudspeaker teams. Humanitarian Information Support Teams provided further support. Employing eight loudspeaker teams in high mobility, multipurpose wheeled vehicles these teams broadcast public service announcements to people who stayed with what remained of their homes and to those whose radios and televisions had been destroyed.

COMMONWEALTH OF INDEPENDENT STATES (CIS)

SOF personnel were deployed to the former Soviet Union during Operation PROVIDE HOPE to provide linguistic and liaison support for the delivery of humanitarian aid and supplies. SOF personnel, proficient in Russian, facilitated the safe passage of U. S. aircraft through restricted air corridors.

In Khabarovsk, Russia, SOF worked with Russian Spetsnaz (Special Purpose, i.e. Special Operations) personnel and national-level officials to coordinate initial aid management, ground operations, and physical security. In Dushanbe, Tadzhikistan, the U.S. SOF detachment landed near intense ethnic and political fighting and worked with the Ministry of the Interior and its special purpose troops to ensure the safety of humanitarian assistance personnel and aircraft, and the physical security of 20 tons of urgently needed medical supplies.

MONGOLIA -- TRANSLATION SERVICES

SOF often supports new regional initiatives involving other foreign military forces. The highlight of one such mission in Ulan Bator, Mongolia occurred when a parachute qualified female PSYOP linguist became the first U.S. soldier to jump with the Mongolian Armed Forces and was authorized to wear Mongolian jump wings. Proficient in Russian, the specialist deployed for six months as a liaison between the U.S. Defense Attaché Office and the Mongolian Ministries of Defense and External Relations. Her primary mission was to teach English to Mongolian officers, officer cadets, and the Chief of the Mongolian General Staff. She received her wings after participating in airborne operations, parachuting from a Soviet MI-8 helicopter with elements of the 184th Mongolian Parachute Regiment.

SOMALIA -- OPERATION PROVIDE RELIEF

In August 1992, President Bush ordered the Department of Defense to begin emergency airlifts of food in what became known as Operation PROVIDE RELIEF. An Army Special Forces company provided the increased security necessary for the supply airlifts. By November 1992, however, the situation had deteriorated further, especially in southern and central Somalia. The prime missions for the U.S. forces in Operation RESTORE HOPE, which began in early December 1992, were to secure the major food distribution points as well as air and seaports, guard relief convoys, and assist relief organization efforts. These missions were succeeding when the original Humanitarian mission was expanded in early 1993 to include neutralizing the various competing native armed factions.

1993

SOF AROUND THE WORLD

More than thirteen thousand U.S. Special Operations Personnel (13,454 men and women) were deployed around the world to 101 countries during 1993.

ASIA

CAMBODIA

In Cambodia, land mines are responsible for over 300 casualties or deaths per month. A PSYOP battalion deployed with and supported the United Nations and the Cambodian Mine Action Center (CMAC) by producing an extensive variety of mine awareness products such as leaflets, posters, bulletins, banners, and cards. The team worked closely with the Cambodians and other international groups, assisting in the mine awareness and mine clearance programs to educate the people about the dangers of unexpended munitions.

KOREA

The largest SOF field training exercise (FTX) in the free world - JCS Exercise Foal Eagle - takes place annually in the Republic of Korea (ROK). The FTX combined the ROK Special Forces Brigades, a U.S. Special Forces Battalion, U.S. and ROK Navy SEALs, and a U. S. Air Force Special Operations Group to test the ROK military's defense capabilities.

MARSHALL ISLANDS

In March, the United States Coast Guard towed a refugee ship with over 500 Chinese aboard to Kwajalein Atoll. PSYOP and CA personnel were deployed in Operation PROVIDE REFUGE to act as liaison between the installation commander and the refugees and provide Humanitarian assistance.

EUROPE

BOSNIA-HERZEGOVINA

In response to growing international concern about wide-spread starvation in the civil-war-torn republics of the former Yugoslavia, a 15-member PSYOP Task Force was deployed to the United States European Command in February of 1993 to participate in Operation PROVIDE PROMISE. Their mission was to support anticipated United States airdrops of humanitarian relief supplies to isolated pockets of Bosnian Muslims in remote areas. To do this, they produced a wide variety of products including theater and Joint Task Force-level PSYOP plans and annexes, prototype leaflets, posters, handbills, radio and loudspeaker messages for all potential contingencies. The 960,000 PSYOP- prepared leaflets were dropped on the night preceding the first U.S. airdrops of relief supplies stressed the impartial, humanitarian nature of our assistance and cautioned the people not to approach the area until all the heavy food pallets had landed.

YUGOSLAVIA

SOF teams from within the European theater supported Operation PROVIDE PROMISE, the UN humanitarian aid effort for the former nation of Yugoslavia. Rescue teams composed of Air Force Special Tactics combat control and pararescue personnel, Army Special Forces troopers, and Navy SEALs were provided movement, resupply and medical evacuation support by USAF SOF MH-53J helicopters and HC-130 aerial refueling aircraft.

MIDDLE EAST

JORDAN

EARLY VICTOR 93 was a joint/combined SOF exercise conducted with 800 Jordanian military and 545 SOF personnel. Despite a two-year hiatus, since the previous exercise, the high degree of participation and cooperation of the Jordanian Armed Forces throughout the exercise highlighted Jordan's desire to maximize the training opportunity and to enhance United States-Jordanian military relations. Units from the Special Operations Command, Central (SOCCENT) headquarters, Special Forces, Special Operations Aviation, NSW Task Groups, and Air Force Special Operations Command (AFSOC) were involved with the exercise.

KUWAIT

1993 was a year of continued SOF presence in Kuwait. U.S. troops lived and trained with the Kuwaiti forces on a daily basis.

PAKISTAN

For the first time since the late 1980s, U. S. military forces were deployed to Pakistan in 1993 to participate in a bilateral exercise called *Inspired Venture*. SOF led the way as elements from Special Forces and Headquarters SOCCENT deployed to Cherat in the North-West Frontier Province, south of Pershawar. Training was conducted in demolition, rappelling, direct action, airborne operations, and small arms. The success of the exercise led directly to an invitation from Pakistan for SOF personnel to participate in a Himalayan climbing expedition. SF personnel trained with their Pakistani counterparts before beginning their climb. Although the expedition failed to reach the summit due to severe weather, the experiences and the hardships shared by all members of the climbing party paved the way for future bilateral cooperation.

AFRICA

ETHIOPIA

A 1993 SOF-led humanitarian effort was the first to help the Ethiopian people clear their ordnance-strewn land following years of civil war. In support of this effort, a Special Forces company deployed to Debre Zeit in Shewa province, southeast of Addis Ababa, for a combined/bilateral ordnance clearing training exercise with Ethiopian forces. The training included engineering demolitions, ordnance disposal, mine clearing and ordnance handling and storage methods. This training gave the host nation a safe means of ordnance disposal and handling and storage of munitions. In addition, a PSYOP unit produced ordnance awareness and first aid handbooks and training outlines. The overall success of this exercise and the rapport established by SOF resulted in Ethiopia's extending an invitation for U.S. forces to return and build on this relationship.

SENEGAL

SOF personnel served in multiple roles on a variety of humanitarian missions. In a medical readiness exercise, MEDFLAG, Special Forces personnel, in conjunction with the Senegalese Army, provided command and control services and training teams to the Senegalese military medical establishment. This humanitarian mission treated more than 4,700 people at multiple sites within Senegal.

SIERRA LEONE

A Special Operations Command, Europe (SOCEUR) Joint Task Force, consisting of SF teams, Special Tactics personnel, and an aviation element, successfully evacuated noncombatants following a political coup. While Special Tactics personnel provided air traffic control and command and control communications, the other SOF units successfully removed 448 civilian and military personnel and safely recovered $325,000 worth of U.S. Air Force medical equipment.

THE CARIBBEAN

BAHAMAS -- DISASTER ASSISTANCE

Not only did Hurricane Emily wreak havoc in Florida and Louisiana, in 1993, it also virtually brought the Bahamas to a standstill. It particularly devastated the island of Eleuthera where SOF were immediately dispatched to render medical assistance, assess damage, organize a relief effort, evacuate displaced persons, and distribute much needed medical supplies until civilian organizations were able to take charge. The actions of the SOF teams saved lives, minimized property damage, and helped maintain law and order.

BARBADOS, ST. LUCIA, GRENADA

PSYOP Military Information Support Teams (MISTs) deployed to these islands in support of the U.S. Embassy's Narcotics Affairs Section to work with the host-nation committees to develop drug awareness campaign. In each of the countries, SOF personnel assisted in creating products that highlighted the negative effects of drugs on individuals, families, and society. The message was disseminated primarily through television commercials and bumper stickers.

DOMINICAN REPUBLIC

A SOF PSYOPS Military Information Support Team (MIST) was also deployed to the Dominican Republic to work with the United States embassy and National Directorate for the Control of Drugs on drug awareness products directed toward school age children. The information team developed coloring books, videos, and radio spots to reach this audience.

JAMAICA

PSYOP teams deployed to Jamaica at the request of the American Ambassador to support the U.S. Embassy's Narcotics Affairs Section and assist the Jamaican government in informing the populace about the dangers of drugs to Jamaican society. The team worked with a composite Jamaican committee that included both government and non-government agencies. The common goal was reducing drug use on the island.

LATIN AMERICA

GUATEMALA

A SOF PSYOP Team developed a range of counter-drug information products in coordination with the Guatemalan government, the Department of State's Bureau of International Narcotics Matters, and the United States Information Service (USIS). Products included pamphlets designed to educate the people concerning the new counter-narcotics activity law and the dangers of drugs to Guatemalan society.

BOLIVIA

In 1993, U.S. Navy SEAL platoons trained Bolivian forces in small unit tactics, marksmanship, helicopter, and small boat insertions and extractions, and basic demolition techniques. This program greatly increased the effectiveness of both Bolivian Police and Navy efforts to interdict narcotics and precursor substances along Bolivian waterways.

COLOMBIA

Working with a host of agencies including the Colombian Navy and Army, the National Police, the Directorate of Narcotics, the U.S. Embassy's Narcotics Affairs Section, and the USIS, SOF personnel assisted in developing opium eradication campaigns, countering narco-terrorism, and supporting internal defense. Other SOF efforts have supported the United States Drug Enforcement Administration's interdiction strategy.

THE HORN OF AFRICA

SOMALIA

SPECIAL FORCES teams provided increased security for food and relief supply airlifts in Operation RESTORE HOPE. Between August 1992 and February 1993, they assisted in delivering more than 30,000 metric tons of food and relief supplies in Somalia, 70 percent of which was conveyed by the United States. SF teams also worked with local clan leaders to enable delivery of humanitarian relief and upon occasion supported Task Force Ranger.

CIVIL AFFAIRS teams assisted the Commander of the Joint Task Force in Somalia with planning at all levels. They negotiated labor disputes; interacted with local clans to locate snipers and stolen or lost U.S. military equipment; coordinated military support tot relief agencies and clan damage claims; and enhanced relationships between civilians and military. This full integration of SOF-a-lesson-learned from the Gulf War-facilitated communications between UN and U.S. forces.

ARMY Special Operations Aviation (SOA) units were also deployed. They provided aerial infiltration/exfiltration, aerial resupply, aerial security and supporting fire, and airborne command and control. An integral part of overall Task Force operations, they flew numerous missions, including close air support.

ARMY RANGERS (Task Force Ranger) were integral to the security of many relief missions during Operations PROVIDE RELIEF and RESTORE HOPE. In the latter phases of the deployment the Rangers were called upon to be the focus of a major quick reaction mission. At mid-morning of the 3rd of October 1992, the Rangers were tasked to conduct an immediate raid on a location where a number of dissident Somali leaders were meeting. The mid-day raid, which was executed superbly and successfully capturing 20 of the dissident leaders. However, the quick raid turned into an intense and prolonged urban defensive battle, when a helicopter was brought down by a Soviet designed shoulder fired Rocket-Propelled Grenade (RPG) and another by a hail of Somali small arms fire during the extraction. Rather then withdraw, the Rangers went to the defense of the downed aircrews. The Rangers, with their accompanying Special Tactics Team and supporting helicopters found themselves in the center of the most brutal military action to take place in Somali. The local Somali militia, including women and young boys, thought they would have a field day shooting at the now-surrounded Americans, as if they were fish in a barrel. The action, which lasted more than six hours, resulted in 18 American fatalities and 70 wounded, and more than six-hundred Somali killed or injured. Two of the American fatalities were a Special Forces Sniper team that volunteered to enter the fray to protect one of the downed aircrews. After exhausting all of their rifle ammunition in a prolonged defense of the aircrew, during which they both were severely wounded, both continued the fight with their pistols until killed. Both were awarded the Congressional Medal of Honor for their Valor.

USAF Special Tactics teams served in various missions in Somalia, including ground operations support and air traffic control at Mogadishu airfield. Because of their dual orientation in air and ground operations, they effectively meshed Special Operations air and ground forces' efforts, especially during complex missions such as personnel insertion/extraction, close air support, on-target advisories, and attack control. During Task Force Ranger, Special Tactics pararescue personnel, members of the joint SOF medical team, set up a casualty collection point, provided expert medical treatment for injuries ranging from life-threatening gunshot and shrapnel wounds to limb and shock trauma, and coordinated the evacuation of wounded personnel.

Arlington National Cemetery, Veterans' Day 1993
President Bill Clinton

Not enough of our fellow Americans know the real story of Mogadishu on October 3rd - a fight in which [SOF] demonstrated great ability, success and unbelievable valor. During that raid, a Black Hawk helicopter was downed. Despite this set back, the Special Operations Forces conducted their raid with precision, apprehending 20 people suspected of involvement in the murder of United Nations peacekeepers in the Somali mission. At that point, they could have pulled back to safety, confident in the success of their mission. After all, what they had come to do was over. But they share an ethic that says they can never leave a fallen comrade behind.

So some 90 of them formed a perimeter around the downed aircraft in an attempt to retrieve the wounded and dead. They found they could not dislodge the body of one pilot, but they refused to leave him behind. They braved hours of the fiercest enemy fire. Eighteen of them ultimate perished; over 70 were wounded. They exacted a terrible toll on their adversaries: casualties 10 times as great.

I want to thank them. And I want you to let them know that we know they did their mission well and that we are proud of them.

SOF OPERATIONS 1994-1996

The number of SOF deployments, personnel involved, and missions accomplished have continued unabated and increase in number each year, often manifesting themselves with new complexities and challenges. In 1996, the total number of SOF deployment missions exceeded a thousand commitments, some involving hundreds of SOF personnel and extending for months on end. Operations in Haiti, Somalia, Rwanda, Bosnia-Herzegovina represent a few of the larger missions.

These and the hundreds of lesser known missions have reinforced and highlighted two critical realities. The first and most fundamental, is the recognition Special Operations Forces possess a tremendous range of capabilities that can be used in both peace and war, and when used in conjunction with conventional and strategic forces can provide the Joint Force Commander a capability far greater than the individual parts. Second, the full impact of Special Operations Forces is most effective when SOF capabilities and limitations are known to decision makers, and SOF is fully integrated into the Joint Campaign Planning from the beginning.

The following summary, based on contingency preparations for the U.S. intervention into Haiti -- Operation Uphold Democracy -- is illustrative of one dimension of the challenge of adopting to new situations and opportunities.

In mid-September 1994, the aircraft carrier *USS America* (*CV-66*) set sail for Haitian waters with 64 helicopters on-board configured to conduct a two phased major combat assault to help remove the Haitian military Junta from power and return the reins of government to the elected officials. The helicopter force was a major segment of the Joint Special Operation Task Force (JSOTF) that was to spearhead the operation. The five dozen helicopters came with more than a thousand soldiers and aircrew.

The need to conduct the combat assault was avoided at the last minute. The daring and delicate carrot and stick diplomacy of former President Jimmy Carter and former Chairman of the JCS Colin Powell persuaded the Haitian leadership to step down thus avoiding bloodshed. However, given the potential for unrest and violence among the population the waterborne Joint Special Operations Task Force (JSOTF) remained intact and operated in a mixed security and humanitarian assistance role for the following five weeks.

Planning for the possible combat operations had begun quite some time before, but on a contingency basis against an ever changing political and operational backdrop. Initial plans called for the JSOTF to base all its helicopter assets at Guantanamo, Cuba and launch operations from there. However, due to continuing influx of refugees and media the JSOTF began to look for ways to decrease its visible presence. Although the prospect of using a maritime platform of some sort as the SOF assault base had been surfaced early in the planning, the basing and staging options had to be kept open and revised frequently because of changes in ship availability.

Crippled Eagle

The flexibility and maneuverability of an afloat platform make it a very attractive alternative to support special operations missions. In addition the unique operational circumstances afforded by the lack of enemy air or naval threat, and the fact that the JSOTF would exercise tactical control of the launch platform greatly enhanced the viability of this option within the SOF community.

Throughout the spring and early summer, while the SOF planners waited for a definitive answer on which ship would be available as the forward staging base, they developed a range of modular force packages for every possible size Navy platform that might be made available. This included several classes of aircraft carriers and a range of Marine Corps amphibious assault ships that came in different sizes and configurations. The *America*, (*CV-66*) a *Kitty Hawk* class carrier and a *Tarwara* class helicopter assault ship were representative candidates.

When the *America,* a Norfolk, Virginia-based ship was declared available in late August, the planners developed numerous options as to which of the SOF force modules could be put on-board. The JSOTF commander made the final basing/staging decision based on three primary criteria: reducing the JSOTF's visibility at Guantanamo; maintaining ground force unit integrity; and ensuring airspace deconfliction in the target area. The helicopters, mostly Army, came in all manner of shapes and sizes, and most were unable to fold their rotor blades without turning the procedure into a major maintenance event. A staging/embarkation plan had been designed using a Marine planning procedure called PERMA (planning, embarkation, rehearsal, movement and assault) and an AutoCAD computer program that provided scale drawings of the flight deck and helicopters.

The long range heavy lift Air Force MH-53J Pave Low helicopters, had a geographically separate target set and a specialized ground force to deliver. Therefore, it was decided to leave them at Guantanamo with their attached U.S. Army rotary-wing fire-support assets, while all of the other, shorter legged helicopters went on the *America.*

A training rehearsal was scheduled shortly after the availability notice reached the JSOTF planners, but the Operational Deployment order came before the rehearsal could take place. Due to the short deployment notice, an advance echelon made up of officers and Non-Commissioned Officers (NCOs) from key JSOTF staff functional areas embarked simultaneously with the main operational forces rather than in advance as initially planned.

Although the JSOTF loaded some equipment and personnel on-board the *America* at a Norfolk pier, the bulk of the ground forces were flown on to the carrier from various points along the eastern coast by the assault force helicopters. This approach avoided projecting a large and unusual signature at Norfolk, and allowed the ground forces some additional time for last minute planning and equipment preparation ashore. Once on-board the *America,* the ground personnel disembarked the helos and marshaled and moved to their berthing spaces fairly quickly, however, much of their equipment and supplies had to be man-handled from the choppers to the maintenance and equipment storage spaces. This became a time consuming and arduous task.

During the onshore pre-deployment planning sessions, the ship's planners felt the flight deck crews could reconfigure or spot the deck, i.e., tow each helicopter to its respective takeoff spot, in six hours. The actual effort took twice that long. The spotting challenge was complicated by the fact that specific aircraft/aircrews had been assigned specific missions, which precluded swapping missions or simply arranging the helicopters by type, as had been done in previous "academic" war-gaming sessions. Once the deck-spotting situation had been rectified, preparations began for a rehearsal of the mission night-launch sequence. This daunting challenge involved planning and deconflicting the movement of over 1,000 troops. The movement routes ran from the berthing areas far below the flight deck, through the mess decks and narrow passageways to their equipment. And continued up to the flight deck, in chauks (airlift groups). There they were met by flight deck personnel and a crewmember from their respective helicopter who led them to their machine.

The planning team had to contend not only with the small passageways of the carrier, which are not designed for troops with rucksacks, but with the fact that most of the ground forces had little or no experience operating in a shipboard environment. The planners succeeded in working out primary and alternate routes, using both elevators and ladders, for each group (aircrews and ground forces). The movement flow was aided by prepositioning crew-served weapons and ammunition in the helicopters. And by staging personal ammunition with the other gear in guarded areas of the hangar deck.

The initial D-day assault plan called for two major launches separated by 45 minutes, requiring a second major deck spotting. During the rehearsal of the launch sequence, philosophical differences between SOF aviation and carrier aviation procedures came to the fore. Carrier flight deck operations require tight control and strict adherence to a detailed timetable. Each decision or deviation must account for elevator runs, winds across the deck and ship's maneuvering room, availability of the search and rescue helicopter, aircraft refueling crews and locations, Hazards of Electromagnetic Radiation to Ordnance (HERO) conditions, and deck spotting for future operations.

The intricacies of launching from a maritime platform (particularly one that was underway), were not initially understood by the SOF personnel. The SOF flight crews were accustomed to the more open spaces of an airfield and an orderly, but more flexible launch flow as modifications in the takeoff sequence were frequently dictated by changes in the combat situation or target priorities. Conversely, the ship's company did not initially grasp the ever-changing nature of assault force mission profiles. Eventually both learning curves merged, and flight deck operations smoothed out, something that would have occurred much earlier if a "live" rehearsal had been possible.

Much of this merging involved non-carrier standard procedures, such as using the entire flight deck as one big landing zone, limiting the number of Landing Signalman Enlisted (LSE), and employing unique deck-lighting techniques. In order to maximize the space available, helicopter takeoffs and landings were made from elevators and on both the starboard and port sides of the ship, a deviation from normal carrier flight operations. The density of traffic on the flight deck led to using only one LSE for flight or element departures, but each recovery was individually controlled by an LSE. As for lighting, all night aircraft departures and recoveries were made with the aircrews using Night-Vision Goggles (NVGs), while very dim deck lighting was used to provide the deck crew a degree of safety they would not have had in total black out conditions. For the most part, the flight deck personnel did not have NVGs, which were routinely used by SOF aviation aircrews, the Special Tactics Combat Controllers and the SOF ground servicing crews.

Ultimately, there were no H-hour combat assaults, and the JSOTF moved into sustained non-combat support operations. The peaceful nature of the American force introduction, and lack of armed resistance, changed the nature of the mission and required a totally new round of planning and a different set of factors to be considered.

Overall, the experience was judged to be positive, and many lessons of joint interoperability were relearned. The first among these being early joint planning is essential. Second, cohesion within the planning team is vital. Third, a live rehearsal of all aspects of the mission is essential particularly when any new undertaking or change in operating procedures is anticipated or there is an identifiable or the possibility of a predictable deviation from the norm.

Our national security will be faced with more and more regional challenges to include quick reaction peacekeeping and security operations. The well rehearsed use of a blend of conventional and unconventional assets -- such as demonstrated on-board the *America* and throughout *Operation Up Hold Democracy* -- provide yet another example of the need for early cooperation and hands-on joint-combined arms training to ensure the most effective of our military forces:

> No one knows for sure what the future security environment will be like, but it is safe to say that it will be at least as challenging as the present one.
> General John M. Shalikashvili,
> Chairman of the Joint Chiefs of Staff

APPENDIX TWO
AMERICAN PROFILES

In one of his most famous public speeches, given to a Joint Session of Congress on April 20, 1951, General of the Armies Douglas MacArthur said, "Old soldiers never die, they just fade away." General MacArthur's prophecy is only partially true, as the following brief summaries of the careers of ten members of the JTF 79-1 reflect.

COMMANDER JTF 1-79

James Vaught was drafted into the U.S. Army in 1945 while in his 2nd year in the Corps of Cadets at the Citadel. He received his commission in February 1946, and served in WW II, and in the Korean "police action" and the Vietnam "conflict." After the release of the hostages and the shutdown of JTF 1-79, he returned to the Army staff as Director Operations, Mobilization and Readiness. Subsequently, he was the Commanding General of the Combined Forces Korea. In December 1981, in an exchange of correspondence with two of his former JTF 1-79 intelligence officers (who viewed events north of the Korean DMZ as potentially ominous and who had communicated these thoughts to "Hammer"), he provided a brief handwritten response: "If they come South, I will go North!" He retired from the Army in 1983 at the rank of Lieutenant General after 38 years of service. He is now self-employed in the international business community.

CHIEF OF STAFF (AND DIRECTOR OF OPERATIONS) JTF 1-79

Jerry King enlisted in the U.S. Army in 1955, rose to the rank of sergeant in 14 months and was commissioned into the infantry shortly thereafter. He was one of several DOD personnel detailed to the CIA in 1960 to assist in training the Cuban expatriate force that was to return to Cuba and begin a counter-revolutionary movement to oust Fidel Castro and his communist regime. In 1961, he had to stand by helplessly and witness the decimation of the outnumbered and out-gunned force he had assisted in committing to the beaches of the Bay of Pigs. He served two tours in Vietnam as a Special Forces officer. Colonel King left the JTF staff in mid-1980 to form the much-needed DOD "scout" element. Later, he served as Commander of CENTCOM Special Operations Command (SOCCENT), laying much of the foundation for the later success of SOF in the deserts of Iraq and Kuwait. He retired in 1987 at the rank of Colonel, and went back to school, earning a Ph.D. in American history and assuming the role of the college Don.

CHIEF OF COMBAT CONTROLLER TEAM

John Carney was commissioned a second lieutenant in the Air Force in 1964, and after several months in training was assigned to duty in Vietnam as a combat controller. After this tour, he was assigned to the Air Force Academy as an instructor. From 1975-79, John served as the principal

Special Operations Combat Controller Trainer for the Military Airlift Command. In November 1979, he was assigned to JTF 1-79 as Chief of the USAF Combat Controller Team. In March 1980, Major John Carney was flown into Desert One to "walk the ground" and emplace landing beacons. He bore the responsibility to certify to COMJTF 1-79, General Vaught, Charlie Beckwith and Colonel Jim Kyle that Desert One could support the landing impact of a loaded C-130 and could serve as a landing /transfer site for the rescue forces. Subsequent to the deactivation of JTF 1-79, John Carney became Commander of an Air Force CCT Special Mission Unit assigned to the newly-created Joint Special Operations Command (JSOC) at Fort Bragg. In this capacity, he was involved in the quick-reaction planning for Operation Urgent Fury in 1983 and was one of the first Americans to land on Grenada. He retired from the Air Force in 1984 as a Lieutenant Colonel. He was recalled to active duty six months later as a Colonel and assigned as Director of Combat Control and Pararescue Operations for MAC with the mission of creating a unique USAF Special Operations capability. In 1987, he became the first commander of this newly-created USAF Special Tactics Group, a key element of the new Air Force Special Operations Command. In this capacity, he was heavily involved in the planning and coordination of USAF Special Tactics participation in Operation Just Cause and led the unit deployment. John Carney retired as a Colonel in 1992 and is currently working in private industry, often in international ventures.

EUROPEAN COMMAND LIAISON OFFICER TO JTF 1-79

James G. Magee received a commission in the United States Marine Corps in 1966 and served as a Marine Infantry commander throughout most of his career, interspersed with several joint assignments including a tour with the European Command's Special Operations Task Force Europe (SOTFE) in Germany. On 13 November 1979, he became the European Command Liaison Officer to JTF 1-79. Major Magee continued in that role throughout the 444 days of the hostage crisis and beyond to include coordinating the security arrangements for the hostages' stay in Germany, pending their return to Washington at the end of January 1981. Subsequent to the dissolution of JTF 1-79, he completed his tour with the Special Operations Task Force Europe (SOTFE). In 1983, he was selected to form the cadre of the 2nd Light Armored Vehicle Battalion, serving as its first commander until 1986. After a tour as Director of Operations, Fleet Marine Force, Europe and as senior Special Operations staff officer at Headquarters USMC, he served as Commander, USMC Security Force Battalion with worldwide anti-terrorism responsibilities. He retired from the Marine Corps in 1993 as a Colonel. At Colonel Magee's retirement, General Al Gray, the 29th Commandant of the Marine Corps, gave an impromptu tribute to Jim Magee that the was highpoint of the retirement ceremony. Jim Magee is now employed as a senior executive of a security product development firm.

"TROOPER SAM" JTF 1-79

"Sam" is representative of the hundreds of enlisted personnel that make the U.S. military a living organism. Sam enlisted in the USAF in the mid-1970s and was serving as a flightline mechanic at the rank of E-4 when the hostage situation broke. Recognizing that his native command of the Farsi and knowledge of the culture might be of assistance to a possible rescue effort, Sam offered his services. His Squadron Commander contacted Air Force Intelligence, which in turn contacted the DIA, and orders were cut dispatching Sam to Washington. Sam's commitment was extraordinary, and his talent multi-fold. He was selected, with the concurrence of Charlie Beckwith, to be a member of the Delta support team that would enter Tehran in advance of the rescue force and assume the support function from the CIA team. The day before the mission was to be launched, an Iranian road crew dug a four-foot deep and three-foot wide ditch across the only access road out of the warehouse compound hiding the trucks that were to move Delta to the embassy. "Pleading" that his boss would "skin him alive" if the vehicles could not get out, and bribing with a case of cold beer, Sam managed to get the ditch refilled. He was also instrumental in getting all the vehicles in running order; at least two had dead batteries and two others needed tune-ups. Sam's greatest contribution came after the mission abort. He assumed the role of safety net and helped the other three members of the team leave the country, then went underground for a week to be in a position to assist should any of them be picked up at the airport and jailed. Subsequent to the deactivation of JTF 1-79, Sam was one of several USAF personnel who were offered service transfers to the Army. Sam went to helicopter flight school and began flying as an Army Warrant Officer.

THE OPERATORS -- Special Forces Soldiers All

The members of the Army Special Forces Community that supported JTF 1-79 were as diverse as their ability to consistently hit the bull-eye at 100 yards was uniform. Major Logan Fitch, who commanded "Blue" Element, had the responsibility for clearing half of the Embassy compound, while Captain Peter Schoomaker had "Red" element and the other half of the compound. Captain Jim Knight commanded "White Element," whose mission was to seize and secure the extraction corridor from the embassy to the stadium. Captain William G. "Jerry" Boykin was responsible for securing the stadium for the extraction of the hostages and the rescue force. Major Jesse Johnson had been charged by Charlie Beckwith with the responsibility of overseeing the two roadblock teams at Desert One. Master Sergeant Paul Lawrence was one of the Delta "shooters." Sergeant Stewart O'Neil was one of the MFA mission team members from Berlin. All were at Desert One. All risked their lives to help others, but none more so than Paul Lawrence and Stu O'Neil, who ran back into the burning C-130 and pulled the Air Force communications specialist, Sergeant Joe Beyers, from the debris of the burning wreckage. Stu O'Neil left the Army at the end of his enlistment, went to college, and is now Doctor Stewart O'Neil a highly respected physician. Sergeant Paul Lawrence is now a government civilian with the United States Special Operations Command. Captains Boykin, Schoomaker, and Knight and Major Johnson continued to serve in the Special Forces. Logan Fitch became an investment banker in Dallas. Jesse Johnson followed Jerry King's footsteps and became Commander of the CENTCOM Special Operations Command, focused on the Arabian Gulf. During Desert Storm, he was the senior Special Operations officer on General Schwartzkopf's' staff, and the first American to reenter the American Embassy in Kuwait City. Pete Schoomaker and Jerry Boykin stayed closer to counter-terrorist work, each eventually serving as the Commander of Delta. In 1991, Lt. Colonel Boykin attended the Army War College and researched the politically torturous road of the legislation that eventually created the U.S. Special Operations Command. Much of his work has found its way into Chapter 11, "Competing Perspectives." Peter J. Schoomaker rose to the rank of General and assumed Command of the Joint Special Operation Command (JSOC) on 7 July 1994, subsequently served as Commanding General of the Army Special Operations Command, and became CINCSOC, the Commander-In-Chief, United States Special Operations Command in 1997.

THE INTELLIGENCE CADRE

The JTF 1-79 intelligence cadre during the first five months numbered only three officers -- two Army, Major Dick Friedel and Captain Tim Casey, and one Air Force, the author. All volunteered to go to Teheran in the frustrating days of November 1979, when reliable information was limited but rumors and wild speculation were rampant. After the mission abort, one of the trio, the former Blue Light G-2 and SF officer signed on to the CIA and immediately disappeared into the shadows of that world. The two remaining officers were augmented by three new recruits: one Army, one Marine and one Air Force (Captain Sam Scott, Captain Tim Conway, and Major Dave Prevost). After the hostages were released, all five returned to their respective jobs with a wealth of experiences not normally attainable in an ordinary career. Representative of this diversity were the follow-on assignments of the original member of the JTF intelligence cadre. After concluding his JCS tour, he was assigned as Commander of a one-of-a-kind intelligence unit at Nellis Air Force Base. From there, he was selected to be Chief of Intelligence for 12th Air Force, which had just been designated with Latin American contingency responsibility. In this capacity, he routinely traveled the potential Area of Operations (AO) including Nicaragua. Subsequently, he was transferred to Panama as the Director of Operational Intelligence for the U.S. Southern Command, splitting his energies between Nicaragua, El Salvador, Bolivia and Panama. After witnessing the beginnings of unrest and the potential for confrontation that was increasing in Panama, he was selected by Major General Patterson to be the Director of Intelligence for the newly-created Air Force Special Operations Command at Hurlburt Field, Florida. In March 1988, he was dual-hatted as the J-2 for the Joint Special Operations Task Force, created at the request of the Commander of the Southern Command, to begin planning the neutralization of the Panamanian Defense Forces. He retired in mid-1988, completing 32 years of service including duty in MAC, SAC, TAC and the Air Staff, and more than 16 years in joint service assignments and JTFs including: MACV, NATO, REDCOM, the Office of Joint Chiefs of Staff, and the United States Southern Command.

COMMUNICATION SPECIALISTS

Staff Sergeant James Nelson and Sergeant Chris Nelson were part of the Communication team deployed from the Joint Communication Support Element (JCSE) at Mac Dill AFB to operate the JTF 1-79 communications network. Members of the JCSE had been supporting REDCOM and its predecessor STRIKECOM for more than 20 years. JSCE was a joint organization, largely composed of Army and Air Force communicators, that had been truly "joint" in its philosophy and function. Several different JCSE teams supported JTF 1-79 from November 1979 through June 1981, when the communications responsibility for supporting the new JTF (i.e., JSOC) was turned over to a team referred to as the JCU (Joint Communication Unit). JCSE/JCU personnel were equally at home with strategic or tactical communications. It had been JCSE personnel that had provided the communications packages for REDCOM's JTF 7X. This support included parachute-qualified communicators organized into two-three man Quick Reaction Element (QRE) teams that jumped in with the Rangers and the CCT. Jim and Chris Nelson, a husband and wife communications team, were representative of the many support personnel who worked long and hard, and upheld their part of the rescue chain. One of the Nelsons' last contributions to the mission was a pen-and-ink-colored representation of the reverse side of the Humanitarian Service Medal (an outstretched hand). The sketch, along with a copy of another amateur military artist's (Ren Wicks) oil color rendition of the eight RH-53 helicopters departing the *Nimitz*, plus the words "The greatest failure is the failure to try" were given to "a little old lady in tennis shoes" at DMA. She demonstrated her artistic and photographic flare and combined the three elements into a composite image that captured the essence of the rescue mission.

APPENDIX THREE

Joint Task Force 1-79 Roster
As of 24 April 1980

LOST AT DESERT ONE

Harold L. Lewis, Jr. Captain, Pilot C-130, USAF
Lyn D. McIntosh, Captain, Copilot C-130, USAF
Richard L. Blakke, Captain, Navigator C-130, USAF
Charles T. McMillian, Captain, Navigator C-130, USAF
Joel C. Mayo, Technical Sergeant, Flight Engineer C-130, USAF
Staff Sergeant Dewey L. Johnson, Crewmember RH-53, USMC
Sergeant John D. Harvey, Crewmember RH-53, USMC
Corporal George N. Holmes, Jr. RH-53, USMC

***

JTF Helicopter Detachment
(Alphabetically by Service)

U.S. Air Force
Rakip, Russell, E.

U.S. Navy
Allen, Terry
Davis, Rodney
Diascuk, John
Mingo, Robert
Scurria, James
Thomas, Stanley

U.S. Marine Corps
Beach, Dean
Beaucamp, Richard
Bird, Daniel
Buchanan, William
Coffin, Jeffrey
Cook, Larry
Dehoust, Walt
Doroski, David
Fiori, James
Harold, Joseph
Harvey, John D.*
Higley, Thomas
Hoff, William
Holmes, George, Jr.*
Husman, David
Johnson, Dewey L.
Klasek, Dominick
Karch, Henry
Lewis, Dwayne
Lightle, Charles
Linderman, James
Logue, K.D.
McGuire, B.J.
Mueller, Ronald
Neymeyer, Rance
Oldfield, Barney
Petty, Less
Schaeffer, James
Scurria, James
Seiffert, Edward
Sigman, John
Sosa, Larry
Strickland, Phillip
Walt, L.C.

USMC Attachés

Mission Coordinator
Pitman, Charles (Colonel)

Intelligence Officer
Mattingly, Robert (Major)

* Lost at Desert One

Other Members of JTF 1-79 by Service and by Rank

U.S. Marine Corps

Lt. Colonel
Neff, Robert

Major
Magee, James G.

U.S. Navy

Captain
Butterfield, John A.

Commander
Wyers, Maynard R.

Chief Yeoman
Collins, William A.

U.S. Army

Major General
Vaught, James B.

Colonels
Balaban, Bernard
Barkett, John S.
Beckwith, Charlie A.
Foley, William R.
King, Jerry M.
Olchovik, Stanley
Sperandio, John
Thompson, Joe N.

Lt. Colonels
Ahrens, Roger W.
Arkangel, Carmelito, Jr.
Dieck, Peter F.
Hammond, George
Johnson, Jesse L.
Matthiesen, Jerry A.
Nightingale, Keith M.
Olmstead, James
Phillips, Charles
Potter, Richard W., Jr.
Salander, James M.
Savory, Carlton G.
Shaw, Hubert S.
Thompson, Joseph
Williford, Sherman H.

Majors
Adler, Herman
Bender, Nathan J.
Bowen, Marshall J.
Boykin, William G.
Burruss Lewis H., Jr.
Cagle, Donald
Custer, Norman
Elmore, Darrell G.
Fitch, Logan D.
Friedel, Richard B.
Klain, Elliott
Long, Wayne E.
Meadows, Richard
Ohl, William C.
Roberts, James Q.
Schoomaker, Peter J.
Slay, Robert
Smith, Edwin K., III
Thompson, Peter
Tisdale, Tyrone T.
Torres-Cartagena, Jorge L.

Captains
Casey, Timothy J.
Deane, William H.
Gowdy, Willard P.
Grange, David L.
Iagulli, James
Ishimoto, Wade Y.
Knight, James F.
McClellon, Johnie

Moran, William
Schwitters, James H.
Toomy, Robert
Wright, Steven J.

1st Lieutenants
Milam, Thomas
Provost, John
Richardson, Wayne
Wall, Tommy T.

Warrant Officers
Bryda, Michael
Byard, Harry J.
Clarkson, Philip D.
Lamonica, John C.
Zeisman, Paul A.
Donau, Charles R.
Hollingsed, Michael J.
Sykes, Larry
Stanley, John W., Jr.
Vona, Russell R., II
Welsch, William L.

Sergeants Major
Cheney, David
Foreman, Forrest K.
Grimes, William R.
Haynes, Ratchford P.
Joplin, Jack G.
Macias, Angel
Schalavin, Jan
Shumate, Walter L.

Master Sergeants
Almueti, Andy M.
Bolton, Robert L., III
Bridge, Richard A.
Candelaria, Angel C.
Clemmens, John M., Jr.
Czarnecki, Ronald C.
George, Roger L.
Headman, Rodney L.
Lawrence, Paul A.
Martin, John R..
Moston, Gary M.
Ravitz, Alan
Sharon, Leon E.
Simmons, Donald G.
Smith, Kerby A.
Spencer, Eugene
Taitano, Norman C.
Waite, Michael P.
Westfall, Edward H., Jr.
Wolfe, Dennis E.

Sergeants First Class
Adams, Herman L., Jr.
Alvarez, Deciderio
Briere, Donald L.
Brown, Kent H., Jr.
Brown, Marshal L.
Bugarin, Edward U.
Burney, Jerry L.
Chapman, Guy L.
Chewey, Junior L.
Cooper, Bradley
Corbett, Thomas B.
Crawford, Norman F.
Cronin, William F., III
Dengerud, Durwin D.
Feeney, Donald M., Jr.
Flanagan, George M.
Fontana, Gerald
Freedman, Lawrence N.
Gentry, Mark S.
Hall, Terry L.
Haney, Eric L.
Hanson, Phillip L.
Hobson, Daniel F.
Hoeffer, Randall A.
Hoffman, Steven T.
Hurley, Patrick R.
James, Frank J.
Jeter, Killis W., III
Jones, John W.
Knotts, James L.
Krieger, Billy
Lemke, Clemons E.
Little, Robert D.

Mathers, Danny L.
McEwan, John C.
McKenna, Frank 0.
Miller, James A.
Mims, John P.
Moniz, Earl J.
Morgan, Cecil W.
Morton, Billie D.
Murphy, Steven
Nickel, Glen M.
Potter, John G.
Presley, Eulis A.
Purdue, Keith W.
Purdy, Donald E.
Reves, Harrison
Rigo, David C.
Roberts, James D.
Rodriguez, Rodolfo D.
Shelton, Donald J.
Shelton, James V.
Spivey, Kenneth W.
Suggs, Raymond E.
Sumakeris, Joseph J.
Troller, Gerald R.
Urbaniak, Bruno
Vincent, Rolland E., Jr.
Waldo, Arthur L.
Wick, Melvin L.
Wilderman, William J.
Wilson, Robert R.
Yancey, John M. J--.
Zumwalt, William L.

Staff Sergeants
Abel, Christopher W.
Banta, Irvin J.
Berryhill, Roger D.
Bullock, Randall A.
Chrisman, Donald W.
Cook, Joseph
Crawford, Iain T. R.
Delaihoussaye, Derek A.
Donovan, William
Fish, Francis W., II
France, William C., III
Gainey, Gregory
Gandee, Alfred L.
Guest, William
Holt, Kenneth R.
Honaker, Reginald H.
Hotle, Barry T.
Huber, Jeffrey L.
Kaita, Bernhard W.
Kalua, Michael A.
Kuenstle, Robert
Lambert, Thomas B.
Laws, Charles
Lewis, Frederick J.
Littlejohn, David R.
Lostan, Azzam
Moore, Michael T.
Mushrim, Thomas L.
O'Callaghan, James P.
Owens, James R.
Pechtel, Douglas G.
Pelaiz, Manuel R.
Pitts, John D.
Rogers, Jack
Staples, Glen A., Jr.
Steele, Larry A.
Thompson, Joseph
Vanborkulo, Peter, Jr.
Vining, Michael
Vlasko, Donald F., Jr.
Westling, Carlos C.

Sergeants
Ashe, Franklin
Baillaigeon, Mark
Bowman, Francis
Burrows, Richard
Hyde, Selmer
Kampmeir, Roy
Kinny, James
McGirr, Michael T.
Muro, Daniel
Nieves-Nieves, Ruben A.
Noyes, Michael
Nunez, Wilson
O'Neil, Stewart K.

Perez, Juan M., Jr.
Peters, Gene
Phillips, James
Pirtle, Donald J.
Ripepi, Joseph
Sisk, David
Smith, Blase W.
Smith, Larry
Swyenburg, Jeffery
Syouf, Helal S.
Tietjen, Michael
Yates, Mannifred

Corporals/Spec Fours
Beck, Roger
Berkan, David
Bowman, Francis P.
Chapman, Roger
Collicot, Arvin J.
De Rinzo, Frank
Evans, Stanley C.
Fletcher, Mark
French, Daniel
Friedman, Joseph
Gilbert, Edwin
Gooding, Marty
Hogue, Steven
Horsley, Roy
Hudachek, John
Kaylor, Wesley W.
Lamb, Richard
Lewis, David
Love, Peter
Martin, Kenneth
Kassey, Kurt L.
Navarro, Henry
Noble, Gary
Principe, Joseph
Ray, Charles
Rhash, Raymond
Rodrigues, Hector
Rubio, Robert, Jr.
Sampson, Michael
Schneider, Kurt
Scott, Eric
Shields, Gordon
Smith, Donald
Stewart, James
Taylor, Mark
Tomazin, James
Turner, Horace
Weeks, Bryan K.
Young, Gordon

Privates First Class
Brantley, Arnett
Clement, Kenneth
Dee, James
Dodson, Dennis
Fooks, Charles
La Flex, Joseph
McCalip, Slade
Morrow, Keith
Pflaum, Michael
Reed, Bobby
Resil, Fritz
Sparks, James
Warf, Makie
White, William

Privates
Hitchcock, Michael
Kolhof, Kerry
Long, Warren
Miller, James
Parker, Bret
Spayd, Timothy

DA Civilians
Waananen, Ronald C.

U.S. Air Force

Major General
Gast, Philip C.

Colonels
Keating, Richard
Kyle, James
Moore, Eugene A.

Pinard, Robert N.
Wicker, Thomas J.

Lt. Colonels
Bateman, John P.
Bonham, Lawrence D.
Bradley, Thomas P.
Brenci, Robert L.
Casperson, David I.
Crane, William M.
Drohan, John A.
Gallagher, John A.
Gamble, John E.
Graham, Bobbie Gene
Guidry, Roland D.
Hall, Lannie W.
Horton, Claude R.
Jones, Ronald L.
Lawrence, Robert
Lenahan, Rod
Livesey, James A.
McCarron, Thomas L.
Michaels, Ronald
Oliver, Kenneth D.
Postles, William T.
Smith, Lester C.
Turczynski, Raymond, Jr.
White, Flurin D.
Wilson, John H.

Majors
Anderson, Frank W.
Anderson, John R.
Bagby, Alva E., III
Barratt, George R.
Blum, David J.
Brown, Alan H.
Buchanan, Donald
Butler, Clyde, II
Cairns, Darin T.
Carney, John T., Jr.
Casteel, Terence L.
Couvillon, M.
Darden, Russell B. G.
Deegan, William F., Jr.
Diggins, William H.
Duke, James D.
Gilbert, Clifford
Hawkins, John E.
Houston, Carl S.
Horne, William K.
Jahnke, Terance L.
Johnson, Harry
Kirk, James M.
Logan, John M.
Overstreet, Michael D.
Ozolins, John
Pena, Juan, Jr.
Pumroy, Fredrick L.
Roberts, James N.
Rumple, Paul W.
Schwall, Arthur W., Jr.
Stock, John
Terry, William R.
Thomas, John W.
Toles, Stephen L.
Toth, George R.
Ulery, Douglas L.
Uttaro, Gerald J.
Waali, Douglas R.
Weaver, John V.0., Jr.
Wells, Frank
Werling, Wesley T.

Captains
Bakke, Richard L.*
Bennes, James, II
Beres, Thomas M.
Bishop, Dennis R.
Blohm, Jeffrey A.
Bolduc, Paul R.
Brennan, Joseph A.
Buley, Stephen L.
Burke, Stephen
Butler, Thomas W.
Bysewski, Robert H.
Chaplvian, Clayton J., Jr.
Contigququlia, Joseph J.

---

* Lost at Desert One

Conway, Jerome F.
Cummings, Michael A.
Daley, Judson D.
Davenport, David L.
Dickensheets, James
Dickinson, Jack R.
Downey, John E., Jr.
Drake, Leslie R.
Driver, Michael A.
Dungan, Michael A.
Earle, Bobby F.
Ellis, Donald S.
Else, Steven E.
Ferkes, George C.
Filler, Michael R.
Fleming, Stephen, A.
Galloway, Samuel-E.
Garbe, Steven E.
Godby, Terry
Hamilton, M. J.
Happe, Michael L.
Harrison, Jeffrey B.
Hicks, Raymond P.
Honaker, Robert L.
Jaczinski, John S., III
Johnson, Douglas A.
Jubelt, Martin P.
Kegel, John P.
Kelly, James D.
Langenhan, James L.
Lavender, Stephen D.
Lawrence, James D.
Lee, Clark P.
Leeman, Kevin H.
Lewis, Ellen K.
Lewis, Harold L., Jr.*
Lewis, Robert M.
Lovett, Charles R.
Lucyshyn, William
Luginbuhl, Robert T., Jr.
McBride, J. J.
McClellan, Michael
McIntosh, Lyn D.*
McMillan, Charles T., II*
Michael, John R.
Miller, Robert L.
Nimmo, John A.
Norris, Basil S., Jr.
Novy, Dennis E.
O'Keefe, Lawrence J.
Osborne, William E.
Pearson, John G.
Peppers, Gregory S.
Perkumas, Joseph D.
Poole, Kenneth H.
Prater, Timothy C.
Pugh, James R., III
Rakip, Russel E., Jr.
Remington, Michael D.
Rice, Dean E.
Robb, William P.
Robbins, Richard A.
Robinson, Neal T.
Rorabaugh, James D.
Ross, William W.
Saier, William E.
Sanderson, Mark R.
Scearse, Michael D.
Schultz, Robert G.
Sherkus, John P.
Siegel, Donald C.
Sliwa, Brian A.
Smilek, John M.
Solomon, Harold L.
Sonner, Maurice F., II
Springler, Edward C.
Stephens, Larry M.
Srubbe, Steven J.
Sumida, Michael K.
Tanner, Ronald L.
Tharp, Russell E.
Thigpen, Jerry L.
Thom, Wayne L.
Townsend, John G.
Tucker, Lester P.
Valenta, David L.

---

* Lost at Desert One

Villarreal, Xavier G.
Viray, Richard G.
Weaver, Warren I.
Williams, Myron E.
Williamson, Charles
Witzel, John C.
Yagher, Ray A.
Young, Karl B.
Youngblood, Herman
Ziegenhorn, Russ
Ziegler, Davis R.

1st Lieutenants
Ayer, Clyde C.
Drosezko, Joseph M.
Ford, Charles D.
Guida, Vincent J.
Harrison, Jeffrey B.
Hudson, Robert W.
Jaskey, Armas J.
Mongillo, Robert J.
Novy, Dennis E.
Prater, Timothy C.
Riley, Lin A.
Rund, Berton B.
Sharpe, Ronald C.
Smith, Gerald R.
Vancil, Stephen P.
Wildermuth, Mark
Wilson, Michael N.
Yaggi, Ronald D.

2nd Lieutenants
Moushon, Allen A.
Strang, Michael E.

Chief Master Sergeants
Harris, Fred 0.
Kindle, Buie E.

Senior Master Sergeants
Davis, Richard G.
Eller, Sherman E.
Foster, Stephen L.
Gerkey, John M.
Hodgson, Olive
Humphrey, Arthur W.
Keeserling, Wayne
Messer, Clawson L.
Patterson, Kenneth D.
Turcotte, Albert J.
Wiley, Atwell L.

Master Sergeants
Allen, Frederick R.
Almanzar, Roberto L.
Appleby, Gerald A.
Banks, Freddie L.
Beavers, William D.
Boudreaux, Don
Brandmeier, Gary E.
Bryan, Michael R.
Capps, Roger L.
Chitwood, Robert A.
Cole, Reuben S.
Daigenaut, Thomas
Denoi, Anthony G.
Doyle, Ray C.
Duncan, 0. B.
Garrett, Jerry W.
Gowdy, Clyde C.
Hawkins, George W., Jr.
Jackson, Johnas
Jenkins, Fred E.
Katalik, John F., Jr.
Kirby, Edward F.
Lampe, Michael I;
Larsen, William H.
Maddux, Harold D.
McGill, Ronald
Michaud, H. L., Jr.
Mink, John W.
Plain, R.T., Jr.
Puskas, Francis J.
Ray, Dennis C.
Russell, Daniel G.
Schugman, John
Sheldon, Joseph G.
Sikes, Bobbie K.
Skorupski, Francis J.

Williamson, Bruce B.
Wilson, Garnett E., Jr.

Technical Sergeants
Allen, Arthur F.
Allen, Warren S.
Aokin,S, Lewis G.
Arviso, Rodney
Bancroft, Kenneth L.
Barthlett, Raphael M.
Beach, Fred E.
Boknevitz, T.A.
Booe, Stephen R.
Boughton, Gary L.
Bracken, Jack G., Jr.
Brown, Mitchell
Capps, Roger L.
Charvat, James
Chesser, James D.
Davis, Eurial, Jr.
Diehl, Richard A.
Ferrell, Ben R.
Folley, Donald H., Jr.
Gingrich, William R.
Gonzalez, Manuel L,
Grisham, Denny M.
Haman, Kenneth F.
Hamilton, James
Hassler, Michael L.
Holloman, Barry P.
Hollyfield, J.J.
Hosenbackez, M.
Hughes, Charles W., Jr.
Janes, Ronnie M.
Jerome, William R.
Juniper, Thomas
King, Arthur
Koren, John A.
Kowalik, James A.
Lippens, William A.
Lutterman, James H.
Marbry, Michael R.
Martin, Mark S.
Mattison, John W.
Mayo, Joel C.*
Mays, Rex D.
Miller, George S.
Newberry, Dwight A.
Nichols, Robert W.
Ray, Dennis C.
Roeder, Robert L.
Schutee, Jerry L.
Smith, Stephen, Jr.
Strange, Edward B.
Torres, Jose L.
Underwood, Robert B., Jr.
Vandemark, Theodore C.
Wacht, Thomas A.
Welty, Frederick
West, James E.
Wilkins, Barry W.
Winters, Dean F.
Winters, Wayne A.
Wood, Walter E.

Staff Sergeants
Anderson, Jerry L.
Arija, Nasamichi
Arooji, Fred
Beattie, Larry J.
Beeman, Jerry
Beyers, Joseph J.,III
Bloomfield, Larry A.
Boeninghaus, Leonard
Bogisich, Guy W.
Bramer, Virgil C,
Bupp, Larry L.
Burrus, Larry B.
Calhoun, Ronald, Jr.
Chamess, James L.
Clain, Barry W., Jr.
Clark, Dannie
Clark, Kenneth W.
Coons, Raymond L.
Corbett, S.G.
Cowan, William D.
Cruz, Freddy Adamos

---

* Lost at Desert One

Daughtery, William E., Jr.
Davis, Chester G.
Davis, Teddie C.
Devine, James B. Iv
Diaz, Salvador
Diehl, Richard A.
Duncan, Roy S.
Felton, John T.
Fleming, Charles A.
Fowle,R, Harold W.
Fredricksen, David A.
Galt, William R.
Graczyk, James A.
Grant, Clint A.
Haase, James K.
Hall, James C.
Harrison, D. L.
Hensley, Dana B.
Hickman, Roland C.
Holly, Jackie D.
Holmes, James A.
Huff, Andrew J.
Ingram, Kenneth R.
Jacobs, Wilburt L.
Jimenez, Ray A.
Joy, James B.
Justice, James A.
Kahler, Ricky E.
Kane, Robert J.
King, William M.
Kramer, Frederick
Labit, James M.
Latona, Vincent A. S.
Latona, Vincent A. Sr.
Lawrence, William H.
McCoy, William
McKee, Kenneth F.
Maston, Leverious D., Jr.
Milburn, William F.
Mize, Horace T.
Mock, Thomas L.
Necker, William, Jr.
Page, Robert S.
Parchment, Earl
Perez-Murales, C.
Permenter, Randall
Pettry, Bruce L.
Price, James H.
Reid, Joseph D.
Reschetinkow, George
Roessling, Bernard
Rought, Burton C., Jr.
Sanchez, Richard T.
Silva, Clyde S.
Stevens, Charles D.
Stigar, Andrew J.
Tafoya, William A.
Tate, Billy J., Jr.
Taylor, Frederick
Teaford, Edward L.
Thomas, Ronald J.
Town, Dale R.
Treadwell, Roy, Jr.
Vadnais, Thomas R.
Valenzuela, Luis E.
Varnadore, James B.
Vecchione, Miguel
West, Richard W.
Whalen, Daniel 0.
Williams, David N.
Wilson, Ernest W.
Witherspoon, Wesley B.
Wolf, Bradley M.
Wollmann, Rex V.
Zummer, Ronald L.

Senior Airmen

Abirached, Amin
Alwerdt, David C.
Arthur, Steve P.
Barton, Keith G.
Bigham, Roy L.
Blanks, Keith A.
Bowman, Milton R.
Busha, Mark A.
Bradshaw, Dennis R.
Bridger, Richard W.
Bryant, John
Cardenas, Gary H.
Carter, Dana A.

Chiras, Bruce A.
Clancy, Joseph J., Jr.
Clark, John W.
Cooney, E. J., Jr.
Dahl, Dewey D.
Davis, George L.
Dawley, Ronald J.
Disalvo, Joseph, Jr.
Duffie, Michael G.
Evans, Arthur L.
Fullan, William C.
Finnerty, Joseph W.
Forest, Rodney B.
Garrett, Randy E.
George, Johnny
Green, Gary L.
Greene, Paul .
Grossman, M. T.
Hagge, Eugene R.
Hare, Clifford M.
Harrington, Joseph M.
Hartman, Stephen E.
Hayes, Martin
Henrie, Robert D.
Heard, John R.
Herdman, Bradley A.
Hernandez, Louis, Jr.
Herndon, Dewight L.
Hooper, Gregory L.
Hosler, Michael L.
Houghton, Lawrence
Howland, Jeffrey D.
Jones, Toy L., Jr.
Judkins, James D.
Kark, Donald L.
Lindsey, Robert A.
McClain, James W., Jr.
McCluskey, James
McCunney, Steven A.
McDaniel, Harry A.
Masenburg, Timothy
Massey, James R.
May, David L.
Mayes, David L.
Metherell, David H. R.
Meyers, Daniel
Miller, Laurence D.
Moore, Charles E.
Nicholson, Bruce W.
Parabis, Daniel P.
Poston, Larry E.
Price, Anthony R.
Randlett, Kevin
Reeder, Thomas H.
Romero, Alfred A.
Rowe, Jessie J., III
Sandrow, John R., Jr.
Schultz, Jerome H.
Shankle, Matthew J.
Shaver, Thomas
Skelton, Michael A.
Slavings, Chester
Skinner, Derral
Smith, Donald K.
Smith, Henry F.
Smith, Thomas G.
Snodderly, Dewayne P.
Spence, Edward I.
Sulzberger, Paul E.
Thompson, Martin E.
Thompson, Tommy
Tindall, Charles E.
Vaisvilas, Thomas R.
Wallingford, J. T.
Walsh, Lawrence G.
Walter, William B.
Williamson, Joel
Wright, Daniel B.
Ziarniak, Michael J.

Airmen First Class

Barndollar, Glenn
Bateman, David C.
Blas, Ishael
Bradley, Michael J.
Brosius, Thomas G.
Brown, David R.
Caplinger, James D.
Cardenas, Carlos
Carlisle, Jonathon

Chiarell, Jerald
Cornell, Nikki A.
Crawford, David S.
Crimmins, John R.
Daniel, Kevin F.
Davis, Thomas K.
Delong, Scott A.
Denis, Gary R.
Doane, Matt G.
Dryer, Robert A.
Durington, Daniel E.
Eggum, D. S.
Evans, Alan T.
Feuser, Mark L.
Forster, Anthony M.
Frank, Jerry D.
Goshia, Jerry D.
Gray, Lewis E.
Greffrath, William
Grondin, Mark
Hassel, Fredrick R.
Henry, Terry L.
Holt, Gary D.
Hooten, Eric J.
Houghton, Lawrence J.
House, John P.
Johnson, Douglas A.
Johnson, Juan R.
Kerstetter, David
King, Ricky L.
Larson, Mitchell D.
Lowther, Dennis L.
McKee, Jerry E.
Maloney, Stephen L.
Marine, James L.
Martin, Robert A.
Melanson, John A.
Miller, Randy L.
Mondragun, Michael
Mudge, Rodney J.
Neal, Douglas J.
O'Brien, Joseph
Ohms, William E.
Osterhout, Mark
Peters, Craig E.
Pogue, Perry L. J.
Price, Michael D.
Ramirez, Alan T.
Rinehart, Randall L.
Robb, Ernest E., Jr.
Roundtree, Richard R.
Rumple, Kevin D.
Rutkowski, Kevin J.
Ryan, Robert P.
Sabato, Frank V., Jr.
Sanfilippo, C.
Shear, Alex D.
Sistrunk, Steven T.
Sleggs, Randall L.
Spera, William
Suarez, Anthony V.
Sutton, James R.
Thompson, D. E.
Tidruw, Mark D.
Tootle, William V.
Tracy, Ricky W.
Veenstra, Richard M.
Vincent, John
Wadding, Mark R.
Walton, Hyram L.
Welsh, Dale E.
West, Douglas S.
Whitt, Thomas E.
Wilhelm, Matthew L.
Woods, Charles F., Jr.
Young, David B.

Airmen
Amos, William L.
Carpenter, Philip J.
Cimatu, Vincent P.
Jones, Cardell
Laniog, Romeo M.
Shimono, Mark Wayne K.

Airman Basic
Schod, Christopher

-End Of Roster-

GLOSSARY

CJCS (Chairman of the Joint Chiefs of Staff). Formal title of the Presidentially-selected senior military officer of the U.S. Armed Forces. The CJCS is the designated military advisor to the President and, in partnership with the Secretary of Defense, the Secretary of State, and the President, constitutes the National Command Authority (NCA). Within this context of civilian control, major force deployments outside the U.S. are authorized by the Secretary of Defense and directed by thc Chairman to the Unified Commands and Military Services through the JCS staff -- Office of the Joint Chiefs of Staff.

JCS (Joint Chiefs of Staff). Formal title of the Chiefs of the four military services when operating in their Joint/corporate role as senior United States military deliberation body. Members of the JCS include the Chiefs of Staff of the Army and the Air Force, the Chief of Naval Operations, the Commandant of the Marine Corps, and the *Chairman* of this corporate body, the senior American Military Officer on active duty.

OJCS (Organization of the Joint Chiefs of Staff). Also called the Joint Staff. Officers, enlisted personnel and dedicated civilians who develop policy, review plans, monitor resources and coordinate action in support of and between the Unified Joint Commands and the Military Service staffs. Organized along traditional staff functions: J-1, Personnel; J-3, Operations; J-4, Logistics; J-5, Plans; J-6, Communications. The Defense Intelligence Agency acts as the J-2 and provides Intelligence Support.

Rangers. Well-trained, parachute-qualified, light infantry capable of operating in a wide range of geographic and climatic conditions. Organized in 600-man battalions, Ranger forces typically operate in company-sized units of approximately 200 men, with platoon and squad elements given task assignments within the context of the overall mission. Behind-the-lines raiding has been the focus of Ranger training and missions since their creation during the revolutionary war.

REDCOM ([United States] Readiness Command). This command, deactivated in 1987, was responsible for operating, managing and executing the JCS five-year joint exercise plan and training service component elements to operate as a Joint Task Force or as a Joint Special Operations Task Force. Other missions and duties included coordinating and overseeing the preparation and deployment of contingency and/or Army and Air Force reinforcing forces from the continental U.S. to overseas theaters. It also was charged with maintaining and exercising a cadre staff and support core to deploy as the lead Command and Control elements of a Joint Task Force (JTF).

SOF (Special Operations Forces). Umbrella term for a segment of the U.S. military force structure, regardless of military service, which has been designated, trained and equipped to carry-out a range of missions not normally assigned to conventional forces. The Army, Navy and Air Force have forces trained, equipped and designated as Special Operations Forces. When the Iran rescue force was constituted in 1979, many of the Special Operations Forces and capabilities that exist today did not exist. The principal SOF available at the time were Army Special Forces personnel, Army Ranger units, Air Force Special Operations transports (C-130s) and Combat Controller Teams. The 1998 force structure includes Special Mission Units, Navy Special Warfare units, Air Force Special Tactics Squadrons, as well as Psychological and Civil Affairs units.

SOW (Special Operations Wing). An operational Air Force unit consisting of several squadrons of C-130 medium-range transport aircraft. The aircraft are specially equipped, and crewed by specially-trained fight personnel. Their mission is to deliver Special Operations personnel of all services into the mission area undetected, resupply them as necessary, and provide gunfire and surveillance support to American personnel on the ground. At the time of the Iran rescue effort, there was only one understrength wing and three small squadrons, and no long-range helicopter capability. A parachute-qualified combat control element was attached to the wing and each of the squadrons to provide coordination between the SOF personnel on the ground and the supporting aircraft.

Special Forces Group. A Special Forces Group is primarily a personnel, administrative, leadership, training and logistic structure designed to support a number of Operating Detachments of differing sizes. The smallest is a 12-man team called an "A" Detachment. A "B" Detachment is a larger operating force, typically less than 36 personnel, often composed of several "A" Detachments operating in concert. A "C" Detachment is primarily a Command and Control element designed to coordinate the actions of a number of "A" and "B" Detachments. The primary mission of these Army Special Forces units is to conduct training of indigenous and or allied personnel, although they are capable of applying military combat skills in reconnaissance or Direct Action (DA) missions.

Unified Command. Term applied to a Joint Theater level (geographic) or a national level Joint Functional Command of the U.S. Armed Forces. As of 1997, there are five Unified Theater Commands: European, Pacific, Atlantic, Southern (Latin America), and Central Command (Southwest Asia/Middle East). There are also four national level joint functional Commands: Transportation, Strategic, Space, and Special Operations. Each is composed of combat and support elements from two or more military services. These entities are referred to as "component commands" or "service component commands."

BIBLIOGRAPHY

The first three works listed are the only first-party source narratives published to date regarding the rescue attempt. Each has a different perspective, based on the role of the author. Each was somewhat removed from the day-to-day workings and considerations of the JTF 1-79 staff; thus, these previously published works fall short (through no fault of the authors) of telling many of the other aspects of both the initial rescue effort and the follow-on efforts. The fourth work is an Iranian construction of the mission, based on their interpretation of the maps, charts, photographs and notes left on the abandoned rescue helicopters. It is laced with "revolutionary" propaganda aimed at the U.S., and with accusations aimed at Iranians who allegedly did not support the revolution or the Iman.

FIRST-PARTY BOOKS

Beckwith, Charlie A., Colonel (U.S. Army, Retired) and Knox, Donald.*Delta Force*. New York: Harcourt, Brace, Jovanovich, 1983.
Comment: Written by the first Commander of the 1st Special Forces Operating Detachment DELTA and the senior ground force rescue planner. This work details the author's crusade that led to the creation of DELTA, its journey to operational status, and segments of the unit's training and preparation for the rescue mission and the bitter disappointment at the abort and the "failure of the helicopter force to measure up."

Carter, Jimmy. *Keeping Faith: Memoirs of a President.* New York: Bantam Books, 1982.
Comment: The subject of the Iran hostage situation told from the perspective of a very human, concerned and caring President (pp. 433-524, 590-596) paints the political background at the highest level of national policy and responsibility. It stops with the release of the hostages on 20 January 1981, the former President no longer being privy to the details learned after that date.

Kyle, James H., Colonel (USAF, Ret). *The Guts to Try.* New York: Crown, 1990.
Comment: Written by the JTF 1-79 Senior Air planner for the C-130 force, subsequent to the publication of DELTA FORCE. It tells the story of the April rescue attempt with a focus on the aviation aspects of the mission. It is limited to the operational planning and training of the initial rescue mission and the events that transpired at Desert One. In its closing chapter the author sets forth a set of rationales for the mission abort.

Iranian Student Construct: Tabas: Folly of The Mammoth -- A look at the Adventure of Tabas. Compiled/printed in Farsi, on sale in Iran in 1980, by the "Moslem Youth Following the Path of the IMAM" (28 Khordad 1360)
Comment: This booklet, compiled by the "Students" that held the American Embassy Hostages captive, is their attempt to reconstruct of the rescue mission. It is based on classified material left in the helicopters at Desert One as well as numerous American newspaper and magazine sources, such as *Aviation Week*, *Time Magazine* and the *Houston Chronicle*. It is flavored with a substantial amount of propaganda and condemnation of members of the Iranian civil government and senior Iranian

military officers. Some is based on purported CIA documents found in the Embassy. A variety of allegations imply that secular and military officials were part of a larger plot supported by the CIA to undermine the Islamic fundamentalist revolution.

ORIGINAL DOCUMENTS

Maps and photographic material left behind in the helicopters was acquired from Iranian authorities by a major U.S. television network within days of the abort and used as a basis for a speculative reconstruction of the mission beyond Desert One. This material is the same as that used in the "Student" booklet.

Freedom of Information Act (FOIA) Documentation. *The Washington Post*, among others, submitted a number of FOIA requests to the Department of Defense for material relating to the rescue operation. During the course of responding to these requests, JTF 1-79 files, documents and planning material were reviewed by team of officers, none of whom had been involved in the rescue effort. A large segment of the material was released, although in some cases with selected terms and names blackened and classified photography excised. Overall, more than seven boxes of copies of original working papers, correspondence and messages were released to the public domain. Given the mundane and matter-of-fact nature of the documentation and the absence of sensational revelations, the *Washington Post*, which had contemplated a book "expose," and CBS, which had considered producing a movie on the rescue attempt, terminated their efforts. Ref: FOIA 92-FOI-0640/L - 07 May 1992.
Comment: The author reviewed this material, recognized most of it and found it to be a comprehensive and accurate body of information, that presented events as they happened, and has included a representative collection of the material in the manuscript.

"Credible Sport," Project Summary Video. Prepared by Lockheed-Martin-Marrietta Company (Circa 12/80-2/81) from original project/test footage (August-October 1980). Running Time: 16 minutes. Traces the requirement and development effort of the Super Stol C-130 project.

RELATED STUDIES

Boykin, William G., Colonel (U.S. Army). "Study Project: Special Operations and Low-Intensity Conflict Legislation." U.S.Army War College, Class of 1991.
Comment: The author of this paper was one of the Delta Force tactical commanders during the Iranian rescue attempt. He later served in the Joint Special Operations Command and as Commander of Delta. This work traces the heritage of the Congressional Legislation that created the U.S. Special Operations Command.

Collins, John M. (Senior Specialist in National Defense). *Special Operations Forces: An Assessment 1986-1993*. Washington, D.C.: Congressional Research Service, Library of Congress, July 30, 1994.
Comment: This study was undertaken at the request of the Senate Committee on Armed Forces, which, in an April 1993 letter to the Director of the Congressional

Research Service, stated that it would be helpful to assess the current and future capabilities of U.S. Special Operations Forces. This study covers many aspects of force capabilities and readiness not normally addressed, such as education and training.

United States Special Operations Forces Posture Statements (1992, 1993, 1994, 1995).
Comment: An annual publication produced by the Assistant Secretary of Defense, Special Operations/Low Intensity Conflict in conjunction with the U.S. Special Operations Command. This "Report to the stockholders, the U.S. citizenry," provides a review of SOF activities during the previous year and a status report on current SOF capabilities and future initiatives.

OTHER READINGS

Bolger, Daniel P. *Americans at War.* Novato, CA: Presidio Press, 1988.
Comment: Hindsight analysis based on third party sources, adds little if anything to the history of events. See, in particular, "Chapter 2: Dust and Ashes," 99-168.

Christopher, Warren. *American Hostages In Iran: The Conduct of a Crisis.* New Haven: Yale University Press, 1985.
Comment: An excellent political case study from respected diplomatic officials and policy authorities. The nuts and bolts of the negotiating process is covered in detail and analyzed objectively. Each section of this work was written by a different official or authority. Warren Christopher, one of the principal U.S. negotiators in the hostage crisis, wrote the introduction that sets the stage for the scope of the work and includes a brief review of each of the subsequent chapters. Chapters 3 and 10 are of particular interest. Chapter 3, written by Gary Sick, discusses the Military Options and Constraints. Chapter 10, the concluding chapter, written by Abraham Ribicoff, brings together some of the principle themes of the work, and offers thoughts on the significance of the Iran Hostage Crisis for the future.

Emerson, Steven. *Secret Warriors.* New York: G.P. Putnam's Sons, 1988.
Comment: Highly interesting synopsis which includes an overview of many of the organizations that, according to the author, evolved after the April rescue attempt. See, in particular, "Chapter 1," 12-26.

Kennedy, Moorehead. *American Hostage in Iran: The Ayatollah in the Cathedral.* New Haven: Yale University Press, 1985.
Comment: Moorehead Kennedy was one of the State Department officers detained as a hostage the full 444 days. His wife was instrumental in organizing FLAG, the hostage family support group, and in keeping the hostage issue in the forefront of the weekly newsmagazines.

Laigen, Bruce.*Yellow Ribbon: The Secret Journal of Bruce Laigen.* New York: Brassey's, Inc., 1992.
Comment: Ambassador Laigen was the senior American diplomat detained by Iranian authorities, allegedly for his own protection. This work, essentially a day-by-day dairy, presents his view of the crisis as it unfolded for the MFA trio.

Martin, David, and Walcott, John. *Best Laid Plans*. New York: Harper and Row, 1988.
Comment: Succinct action summary, includes a vignette on "Eureka" reporting. See, in particular, "Chapter 1: Desert One," 6-42.

Queen, Richard. *Inside and Out, Hostage to Iran Hostage to Myself*. New York: Putnam Press, 1981.
Comment: In the early 1980, the Iranian authorities became aware that Richard Queen had a medical condition that they could neither diagnose nor treat. In an effort to avoid any major American action that might be undertaken because of his possible death, Queen was released in mid-1980 on humanitarian grounds. During his period of detention, he was one of five Americans *not* dispersed to the four winds after the rescue abort. Queen, the women hostages, and two elderly men continued to be detained in the Chancery until he was released in June and they were transferred to one of the prerelease sites in northern Teheran in mid-December 1980.

Ryan, Paul B., Captain (USN, Ret).*The Iranian Rescue Mission*. Annapolis, MD: Naval Institute Press, 1985
Comment: This book is an academic criticism of the mission based largely on the unclassified Holloway Report. The work is flawed by numerous technical errors and voids which reflect a lack of substantive research and a definitive lack of understanding of Special Operations and USAF operations. The majority of the sources/interviews cited are Naval or Navy-associated personnel. None of the JTF staff, Delta Force, or the USAF element are listed as references.

Special Forces and Missions. Alexandria, VA Time-Life Books, 1991 (The New Face of War Series].
Comment: Compiled in a highly readable style, much of this treatment was drawn from first person sources and contains some of the only published photos of actual material used during the operation. See particularly, "Chapter 4: Catastrophe at Desert One," 124-163.

Waller, Douglas C. *The Commandos*. New York: Simon & Schuster, 1994.
Comment: The first half provides a comprehensive rundown on Special Forces and SEAL selection and training, and a rare look at the training of the USAF Special Operations Aircrews. The second half provides an extensive treatment of U.S. Special Operations Forces in Operation Just Cause and Operation Desert Storm.

NEWSPAPERS AND MAGAZINES

Becker, Joseph D., Major (USAF). "Special Operations Afloat." *Armed Forces Journal International* (February 1996): 18-20.
Comment: Contemporary article summarizes SOF use of an aircraft carrier as Joint Special Operations headquarters and staging base for a helicopter assault force targeted to spearhead the anticipated combat intervention into Haiti in the fall of 1994.

"CBS is Developing a Movie on Attempted Raid in Iran."*Washington Star*, 10 February 1981.

Comment: The production was to be developed by T.A.T. Communications and Stonehedge Productions, with Dick Berg as executive producer. Tom Capra, a former senior producer for *20-20*, was to produce and supervise the research.

"Debacle in the Desert." *Time Magazine* (5 May 1980): 12-31.

Comment: This article (plus several others in this issuc) provides a summary of the rescue effort and a collection of color photographs of the hostages originally published in the German magazine *Stern*, before the rescue attempt.

Halloran, Richard. "Military is Quietly Rebuilding its Special Operations Forces." *New York Times*, 19 July 1982.

Comment: Article states that funding was included in the proposed 1983 DOD budget to pay for a range of improvements, including communications equipment, additional air transportation, and expanded joint-service exercises.

Martin, David C. "Inside the Rescue Mission." *Newsweek*, July 12, 1982.

Comment: Based partially on an interview with Dick Meadows, one of the four Americans who entered Iran prior to the rescue effort to conduct a final reconnaissance and facilitate the movement of Delta force from their insertion point to the Embassy.

Scott Armstrong, George C. Wilson, Bob Woodward. "Scope of Hostage Mission Unfolds: Debate Rekindles on Failed Iran Raid." *Washington Post*, 25 April 1982.

Comment: Based on interviews with several members of the Carter administration and CIA officials. Highlights a call by Admiral Stansfield Turner, the former head of the CIA during the Iranian hostage situation, to conduct another investigation and review of the operation for lessons learned. Includes a statement by General David Jones that there is no value to be gained in another investigation and the energy would be better spent in enhancing the capabilities to respond in the future.

"Special Report: A Grim Thanksgiving." *Newsweek* (December 3, 1979): 44-65.

Comment: A good, quick treatment of the political and situational background of events in Teheran and a presentation on some of the key Iranian figures. Includes a summary of the assault on the U.S. Embassy in Pakistan, an attempted "copy cat" event which took place within a week of the Teheran take over (56-57). "Mecca and the Gulf" (58-61) summarizes the third, and most violent, event to occur in the Islamic world in this time frame -- the seizure of the Grand Mosque by a small group of armed religious extremists who killed and injured hundreds of Islamic Pilgrims before being subdued by Saudi Arabian Security Forces. A long-range photo enlargement (58) shows an Air Force C-5A wide-bodied transport aircraft loading USN CH-53 for "possible" minesweeping missions in the Gulf.

Wilson, George C. "For Rangers in Egypt, Bunker 13 Proved a Harbinger of Future." *Washington Post*, 25 April 1982.

Comment: Although not precisely correct in a few points, this short article provides another insight into the final hours of mission preparation.

ABOUT THE AUTHOR

Mr. Lenahan served in a variety of intelligence and support positions in a wide range of commands and forces during his military career. These included U.S. Air Forces Europe, the Strategic Air Command, the U.S. Military Assistance Command, Vietnam (MACV), 4th Allied Tactical Air Forces (NATO), the U.S. Readiness Command, the Organization of the Joint Chiefs of Staff, the USAF Tactical Fighter Weapons Center, the U.S. Southern Command, and the USAF Special Operations Command as well as numerous Joint Task Forces.

Mr. Lenahan has also authored numerous defense-related publications, including: *Guide to Indications and Warning Analysis* (1972); *Soviet Military Exercises: A Ten-Year Review* (1973); *Soviet Military Service Training: A Ten-Year Review* (1974); *Soviet Tactical Reconnaissance Multi-Source Review* (1975); *Operation Analysis-Terrorism Counter Force Planning* (1978); *Intelligence Guide for Joint Contingency Operations* (1979); *Guidelines for Crisis Response Management* (1981); *Deception in Support of Military Operations* (1982); *Consumer Guide for Effective Intelligence* (1989); *Intelligence Officer's Guide to Special Operations* (1990); and *Counter Force Actions Survey, 1976-1986* (1991). In 1993-94, Mr. Lenahan compiled a book-length case study for the National Defense University about the political-military events leading up to Operation Just Cause.

Colonel Lenahan retired from the U.S. Air Force in 1988. He is now employed in the private sector and is working on a book about Operation Just Cause.